Italy

Perfect places to stay, eat & explore

Contents

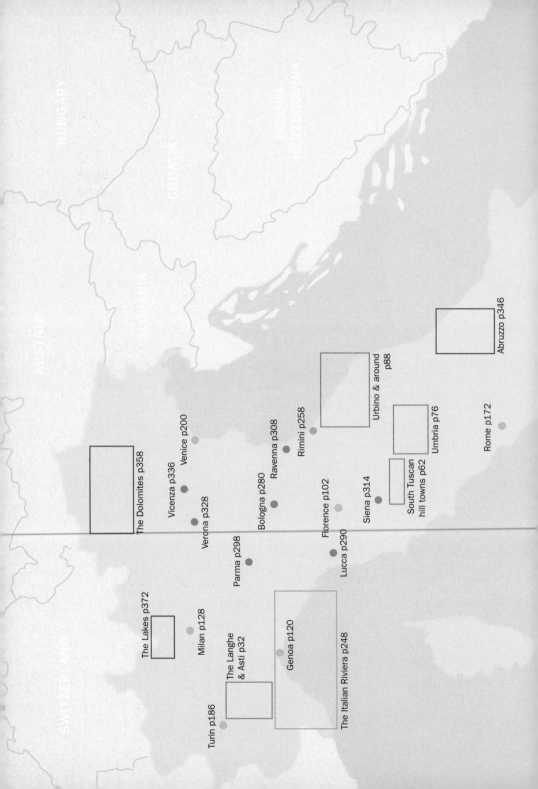

SWITZERLAND
AUSTRIA
HUNGARY
SLOVENIA
CROATIA
BOSNIA HERZEGOVINA

The Dolomites p358

Vicenza p336
Venice p200
Verona p328

Parma p298
Bologna p280
Ravenna p308
Rimini p258

Urbino & around p88

The Lakes p372
Milan p128

The Langhe & Asti p32
Genoa p120

Turin p186

The Italian Riviera p248

Lucca p290
Florence p102
Siena p314
South Tuscan hill towns p62
Umbria p76

Abruzzo p346

Rome p172

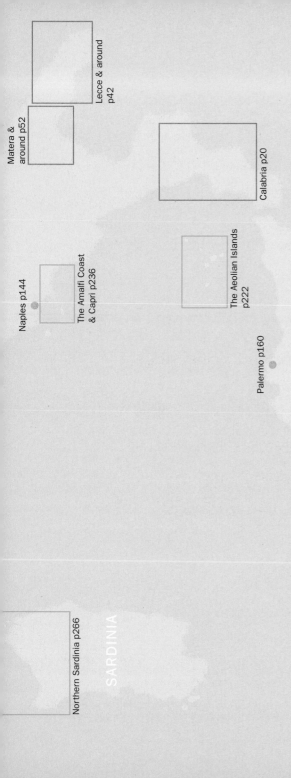

Italy

Northern Sardinia p266

SARDINIA

Matera &
around p52

Lecce & around
p42

Naples p144

The Amalfi Coast
& Capri p236

Calabria p20

The Aeolian Islands
p222

Palermo p160

SICILY

- Rural Idylls pp18-99
- Cities pp100-219
- Coast & Islands pp220-277
- Small Gems pp278-343
- Lakes & Mountains pp344-383

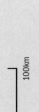

0   100km

Published by Time Out Guides Ltd, a wholly owned subsidiary of Time Out Group Ltd.
Time Out and the Time Out logo are trademarks of Time Out Group Ltd.

© **Time Out Group Ltd 2008**

10 9 8 7 6 5 4 3 2 1

This edition first published in Great Britain in 2008 by Ebury Publishing
A Random House Group Company
20 Vauxhall Bridge Road, London SW1V 2SA

Random House Australia Pty Limited 20 Alfred Street, Milsons Point, Sydney, New South Wales 2061, Australia
Random House New Zealand Limited 18 Poland Road, Glenfield, Auckland 10, New Zealand
Random House South Africa (Pty) Limited Isle of Houghton, Corner Boundary
Road & Carse O'Gowrie, Houghton 2198, South Africa

Random House UK Limited Reg. No. 954009

For further distribution details, see www.timeout.com

ISBN: 978-184670-046-0

A CIP catalogue record for this book is available from the British Library

Printed and bound by Firmengruppe APPL, aprinta druck, Wemding, Germany

The Random House Group Limited supports The Forest Stewardship Council (FSC), the leading international forest
certification organisation. All our titles that are printed on Greenpeace approved FSC certified paper carry the FSC logo.
Our paper procurement policy can be found at http://www.rbooks.co.uk/environment

Introduction

Welcome to *Time Out Italy: Perfect places to stay, eat & explore*, one in a new series of guidebooks that picks out the very best of a country. We've chosen 30 of Italy's most inspiring destinations and for each of them singled out the hotels, restaurants, sights, shops and venues that can't fail to please. We hope that in this way you'll find exactly what you need both for planning a visit and then for enjoying it.

Since we kicked this series off with one of the world's most treasure-filled countries, choosing the 30 destinations was no easy job. The big cities and great centres of art and architecture selected themselves. With the remainder, our aim was to paint a picture of Italy in all its diversity, at the same time as finding a balance between the must-sees and the lesser-known gems. The hill towns of south Tuscany, cherished by visitors for centuries, stand alongside the wildernesses of Abruzzo, one of the few areas in western Europe where wolves still roam. We hope that the combined effect is to evoke the disparate character of Italy's cultural riches, flavours and landscapes and provide the reader with a varied compendium of holiday options. For this reason, our out-of-town chapters do not aim to cover an entire region: we have focused on particular areas rich with interest (and lovely places to eat and sleep).

Built in the 1800, Palazzo Papaleo in Otranto, is one of the finest hotels in Salento, Apulia.

HOTEL
PALAZZO PAPALEO
Otranto
★★★★★
Tel. +39 0836 80.21.08
www.hotelpalazzopapaleo.com

Recently restored to its timeless beauty, **Palazzo Papaleo** is the only 5 star hotel in the East Coast of Salento in Apulia. With 10 rooms, each with a unique personality and sophisticated furnishings, this boutique hotel retains the charms of history while giving you total comfort.

The Hotel is located in the enchanting historical centre of Otranto, just steps away from the blue sea of the Adriatic. With two bars, a Turkish bath, a wide Jacuzzi, and a solarium, **Palazzo Papaleo** is there to pamper your senses… Imagine sipping a cocktail at sunset on the splendid roof terrace overlooking the fabulous bay of Otranto in a truly welcoming and unique atmosphere.

Just 20 minutes from the Hotel, you find Le Campine a splendid retreat in the Salento countryside. Imagine beginning you day with Ashtanga Vinyasa Yogo, near a swimming pool immersed in nature. Imagine meditating surrounded by olive trees in a heaven of peacefulness. Imagine abandoning yourself in the hands of an experienced Ayurveda therapist. (www.lecampineresort.com – info@yogainsalento.com).

You don't have to imagine any longer.. call today to book your holiday, spaces are limited in both locations.

We've chosen our destinations in collaboration with our consultant editor, Tim Jepson, and our team of writers, all Italy specialists and many of them resident in the country (you can read about our contributors on page 12). All are passionate about Italy, and many of the places they've included are their personal discoveries and favourites. But, inevitably, the selection of destinations and venues is subjective, and we apologise in advance if we've missed out any of your favourite places. Write and tell us, and we'll put them on the list for Volume 2.

We've paid serious attention to finding you some unforgettable places to stay. Our listings include the latest showpiece fashion hotels, standard-bearing city landmarks, country estates, and *palazzi* where you'll be treated like royalty. But they also take in ex-monasteries, cave dwellings, conical *trulli* houses and at least one entirely renovated village, as well as restaurant rooms, B&Bs and *agriturismi* (working farms, whose produce is served up on your plate). Most are personally owned and run, with a sense of pride and a beguiling eye for detail.

Our restaurant and café reviews take into account that, in Italy, food is never merely sustenance. If you want to keep up with the latest trends, you'll find many cutting-edge critical favourites here, but we've given equal weight to the village restaurants where the staff are as much keepers of the flame as restaurateurs, serving the best local ingredients with a time-honed perfectionism. For every destination, we've made a point of tracking down the best places to try the regional dishes that are at the heart of Italian cuisine.

A word about the listings. The euro symbols indicate the price bracket of a venue: €=budget, €€=moderate, €€€=expensive and €€€€=luxury. Unless otherwise stated, all venues accept Visa and MasterCard credit cards. Many restaurants and, particularly, hotels are hidden away deep in the countryside. We've indicated a location relative to a nearby town or village but do consult the venue's website for detailed directions.

All our listings are double-checked, but businesses do sometimes close or change their hours or prices, so it's always a good idea to call a venue before visiting. While every effort has been made to ensure accuracy, the publishers cannot accept responsibility for any errors this guide may contain.

DISCOVER OVER 75 PRESTIGIOUS BOUTIQUES
A.G. SPALDING & BROS., CALVIN KLEIN JEANS,
CAMPER, ELENA MIRÒ, FRETTE, FURLA,
GUESS, LINDT, NIKE, PINKO, PUMA,
SAMSONITE, TRIUMPH, TRUSSARDI JEANS,
VERSACE **AND MANY MORE**

MILAN
FIDENZA ❀ VILLAGE
OUTLET SHOPPING

CHIC OUTLET SHOPPING®
2008-09
FIDENZA VILLAGE

DISCOVER FIDENZA VILLAGE,
1 OF EUROPE'S 9 CHIC OUTLET SHOPPING®
VILLAGES, WHERE YOU'LL FIND PREVIOUS
SEASONS' COLLECTIONS FROM THE WORLD'S
LUXURY FASHION AND LIFESTYLE BRAND
NAMES REDUCED BY UP TO 70%*,
EVERY DAY, ALL YEAR ROUND.
9 VILLAGES, 9 DESTINATIONS.

*"this is all about
the ultimate luxury
of spending less..."**

fidenza ❀ village
OUTLET SHOPPING

www.FidenzaVillage.com

Contributors

Tim Jepson, consultant editor for *Time Out Italy*, has lived in Rome, Venice and Umbria for six years, and has been visiting for 25 years. He has written over 20 books and guides to the country (including five for *National Geographic*) and numerous articles for the *Daily Telegraph*, *Vogue* and *Condé Nast Traveller* among others.

Ros Belford is a writer and editor who spends as much time as she can on the Aeolian island of Salina.

Karl Blackwell lived in Milan for many years, teaching photography and spending his spare time travelling around Lombardy snapping photos. He travels back to Italy as often as he can, and has a fondness for Fiat 500s.

Paul Bradshaw, publisher and editor of *Straight No Chaser* magazine for the past two decades, has travelled the globe nurturing a community devoted to 'intergalactic sounds – ancient to future'. He is currently working on *Straight No Chaser – The Book* and can be found blogging online at www.straightnochaser.co.uk.

Nick Bruno is a freelance journalist, travel writer and photographer based in Scotland and Italy. His work may have taken him around the globe but he still reckons that the Bay of Naples is the most compelling and beautiful place in the world, if you don't mind a few rough and roguish edges. And the food's to die for.

Julia Burdet is based in Florence and is the editor of *Bridge for Design* magazine. She has also written for the *Sunday Times Travel* magazine and *Grand Designs* and is a regular contributor to the *Time Out* guide to Florence.

Carla Capalbo is an American-born, freelance food and wine writer who has lived in Italy for 18 years and won the 2007 Luigi Veronelli prize for Best Foreign Language Food and Wine Writer in Italy. She writes regularly for *Decanter* and *Olive* magazines; her most recent book is *The Food and Wine Guide to Naples and Campania*.

Andrew Copestake is a freelance writer and travel editor of *GT Magazine*. His work has taken him across the globe, but when he needs a holiday he always returns to Italy.

Natasha Foges is a freelance writer and editor who divides her time between London and Rome. She is a regular contributor to *Time Out*'s Rome guide and has written about Italy for the *Daily Telegraph* and the *Observer*.

Paul Lay is the author of *Real Italian Food*, and is currently writing and researching a history of Venice and its influence on the English Civil War.

Jonathan Lee is a writer and broadcaster who divides his time between London and Italy. He is the author of *50 Great Escapes, A Global Guide to Creativity*, and a contributor to the BBC and the *Guardian*.

Melanie Leyshon has edited the *Les Routiers Hotel and Restaurant Guide*, and travelled extensively throughout Italy as deputy editor of *Food and Travel* magazine.

Leonie Loudon lived in Naples and Rome for six years, travel writing and teaching English. She got the seven-year itch and moved back to London in 2007, but is missing *il bel paese* already.

Lesley McCave is a freelance writer and editor living in Los Angeles. Her love affair with Italy began with a trip to Florence in 1995, and since then she has made regular visits to the country that first turned her on to the joy of proper coffee.

Katie Parla is a freelance writer, sommelier and food expert living in Rome. Her passion for wine and food continually bring her back to the Langhe.

Ron Pasas is a travel writer from the old school: a wanderer, risk-taker, poet and spy. When Ron is not speeding along the Amalfi Coast in a three-wheeled van, he can be found snapping away with his Rolleiflex in the back streets of Naples.

Gillian Price is a travel writer and photographer who lives in Venice but spends most of her time walking in her beloved Dolomites. She has authored outdoor guides to most of Italy.

Alessandra Santarelli is a Brussels-born photographer. Half-Italian and half-American, Alessandra divides her time between Rome and London, and has contributed to many travel guides around the world.

Cyrus Shahrad is a snowboarder and journalist who spent his teenage years riding the mountains of Italy and his twenties writing about them. He has recently completed a book on the Vatican and is currently busy editing a guide to Malta.

Paul Shawcross is a freelance travel writer and photographer specialising in Italy and France. His main interest is writing and revising travel guides but he also contributes illustrated articles to several well-known magazines.

Marina Spironetti is a Milan-born photographer who lived in Umbria for many years before moving to London. She still has a house near Orvieto and gets back there whenever she can. Her travel and reportage pictures are regularly featured in Italian and English newspapers and magazines.

Paul Sullivan is a freelance music and travel journalist and photographer. He loves Italy for many reasons and is currently obsessed with exploring the culture, history and culinary heritage of the Mezzogiorno.

Nicky Swallow is a freelance travel writer living in Florence, and a regular contributer to the Time Out guides to Florence, Venice and Rome. She likes to spend time in Umbria, finding it a peaceful refuge from tourist-worn Tuscany.

Charlotte Thomas is a freelance writer and artist who divides her time between London and the Veneto. She has contributed to several Time Out publications on northern Italy.

Christine Webb is a freelance journalist and photographer living in Sansepolcro, Tuscany. She has been a regular cover story contributor to *Italy* magazine and is currently working on a book of her photography.

Contributors by chapter
The Italian Riviera Paul Shawcross. Genoa, Verona Jan Fuscoe. Turin Ruth Jarvis. The Langhe & Asti Katie Parla. Milan, Rome, Florence, Venice Lesley McCave (*A race of heroes* Ron Pasas; *Palladian dream* Charlotte Thomas; *Michelin man* Carla Capalbo). The Dolomites Gillian Price (*High-altitude hotel heaven* Julia Burdet; *Sellavation* Cyrus Shahrad). Vicenza Charlotte Thomas. Ravenna, Rimini, Urbino & around, Matera & around Leonie Loudon (*Club class* Paul Bradshaw). Bologna, Parma Andrew Copestake (*Petrolhead passions* Paul Lay). Siena, South Tuscan hill towns Christine Webb. Lucca Paul Lay. The Lakes, The Amalfi Coast & Capri, Naples Ron Pasas. Lecce & around Natasha Foges (*Liquid gold* Jan Fuscoe). Palermo Jonathan Lee. The Aeolian Islands Ros Belford (*Smooth sailing* Jael Marschner). Umbria Nicky Swallow. Northern Sardinia Melanie Leyshon. Abruzzo, Calabria Paul Sullivan.

Time Out Guides Limited
Universal House
251 Tottenham Court Road
London W1T 7AB
Tel + 44 (0)20 7813 3000
Fax + 44 (0)20 7813 6001
Email guides@timeout.com
www.timeout.com

Editorial

Editor Jan Fuscoe
Copy Editors Edoardo Albert, Simon Coppock, Jonathan
Derbyshire, Will Fulford-Jones,
Charlie Godfrey-Faussett, Cathy Limb,
Holly Pick, Lisa Ritchie, Elizabeth Winding
Consultant Editor Tim Jepson
Listings Editors Katie Parla,
Marianna Raffaele, Julien Sauvalle
Proofreader Simon Cropper
Indexer Ismay Atkins

Managing Director Peter Fiennes
Financial Director Gareth Garner
Editorial Director Ruth Jarvis
Deputy Series Editor Dominic Earle
Editorial Manager Holly Pick
Assistant Management Accountant
Ija Krasnikova

Design

Art Director Scott Moore
Art Editor Pinelope Kourmouzoglou
Senior Designer Henry Elphick
Graphic Designers Gemma Doyle, Kei Ishimaru
Digital Imaging Simon Foster
Advertising Designer Jodi Sher

Picture Desk

Picture Editor Jael Marschner
Deputy Picture Editor Katie Morris
Picture Researcher Helen McFarland
Picture Desk Assistant Troy Bailey

Advertising

Sales Director Mark Phillips
International Advertising Manager
Kasimir Berger
International Sales Consultant Ross Canadé
International Sales Executive Charlie Sokol
Advertising Sales The Florentine
(Florence & Tuscany); Conversa (Turin);
Fabio Giannini (Venice)
Advertising Assistant Kate Staddon

Marketing

Head of Marketing Catherine Demajo
Marketing Manager Yvonne Poon
Sales and Marketing Director
North America Lisa Levinson

Production

Group Production Director Mark Lamond
Production Manager Brendan McKeown
Production Controller Caroline Bradford
Production Coordinator Julie Pallot

Time Out Group

Chairman Tony Elliott
Financial Director Richard Waterlow
Group General Manager/Director
Nichola Coulthard
Time Out Magazine Ltd MD Richard Waterlow
Time Out Communications Ltd MD David Pepper
Time Out International MD Cathy Runciman
Group Art Director John Oakey
Group IT Director Simon Chappell

Maps Kei Ishimaru.

Back cover photography by Jonathan Perugia, The Rocco Forte Collection and Marina Spironetti.

Photography pages 3, 43, 48, 52, 56, 59, 89, 92, 95, 96, 346, 350, 353, 354, 400 Alessandra Santarelli; pages 3, 40, 63, 66, 102, 108, 109, 113, 117, 118, 128, 132, 134, 138, 139, 141, 173, 176, 181, 185, 186, 192, 198 Gianluca Moggi; pages 3, 76, 80, 83, 86, 266, 271, 272, 275, 308, 400 Marina Spironetti, pages 3, 222, 229, 233, 234 Jael Marschner; pages 20, 26, 29, 30, 400 Agnese Sanvito; pages 32, 36, 40, 121, 145, 148, 157, 151, 237, 241, 245, 248, 255, 256, 281, 285, 299, 304, 400 Karl Blackwell; page 47 Heloise Bergman; page 47 Tricia de Courcy Ling; pages 66, 136, 154, 245, 290, 295, 315, 320, 323 Jonathan Perugia; page 66 Ming Tang Evans; page 66 Rob Greig; page 74 Corbis; pages 121, 237, 245 Jan Fuscoe; page 121 Centro Video del Comune di Genova; page 134 Piero de Grossi; pages 160, 166 Assessorato Al Turismo; pages 160, 170 Jonathan M. Lee; page 160 Mark Phillips; page 165 Joll Biletta; page 183 Brescia Tourism; pages 201, 209, 212, 217, 218, 329, 334, 337, 341 Olivia Rutherford; pages 201, 218 Alys Tomlinson; page 241 Wagner Tours; page 259 Photographic 'Common Councillorship' Tourism of Rimini; page 271 Design Hotels; pages 281, 306 Ferrari S.p.A; page 281 A.P.T.; page 281 Luciano Leonotti; page 303 Giancarlo Tovo/ Pho-to.it; page 308 G.Liverani; page 319 A.P.T. Siena; page 329 Baglioni Hotels; pages 333, 372, 379, 382 Cesare Cicardini; pages 337, 341 Consorzio Vicenza è; pages 358, 362 Tourist Office Val Gardena; page 358 Südtirol Marketing/ Laurin Moser; page 370 4 Corners Images/ Giovanni Simeone; pages 372, 380 Distretto Turistico dei Laghi; page 376 www.hotelvillacrespi.it; page 382 Alessi S.p.A..

The following images were provided by the featured establishments/ artists: pages 36, 48, 56, 63, 66, 70, 73, 124, 132, 165, 166, 170, 203, 242, 255, 263, 264, 271, 320, 323, 326, 365, 366, 369, 376.

The Editor would like to thank Ilaria Bardessono, Damir Biuklic, Thomas Cameron, Giulia Capello, Erika Carpaneto, Marian Fuscoe, David Howells, Filippo Liguoro, James Mitchell, Paola Musolino, Diriye Osman, Marianna Raffaele, Samira Shackle, Jesse Whittock and all contributors to previous editions of *Time Out*'s Italian guides, whose work forms the basis for parts of this book.

Venice Airport less than 1.5 hours from the Dolomites and the Veneto Mountains

A holiday away from it all to discover another way of life

Republic.

There is then the incredible Dolomite area with the "Pail Mounts" in the province of Belluno: the fantastic rocks in Cadore, Valle d'Ampezzo, Agordino, Zoldano. The gentle slopes in Feltrino, Val Belluna, Alpago, Peralba, Three Lavaredo Peaks, Tofane, Marmolada, Civetta, Vette Feltrine, Monti del Sole, Schiara - these are just a few of the myriad of jewels.

The Dolomites and Veneto Mountains. Which from the sea of this generous land gather a thousand different shades and features. Large and small lakes, the gurgling cool streams, the rivers seeped in history that wash by the cities and towns that are still on a human scale.

The Veneto Mountains have all the flavour of the Venice sea that generated them millions of years ago. From that sea they gradually have been formed to reach us today. The gentle slopes of the sub-alpine area and the green plateaus lead to the breathtaking peaks of the Dolomites - the most beautiful are found in the Veneto. From Lake Garda with the reflection of Mount Baldo to the distinct Lessinia which indulgently looks over ancient Verona. From the Vicenza mountains with the precious Recoaro waters, to the Astico and Posina Valleys and beyond to the proud Asiago Plain with its seven municipalities.

From Mount Grappa to the sunny, generous Montello hills around Treviso, the Treviso Prealps with the Cansiglio Plateau, the ancient "Bosco da reme" (Wood for oars) of the Serenissima

The green pastures tinged with the colours of a still uncontaminated nature, the meadows leading to the perfumed shady woods that are perfect for a walk to relax body and mind and where there is the chance of coming across precious species of fauna - a trait that the Veneto Mountains still offer us. Perhaps simple things, but true and within the reach of us all, which is what counts for both the hurried tourist and those who want to discover all the hidden features of the nature and ancient and modern creations of the Veneto people.

The Veneto Mountains. Generous nature within the reach of us all that never disappoints. Genuine, sometimes delicate sometimes strong, flavours like the mountains that protect our coveted rest. This same nature is generous in all

the thousands of leisure opportunities in the mountains, be it on foot, horse or bike or sailing on the lakes or gliding in the clear skies. There is then the winter season that has just closed, when the snow redesigns the landscape and the pace of life when the splendid Dolomites and Veneto Mountains are perfect, with breathtaking downhill runs on skis or snowboards and long cross-country ski treks and invigorating walks on the "ciaspe" or snowshoes. No matter where you go in the Dolomites and Veneto Mountains you will enjoy a full and complete holiday with the wonderful hospitality that the Veneto mountain people proudly offer. It is a holiday away from it all to discover another way of life.

In the heart of the Dolomites, surrounded by impressive mountains such as the Tofana, the Faloria, the Cristallo or the Cinque Torri Group, the Ampezzo Valley is considered since time immemorial one of the best holiday destinations in Italy.

Host of the Olympic Winter Games in 1956, Cortina is known as the "Queen of the Dolomites", and its natural beauties are a constant attraction for those who regard the mountains as a relaxing place away from the crowd and those who seek somewhere special for Winter and Summer holidays. Cortina has also the privilege to be a Partner in the exclusive Association BEST OF THE ALPS which has been joining the best-known alpine resorts in five countries united by a mountain range 746 km long - the Alps.

extreme sports to relaxing wild spotting among woods, rocks, "rifugi", lakes, waterfalls in the most pleasant mountain climate even when it rains!

During all Summer, Spring and Autumn time Cortina is a real Eden for mountain lovers. The Ampezzo Valley offers a wide variety of hikes, vie ferrate, climbing routes or easy rambles in an adventurous discovery of breathtaking sceneries.

Mountain bike lovers are spoilt for choice with the great number of possibilities in the Dolomites. For the keen historians an excursion to the largest Great War Museum in the Dolomites is a must.

Winter. The world-wide fame of the "Queen of the Dolomites" is due not only to its superb landscape, but also to the high quality of its facilities, which guarantee skiing from December through April. Apart from skiing, a whole range of alternative activities are on offer to keep even the most demanding visitor happy. And after a hard day of snow, you can pamper yourself in a cozy, traditional hotel or with a visit to some high class shops, traditional craft workshop or one of the famous art galleries in the town. And food lovers really will be satisfied for choice, with a huge variety of restaurants and refuges just waiting to welcome you.

Cortina D'Ampezzo Events

Curling 2010:
Men's World Championship

Bob Sleigh & Skeleton 2011:
F.I.B.T. World Championships

Alpine Ski 2013:
Candidate for the FIS Alpine World Ski Championship

New Congress Center "Alexander Girardi Hall":
Capacity 600 people

Spring & Summer. A unique variety of adventures with close contact to nature, from

Veneto
From Earth to Sky
www.veneto.to

Rural Idylls

Calabria

In a country rammed to the rafters with priceless art, designer fashion and tourists, Calabria keeps it real. Although it swaps the peacock strut of the north for some hard-nosed *mezzogiorno* swagger, Calabria isn't short on attractions: sand, sea and sunshine, of course; but also colourful history, vivid, sometimes surreal landscapes, and local character in spades.

From top, left to right:
Tropea beach; Capo
Vaticano; Tropea's
Cattedrale Normanna;
La Sila National Park;
Tropea beach.

What sets Calabria apart from the rest of its southern (and northern) neighbours is its rough-edged provincial character and rugged physical charms. Surrounded by two seas (the Tyrrhenian to the west, Ionian to the east), the region flaunts about 800 kilometres of coastline, much of it stunning, a lot of it relatively unexplored; but it also contains a vast inland expanse of jagged mountains, rolling hills and rippling plateaux.

The same coastline that lures the summer hordes today (especially on the west coast) has long been Calabria's Achilles heel. The first sea-bound colonisers were the Greeks, who founded cities such as Reggio di Calabria, Sybaris, Crotone and Locri. Subsequent rulers included the Byzantines, Normans, and, after it was swept into the medieval Kingdom of Naples, the Swabians, Spanish, Habsburgs and Bourbons, among others – until unification in 1861.

This chapter focuses on the south of the region. The 'Calabrian Riviera' is the name given to the myriad resorts and villages that are strung out along Calabria's Tyrrhenian coast, from Praia a Mare in the north down to Reggio di Calabria in the south. The diamond in this coastal tiara is Tropea – as proved by the crowds of visitors in August. Built on the edge of a series of steep cliffs, its elegant medieval centre, interesting jumble of architectural styles (Norman and Arabic, Baroque and Renaissance) and superb beaches make it a showpiece for the whole coast.

La Sila is one of Calabria's three principal parks. Less mountainous than Il Pollino to the north, and less wild than the Aspromonte to the south, it's more grand plateau than mountain range, though it does contain some serious peaks.

Immaculately preserved Gerace is a stunning medieval town set out on a trio of plateaux and perched atop a 500 metre vertical rock with views across the sprawling Ionian coast.

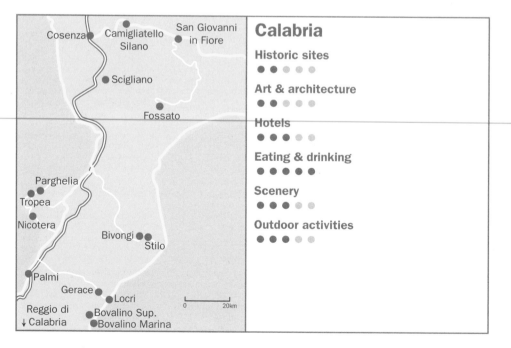

Calabria

Historic sites
● ● ● ○ ○

Art & architecture
● ● ● ○ ○

Hotels
● ● ● ● ○

Eating & drinking
● ● ● ● ●

Scenery
● ● ● ○ ○

Outdoor activities
● ● ● ○ ○

Stay

Having developed its tourist infrastructure relatively late (at least, by Italian standards), Calabria doesn't yet match the wide range of accommodation options offered by most of Italy's regions further to the north. *Agriturismi* and B&Bs are fairly widespread, but only in larger towns such as Tropea, Scilla and Gerace is there any real diversity.

B&B Calabria

Scigliano *Borgo Diano, Via Roma 7 (0984 966 150/ www.bedandbreakfastcalabria.it). €.*
This cosy B&B offers simple rooms in one of the tiny connected hamlets that make up the area of Scigliano. The building was once the local bakery and has some associated idiosyncrasies: room one, for example, offers upstairs access via an enormous trap door. The owners, the amiable Esther van der Linde (Dutch) and Raffaele Ripoli (Italian), are passionate about the area (Ripoli grew up here) and are a mine of information. Wonderful valley views are available just a short stroll away.

La Casa Di Gianna

Gerace *Via Paolo Frascà 4 (0964 355 024/www. lacasadigianna.it). €€€.*
The owners of this early 20th-century patrician residence play up its 'home from home' atmosphere, and although there are some grand features, such as an expansive marble staircase, high ceilings and vast windows, the hodgepodge of approximate period style and more modern elements gives it the feel of a family house. The ten bedrooms are in the same vein: each one has a different decor, with such old-fashioned touches as hand-embroidered linens, oriental rugs on the polished wooden floors and, in the suite, a four-poster bed and en-suite jacuzzi. The traditional restaurant has a lovely covered terrace. Hidden away just off the main drag, the hotel is perfectly placed for exploring the town.

Il Convento

Tropea *Via Abate Sergio 10 (347 509 0576 mobile/ www.ilconvento.com). €€€.*
Built into the cliffs overlooking the seafront, Il Convento is smack in the centre of the city. As the name suggests, the place used to be a convent – built in the 13th century, but added to until the 17th – and has been sensitively converted into apartments. The two main spaces available to rent, Sole and Luna, are a gorgeous mix of the rustic and modern, with atmospheric features such as stone walls (even in the bathroom) and barrel-vaulted ceilings. The larger Luna (sleeps four to six) has contemporary, split-level loft styling in striking contrast with the rustic space. Both apartments have fully equipped kitchens and terraces with sea views.

Il Giardino di Gerace

Gerace *Via Fanfani 8 (0964 356 732/338 485 1481 mobile). €€€.*
This pretty, unassuming bed and breakfast, run by the Scaglione family, is hidden away down a warren of streets.

The eponymous garden provides a colourful welcome, and the four rooms are basic but charming, all featuring parts of the original 16th-century building. Despite being within striking distance of Gerace's main drag, it's incredibly peaceful, and the sweeping views (which span a ninth-century Byzantine church and a dilapidated palace where Edward Lear once stayed) are among Gerace's best.

Hotel Aquila & Edelweiss

Camigliatello Silano *Viale Stazione 15 (0984 578 044/www.hotelaquilaeedelweiss.com). Closed 8-22 Dec. €€.*
The façade of this family-run establishment is undistinguished, and dimly lit corridors and old-fashioned wood panelling seem stuck in a *Shining*-era timewarp, but the bedrooms, done up in a dated but inoffensive standard-issue-hotel style, are clean, reasonably large and comfortable. The buffet breakfast is also good – in fact, the downstairs restaurant serves up some of the region's best local cuisine.

Panta Rei

Parghelia, near Tropea *Località Marina di San Nicola (0963 601 865/www.hotelpantarei.com). €€€.*
Nestled cosily amid trees around 5km along the coast from Tropea, Panta Rei is a luxury four-star spot offering four suites and 17 standard doubles, 11 of which are arranged around a large pool. An air of refinement prevails, enhanced by its antique furnishings and some wonderfully old-fashioned service. The hotel has everything you need, from game rooms and a bar to boat trips and car transfers. There's also a great self-service lunch buffet down on the private beach (€25, June-Sept daily).

Porto Pirgos

Parghelia, near Tropea *Località Marina di Bordila SS 522 (0963 600 351/www.portopirgos.com). €€€.*
Set high above the coast in extensive grounds covered with eucalyptus, olive trees and bouganvillea, this stylishly converted 19th-century villa is quiet and discreet, but a shuttle runs guests into Tropea several times a day. The hotel has just 18 rooms, but facilities befitting a larger establishment: private beach, two pools (one right on the beach), two restaurants – a formal room in the villa and a more casual spot on the beach – plus spa and tennis courts. Rooms are spacious and refined, many with antique brass beds, terracotta-tiled floors and private terraces.

Residenza Il Barone

Tropea *Largo Barone (0963 607 181/www.residenza ilbarone.it). €€.*
Conveniently located on the central piazza Ercole, this stylish hostelry occupies the three upper floors of a 1700s building. Some of the old world charm remains – parts of the staircase and some of the ceilings are original – but the rooms have mostly been decorated in the minimalist style de jure today, with tiled floors, coffee-and-cream colour schemes, wooden furnishings and modern touches like plasma TVs and Wi-Fi. Apart from the small roof terrace (where you can take breakfast and enjoy the 360-degree views that reach to the coast) there's a lack of public areas, but with Tropea literally on your doorstep, you probably won't miss them.

Time Out
Travel Guides

Worldwide

All our guides are
written by a team of
local experts with a
unique and stylish
insider perspective.
We offer essential tips,
trusted advice and
honest reviews for
everything you need
to know in the city.

Over 50 destinations
available at all good
bookshops and at
timeout.com/shop

Time Out
Guides

Torre Camigliati

Camigliatello Silano *Parco Old Calabria (0984 578 200/www.torrecamigliati.it/www.oldcalabria.org). €€.*
Set in the heart of the Sila Grande, Torre Camigliati is a listed 18th-century baronial hunting lodge. It has recently been transformed into a cultural centre devoted to local arts and crafts, with a literary dimension inspired by the writings of 'grand tour' travellers to the region, especially Norman Douglas, author of the 1915 travelogue, *Old Calabria*. Surrounded by a 200 acre private estate, it's a tranquil place. The 12 main rooms have been kitted out in period style (iron beds, antique wardrobes), and some nearby workers' cottages have also been converted into swish apartments. Guided (and non guided) historical and literary walks and excursions to nearby places of interest are gladly arranged.

Eat

Foodies will be glad they came to Calabria. The region boasts a multitude of mouth-watering specialities, which lean largely towards the Mediterranean (olives, citrus figs, almonds). The coastal areas are inevitably brimming with great swordfish and baccalà dishes, while the mountain territories tend towards meats, especially pork.

Some of the local delicacies you're sure to come across are sweet red onions, spicy salami paste known as 'nduja and the ubiquitous *peperoncino*. The Sila is also well known for its formidably tasty porcini mushrooms.

Nightlife is limited to Tropea and a smattering of clubs out towards Capo. During summer, bars like La Munizione are packed most nights (from midnight), and clubs like Suite (www.suite disco.it) in Capo pump out bass-heavy club beats for post-beach party people.

Da Cece

Tropea *Largo Toraldo-Grimaldi (0963 603 219). Open Mar-Oct noon-2.30pm, 7.30pm-midnight daily. Traditional Italian. €€.*
Family-run Cece (pronounced 'che che') is reckoned by many to be the best restaurant in town – and for good reason. In summer, tables are arranged outside in the handsome piazza, and friendly staff run back and forth from the kitchen, serving high-calibre house specialities such as *spaghetti con cipolla* (red onion cooked with red wine) and *spaghetti con moscardini* (baby octopus). The romantic ambience keeps both locals and visitors coming back for more.

Hosteria Italiana

Tropea *Via Boiano Dardano, near Duomo (0963 61113). Open Mar-Oct 7am-midnight daily. Modern Italian. €€.*
Bored of traditional regional specialities? A wine bar in the quieter months, in peak season this funky joint turns out innovative dishes that mirror its chic interior (think

Moroccan-influenced decor with a suitably hip soundtrack), and draws a diverse young crowd. The kitchen gives local dishes such as swordfish and 'nduja new spins, and there's a daily brunch menu (11am-5pm) featuring such hangover-busting standbys as eggs Benedict and french toast.

> ## "The coastal areas are brimming with great swordfish and baccalà dishes, while the mountain territories tend towards meats."

Hotel Aquila & Edelweiss

Camigliatello Silano *Viale Stazione 15 (0984 578 044/www.hotelaquilaedelweiss.com). Open 12.30-2.30pm, 7.30-9pm daily. Traditional Italian. €€€.*
The surroundings may be rather unfashionable, but book a table in this hotel's sprawling, old-fashioned dining rooms and you'll be in the very capable hands of the D'Amico family, who have been running the place since 1948. The kitchen turns out typical Calabrian classics such as soups (the courgette and bean soups are particularly recommended), roast meats, saddles of rabbit and ravioli. To finish off, the unforgettable mint ice-cream is made with local wild mint.

La Munizione

Tropea *Largo Duomo 12 (347 808 0511). Open Mar-Oct 7pm-6am daily. Meals served Mar-July, Sept, Oct 7pm-midnight daily. Bar/restaurant. €€.*
You can't miss this lively Tropea bar: it's right next to the Duomo. Not only does it boast the best terrace views in town, it serves up decent Calabrian and Italian classics. In summer, a DJ spins a selection of house and disco grooves. The cocktail bar, located outside on the terrace, gets busy from around midnight onwards, serving up feisty drinks to Tropea's beautiful people until the wee hours.

La Tavernetta

Camigliatello Silano, La Sila *Campo San Lorenzo 14 (0984 579 026/www.latavernetta.info). Open noon-3pm, 7-11pm Mon, Tue, Thur-Sun. Closed 20 Nov-8 Dec. Traditional Italian. €€€.*
La Tavernetta, 5km from Camigliatello Silano, is one of the Sila's stand-out restaurants. It used to be a rustic gem, but a recent refurbishment has transformed it into a much more contemporary space. However, its network of arched, boldly coloured rooms has plenty of character, and the menu has retained its traditional emphasis. Risottos, soups and roasts are rendered superlative with fresh, farm-reared meats, hand-made pastas, organic cheeses and local porcini. The international wine list, with some heavyweight French and Italian vintages, is very seductive.

From top, left to right: La Casa di Gianna (2); Il Convento (3); Torre Camigliati (2).

La Terrazza
Gerace *Via Nazionale (0964 356 739). Open 12.30-2.30pm, 7.30pm-midnight Mon, Wed-Sun. No credit cards. Traditional Italian. €€.*
La Terrazza serves hearty, homely local cuisine on a rooftop terrace bedecked with wooden tables, traditional red and white tablecloths and handwritten laminated menus. The views are great and the food is everything you'd hope for from a place that's been run by the same family for over 20 years: tasty antipasti ('alla Calabrese' is highly memorable), fabulous pastas and pizzas. Portions are generous, and service is speedy yet relaxed. If there's something you like that doesn't appear on the menu, ask: the chefs here apparently like a bit of a challenge.

Vecchio Forno
Tropea *Via Caviano, off corso Vittorio Emanuele III (347 311 2416 mobile). Open Mar-Nov 7pm-midnight daily. Pizzeria. €.*
Ask any Tropean where to go for pizza and they'll point you in the direction of Vecchio Forno. Snuggled in the joint of the medieval elbow that is via Caivano, this is the city's oldest, best and cheapest pizzeria. The set-up is simple – wooden tables laid out along the streets. Inside, the century-old wood oven turns out pizzas topped with everything from potato to 'nduja. Expect to queue after 8pm during peak periods. Takeaways are available.

Explore

TROPEA & THE CALABRIAN RIVIERA

Tropea's centre is set around piazza Ercole (named after Hercules, the mythical founder of the city) in a tangle of small, cobbled lanes and squares. You can see most of the key sights on foot. To the east is the Romanesque-Norman Largo Duomo, one of the key sights of the city. A few metres further, near the ever-popular La Munizione bar, a plaza gives vertiginous views over the marina. Tropea's main drag, corso Vittorio Emanuele III, runs from the bustling piazza Vittorio Veneto, with its tree-shaded benches, cafés and *gelaterie* in the north, down to the abrupt cliffs, sandy beaches and stunning seaside views in the south.

The city rests on a gorgeous stretch of coastline that is well worth taking some time to explore. The most immediate section – bulging with bronzed Italians and smatterings of paler, more self-conscious northern Europeans in summer – is known locally as the Costa degli Dei (Coast of the Gods), and stretches from Pizzo in the north, where you'll find quieter beaches such as Zambrone and Parghelia, to Nicotera and the Capo Vaticano in the south.

> ## "Capo Vaticano's soaring cliffs, turquoise seas and swaying Mediterranean vegetation make it one of the most popular sections of the Tyrhennian coast."

Capo Vaticano, just 15 minutes from the city by car or bus, is particularly stunning: soaring cliffs, turquoise seas and swaying Mediterranean vegetation make this one of the most popular sections of the Tyrhennian coast. Although certain stretches will be busy during summer – especially beaches such as Grotticelle – there are a number of smaller, less crowded strips that can be discovered without too much effort.

South of Palmi lies another well-known stretch of coast, the Costa Viola, so called because of the sea's purplish hue at sundown. Though most of the towns along here are forgettable (such as Villa San Giovanni, a major ferry crossing point for Sicily), the vibrant town of Scilla is worth a stop, as is nearby Bagnara (both famous for swordfish). At the southernmost point of the coast, the capital, Reggio di Calabria, holds few attractions beyond its world-class museum.

Cattedrale Normanna
Tropea *Largo Duomo (0963 61388/0963 61034). Open Oct-Apr 6.30-11.45am, 4-5pm daily. May-Sept 6.30-11.45am, 4-7.30pm daily. Admission free.*
This 11th-century cathedral is the bomb. Or rather, it contains a bomb – two, to be precise, both unexploded and dating from World War II when the Allies bombed Tropea (they sit alongside a grateful prayer to the Madonna). The imposing Norman structure was remodelled in Gothic style and given another facelift following the famous earthquake of 1905. Within the stately interior are fragments of medieval tombs, as well as the celebrated 14th-century icon of the Virgin Mary of Romania.

Museo Nazionale della Magna Grecia
Reggio di Calabria *piazza de Nava 26 (0965 812 255/ www.museonazionalerc.it) Open 9am-7pm Tue-Sun. Admission €6; €2 reductions.*
The main reason that visitors have for coming here is to see the world-renowned Bronzi di Riace: two full-size Greek bronzes of young, nude, bearded warriors that were discovered off the coast of Calabria in 1972 and were subsequently dated to around 460BC. And while the statues are definitely the main attraction, there are lots more

fascinating objects on display here, including iron age exhibits, funeral objects for accompanying the dead to Hades, modern works of art and an underwater archeology department. Guided tours are available in English.

Ruffo Castle

Scilla *Rocca di Scilla (0965 704207/0965 754704). Open 8.30am-7.30pm daily. Admission €1.50.*
Scilla, an attractive fishing village at the entrance of the Straits of Messina, is still dining out on its Homeric associations (the village marks the spot where the mythological Scylla changed into a sea monster in *The Odyssey*). Its Norman castle, which clings to a spur that stretches out to sea, is one of the area's main sights. Constructed between the eighth and ninth centuries, its irregular bulk holds regular art exhibitions and conferences.

PARCO NAZIONALE DELLA SILA

La Sila (0984 537 109/www.parcosila.it) is comprised of three sections: Sila Grande, the smaller Sila Piccola and the misleadingly named Sila Greca, which has actually been an area of Albanian settlement from the 1500s. Despite the subdivisions, the park functions as a continuous, congruous whole – one that's every bit as sylvan as the name suggests.

Coniferous forests, dense woodlands, hidden caves and dramatic valleys conspire to create a lush, peaceful habitat that hosts some of the region's most diverse wildlife: roe deer, wild boar, black woodpeckers, peregrine falcons and eagle owls included. A great outdoor playground, the park is equipped for activities of all kinds, including hiking, fishing, mountain biking, canyoning, hang-gliding, canoeing, horse riding, skiing and snowboarding.

La Sila's official tourist centre is Camigliatello Silano, a somewhat functional town to the south of the park with a reasonable selection of accommodation and eating options, decent skiing facilities and a dedicated tourist office supplying maps and advice for exploring the area. There are also two official Parco Sila visitor centres (one at Cecita Lake, another at Taverna), which offer information and 32 itineraries through the park.

Visitors looking to get off the beaten path might enjoy Torre Camigliati, a restored 18th-century baronial hunting lodge set in extensive, idyllic grounds and run by descendants of the original owners, the Barracco family. It's part cultural space (offering walking and historical itineraries through the region, permanent in-house exhibitions and a nearby museum, La Nave della Sila), and part literary centre, celebrating the visions of 'grand tour' travellers from the 18th to the 20th centuries, especially Norman Douglas, author of the 1915 account *Old Calabria*. Torre Camigliati also offers rooms and self-service

apartments, and makes a great base from which to explore the area.

From here you can strike out along the 'strada della vette' ('road of the peaks'), a 13-kilometre romp through woods that takes you to three of the park's main peaks – Monte Scuro, Monte Corcio and Monte Botte Donato – before descending down to Lago Arvo and the lakeside resort of Lorica. This same route is accessible by car. From the Albanian town of Acri in the north it's possible to drive down to Cecita Lake (detouring to the official trail hub of La Fossiata if hiking is your thing), through Camigliatello Silano and the 'strada della vette' towards Lorica and Lago Arvo, before heading towards Villagio Mancuso and Catanzaro.

Other highlights worth making a detour to are the striking Byzantine village of Santa Severina; the wood-framed houses of Villaggio Mancuso; Rossano, with its aristocratic buildings and cathedral housing the world-renowned *Codex Purpureus*; and the cliff-top village of Civita, which has dramatic views of the Gole del Raganello and houses the Museo Etnico Arbëresh (piazza Municipio 9, 0981 73 019, www.civita.info, open 5-8pm Tue-Sun, admission free), which charts the historical settlement of Albanians in the area from the 15th century on.

Museo Diocesano, Rossano Cathedral

Rossano Calabro, Discesa Duomo (0983 525263). Open Museum Oct-June 9.30am-12.30pm, 4-7pm Tue-Fri; 10am-noon, 4.30-6.30pm Sat, Sun. July-Sept 9am-1pm, 4.30-8pm daily. Admission €3. Cathedral Oct-May 8am-noon, 4.45-8pm daily. June-Sept 7am-noon, 4.45-8.30pm daily. Admission free.
In Rossano's 11th-century cathedral lies one of the most important church documents in Italy: the *Codex Purpureus Rossanensis*. One of the oldest surviving illuminated manuscripts of the New Testament, the document – so called because of the reddish colour of its pages – was thought to have been created in Palestine in the sixth century and brought to Italy by monks fleeing the Muslim invasions. Penned in silver ink, the 188-page codex contains the text of the Gospel of Matthew and the majority of the Gospel of Mark (a second volume is apparently missing), as well as a prefatory cycle of illustrations.

La Nave della Sila

Camigliatello Silano, Torre di Camigliati, Parco Old Calabria (0984 578200/www.oldcalabria.org). Open Aug 10am-2pm, 3.30-7.30pm daily. Sept-July by appointment. Admission Aug €1; Sept-July €2.
This large, modern space is a recent addition to the Torre Camigliati estate. Mixing installations (including a replica of a ship's cabin) with lucid illustrations, enlarged photographic prints and newspaper articles, the museum posits a fascinating insight into the history of the Calabrian diaspora. A big draw for locals is the extensive database that can be used to trace family histories back several generations. Also drawing them in is the adjacent café, which serves a powerful espresso.

La Tavernetta.

From top, left to right: La Cattolica; Gerace Cathedral; La Sila National Park; Tropea's belvedere.

GERACE

Present-day Gerace emerged from the ruins of nearby Locri, which was laid low by repeated pirate raids and endemic malaria, in the eighth century. The city was conquered briefly by Saracens before returning to Byzantine control and, eventually, falling under Norman rule. The main attractions are still the Norman castle (physically out of bounds due to the precarious state of the walls and paths) and the impressive cathedral, Calabria's largest, of the same period. There are also several smaller churches within easy reach. Although Gerace is the primary draw to the area, Locri – a functional, workaday town that boasts little in the way of attractions – does have some interesting ruins and a glut of good beaches. Stilo (an hour away by car) also offers the chance to see the region's oldest Byzantine church, La Cattolica.

La Cattolica

Stilo, 1hr from Gerace *Via Cattolica, close to Piazza S Giovanni (0964 776006/www.lacattolicadistilo.it). Open 8am-8pm daily. Admission free.*
Its image reproduced on many a brochure and postcard, Stilo's small, square brick church is one of the architectural highlights of the area. It's about an hour's drive from Gerace, but worth the detour. Built in the ninth or tenth century and restored in the early 1900s, it sits at the foot of a mountain. The three naves are held up by a quartet of pillars and contain remains of Byzantine frescoes. The church's distinctive domes are illuminated by mullioned windows. Nearby Bivongi is home to the equally lovely Byzantine-Norman basilica of San Giovanni Theristis.

Gerace Cathedral

Via Circonvallazione, close to Piazza del Tocco (0964 356323/0964 356828). Open Apr-July 9.30am-1pm, 3-8pm Tue-Sun. Aug 9.30am-1pm, 3-9pm Tue-Sun. Sept-Oct 9.30am-1pm, 3-7pm Tue-Sun. Nov-Mar 9.30am-1pm, 3-6pm Tue-Sun. Admission €1.50.
Founded in 1045 by Robert Guiscard and enlarged by Frederick II in 1222, Gerace's Norman cathedral is an impressive sight. The stately interior is plain and unadorned, with a mix of columns said to have come from the ancient Greek and Roman temples found in Locri. Behind the altar sits a virgin and child by the Pisa school. The Greek-cross-shaped crypt has a floor in Gerace mosaic, and there's an interesting display charting the restoration.

Locri Epizefiri ruins & museum

Locri *Contrada Marasa' (0964 390 023). Open 9am-7.30pm Tue-Sun. Admission €2; €1 reductions.*
About 3km beyond Locri lie the city wall ruins of the Greek city Epizefiri. An ongoing excavation, the site harks back to the seventh century BC. Only vestiges can be seen, though the original measured around 8km in circumference. The ruins are spread over a wide area amid olive groves and orchards, so transport is useful, although the most interesting sights – a fifth century BC Ionic temple, Roman necropolis and fourth-century Graeco-Roman theatre – can all be reached on foot. The museum is worth a look before you set off, as it has a decent overview of the site and its finds.

Factfile

When to go

August – when the Italians take their holiday and the rest of the country closes down – is the most crowded month, and accommodation should be booked well in advance. However, the weather is pleasanter in spring and early autumn, and the crowds are thinner.

Getting there

The closest airport is Aeroporto Internazionale di Lamezia Terme (www.sacal.it 0968 414 333), 64km from Tropea. The railway station is 2km from the airport and connects directly with Tropea (1 hour, www.trenitalia.it).

Getting around

Four buses run from Tropea to Capo Vaticano every day (June-Sept, 20mins).

Tourist information

Cosenza tourist office, piazzetta Toscano (0984 813336). Open 9am-1pm, 3-6pm Mon, Thur; 9am-1pm Tue, Wed, Fri.
Cosenza Assessorato al Turismo, via Galliano 6 (0984 814527). Open Mon, Wed 10am-noon; 4-5pm Thur.
Sila Point, Via Forgitelle, Camigliatello Silano (0984 578031). Open Oct-May 8am-2pm Mon-Fri. June-Sept 8am-2pm, 3-6pm Mon-Fri.
Tropea Tourist Office, piazza Ercole (0963 61475). Open Oct-May 9am-1pm, 3.30-7.30pm daily. June-Sept 9am-1pm, 4-8pm daily.
APT Reggio di Calabria, Via Roma 3 (0965 22530). Open Oct-Mar 7.30am-1.30pm, 2.30-5.30pm Mon, Wed; 7.30am-1.30pm Tue, Thur, Fri. Apr-Sept 7.30am-1.30pm, 2.30-5.30pm daily.

Internet

Virus Informatica Via Provinciale 97, S Domenica di Tropea (0963 669 970). Open 9am-1pm, 4-8pm Mon-Fri; 9am-1pm Sat.
Cosenza Internet Café, via Falcone 48 (0984 408351). Open 7am-10pm daily.
Reggio di Calabria Internet Point Santagati, via Briatico 44 (0965 752 705). Open 2.30-8.30pm Mon; 10am-1pm, 2.30-8.30pm Tue-Sun.

Clockwise from top left:
Alba; pastries from Alba;
vineyards near Alba,
Castello Falletti in Barolo;
Enoteca Regionale di
Barola.

The Langhe & Asti

Halfway between the Alps and the Mediterranean lies the Langhe. It's only 80 kilometres south-east of the factories and bustle of Turin, but in terms of character, it couldn't be more distant. Vineyards cling to dramatic slopes, whose peaks are studded with enchanting medieval towns. The morning fog that sits on the looming castles, Gothic churches and defensive towers gives the area a fairytale feel. But it's the unpretentious approach to food that draws visitors from all over the world in search of the ideal meal and the perfect bottle of wine.

Wine has been produced in the Langhe for more than 2,000 years, using dozens of native grapes that thrive in the region's various microclimates. Grape cultivation was perfected by the Romans soon after they conquered the territory in the first century BC. The modern Italian wine industry was born during the late 19th century, in the latter days of Piedmont's Savoy monarchy. By the late 20th century the Langhe was turning out nebbiolo-based reds that compete with those of Bordeaux and Burgundy for their quality, elegance and capacity for ageing. Employing a mixture of traditional methods and cutting edge technology, the region's producers now coax the best from the stubborn nebbiolo, acidic barbera, fruit-driven dolcetto and aromatic moscato grapes. Many of the area's vineyards are hands-on, family-run operations; tours are often given by the vineyards' owners.

Centuries of invasion and civil war have left fortified towns and imposing castles in their wake; Barolo, Monforte d'Alba and Barbaresco are just a few of the towns with castles adding definition to their skylines. Today, the historic centres of the Langhe's main towns are found within the fortified circuits of medieval bastions, where cathedrals dominate the main squares and tangled medieval streets radiate out towards the city walls.

North of the Langhe, in the hilly Monferrato region, is Asti. Its history is similar to that of the Langhe, with its strategic location ensuring it was hotly contested by noble families and European monarchies. And like its neighbours in the Langhe, Asti is a town where food and wine reign supreme.

Turin

0 5km

Asti

Costigliole d'Asti

Castiglione
Tinella

Barbaresco

Alba

Santo Stefano
Belbo

Barolo

Monforte d'Alba

The Langhe & Asti

Historic sites
● ● ● ● ●

Art & architecture
● ● ● ● ●

Hotels
● ● ● ● ●

Eating & drinking
● ● ● ● ●

Scenery
● ● ● ● ●

Outdoor activities
● ● ● ● ●

Stay

Agriturismo Cascina Papaveri
Costigliole d'Asti *Strada Chiesa San Michele 8 (0141 962 044/www.cascinapapaveri.com). Closed late Nov-Feb. €€€.*
Perched in the green Monferrato hills, this working organic farm provides all-inclusive breaks with five-star facilities. The rooms are stylish and understated, with flatscreen TVs and sumptuous views. Guests are instructed in the nuances of Piedmont's food and wine culture in a state-of-the-art kitchen, and treated to market and winery visits. Pilates classes are run in the studio, and there are two pools in which to burn off some of the calories you've added.

Albergo Castiglione
Castiglione Tinella *Via Cavour 5 (0141 855 410/www.albergocastiglione.com). Closed mid Dec-mid Mar. €€.*
Albergo Castiglione, located in the centre of a charming village just east of Alba, is an ideal base for exploring the Langhe. The rooms are tasteful and simply furnished; some come with their own private terraces. All guests have access to La Castagna, a pool and spa centre with spectacular views over the moscato vineyards. The owners also rent out two mini apartments with kitchens in the 17th-century Palazzo dei Monferrato, not far from here.

Albergo San Lorenzo
Alba *Piazza Rossetti 6 (0173 362 406/ www.albergo-sanlorenzo.it). Closed 2wks Aug. €€.*
Set in a restored 18th-century building in a quiet square, San Lorenzo is just metres away from Alba's busy main streets and squares. The 11 no-frills double rooms are spacious, clean and soberly decorated; the communal reading room exhibits the same minimalist decor. Staff are friendly and forthcoming, and there's on-site parking for patrons with cars.

Poggio Sul Belbo
Santo Stefano Belbo *Loc Robini Strada Quassi 12 (0141 840 407/www.poggiosulbelbo.com). Closed mid Nov-Mar. €.*
At the top of a winding 5km ascent from the centre of Santo Stefano Belbo, this well-appointed B&B is run by Anglo-Italian owners Maggie and Natale Bauducco. The four spacious rooms are furnished with brightly coloured linens and antique furniture; each has a balcony or patio with sweeping views over Barbera's vineyards and the Langhe hills beyond. Breakfast is served on a panoramic patio from which, on a clear day, the Alps are visible in the distance. Wine and truffle tastings, spa outings and yoga classes can be organised for guests.

Relais San Maurizio
Santo Stefano Belbo *Loc San Maurizio 39 (0141 841 900/www.relaissanmaurizio.it). Closed 3wks Jan, Feb. €€€.*
The 31 rooms at this former Franciscan monastery are divided between the main house and the old barn, occupying the former monks' cells and the stables. Each room is decorated with eclectic pieces and fine antiques; some have open fireplaces. The spa is known for its grape extract-based treatments, and the Michelin-starred restaurant serves creative haute cuisine in the brick barrel vaults of the old wine cellars.

> "The Langhe is a gastronome's paradise: conventional local wisdom states that fatty food is good for you as long as it's washed down with a glass of wine."

Eat

The Langhe is a gastronome's paradise, where conventional local wisdom states that fatty food is good for you as long as it's washed down with a glass of wine. Restaurants range from simple working farms to Michelin-rated affairs.

Meals here begin with antipasti such as *vitello tonnato*, cold sliced veal paired with a rich mayo and tuna sauce, or *carne cruda*, beef carpaccio seasoned with oil, lemon and parmigiano. There's also the love-it-or-hate-it *bagna cauda*, a butter and anchovy sauce that comes out in winter. First courses are dominated by homemade pastas such as *tajarin* (thin hand-cut strips of egg-based pasta) and *agnolotti del plin* (stuffed ravioli). River fish such as trout pop up on the occasional menu, but the Langhe is best known for its meat: veal, steak and game, served grilled, braised or stewed. The area is Italy's capital of hazelnuts, nougat and chocolate; traditional desserts include *torta di nocciola* (hazelnut cake), *semifreddo al torroncino* (frozen nougat custard) and *bunet al cioccolato* (chocolate pudding).

You'll have just as much of an appetising choice when you reach the wine list. Roero Arneis, produced in the nearby Roero hills, is a fresh, floral white that makes a pleasant aperitif, and the aromatic white moscato grape is used to make sparkling Asti Spumante and still Moscato d'Asti, often drunk with desserts. But the Langhe is best known for its excellent reds. Nebbiolo is used to produce the full-bodied Barolo and Barbaresco, and dolcetto and barbera are used to make versatile wines of the same name.

Clockwise from top left:
Relais San Maurizio (3);
biscuits, sweets and
truffle oil from Alba.

L'Angolo del Beato
Asti *Via Guttuari 12 (0141 531 668/ www.angolodelbeato.it). Open 12.30-3pm, 7.30-10pm Mon-Sat. €€€. Traditional/regional Italian.*
L'Angolo del Beato's tiny front door, tucked away in the heart of Asti's medieval quarter, resembles not so much a restaurant but a private home. The menu served in its simple, stylish interior focuses on regional fare; the kitchen allows the seasonal ingredients to speak for themselves without overly complicating matters. Specialities include *fiori di zucca ripieni di fonduta* (zucchini flowers stuffed with fondue) and *brasato di bue* (braised ox); the impressive cellar stocks some 400 labels.

La Cantinetta
Barolo *Via Roma 33 (0173 56198). Open 12.30-3pm, 7.30-10pm Mon, Tue, Fri-Sun; 12.30-3pm Wed. Closed mid Feb-mid Mar, 2wks July. €€€. Traditional/regional Italian.*
The Chiappetto brothers have been serving innovative cuisine in Barolo since 1995. Although plenty of traditional dishes make an appearance on the menu, more unusual options abound, among them *l'uovo in pasta* (a large ravioli filled with runny egg yolk and topped with finely grated white truffle) and *finanziera alla piemontese*, a concoction combining sweetbread, liver, cockscomb and mushrooms. The best seats in the house are on the back terrace, with its sweeping views over the hills and nebbiolo vineyards.

La Ciau de Tornavento
Treiso, 7km from Alba *Piazza Baracco 7 (0173 638 333/www.laciaudeltornavento.it). Open 12.30-3pm, 7.30-10pm Mon, Tue, Fri-Sun; 7.30-10pm Thur. Closed Feb. €€€€. Modern Italian.*
Chef Maurillo Garol crafts an array of innovative dishes in a formal setting at this Michelin-starred temple of haute cuisine; the sum of his endeavours is a superlative dining experience. The main dining room and summer patio offer panoramic views over Barbaresco's nebbiolo vineyards; appropriate, really, given that the cellars contain a dizzying 1,000 labels.

La Gibigianna
Barbaresco *Via Torino 26 (339 481 5927 mobile/ www.lagibigianna.it). Open 9am-8pm Mon, Wed-Sun. Closed Jan. €. Enoteca.*
This cosy, relaxed enoteca is run by the amiable, passionate Francesco Gigliotti. The ground floor is a bright, sunny space that looks out on to Barbaresco's main street; upstairs, a few more tables look out on the piazza Municipio, and diners can also eat on the patio during summer. There are more than 100 Barbaresco labels on the menu, that can be paired with cold plates of cheeses or cured meats, along with olive oils, pastas and chocolates to take away.

Osteria dell'Arco
Alba *Piazza Savona 5 (0173 363 974/ www.osteriadellarco.it). Open 12.30-3pm, 7.30-10.30pm Tue-Sat. €€. Traditional/modern Italian.*
The crisp white linen and sparsely decorated dining room at Osteria dell'Arco suggest formality, but the service and atmosphere are more down to earth. All the dishes showcase local produce and seasonal ingredients, with traditional recipes indicated by the Slow Food movement's trademark snail. The delicate *tajarin*, served with butter and sage or sausage ragù, is delectable, and *lumache al verde* (snails in parsley pesto) are a must for mollusc fans.

Ristorante Stazione
Santo Stefano Belbo *Piazzale G Manzo 6 (0141 844 233). Open 12.30-3pm, 7.30-10.30pm Mon, Tue, Fri-Sun; 12.30-3pm Wed. €€. Traditional/regional Italian.*
From the outside, there's little indication that this place is a restaurant, save for the telltale sound of the sizzling grill and clink of dishes escaping from a front window. Although the interior decorator didn't quite get it right in the two dining rooms, one homely and the other decorated in ultra-modern fashion, the chef certainly does, with an array of formal yet moderately priced Langhe cuisine. Traditional dishes abound, from *tajarin* to *semifreddo al torroncino*.

La Salita
Monforte d'Alba *Via Marconi 2a (0173 787 196). Open 7.30-10pm Wed-Sat; 12.30-3pm, 7.30-10pm Sun. Closed Jan-mid Mar, 2wks Sept. €€. Osteria.*
In an area known for its Michelin-starred restaurants (with prices to match), La Salita is a pleasantly informal alternative. Much like the decor, the food is modern, light and simple. The inimitable *coniglio al forno*, oven-roasted rabbit with tomatoes and olives, is not be missed; the kitchen also offers an appealing twist on a local staple, serving *carne all'albese* 'con erbette' (delicate slices of raw meat served with oil and herbs, instead of the traditional lemon and parmigiano). The wine list is sensational.

> **"Maurillo Garol's temple to haute cuisine offers views of the nebbiolo vineyards; appropriate, given that the cellar contains 1,000 labels."**

La Vecchia Carrozza
Asti *Via Giosue' Carducci 41 (0141 538 657). Open 12.30-3pm, 7.45-10pm Tue-Sun. €€. Traditional/regional Italian.*
Housed in the converted stables of an old palace, Vecchia Carrozza is known for its superb and typically Astigiani cooking. Take note of the menu at the entrance, because you won't see it again, and don't get your hopes up over any one dish: from the mouthwatering array of dishes, the kitchen only prepares those that are in season. The tantalising dessert tray, displaying a dozen local indulgences, is near-impossible to resist.

Explore

ALBA

Alba was established as a Roman colony in 89 BC, and its historic centre is encircled by the old Roman city walls. Medieval towers rub shoulders with baroque churches and Renaissance palaces, but don't be deceived: this is a modern city, stocked with posh eateries, gourmet shops and chic wine bars.

Via Vittorio Emanuele, the main thoroughfare, is lined with cafés and restaurants. At its southern end is piazza Savona, where the locals come to see and be seen while sipping a glass of wine; at its northern tip stands the monumental piazza Risorgimento, home to the austere Cattedrale di San Lorenzo. The square of piazza Pertinace, just west of piazza Risorgimento, is the site of the Baroque church of San Giovanni Battista, in front of which the underground ruins of the Roman temple of Jupiter are visible.

For nearly 80 years, Alba has been celebrating the white truffle, its most precious export, at its annual Fiera Nazionale del Tartufo, which is held over five weeks each autumn. The festivities aren't solely culinary: one day is dedicated to the Palio degli Asinelli, or donkey races, which cock a snook at the grander affair held in Asti. In the spring, wine is celebrated at the Vinum festival.

"First run in 1275, the palio in Asti, on the third Sunday of September, predates its Sienese counterpart by more than four centuries."

Cattedrale di San Lorenzo
Piazza Risorgimento (0173 440 000). Open call for details. Admission free.
The towering spires of Alba's red brick Gothic cathedral, built during the 12th century, punctuate the town's skyline. Inside, the decoration and architecture range from the sober to the exuberant – the result of restyling in the 15th and 17th centuries. Of particular interest is a 1512 wooden chorus by Bernadino Fossati, inlaid with scenes of city life, and a stirring Crucifixion altarpiece. Major excavations in the central nave, slated for completion in April 2008, should reveal more about the cathedral's intriguing medieval and ancient layers.

Museo Civico Archeologico e di Scienze Naturali Federico Eusebio
Via Vittorio Emanuele 19 (0173 292 473/www.eusebio-online.it). Open 3-6pm Tue-Fri; 9.30am-12.30pm, 3-6pm Sat, Sun. Closed 2wks Aug. Admission €4. No credit cards.
The museum's ground floor is dedicated to the civilisations that have occupied the Langhe from the Neolithic age to the Roman epoch. Especially intriguing are the faithfully reconstructed Copper Age tomb, and the frescoes and artefacts from the forum, theatre, villas and temples of Alba Pompeia. The upper level covers the Langhe's natural history, with fossils of flora and fauna and specimens of exotic plant life.

ASTI

Although its name may bring to mind clinking flutes bubbling with Asti Spumante (once sickly but recently much improved), Asti has much more to offer. Today it's an elegant, manicured city, with a noble air and carefully-restored historical centre.

During the Middle Ages, Asti became one of northern Italy's most powerful political and commercial centres. Pristine Gothic architecture and fine medieval towers testify to its medieval glory. However, the 17th and 18th centuries saw the town attacked and invaded by Austrians and Spaniards seeking control of Monferrato, and it wasn't until the 19th century that Asti would once again become an economic force.

The town's gateway is piazza Campo del Palio where, on the third Sunday in September, Italy's most historic horse race takes place: first run in 1275, the Palio in Asti predates its Sienese counterpart by more than four centuries. Weeks of festivities lead up to the event, and thousands of spectators watch as teams compete in a bareback race for victory and a year's worth of bragging rights. However, it's far from the only event in September: the month is dedicated to wine and food festivals, the most important of which is the two-week Douja d'Or.

Due north of the Campo is piazza Alfieri, named after the 18th-century writer who is Asti's most famous son. From here, the corso Alfieri runs east and west, lined with palaces, museums and churches. At its eastern end is San Pietro in Consavia, a church and cloister that houses the Museo Archeologico e Paleontologico. The western half of corso Alfieri cuts into Asti's medieval heart and ends near the Palazzo Alfieri and Torre Rossa (red tower). Just north of the corso is Asti's cathedral.

Cattedrale
Piazza Cattedrale (0141 592 924). Open 8.30am-12.15pm, 3-5.30pm daily. Admission free.
Built between 1309 and 1354, Asti's cathedral is dedicated to Our Lady of the Assumption and has changed little from

its ancient plan; its red brick exterior is quintessential Piemontese Gothic. The original entrance façade features three fine portals surmounted by rose windows, though the entrance is now on the cathedral's south side. The interior has undergone major renovations over the centuries, most notably during the Renaissance, when Gandolfino da Roreto decorated the side chapels. A chapel in the left aisle is home to a painting of Sant'Aventino, known to Astigiani for miraculously curing headaches.

Chiesa Collegiata di San Secondo
Piazza San Secondo (0141 53006). Open 10.45am-noon, 3.30-5.30pm Mon-Sat; 3.30-5.30pm Sun. Admission free.
Another sterling example of Piemontese Gothic, San Secondo was built on the site of San Secondo's martyrdom and burial; relics of Asti's patron saint are housed in the ninth-century crypt. Constructed between the 13th and 15th centuries, its exterior is similar to that of the cathedral. Inside, the Chapel of San Secondo houses historic victory banners from the city's annual Palio, portraying San Secondo as a knight on horseback.

Complesso Medioevale di San Pietro in Consavia – Museo Archeologico e Paleontologico
Corso Alfieri 2 (0141 353 072). Open May-Sept 9am-1pm, 4-7pm Tue-Fri; 10am-1pm Sat; 4-7pm Sun. Oct-Apr 9am-1pm, 3-5pm Tue-Fri; 10am-1pm Sat; 3-6pm Sun. Admission free.
Built in several stages, this complex is one of Piedmont's most important historic sites. The oldest building is the 12th-century Romanesque baptistery, dubbed the Rotonda. Originally dedicated to the Holy Sepulchre, it was claimed by the Knights of the Holy Sepulchre in the 13th century, who rededicated it to San Pietro and added a cloister and hospital for pilgrims. The last major addition came in the 15th century with the addition of the Gothic Aula Valperga, probably intended as a funeral chapel for the noble Valperga family. Today, the cloister is home to Asti's archaeology and paleontology museums.

BAROLO

Barolo's skyline is dominated by the tenth-century Castello Falletti, a noble residence that's now a museum and a home to the village's tourist office and Enoteca Regionale. The parish church, San Donato (open 5-7pm Sat, 8-10am Sun), is in the square facing the entrance to the museum. Down the hill along via Roma is the Museo dei Cavatappi (0173 560 539, www.museodeicavatappi.it), dedicated to the history of the corkscrew, and some gourmet food and wine shops that promote local wines.

Indeed, the village's name is synonymous with world-class vino. As you wander through Barolo's streets, it's impossible to escape the stuff. Indeed, it sometimes seems as though all 500 Barolo residents are involved in the production, promotion and sale of the 'king of wines and

wine of kings'. Made from the late-ripening red nebbiolo grape, it's aged for three years in oak barrels (four for Riserva) and is defined by its elegant aromas, from chocolate and coffee to tobacco and leather. It ages well and pairs very nicely with hearty dishes such as braised meat, stews and game.

Castello Falletti & Enoteca Regionale di Barolo
Piazza Falletti (0173 56277/www.baroloworld.it). Open 10am-12.30pm, 3-6pm Mon-Wed, Fri-Sun. Closed Jan. Admission Castle & apartments €4. Enoteca free. No credit cards.
Home to the Falletti family from the 13th to the 19th centuries, the palace's noble apartments, library and salon are opulently furnished with antiques and paintings. Don't miss the remarkable trompe l'oeil tapestries in the Stanza della Marchesa. In the basement, the Enoteca Regionale di Barolo offers wine tastings (€2 for one glass, €5 for three) and sells Barolos from many of the region's main producers.

"As you wander Barolo's streets it seems as though all the town's 500 residents are involved in the production, promotion and sale of wine."

Museo dei Cavatappi
Piazza Castello 4 (0173 560 539/www.museodeicavatappi.it). Open Mar-Aug, Nov, Dec 10am-1pm, 2-6.30pm Mon-Wed, Fri-Sun. Sept, Oct 10am-1pm, 2-6.30pm daily. Closed Jan, Feb. Admission €4.
Next door to the Castello Falletti, Barolo's corkscrew museum displays more than 500 bottle openers, documenting the development of the priceless invention. Drop by for a pit stop between Barolo tastings.

BARBARESCO

The diminutive village of Barbaresco sits on a hill that's enveloped by nebbiolo vineyards. Wine is, indeed, the village's lifeblood, and almost all of its residents are in the business.

Exploring the village won't take more than half an hour, but it's a charming place. The main street, via Torino, is a 300-metre stretch lined with shops, enoteche and restaurants, where, guided by passionate proprietors, you can while away a pleasant afternoon sampling

Clockwise from top left: Enoteca Regionale di Barolo (3); vineyards near Barolo; Alba towers; Alba; Barbaresco.

the local vintages. At one end of the street is the Enoteca Regionale di Barbaresco; at the other stands the Torre del Bricco, a 36-metre defensive tower that's become a symbol of the town.

Enoteca Regionale di Barbaresco
Piazza del Municipio 7 (0173 635 251/ www.enotecadelbarbaresco.it). Open 9.30am-6pm Mon, Tue, Thur-Sat; 9.30am-1pm, 2.30-6pm Sun. Closed Jan. Admission free.
The town's wine promotion and tourist office resides in the desanctified church of San Donato. The friendly staff provide didactic wine tastings, charging €1.50 a glass and selling bottles from 106 producers. In summer, the church accommodates modern art exhibitions of sometimes dubious quality.

SANTO STEFANO BELBO

Santo Stefano Belbo was settled by the Romans, but the most significant moment in its millennial history was the birth of anti-fascist writer Cesare Pavese in 1908. An annual festival celebrates the life and work of Santo Stefano's most famous son; a library and literary park dedicated to his life and works marks his birthplace on the road to Canelli.

In the town's main square, piazza Umberto I, old men play cards at the numerous bars, while teenagers hang out on the benches. Wine is the topic of many a conversation: the town is a main centre for Barbera wine production.

MONFORTE D'ALBA

Named for the ancient castle (*fortis*) that once stood on the hill (*mons*), Monforte d'Alba is one of the Langhe's most charming hamlets. The site where the castle once stood is now occupied by the 18th-century Palazzo Scarampi (closed to the public); below it, medieval houses and churches cling to the hillside.

Legend has it that in 1028, the people of Monforte, followers of the heretical Catharist sect, were given the choice of renouncing their religious beliefs or being burned at the stake. They chose death, and so the Archbishop of Milan took the vacant town. It was later donated to the Marquess of del Caretto and then controlled by a string of noble families until it was taken by force by the Savoy dynasty in 1703.

In the 20th century, Monforte had an important role in the partisan movement, becoming a centre of anti-fascist militias. Today, it is home to several exclusive hotels and restaurants.

Factfile

When to go
The best time to visit the Langhe is during the autumn season, when towns celebrate the annual grape harvest or local produce (especially truffles). Festivals are held in almost every town; among them are Alba's Vinum e Fiera Nazionale del Tartufo, Dogliani's Sagra del Dolcetto, and Asti's Douja D'Or and Festival delle Sagre.

Consequently, of course, the vineyards are swamped during autumn, and may be less able to accommodate visits and tastings. If you're here for the wine, come in spring and early summer, when new wines are released and their producers are in full PR mode. Be warned that many restaurants and hotels close for all or part of August.

Getting there
The closest airports are Turin Caselle, Malpensa and Linate in Milan, Cristoforo Colombo in Genoa and Cuneo Levaldigi. International trains arrive at Turin, from where three local trains an hour take the 40-minute ride on to Asti. From Asti, connections run to most major towns in the Langhe. However, while it is possible to use Asti or Alba as a base from which to explore the nearby towns by train, it's easier to rent a car.

Tourist information
AstiTurismo – ATL Piazza Alfieri 29, Asti (014 153 0357/www.astiturismo.it). Open 9am-1pm, 2.30-6.30pm Mon-Sat; 9am-1pm Sun. Ente Turismo Alba Bra Langhe Roero, Piazza Risorgimento 2, Alba (017 335 833/ www.langheroero.it). Open 9am-1pm, 2.30pm-6.30pm daily. Enoteca Regionale e Ufficio turistico di Barbaresco (see above). Enoteca Regionale e Ufficio turistico del Barolo (see p39). The Langhe & Roero Card costs €5 and allows free entrance to several of the region's castles and museums. It also offers discounts on entertainment, culinary and sporting events. The card is available at most tourist offices and some museums. For more, see www.turismoinlanga.it.

Internet
Many tourist offices have internet access and Wi-Fi connections; you can also get online at the Museo dei Cavatappi (see p39) and Donat International in Alba (via Gioberti 6, 017 366 504). Otherwise, historic districts usually have at least one shop with internet access for €3-€5 an hour.

Lecce & around

While holidaymakers from abroad have been busy colonising Tuscany for decades, the natives have quietly kept Puglia, the sun-soaked heel of Italy's boot, to themselves. The region is being rebranded as 'the New Tuscany', but its charms aren't so easy to define. There may be hill towns and olive trees, but the area's beauty is wilder and less contained, and its simple, low-key pleasures (pristine sandy beaches, untamed countryside, great food) are amplified by a lack of famous sights. Freed from the obligation to tick off must-see attractions, you can wander at will without bumping into fellow tourists at every turn.

Clockwise from top left: Cattedrale di Santa Maria Annunziata (2); Locorotondo; alley in Otranto; Gallipoli fish market; Otranto ceramics.

Italians make up 70 per cent of Puglia's visitors, but the region is primed for a foreign invasion – and not for the first time. Lying between the Adriatic and Ionian seas, the region has been conquered by just about everyone: the Greeks, the Romans, the Normans and the Spanish. Puglia has been shaped by these many centuries of colliding cultural influences. Today, its dazzlingly hybrid-architecture, from Greek whitewashed houses to grandiose Baroque palazzi and Norman castles to the characteristic *trulli*, are key to its offbeat appeal.

In Baroque Lecce, the lively capital, dubbed 'the Florence of the South', gargoyles loom over medieval alleyways and cherubim cavort across façades, lending the town an other-worldly theatricality. An hour's drive north-west is the Valle d'Itria, home of the *trulli* with their distinctive conical roofs and the 'white towns' of Ostuni and Martina Franca. And the sea is never far away; south-east of Lecce the tip of the Salentine Peninsula curls around the Gulf of Taranto, with unspoiled beauty on either side. Focuses are the historic port town of Otranto on the Adriatic and the island of Gallipoli on the Ionian.

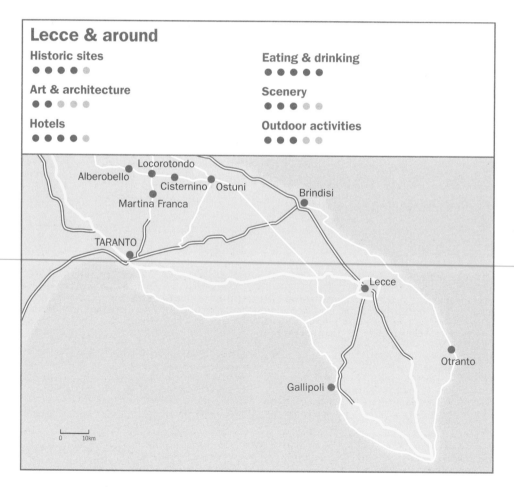

Lecce & around

Historic sites
● ● ● ● ◔

Art & architecture
● ● ◔ ◌ ◌

Hotels
● ● ● ● ◔

Eating & drinking
● ● ● ● ●

Scenery
● ● ● ◌ ◌

Outdoor activities
● ● ● ◌ ◌

Locorotondo
Alberobello
Cisternino Ostuni
Martina Franca
Brindisi
TARANTO
Lecce
Otranto
Gallipoli ●

0   10km

Stay

Acquarossa

Between Cisternino & Ostuni *Contrada da Acquarossa 2, Casalini-Cisternino Road (0804 444 093/ www.acqua-rossa.it).* €€.

A slew of chichi *trulli* resorts have sprung up around the Valle d'Itria in recent years, but this is the real deal. Each *trullo* has its own tiny bathroom and even tinier kitchen, and the decor is appropriately rustic (flagstoned floors, wood-burning stoves, antique furniture). The atmosphere is relaxed: the charmingly ramshackle yard has hammocks, while the sumptuous breakfast (served on lavender-planted terraces) merges comfortably into brunch for late-risers. Check the website for (fairly complex) driving directions.

Balconcino d'Oriente

Otranto *Via San Francesco da Paola 71 (0836 801 529/www.balconcinodoriente.com).* €.

Balconcino d'Oriente is a friendly B&B that offers excellent value for money. There's only four rooms, each decorated with Moroccan-style ceramic lanterns and gauzy curtains, and the cool, mosaic-tiled en suite bathrooms are spotless. The first-floor rooms have private terraces. Served in a cosy, barrel-vaulted room cluttered with tribal *objets*, breakfast is a feast of own-made goodies.

"In the 16th century, this *masseria* served as a watchtower against Ottoman and Saracen attacks, a far cry from its present luxury."

B&B Prestige

Lecce *Via Santa Maria del Paradiso 4 (0832 243 353/ www.bbprestige-lecce.it).* €.

The three rooms at this bijou B&B are spacious and light-filled, with balconies and spick-and-span mosaic-tiled bathrooms. With glorious views of the church, the flower-filled terrace is a pleasant spot for summer breakfasts; in winter, you'll eat by the fire in the folksy sitting room.

Centro Storico

Lecce *Via Vignes 2/B (0832 242 727/www.bedand breakfast.lecce.it). Closed mid Jan-mid Feb.* €.

This 16th-century palazzo makes an elegant and central base. Local *pietra leccese* is much in evidence in the six rooms' star-vaulted ceilings, cornices and niches. The Imperial Suite is the pick of the bunch, a lofty ex-ballroom complete with a balcony overlooking the church of San Matteo, a kitchenette and an antique piano. The vast roof terrace has views of the Duomo's bell tower; a hot tub is planned for 2008.

Il Frantoio

6km NW of Ostuni *Km 874 along SS16 (0831 330 276/www.masseriailfrantoio.it).* €€€.

Il Frantolo is housed in a 16th-century *masseria* (a fortified farm house). But don't let the defences fool you: this is a bucolic utopia. The charmingly disorganised garden is full of glossy peacocks; antiques decorate the lovely, Victorian-style rooms; burstingly ripe fruit and veg grown on the estate go into making exquisite eight-course gourmet feasts in the evenings. Relaxed hospitality prevails: guests are taken for a spin in a vintage car, then plied with potent, own-made *rosoli* (restorative herb liqueurs) after dinner.

Masseria Torre Maizza

Savelletri, 20km NE of Locorotondo *Contrada Coccaro (0804 827 838/www.gesthotels.com).* €€€€.

In the 16th century, this *masseria* served as a watchtower against the recurrent Ottoman and Saracen attacks of the time. It's all a far cry from the luxury of its current incarnation. The stone-paved bedrooms boast designer furnishings, luxe fabrics and chic, minimalist bathrooms; the vast Palm Suites have terraces overlooking the olive groves, each with its own plunge pool. All this, plus a head-spinning array of on-site attractions (an Aveda spa, a golf course, a pool, an award-winning restaurant, even a cookery school), may scupper your sightseeing plans.

Palazzo del Corso

Gallipoli *Corso Roma 145 (0833 264 040/ www.hotelpalazzodelcorso.it).* €€€.

Gallipoli's swankiest hotel is housed in an 18th-century palazzo. The seven rooms feature lashings of marble, plush drapery and generous bathrooms, but it's worth splashing out on one of the suites, complete with vaulted ceilings and four-posters: Perla is popular with honeymooners thanks to the dancing cupids on its original frescoed ceiling. The roof terrace (with jacuzzi) has spectacular views.

Palazzo Personè

Lecce *Via Umberto I 5 (335 408 384 mobile/ www.palazzopersone.com).* €€€.

Open since July 2007, this boutique six-room hotel, café and *enoteca* is a polished affair. The decor comprises an eclectic mix of antiques, quirky auction finds and pop designer pieces. It may be a tried-and-tested formula, but the pairing of 19th-century lamps with hand-embroidered bed linen, not to mention '30s deco chairs with gleaming, ultra-modern bathrooms, feels far from contrived.

Palazzo Senape de Pace

Gallipoli *Via Monacelle 27/39 (0833 266 179/ www.palazzosenapedepace.it).* €€.

The aristocratic Senape de Pace family opened part of their 16th-century home as a B&B in 2007. Opportunities to hobnob with the hosts are rare, but daily tours of their museum-like living quarters on the first floor offer enough magnificent frescoes and priceless antiques to satisfy even the nosiest of guests. The second-floor guest bedrooms may feel slightly spartan in comparison, but they're comfortable enough, with character provided by features such as 16th-century window-frames and antique beds.

Eat

Now the richest region – in agricultural terms – in southern Italy, Puglia presses most of the country's olive oil, and its fertile soil yields remarkable produce. But that wasn't always the case. Worn down by centuries of poverty, Puglia developed a tradition of *cucina povera*: fresh, 'poor' ingredients transformed into culinary masterpieces. Humble vegetables such as *cime di rapa* (turnip tops), *lampascioni* (wild onions) and *ciceri* (chickpeas) are elevated to cult status, while the classic *'ncapriata* (puréed broad beans and wild chicory) and *orecchiette* (little pasta 'ears'), are on every menu. Inland, grilled beef and pork and braised horsemeat are staples; towards the coast, the focus shifts to seafood.

Star grapes that the oenophile should look out for include the intense, bilberry-toned primitivo and full-bodied negroamaro. The latter works best when blended with the aromatic malvasia nera, as in the Salice Salentino DOC.

Alle Due Corti

Lecce *Corte dei Giugni 1 (0832 242 223). Open 1-2.30pm, 8-11.30pm Mon-Sat. Closed 10 days Aug. €€. Traditional Pugliese.*
The menu at this proto-rustic trattoria is in a dialect impenetrable to most Italians (though it's translated into English), and the kitchen serves up seasonal local fare. The stand-out dish is the exemplary *tajeddha*, layered potatoes, rice and mussels. For the more adventurous, *cavallu* (horse) and *turcinieddhi* (goat entrails) are usually on the menu.

> # "Worn down by centuries of poverty, Puglia developed a tradition of *cucina povera*: fresh, 'poor' ingredients transformed into culinary masterpieces."

La Braceria

Locorotondo *Via Cesare Battisti 28 (0804 317 282). Open June, Jul, Sept 6.30-midnight Tue-Sun. Aug 6.30-midnight daily. Oct-May 7-11pm Tue-Sat. €€. Grill.*
Bracerie (grill restaurants with wood-burning ovens) are a Lororotondo trademark, and this is the best of the bunch. Tables line the alley outside in summer, but if you park yourself in the cosy, stone-vaulted dining area, you'll be able to watch your steak spluttering away in the oven. The best of the region's full-bodied reds do justice to the robust food.

Caffè Personè

Lecce *Via Umberto I 5 (333 374 5510 mobile). Open 7.30am-3pm, 6pm-midnight Mon-Sat. €€. Café/bar/enoteca.*
In this land of folksy *trattorie*, the decor of this vogueish restaurant – futuristic white plastic chairs paired with rustic wooden tables and statement art – can arouse suspicions as to the calibre of the kitchen. In fact, the handful of daily dishes (*gnocchetti* in a tomato and basil sauce, say) are impeccably cooked. Personè's owners are award-winning producers of wine and olive oil; downstairs has been transformed into tasting rooms in which you can sup on fine *negroamaro*.

Cucina Casereccia

Lecce *Via Colonnello Costadura 19 (0832 245 178). Open 12.30-2.30pm, 8-11pm Tue-Sat; 12.30-2.30pm Sun. Closed 2wks Aug-Sept, 10 days Dec-Jan. €€. Traditional Pugliese.*
The pleasantly cluttered, unpretentious Cucina Casereccia serves up hearty portions of home cooking. There's no menu, but dishes are likely to include broad bean purée with braised wild chicory, *sagne 'ncannulate* (noodles in an intense tomato and ricotta sauce) and succulent veal meatballs. Booking is advised.

La Maruzzella

Lido Conchiglie, 9km N of Gallipoli *Via Cristoforo Colombo (0833 208 900). Open Apr-Sept 12.30-4pm, 6pm-midnight daily. Oct-Mar 12.30-4pm, 6-10pm daily. €. No credit cards. Fish.*
With its neon strip lighting and plastic picnic tables, La Maruzzella is probably not the place for a romantic soirée. Nonetheless, the fantastic fish and the beachside location make it worth the trek from Gallipoli. Sea urchins are de-spined to form the base for *spaghetti con ricci* on a table front, and steaming bowls of mussels and an array of freshly-fished specimens sizzling on the grill could convert the most dedicated of carnivores. Staff speak little English.

Osteria degli Angeli

Lecce *Via Cavour 4/A (0832 244 250). Open 8-11pm Tue-Sun. €. Pizzeria.*
A local favourite, this no-frills *osteria* is an appealingly raucous place in which to sample some home cooking. The main draw is the generous pizzas, cooked in a wood-fired oven and served with little ceremony on plastic tablecloth-clad tables. For dessert, *pizza alla Nutella* vies with the homemade *sbricciolata*, a *crema pasticcera*-filled crumble, for sheer gluttonous appeal.

Picton

Lecce *Via Idomeneo 14 (0832 332 383). Open 1-2.30pm, 8-11.30pm Tue-Sun. Closed last 10 days June, 1st 10 days Nov. €€. Traditional Pugliese.*
Cordon Bleu chef and gastro-journalist Tonio Piceci dishes up Salentine specialities such as *ciceri e tria* (boiled, crisp-fried pasta with chickpeas) and *gamberoni mmuddhicati* (breaded, spiced and roasted king prawns) at surprisingly reasonable prices. The atmospheric dining room has marble floors and vaulted stone ceilings; framed napkins bearing the signatures of well-fed D-listers line the walls.

Liquid gold

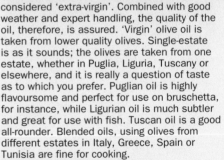

Popeye certainly isn't the only one to appreciate Olive Oyl's special qualities. These days, its beneficial qualities are well known and in certain countries its study is something of an art. So we asked Milvio Avogadro, one of Italy's olive oil experts, to share a few of its secrets.

As well as being Associate Professor of Food Technology at Genoa University, Milvio advises non-European oil producers on how to bring their oils up to EU standards.

How do you determine the quality of the oil?
MA: Tasting olive oil isn't like wine-tasting – oil has a different function, for a start; and unlike many other oil sources, the olive is a fruit, not a seed. This means that it needs even more antioxidants, as, unlike a seed, it doesn't have a hard 'skin' to protect it. That's why the olive is such a special food, because – well protected, and well-managed – it's a wonderful source of antioxidants and flavonoids, and is much healthier than many other forms of fat.

What about extra-virgin, or single estate oils? Are they worth the extra money?
MA: Extra-virgin oil is taken from the first pressing of the olive, but it is also subject to a test of its acidity, oxidation and flavour. It must reach a certain standard or it cannot be considered 'extra-virgin'. Combined with good weather and expert handling, the quality of the oil, therefore, is assured. 'Virgin' olive oil is taken from lower quality olives. Single-estate is as it sounds; the olives are taken from one estate, whether in Puglia, Liguria, Tuscany or elsewhere, and it is really a question of taste as to which you prefer. Puglian oil is highly flavoursome and perfect for use on bruschetta, for instance, while Ligurian oil is much subtler and great for use with fish. Tuscan oil is a good all-rounder. Blended oils, using olives from different estates in Italy, Greece, Spain or Tunisia are fine for cooking.

What's the best way to keep it?
MA: The oil is stored in a dark bottle for a reason, and should be kept out of direct sunlight (which oxidises the oil) in a cool, but not cold, cupboard.

Like a wine, the olive has a personality, and to get the best from it, it must be kept carefully. Unlike a wine, however, the olive can't improve over time; its quality can only be maintained. It is also worth bearing in mind that it loses its beneficial qualities a year after harvest – which usually takes place from the end of November to March. So glug it *pronto*!

Clockwise from top left: Palazzo Personè; Il Frantoio; Palazzo del Corso; La Braceria; Gallipoli fish market; La Braceria.

La Puritate

Gallipoli *Via Sant'Elia 18 (0833 264 205). Open June-Sept 12.30-3pm, 8pm-midnight daily. Nov-May 12.30-3pm, 8pm-midnight Mon, Tue, Thur-Sun. Closed Oct. €€€. Fish.*
It's not cheap, but elegant La Puritate wins the much-contested title of Gallipoli's best fish restaurant. The list of refreshingly frill-less *primi* includes linguine with prawns and cherry tomatoes, and a fresh *spaghettini al limone*, and the choice of fishy *secondi* depends on the daily haul. The serious wine list and own-made desserts are further draws. Book a table in the sea-facing front room.

Ritrò

Gallipoli *Riviera Armando Diaz 1/3 (0833 263 901). Open June-Sept 10am-3am daily. Oct, Dec-May 10am-3pm, 7-11pm Tue-Sun. Closed Nov. €€. International/Pugliese/bar.*
Tucked into a curve of ancient wall overlooking the sea, Ritrò's decked outdoor space has stunning views. Although the menu depends on the day's catch, the kitchen amuses itself with ethnic fusion: mussels with curry, basil and cherry tomatoes is a typical creation. There's also a surprisingly good choice of meaty mains, and an impressive wine list. Sunkissed lovelies flock here at *aperitivo* hour.

Ritrovo degli Amici

Martina Franca *Corso Messapia 8 (0804 839 249). Open 12.30-2.30pm, 7.30-11.30pm Mon-Sat; 12.30-2.30pm Sun. €€. Traditional Pugliese.*
This pint-sized restaurant is a great place in which to sample the local cuisine (though the one exception to the strictly Puglian repertoire, an epic *bucatini all'amatriciana*, rarely to be found outside of Lazio, is worth the culinary detour). Antipasti include a delicate cheese soufflé and an extraordinary *capocollo* pork; mains such as beef *tagliata* with rocket and *grana padano* are simply but expertly prepared. So far, so tempting; but leave room for the divine hot chocolate pudding with orange cream.

Da Sergio

Otranto *Corso Garibaldi 9 (0836 801 408). Open 12.30-2.45pm, 7.30-11.30pm daily. €€€. Fish.*
Whether you plump for an outdoor table with a ringside view of Otranto's lively *passeggiata* or eat in the breezy dining room, a meal in this upmarket spot is a pleasure. Friendly waiters talk you through the platters of antipasti such as octopus salad, grilled cuttlefish and squid marinated with onions, and advise on *secondi*; if you're organised enough to order in advance, go for the fish soup.

Zia Fernanda

Otranto *Via XXV Aprile (0836 801 884). Open Mid June-mid Sept 12.30-3pm, 7.30pm-midnight daily. Mid Sept-mid June 12.30-3pm, 7.30pm-midnight Tue-Sun. €€. Traditional Pugliese.*
Steps from the seafront, this local home-cooking favourite is presided over by the diminutive 'zia' (auntie) Fernanda. Standout *primi* include orecchiette with turnip tops or with tomato and ultra-ripe ricotta, while mains include grilled cuttlefish, swordfish and sea bass and a range of meats.

Explore

LECCE

Wrested from the Greeks by the Romans in the third century BC, Lecce was subjected to relentless invasion in the centuries that followed, finally flourishing under the Spanish in the 15th and 16th centuries. Its beguiling Old Town is now centred on jumbled piazza Sant'Oronzo, the best spot in which to get a sense of the town's eventful history. The remains of a Roman amphitheatre are flanked by 19th-century Venetian-style buildings to the west and fascist-era palazzi to the north, with the Renaissance-Gothic Sedile monument plonked in the middle. It's a busy spot at sundown, thronged with street performers, peddlars and strollers out for an evening gelato. From here, the lively *passeggiata* snakes north to shop-lined via Vittorio Emanuele, the town's main drag. Halfway along, a left turn opens out into the piazza del Duomo, with its heart-stopping ensemble of Baroque buildings in the famously sculptable *pietra leccese* sandstone.

> "The Duomo is a no-holds-barred riot of marble and gold. Get here first thing and have the place to yourself, or visit at night and swoon over the spectacularly floodlit piazza."

Two minutes south is the Castello di Carlo V, a medieval structure that now hosts occasional modern art exhibitions. A 15-minute stroll west is the Museo Provinciale Sigismondo Castromediano (viale Gallipoli 20, 0832 683 503, closed Sun afternoons), housing a striking collection of Greek pottery and tombstones, and artworks from the 15th to 18th centuries.

Piazza del Duomo

Duomo (0832 251 111). Open Duomo 7am-noon, 5-7.30pm daily. Admission free.
The blink-and-you'll-miss-it entrance, which lies off via Vittorio Emanuele, leads to a startling cul-de-sac, the appealingly asymmetrical but nonetheless wonderfully harmonious piazza del Duomo. Inside, the Zimbalo-built

Duomo is a no-holds-barred riot of marble and gold. Get here first thing and have the place to yourself, or visit at night and swoon over the spectacularly floodlit piazza.

Piazza Sant'Oronzo
Open Amphitheatre 5-9pm daily. Concerts held end July to mid Sept. Admission €2. No credit cards.
The town's patron saint gives his name to its main square. A bronze statue of him looms atop the Colonna di Sant'Oronzo, his hand raised (either in benediction or to stop himself from toppling over) and with his back resolutely turned on the ancient Roman amphitheatre behind: unsurprising, since the bishop went to the lions under Nero. The semicircle of second-century amphitheatre was unearthed in the 1930s; the rest is buried beneath the Baroque church of Santa Maria delle Grazie.

San Giovanni Battista
Via Libertini (0832 308 540). Open 7.30am-noon, 5-6.45pm Mon-Sat; 7.30am-noon Sun. Admission free.
Perhaps sensing it would be his final commission, 70-year-old Zimbalo devoted himself wholeheartedly to the facelift of this church in 1691, even offering his own money when funds dried up. The sculptor died in 1710, but work continued until 1728. The result is suitably Zimbalesque, from the florid façade to the altars groaning with baroque detail. The church is thought to be its creator's final resting place, though the location of his tomb remains a mystery.

> ## "Joined to the mainland by a 17th-century bridge, Gallipoli is encircled by a sea of such limpid blueness that it's easy to see why the Greeks gave it the name Kalé polis ('beautiful city')."

Santa Croce
Via Umberto I (0832 241 957). Open 9am-noon, 5-8pm daily. Admission free.
An army of master chisellers started work on the basilica in 1549, finally downing their tools 146 years later. The façade of Santa Croce is a mind-boggling extravaganza of prancing *putti* and exuberant blooms, dominated by a vast rose window. A symbol of the light of Christ, it's hoisted aloft by a merry band of infidels. The excess continues inside, though the uniform creaminess of the stone redeems it from what might otherwise be yet another case of Baroque overkill, as beady-eyed apostles scrutinise the congregation from on high, leafy fronds sprout from corners and garlands thread the 16th-century vaults.

THE SALENTINE PENINSULA

South of Lecce, the landscape flattens and takes on a distinctive Greek flavour. A 40-kilometre drive down the Adriatic coast, dotted with rugged coves, grottoes and ruined watchtowers, is Otranto, a prosperous port town since Roman times, although it suffered badly when, in 1480 the Ottomans besieged it. After fifteen days of defiance the city fell and the rampaging Turks killed 12,000 of the inhabitants. Not satisfied with that, the survivors were invited to embrace Islam. When the local archbishop refused he was sawn in half, while 800 others were beheaded on a nearby hill. Such savagery seems remote now that the walled Old Town has become a likeable resort, the crescent of unspoiled sandy beach drawing sun-worshippers and watersporters. The courtyard of the hulking but not oppressive Aragonese Castello is littered with cannonballs; a five-minute stroll south-east is the minute, fifth-century Byzantine church of San Pietro, emblazoned with bold, richly pigmented frescoes.

On the peninsula's Ionian-lapped southern side is the sleepy island of Gallipoli (not to be confused with the World War I battlefield in Turkey). Joined to the mainland by a 17th-century bridge, it's encircled by a sea of such limpid blueness that it's easy to see why the colonising Greeks gave it the name Kalé polis ('beautiful city'). The attractions are low-key: a clutch of dazzlingly white, pastel-trimmed churches, some great fish restaurants, a few easy strolls along the ancient walls. Rowdy *pescatori* sell their freshly-caught wares portside in afternoon fish auctions, while their wives repair nets in the Old Town's Moorish, whitewashed lanes. Standing sentry by the port, a rotund Angevin fortress and Greco-Roman monumental fountain (currently undergoing restoration) are further reminders of the relentless waves of invaders that washed up on these shores.

Cattedrale di Sant'Agata
Gallipoli *Via Duomo 1 (0833 261 987/www.cattedrale gallipoli.it). Open 8am-noon, 4-8pm daily. Admission free.*
Vast canvasses bedeck Gallipoli's cathedral. Many glorify the martyred St Agatha, who suffered endless trials as punishment for her Christian devotion. Along the nave, ten paintings by Neapolitan artist Nicola Malinconico (1663-1721) tell her sorry tale; her martyrdom is depicted on the magnificent frescoed ceiling.

Cattedrale di Santa Maria Annunziata
Otranto *Piazza Basilica (0836 802 720). Open June-Sept 7am-noon, 3-8pm daily. Oct-May 7am-noon, 1-5pm daily. Admission free.*
Otranto Cathedral's beautiful polychrome mosaic floor, created between 1163 and 1166, intertwines Norman, Greek and Byzantine ideals in a giant 'tree of life' motif. Biblical favourites such as Jonah, cast head-down among the fishes,

mingle with Alexander the Great, the Queen of Sheba and King Arthur, plus a menagerie of elephants, dragons, unicorns and mermaids. Here, too, lie the bones of Otranto's 800 martyrs, beheaded by the Ottomans in 1480. They are preserved in wall-to-wall glass cabinets; the meticulously positioned ensemble of skulls, femurs and ribs has the air of a ghoulish art installation.

Grotta Zinzulusa

Castro, 10km S of Otranto *(0836 943 812/ www.grottazinzulusa.it). Open Apr, May 10am-6pm daily. June, Sept 9.30am-6pm daily. July, Aug 9.30am-7pm daily. Oct-Mar 10am-4pm daily. Admission €4; €2 reductions. No credit cards.*
The most accessible of Salento's *grotte* (a 10km drive down the coast road from Otranto), this warren of passageways is punctuated by spectacular stalactites and stalagmites. The last cavern, 30m high, is daubed with 1950s graffiti left by the workmen sent in to shift the 12m mound of bat droppings that had accumulated there; job done, they used the guano to leave their mark.

THE CITTÀ BIANCHE & THE VALLE D'ITRIA

Ostuni, Martina Franca and Locorotondo, a loose triangle of towns, lie an hour's drive north-west of Lecce and make for good day-trip material. Seen from afar, hilltop Ostuni and Martina Franca, known as 'Città Bianche' (white towns), appear like dazzling mirages.

Established in the first century AD, Ostuni is the more touristy of the two. Its steep, cobbled main drag is lined with trinket shops, though wonderful views of the plains and sea, glimpsed down alleys and over walls, provide some recompense. Meanwhile, Martina Franca's medieval core is full of lovely Baroque palazzos, and a surprising profusion of butcher's shops. The mystery is solved when you learn that the town is home to the finest cured meats in Puglia: sample the local speciality *capocollo* (smoked, cured pork) at the historic Tommaso Romanelli & Co (via d'Itria 8, closed Sun). The Wednesday morning market between via Recupero and piazza d'Angiò is a real feast for the senses.

If Puglia has a trademark, it is its *trulli*: diminutive, conical-roofed limestone huts, built without cement so that when the tax-collectors arrived they could be swiftly reduced to a pile of rubble. Nobody's quite sure why they were only built here in the Valle d'Itria, or when – but similar structures existed in Mycenae in ancient Greece some 5,000 years ago. Pagan and astrological symbols daubed on their roofs add to the mystery. UNESCO-protected Alberobello, a 20-minute drive west of Ostuni, has the biggest concentration, though its appeal is diluted by coachloads of tourists and a glut of shops hawking *trulli*-related tat. Instead, head for the valley's quieter countryside roads. Flanked by mile upon mile of prickly pear and olive trees, they offer plenty of opportunities for *trulli*-spotting, particularly around the sleepy, unspoiled hill town of Locorotondo. From here, look down on the valley's vineyards and silvery olive groves, dotted with Lilliputian dwellings and dream of a life spent in the bright glare of the Puglian sun.

Factfile

When to go
May, June and September are Puglia's most beautiful months, though April and October are pleasantly warm and hotel rates are low. In stifling late July and August, Italian tourists take over. Rain is a rarity, but is most likely between November and February.

Getting there
Brindisi Airport is on Papola Casale (0831 412 141, www.seap-puglia.it). From here, SITA buses (0805 790 211, www.sita-on-line.it) run six times a day to Lecce. The 40-minute journey costs €5 (pay on board).

Getting around
FSE trains (0832 668 111, www.fseonline.it) run from Lecce to Otranto and Gallipoli roughly hourly, changing at Maglie, but the Salento service (0833 541 025, www.salentointrenoebus.it;

mid-June to Sept; 11 daily to Otranto, 40min; 10 daily to Gallipoli; 45min; €1-€4.50) is faster and more reliable.

The SS613 runs from Brindisi, passing through Lecce to Otranto; turn off at Maglie for the SP361 to Gallipoli. For Ostuni, take the SP1bis from Brindisi. From here, there are signs to Martina Franca and Locorotondo.

Tourist information
Via Vittorio Emanuele 23 Lecce (0832 332 463/www.pugliaturismo.com). Open June-Sept 8am-1.45pm (until 1.15pm Sat & Sun), 3.30-8.30pm daily. Oct-May 9am-1pm, 4.30-7pm daily.

Internet
Salento Time via Regina Isabella 22, Lecce (0832 303 686). Open 10am-9pm Mon-Sat; 10am-8pm Sun. Rates €2/hr.

Views of and around Matera.

Matera & around

Basilicata's diverse topography encompasses fertile mountains, stark canyons, sweeping plains and white sandy beaches, but the region's undoubted centrepiece was once its deepest source of shame: Matera's cave dwellings, squalid and crowded until the mid 20th century, but now – along with ancient, frescoed cave churches – being carefully restored.

Basilicata's southern reaches straddle two seas – the Tyrrhenian to the west and the Ionian to the east. Sharing the Pollino mountain range with Calabria to the south, it has its very own rounded peaks in the centre and dozens of Norman castles in the rugged north. But the region's USP is undoubtedly ancient Matera (Sassi di Matera). With its spectacular setting against the barren Murge ravine, cave dwellings and a wealth of churches built of and into rock, this town has been a UNESCO World Heritage Site since 1993. Its haunting beauty has long drawn film-makers, from Pasolini, for his 1964 *Gospel According to St Matthew,* and Mel Gibson, for his controversial *The Passion of the Christ,* to the makers of the recent re-tread of *The Omen.*

The troglodyte dwellings are unimaginably old, freighted with the history of mankind. The caves were first inhabited in the Palaeolithic era, two and a half million years ago; people have been hollowing out and building on to the soft limestone ever since to create an extensive city in the rock. Incredibly, people were still living in these primitive conditions – described by Carlo Levi as 'a schoolboy's idea of Dante's *Inferno*' – until the 1950s, when most of the inhabitants were rehoused. Some refused; the *sassi* were never completely cleared. An association was formed to preserve them, and recently the beginnings of a transformation have been glimmering, with businesses such as hotels and restaurants and even a call centre moving in.

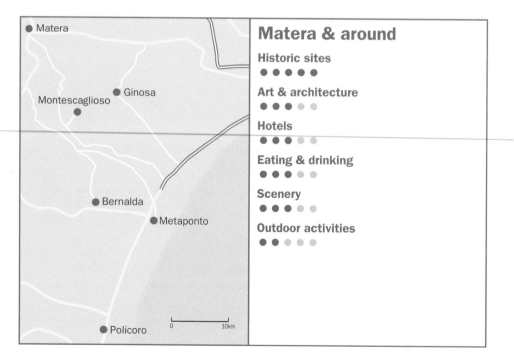

Matera & around

Historic sites
● ● ● ● ●

Art & architecture
● ● ● ● ◦

Hotels
● ● ● ● ◦

Eating & drinking
● ● ● ● ◦

Scenery
● ● ● ● ◦

Outdoor activities
● ● ● ● ◦

Stay

Matera is an ideal base for a short stay in Basilicata. As well as being conveniently placed for exploring the region, many of Matera's *sassi* dwellings have been converted to small hotels and B&Bs – there are also a handful in the new town. But it's a good idea to book ahead as space is limited. For longer stays, the lure of a swimming pool or proximity to the Ionian coast might tip you more towards an *agriturismo*. Ten farms offering accommodation around Matera have clubbed together in a consortium (www.lemasseriedelfalcogrillaio.it).

Affitacamere L'Oasi
Metaponto *Via Lido 47, Metaponto Lido (0835 741 883/338 657 9420/www.metaponto.info). Closed Oct-Apr. €.*
If you want to tumble out of bed and into the sea, this little place above a good restaurant overlooking the beach at Metaponto Lido is perfect. Bedrooms are basic – there's no air-conditioning, just fans – but they're all en suite, perfectly comfortable and available for overnight stays. Most of the hotels here insist on half board and minimum one-week stays in summer. Metaponto Lido is fairly lively in summer – if you prefer peace and quiet, the white sandy beach stretches for miles. With a car you can easily drive further up the coast to a quieter spot fringed by pine woods.

Azienda Agricola Agrituristica Masseria Cardillo
Bernalda *SS 407 Basentana Km 97.5 (0835 748 992/339 384 0600 mobile/www.masseriacardillo.it). Closed Nov-mid Apr. €€.*
Inland from the coast, near Bernalda, this lovely agriturismo set amidst vines has been stylishly transformed from a working farm. Close to the beach and an excellent golf course, the Cardillo also has its own riding stables, tennis courts and swimming pool. There are also bicycles to borrow. Each of the ten pretty rooms has air-conditioning (and central heating) and a little private terrace; the smart sitting room-bar, in the former granary, has comfortable white sofas and fine views – particularly lovely at sunset. There's also a good on-site restaurant.

Azienda Agricola San Teodoro Nuovo
Marconia, nr Bernalda *Contrada San Teodoro (0835 470 042/338 569 8116 mobile/www.santeodoro nuovo.com). €€. Min. stay 2 nights.*
Within a beautiful bougainvillea-covered farm, surrounded by citrus and olive groves, are nine little apartments, each named after a different variety of orange or herb. Charmingly furnished with family antiques – all with air-conditioning, some with kitchenettes – the apartments open on to private patios or gardens. The sea is just 5km away but the San Teodoro has a lovely pool of its own and guests can indulge in treatments at a nearby health spa. Only local ingredients are used in the delicious cuisine.

Hotel Sant'Angelo
Matera *Rione Pianelle-Piazza San Pietro Caveoso-Sassi Caveoso (0835 314 010/www.hotelsantangelosassi.it). €€.*
One of the most upmarket places to stay in the Sassi, the Sant'Angelo is located near the cathedral of San Pietro Caveoso in the Sassi Caveoso. The cave rooms here are amply proportioned, many with flying arches, carved columns and dug-out cubby holes, kitted out with luxurious, stone-tiled bathrooms. Antique furniture provides a dramatic foil for the stark interiors. Located at the top of a steep flight of stairs, rooms on the upper floors have fine views into the mysterious, ancient ravine of the Murge. The hotel is not suitable for those with mobility problems.

> "Converted into a hotel by a charming architect and his wife, it has gorgeous bedrooms, furnished with antiques and luxurious touches, such as bathrobes and Aveda toiletries."

Locanda di San Martino
Matera *Via Fiorentini 71, Sassi Barisano (0835 256 600/www.locandadisanmartino.it). €€.*
Run by a delightful American-Italian couple (Dorothy and Antonio) with ever-smiling Damiano on reception, the Locanda is right in the heart of the Sassi Barisano, with rooms in former dwellings spread over four levels (a lift takes you to the first two). Meandering paths, secret stairs and little secluded terraces give guests privileged views as well as adding a sense of excitement. The whitewashed rooms – all with air-conditioning – are cosy with simple but stylish decor, ceramic lamps, terracotta floors and smart bathrooms. Most have wonderful views over the old town.

Relais Ridola Residenza d'Epoca
Matera *Via Morelli 13, Matera Sud (0835 318 811/www.hotelridolamatera.it). €€.*
The Relais (also known as the Casino) is a charming small hotel in residential 'modern' Matera, in a beautifully renovated rose pink house dating from 1870. Only a 15-minute walk or short drive to the Sassi, it has its own car park, ideal for those touring the region. Converted into a hotel by a charming architect and his wife, it has gorgeous bedrooms, furnished with antiques and luxurious touches, such as bathrobes in the suites and Aveda toiletries. Guests can relax in the pretty little garden, in front of the old stone fireplace in the sitting room or on the sunny first-floor terrace. Breakfasts, including pastries baked to family recipes, are a real treat.

Clockwise from top left: Azienda Agricola San Teodoro Nuovo (3); La Zuppa del Re; local olives; Locanda di San Martino (2).

Eat

Typical Basilicata cuisine revolves around *orecchiette* pasta (usually with broad beans and pecorino cheese), sausages (often with fennel seed), *crapiata* (a bean soup), grilled meats, cheese and vegetables. Donkey and horse meat – traditional fare – are also on many menus. Basilicata produces one of southern Italy's top wines, the Aglianico del Vulture; the best is phenomenally good, as is the mineral water, which is sold across Italy.

Many *agriturismi* and hotels have restaurants open to non-guests, but reservations may be necessary. Coastal resorts are only open in high summer; out of season, head inland for the best places to eat. While you'll find good seafood here, it's likely to be from Puglia, where the seas are deeper.

19a Buca Winery (19th Hole)

Matera *Via Lombardi 3 (0835 333 592/ www.diciannovesimabuca.com). Open 11am-3pm, 7pm-midnight Tue-Sun. Closed 2wks July. €. Enoteca/modern Italian.*

Somewhat of an anomaly at the gateway to the Sassi, this trendy, retro-styled bar, enoteca and virtual golf driving range occupies a warren of rooms that once served as cisterns beneath piazza Vittorio Veneto. Dishes include oysters, salumi (including local smoked venison) and carpaccio of swordfish, goose or wild boar, served alongside a vast range of wines, beers and cocktails. There's even afternoon tea and cakes.

Baccanti

Matera *Via Sant'Angelo, Sassi Caveoso (0835 333 704/www.baccantiristorante.com). Open 12.30-3pm, 7.30-11pm Tue-Sat; 12.30-3pm Sun. Closed Jan. €€. modern Italian.*

At the edge of the Sassi Caveoso, not far from the Murge, this former carpenter's workshop is a romantic location set in whitewashed, candlelit caves. The food and wine are superb, and there's even a gourmet choice of mineral waters. Try the delicious *antipasto del antiquario*: bite-sized pork with apple and leeks, softened dried figs, filled with gorgonzola, potato 'boats' with *cardoncelli* mushrooms and mouthfuls of cod with smoked *scamorza* cheese. Follow with fresh pasta with Pollino truffles and lamb in local Aglianico wine. The cheese trolley and the desserts are works of art.

La Locandiera

Bernalda *Corso Umberto I 194 (0835 543 241/ www.lalocandiera.biz). Open noon-3pm, 4pm-11pm daily. €. No credit cards. Traditional Italian.*

You'll receive a warm welcome at this old-fashioned, gingham-tableclothed locanda in the heart of Bernalda's pretty *centro storico*. The traditional Lucanian fare is excellent, especially starters such as fresh sausages, bean soup or pork livers, the own-made pasta with mushrooms,

mussels and beans or chickpeas. For the main course, there's a wide range of meat dishes as well as salt cod cooked Basilicata-style with peppers.

Nadì

Matera *Via Fiorentini 1/3, Sassi Barisano (0835 332 892/www.ristorantenadi.it). Open 10am-4pm, 7-11.30pm Tue-Sun. €. Traditional Italian/trattoria.*

Close to the entrance to the Sassi Barisano, down the steep steps from Piazza Vittorio Veneto, this friendly little place is popular with the locals. Set in a dark, honey-toned tufa cave, it's ideal for cooling off on a hot day; outside are lots of little wooden tables, perfect for balmy summer evenings. It can get busy, so come early (the service can also be slow). Charcoal-grilled meats – local pork, lamb and fennel sausages – and potatoes are the speciality. There are also some delicious pasta dishes: order a 'tris' to try three of them.

Il Terrazzino

Matera *Vico San Giuseppe 7, Piano (0835 334 119/ www.ilterrazzino.org). Open 12.30-3pm, 7.30-11pm Mon, Wed-Sun. Closed 2wks July. €€. Traditional Italian/trattoria.*

One of the few restaurants in Matera with a terrace overlooking the *sassi* (book ahead), this is reached off piazza Vittorio Veneto (turn left down the alleyway beside the 1930s Banco di Napoli building). Unsurprisingly, it's a fixture on the tourist trail, but the food is reliably good: try the house classics *orecchiette al tegamino* (pasta with tomato, sausage and mozzarella) or minestrone and chickpea soup followed by meat for the main course. Typical desserts include own-made *strazzate* – chocolate and almond biscuits – served with sweet moscato wine.

Pitty

Policoro, 33km SW of Bernalda *Piazza della Pace Y Rabin 9 (0835 981 203). Open June-Sept 12.30-3pm, 7.30-11pm daily. Oct-May 12.30-3pm, 7.30-11pm Tue-Sun. €. Trattoria.*

The attentive Tonino Chiaromonte runs this spick and span trattoria serving excellent seafood. If the trolley laden with *antipasti* such as raw cuttlefish, sea snails, langoustines and the house speciality, grouper with mushrooms and truffle, doesn't tempt you, there are delicious pasta starters such as *cavatelli* with wild asparagus followed by grilled swordfish or mussels from nearby Puglian seafood mecca Taranto. Tonino is not given to writing menus, preferring instead to tell diners himself what the choices are. Trust that he will helpfully steer you in the right direction. There are plenty of good local wines to choose from too.

Vecchia Matera

Matera *Via Sette Dolori 62, Centro Storico (0835 336 910. Open noon-2.30pm, 7.30-10pm Mon, Tue, Thur-Sat; noon-2.30pm Wed, Sun. €. Traditional Italian/trattoria.*

Tucked down a narrow street near the top of the Piano and the Sassi Barisano (reached from via Ridola) is this lovely little spot. A deceptively simple place with excellent food, it has a handful of tables in an inner courtyard and many more in a labyrinthine cave. There are three or four meat dishes on the menu, as well as hand-made *orecchiette* pasta, a selection of fresh seafood, fine bean soups and pizzas baked in a wood-fired oven, accompanied by freshly baked Materese bread and delicious local wine. It's incredibly good value for money, and the service is effortlessly charming.

La Zuppa del Re
Matera *Via Fiorentina 42, Sassi Barisano (0835 332 488). Open noon-11pm Tue-Sun. €. Pizzeria/trattoria.*
A breath of fresh air should rustic charm wear thin, this new pizzeria brings retro style to a whitewashed cave with pop art and bright leather chairs. As well as pizzas, the place serves huge platters of local *salumi* and cheese with roasted vegetables. It has a good choice of wines by the glass as well as beers, and is also an occasional venue for jazz. There are a few tables outside too.

Explore

MATERA

Matera has three key areas: the Piano (the medieval and modern city) rises above the two districts of caves or *sassi* – the Barisano and Caveoso – overlooking the Murge ravine. Beyond the Piano are the new districts, where the inhabitants of the *sassi* were rehoused in the 1950s.

Stairs from the Piano's main square, piazza Vittorio Veneto, lead down to the Sassi Barisano. At the bottom, via Fiorentini takes you to the Murge, where the road bends round into the Sassi Caveoso (otherwise reached from stairs beside Palazzo Lanfranchi off via Ridola).

The Piano has its own charms: an archaeological museum, the Museo Ridola (via Ridola 24, 0835 310058, www.mosa.matera.it, closed Mon) and the nearby Museo Nazionale d'Arte Medievale e Moderna della Basilicata (0835 256262, closed Mon) in Palazzo Lanfranchi, which houses works of art from the 13th to 18th centuries as well as canvases by Carlo Levi featuring people and places from his book, *Christ Stopped at Eboli*. There are also a handful of (non-cave) churches well worth seeing: the 18th-century Chiesa del Purgatorio (via Ridola), featuring macabre carved skeletons in its façade, San Francesco d'Assisi (via del Corso), whose Baroque exterior belies its medieval origins, and the 13th-century San Giovanni Battista (via San Biagio). The Romanesque cathedral (1270), on piazza Duomo has wonderful views, as does the 17th-century San Pietro Caveoso, perched over the Murge, at the crossroads of the two *sassi* districts.

Only a dozen or so of the rupestrian churches of Matera are accessible; there are eight in the two *sassi* districts that can be visited independently, although a good guide will provide insights that will enhance the experience. La Rubrica Sassi (0835 337 374, 334 368 8138 mobile, 338 441 7906 mobile, www.rubricasassi.com) conducts group tours.

To see a few of the other rock and cave churches in the area (there are over 100 of them), you can collect a map from the tourist information office detailing a (fairly hard-going) three-hour walk within the ravine of the Murgia Timone. If your appetite still isn't sated, you'll need a guide to show you more: many are almost impossible to find alone, may be perilously sited or require permission to enter.

Byzantine art was seen as degenerate by the Catholic church. Many of the early medieval frescoes were painted over and the churches were deconsecrated in the 17th century, having been used to house animals or make wine. Shepherds often scratched out saints' eyes in the belief that they would cast the evil eye over their livestock, and the glowing green algae that thrives in the damp caves has also played a part in eradicating much of Matera's original art. For an idea of what daily life was like for someone living in the *sassi*, head for the Casa Grotta in the Caveoso.

"This cave dwelling once housed a family of ten – along with their dogs, chickens and donkey – a status symbol that brought extra warmth to the home but that few could afford."

Casa Grotta
Piazza San Pietro Caveoso, nr Vico Solitario 11 (0835 310 118/www.casagrotta.it). Open 9.30am-sunset daily. Admission €1.50. No credit cards.
A typically furnished cave dwelling, once housing a family of ten, along with their dogs, chickens and donkey – a status symbol that brought extra warmth to the home but that few could afford – in the heart of the Sassi Caveoso. Around 20,000 people lived in similar conditions or worse until the early 1950s. As a museum piece, it's beautifully spick and span , but try to imagine the crowded conditions, the lack of hygiene and the stench that would have permeated the room. Disease may have been rife, but community spirit was unmatched – the latter recreated in the well-conceived new housing developments in up-top Matera.

Views of and around
Matera.

La Cripta del Peccato Originale

14km south of Matera *Contrada Petrapenta (ArteZeta Coop 320 535 0910/www.artezeta.it). Open Booking office 10am-2pm Tue-Sun. Minibus pick up at Piazza Vittorio Veneto. Admission (with tour, booking obligatory) €8. No credit cards.*

Only opened recently, this exquisite rupestrian church – nicknamed the Sistine Chapel of Matera – lies within the property of the Masseria Dragone vineyard. A pioneering project has restored the ninth-century Lombard frescoes, depicting stories from both testaments (highlights are the Creation and Fall from Eden). The work conveys a masterly range of expression, and presents unusual iconography (such as a young-looking, clean-shaven God and a sinfully voluptuous Eve). The unknown painter is known as the Flower Painter of Matera due to the beautiful red poppy-like flowers that unify the imagery.

"This elegant former monastery lost most of its frescoes and the altars were transformed into wine vats when it was leased by the Church to shepherds to house livestock and a winery."

Madonna delle Virtù & San Nicola dei Greci

Via Madonna delle Virtù (0835 336 726/349 718 4357 mobile/www.lascaletta.net). Open 10am-5pm Sat-Sun, reservation only Mon-Fri (call ahead to check opening times). Admission €2. No credit cards.

The easiest churches to find – facing the eerie-looking Murge where the road in the Barisano curves towards the Caveoso – are set on two levels. Downstairs is the church of the Madonna, a basilica with three naves and vaulted arches and cupola dug out from the tufa. In 1674 it was transformed into a Baroque church, most of the original frescoes were painted over and the aspect of the church and entrances altered, by knocking down the original pillars and moving the altar. Every summer, 20th-century sculpture is displayed in the space as part of a regular exhibition running since 1978, and Mel Gibson shot his Last Supper scene for *The Passion of the Christ* here.

Upstairs is San Nicola, damaged when the road was built, which has splendid frescoes, dating as far back as the mid 13th century, including a rare crucifixion with asphodels (a common flower of the Murge) growing at Jesus's feet, a symbol of his future resurrection. Frescoed Santa Barbara and San Nicola show classic Byzantine iconography (the saints face outwards rather than side on, with large eyes,

dark skin, and San Nicola is making the Omega sign rather than the latter-day sign of the Trinity). In the medieval period, the church became a nuns' cemetery – you can see where the graves were dug from the rock, facing the sun.

Museo della Scultura Contemporanea (MUSMA)

Palazzo Pomarici, Via San Giacomo, Sasso Caveoso (320 535 0910/0835 330 582/www.zetema.org). Open Nov-Mar 10am-2pm Tue-Sun. Apr-Oct 10am-2pm, 4-8pm Tue-Sun. Admission €5. No credit cards.

Given the fact that the infrastructure of Matera is carved out of rock, the town makes a fitting location for a museum dedicated to sculpture. Opened in 2006 in a smart cave complex, it showcases works by Henry Moore, Edoardo Paolozzi, Pablo Picasso, Giò and Arnaldo Pomodoro, and a host of other leading lights, many of whom have links with Matera. About 2.5km north-east of central Matera, there's a sculpture park called La Palomba (www.parcoscultura lapalomba.it)

Rupestrian churches of the Sassi Caveoso

Matera *Via Lucana 238 (0835 319 458/www.sassitourism.it). Open Apr-Oct 9am-1pm, 3-7pm daily. Nov-Mar 9.30am-1.30pm, 2.30-4.30pm daily. Santa Barbara rarely open; check ahead. Admission €2.50 per church, 3 churches €5, all 6 €6). Guided tours possible; book ahead on 338 237 0498.*

The Caveoso currently has a circuit of six rupestrian churches open to the public, on a combined ticket. The eighth-century Santa Lucia alle Malve, which is still consecrated for Mass, has fine medieval and Baroque frescoes, whereas the Convicinio di San Antonio, an elegant former monastery containing four churches, lost most of its frescoes and its altars were transformed into wine vats when it was leased by the Church to shepherds to house livestock and a winery. Tiny Santa Barbara, rarely open, is a real gem with exquisite 12th-century frescoes, and Santa Maria de Idris, perched atop a mass of rock called Monte Errone rising above the *sassi* (which stood in for Golgotha in Mel Gibson's *The Passion of the Christ*), has dazzling frescoes of saints, including an unusual *danse macabre*. The others are the adjacent San Giovanni in Monterrone and Santa Maria de Armenis up near the Piano.

AROUND MATERA

En route to the Ionian coast, you pass the medieval monastery of Montescaglioso as well as the pretty villages of Bernalda and Pisticci, both well worth a visit. Bernalda is Francis Ford Coppola's home town; with his nephew Nicolas Cage, Coppola is creating a centre for experimental visual and musical studies here, as well as funding a restoration project for a new hotel. Not far away is Aliano, famous as the place where the writer, politician and artist Carlo Levi was imprisoned under Mussolini in 1935-6. The town is perched on a ravine and dotted with mysterious limestone pinnacles called *calanchi*.

Half an hour's drive (around 30 kilometres) away from Montescaglioso is the little town of Metaponto. Settled by the Greeks in the eighth century BC, the town is known for its ancient ruins as well as for its white, powdery sand beaches, which draw crowds in summer.

Abbey of San Michele at Montescaglioso
Montescaglioso *Piazza del Popolo (334 836 0098). Open Oct-Apr 10am-1pm, 3-5pm Tue-Sun. May-July, Sept 9.30am-1pm daily; 2-6.30pm Tue-Sun. Aug 9.30am-6pm daily. Admission €4 (includes obligatory guided tour, hours vary).*
The first monastery in southern Italy, this 11th-century Benedictine abbey was added to in the Renaissance and Baroque periods. Thousands of pilgrims flocked here, many staying on as hermits, creating the cultural revolution of cave churches across the Murge in Basilicata and Puglia. A pretty place with peaceful cloisters, it is often overlooked by visitors rushing towards Matera.

Carlo Levi Literary Park & Museum
Aliano, 90km from Montescaglioso
Museum Piazza Garibaldi (0835 568 181). Open Oct-Apr 10.30am-12.30pm, 3.30-6.30pm Mon, Tue, Thur-Sun. May-Nov 10.30am-12.30pm; 3.30-7.30pm Mon, Tue, Thur-Sun. Admission €3.
Park Via Martiri d'Ungheria 1, Aliano (0835 568 529/www.aliano.it). Open 9am-12.30pm, 4-7.30pm Mon-Tue, Thur-Sun.

The house to which the artist and writer was banished for a year in the 1930s now has a small museum recording his time in the town – a must for anyone who has read his book *Christ Stopped at Eboli*. A commemorative literary park, including places described in the book, has also been created. Ask for a map at the museum or the park's HQ.

Metapontum
Metaponto Borgo *Museo Archeologico Viale Aristea 21 (0835 745 327). Open 9am-8pm Tue-Sun; 2-8pm Mon. Admission €2.50. No credit cards.*
Tavole Palatine (archaeological site) *SS106 Jonico (no address-follow signs). Open 9am-1hour before sunset daily. Admission free.*
At this ancient Greek site, the remains of a theatre, the foundations of four temples and 15 standing columns of a sixth-century BC Doric temple to Hera can be seen; the museum has a small selection of relics and art from the area.
Around 25km down the coast, west of Policoro, are the ruins of the ancient colony, Heraclea (via Colombo 8, Policoro, 0835 972 154, open 9am to one hour before sunset, admission free), which was all but destroyed in 540 BC. There's little to see here, but the nearby Museo Archeologico della Siritide (via Colombo 8, Policoro, 0835 972 154, open 9am-8pm Tue-Sun, 2-8pm Mon, admission €2) is also used as a storage place for pieces awaiting restoration as they are found (there's ongoing excavation in the area), so there's a changing display of items: terracotta from the sixth to the first centuries BC, bronze plates bearing inscriptions, painted vase fragments, burial treasures and coins.

Factfile

When to go
Most hotels and restaurants in Matera are open all year round. Spring and autumn are peak times. Although Italians tend to head to the beach in high summer, it's becoming increasingly popular with foreign visitors.

Getting there
The nearest airports are Bari and Naples. From July to mid September, the Pugliairbus company (080 531 6186 or 0835 335 611, pugliairbus.aeroportodipuglia.it) connects Bari airport (via the town of Altamura in Puglia) and Matera twice daily. It's free with valid plane ticket. Alternatively, take the bus to Bari Central Station, then FAL train to Matera (you might have to change at Altamura; www.fal-srl.it, 0835 332 861, 080 572 5229). Trains leave approximately every hour and the journey time is between 70 to 90 minutes.
In Naples, the Marino coach (199 800 100, www.marinobus.it) leaves from opposite Naples' Central Station at Piazza Garibaldi to Matera. Buses run three times a day. The journey takes four and a half hours.

Getting around
Matera is small enough to be walkable, but be warned, there is a fair amount of climbing up and down stairs to be done if you're exploring the *sassi*. For trips out of Matera, SITA bus line (0835 385 007, 899 325 204, www.sitabus.it) connects Matera with Metaponto, Bernalda, Policoro, Montescaglioso and Pisticci.

Tourist information
APT Matera Via Spine Bianche 22 (0835 331 817/www.aptbasilicata.it). Open 9am-1.30pm, 3.30-7.30pm daily.
Pro Loco di Bernalda, corso Italia 42, Bernalda (0835 548 516). Open 9am-1pm, 3-7pm daily. This office also has information on Metaponto.

Internet
There are six computers available at The Net, piazza Cesare Firrao, Matera (0835 334 740, www.thenetonline.it). Open 9am-8.30pm Mon-Fri; 3-8.30pm Sat. €1.50 per hour.

South Tuscan hill towns

Within half an hour of Siena are some of the world's most exquisite landscapes: cypress-studded hillsides, the sloping vineyards of Montalcino and Montepulciano, and ancient roads leading erratically to medieval towns and hamlets. It's the stuff of fantasy. Those in the know return here year after year to favourite boltholes; first timers vow to do the same. Busy? Unquestionably. But just because it's well travelled doesn't mean it ceases to charm – there's plenty of beauty to go round. The best of the best: the hill towns of Montalcino, San Quirico d'Orcia, Pienza and Montepulciano.

Clockwise from top left: Sienese woods; Abbazia di Sant'Antimo; views from La Bandita; Montalcino; typical wine vaults; morning coffee.

furnished but amply sized, and there are magnificent views from the rooftop terrace. Note that breakfast is not included and be sure to ask for directions if you're driving.

San Gregorio Residence & Hotel
Pienza *Via della Madonnina 4 (0578 748 059/ www.pienza.net). €.*

Lying just outside the walls of Pienza, San Gregorio offers hotel and self-catering options. The hotel has clean, uncluttered rooms in a restored 1930s theatre, with ample buffet breakfast, swimming pool in summer, massage and spa treatments, while the 16 self-catering apartments are a good-value option for families.

"The food is almost viscerally local: the ingredients that you see on your plate you've probably admired in the countryside."

Villa Cicolina
Montepulciano *Via Provinciale 11 (0578 758 620/ www.villacicolina.it). €€-€€€.*

Villa Cicolina is one of the most beautiful places to stay in Tuscany. Sure, the competition is tough but this villa, with walls covered in frescoes of bucolic scenes and family crests, elegant formal garden and 16th-century chapel, is the Tuscany of sun-deprived northern dreams. The rooms and apartments are furnished with romantic rustic antiques but, lest you think it all stuck in the past, there's an infinity pool with, naturally, great views of the surrounding countryside. Thankfully the service is not at all modern and the food is excellent. There are also three apartments for rent.

Eat

You won't go hungry. You won't find much in the way of exotic, new-fangled food either, but who needs that when the local produce is so good? And if you won't hunger, neither will you thirst, with two of the country's finest wines (Brunello di Montalcino and Montepulciano's Vino Nobile) produced locally.

The holy trinity of the Tuscan diet is bread, olive oil and wine. Bread – deliberately unsalted as a neutral canvas for the food it accompanies – is often used in soups (such as ribollita) and salads (such as panzanella). There is plenty of game, including hare and wild boar; rabbit and beef are also common (though note that the habit of eating steaks was imported in the 18th century by

English aristocrats). Sublime Tuscan white beans are served lukewarm with olive oil and black pepper. The common radicchio may seem bitter at first, but cultivate a taste for it and you'll go on to enjoy the many wild salad varieties.

The one true Tuscan cheese is pecorino, made with ewe's milk. The sheep grazing on the hillsides are more often not there for their milk rather than their meat or wool.

Tuscany produces less wine than Sicily or the Veneto, but its overall value far outstrips that of other regions. Over the last 20 years or so, through the rise of the 'Super Tuscans', whose producers chose to cold-shoulder the Denominazione di Origine Controllata (DOC) hegemony, considering it to produce inferior wines, quality has become the byword here. There's not a traditional winemaker left who would do without the services of an oenologist, and few cottage-industry vine farmers remain.

Red wines dominate, especially at the top end. The principal grape here (as in Chianti to the north) is Sangiovese. The best-known appellations are Brunello di Montalcino and Vino Nobile di Montepulciano, which use exclusively (Montalcino) or predominantly (Montepulciano) Sangiovese in their oaked, tannin-heavy reds.

For more information, including advice on visiting vineyards, contact www.consorzio brunellodimontalcino.it for Montalcino, and www.consorziovinonobile.it for Montepulciano.

Montalcino is well served with *enoteche*. The most imposing establishment is Enoteca Osteria Osticcio (via G Matteotti 23, 0577 848 271, open 9am-8pm Mon-Sat). If you want to buy a bottle or two to take away, try Montalcino 564 (via Mazzini 25, 0577 849 109; open 10am-9pm daily; closed Sun in winter). In Montepulciano, Enoteca per il Pulcino (Via di Gracciano nel Corso, 102, 0578 75871) serves and sells by bottle and from the barrel. The *conzorzio* also has a shop, in Palazzo del Capitano at via Ricci 2 (0578 757812).

Albergo il Giglio
Montalcino *Via S Saloni 5 (0577 848 167/www.giglio hotel.com). Open 7.30-9.30pm Mon-Wed, Fri-Sun. €€. Traditional Italian.*

Tucked away in the historic centre of Montalcino is this excellent family-run restaurant, one of those places people keep returning to year after year. The welcome is warm and the decor is that comfortable muddle that comes with a much-loved old building. There's a big open fire and equally warming small details: pretty prints, oil lamps and bloom vases. Food is almost viscerally local: what you see on your plate you've probably admired in the countryside. Typical dishes might be chestnut cake, ribollita or wild boar stew. The cellar is a serious assemblage of local and Italian wines, with bottles laid down from many vintages and producers. There's also a pretty hotel on the premises should your samplings take you beyond the reach of safe driving.

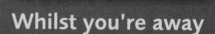

Antico Caffè Poliziano

Montepulciano *Via di Voltaia nel Corso 27/29 (0578 758 615/www.caffepoliziano.it). Open 7.30am-9.30pm Mon-Fri; 7.30am-midnight. €-€€. Café/bar/gelateria.*
Established in 1868 and now exquisitely restored, this was the place where visiting aristocratic families ate and drank, wine deals were struck and intellectuals argued (among them Fellini and Pirandello). Now locals pop in to read the paper in one of the bar's two main rooms. It's ideal for an aperitif and light lunch, or just for one of the splendid desserts. Naturally, local wines are served, including the rated Valdipiatta Vino Nobiles. If the tiny balcony is occupied there is a scenic terrace that seats another 30.

Boccon di Vino

Torrenieri, 10km E of Montalcino *Località Colombaio Tozzi 201 (0577 848 233/ www.bsur.it/boccondivino). Open 12.30-2pm, 7-10pm Mon, Wed-Sun. €€€. Modern Italian.*
Boccon de Vino is one the most expensive restaurants in the area. Still, the price is offset by the views without and the food within: the excellent seasonal menu includes local products such as truffles, wild boar and porcini from Mount Amiata. The wine list will shoot the bill even higher but the selection is first class.

Osteria dell'Acquacheta

Montepulciano *Via del Teatro 22 (0578 717 086/ www.acquacheta.eu). Open 12.30-3pm, 7.30-10.30pm Mon, Wed-Sun. Closed Jan-mid Mar. €. Traditional Italian.*
This is such a popular restaurant that when you book lunch you may well be offered one of two sittings. A busy taverna with a long bar and wooden tables, Acquachetta serves so much home-made pasta that the cook often has to bring in fresh supplies while you're there. It's also known for its steak fiorentina and fillet of veal, both priced by the *etto* (100 grams). In season, there's a white truffle dessert.

Re di Macchia

Montalcino *Via Saloni 21 (0577 846 116). Open 12.30-2pm, 7-10pm Mon-Wed, Fri-Sun. €€. Traditional Italian.*
The Re is one of Montalcino's better restaurants. It's spread over two floors whose classic old-style Tuscan decor, wooden beams and terracotta floors all contribute towards a cosy atmosphere. The short, well thought out menu includes *pinci* (a fat semolina pasta) with wild boar ragu, roast duck breast with Brunello wine sauce, and grilled courgette with aubergines and fresh pecorino cheese: hearty, classic regional dishes.

Ristorante San Giorgio

Montalcino *Via S Saloni (0577 848 507) Open Apr-Oct 12.30-3pm, 7.30-10pm daily. Nov-Mar 12.30-3pm, 7.30-10pm Mon, Wed-Sun. €€. Pizzeria.*
San Giorgio is primarily a pizzeria, but it serves other dishes too, making it a good place to take children while also offering the grown-ups something not involving tomato paste. Dishes include pinci with a meat ragu and almonds, and with 90 seats there'll always be a table available.

Taverna Grappolo Blu

Montalcino *Via Scale Di Via Moglio 1 (0577 847 150). Open 7-10pm Mon-Thur, Sat, Sun. €€. Traditional/modern Italian.*
This cosy and well-liked family run restaurant features in the book *Vanilla Beans & Brodo* by Isabella Dusi, which reveals the intrigues behind the Tuscan village idyll. But there's no myth to the food: dishes here range from the traditional (crostini, sausage and beans) to the more inventive (pheasant al limone). The desserts are divine, the wines local and the place packed at weekends: book ahead.

Trattoria da Fiorella

Pienza *Via Condotti 11 (0578 749 095). Open 12.30-2pm, 7-10pm Mon, Tue, Thur-Sun. €€. Traditional Italian.*
This very popular, small Tuscan restaurant has excellent service and is highly recommended for lunch or dinner. The limited menu features excellent seasonal choices and specials. It's wise to book ahead.

Trattoria Latte di Luna

Pienza *Via San Carlo 6 (0578 748 606/www. portalepienza.it). Open noon-2.30pm, 7.30-9pm Mon, Wed-Sun. €€. Trattoria.*
The reputation of Latte di Luna has spread far and wide thanks to some enthusiastic blog entries and so it's probably best to book ahead. Try the Tuscan antipasti followed by traditional hand-made pasta or bread soup. For mains, we recommend wild boar or *maialino da latte arrosto* (roast suckling pig). To finish try the semifreddo, either orange or hazelnut with a splash of Vin Santo.

Explore

MONTALCINO

Overlooking the Asso, Ombrone and Arbia valleys, dotted with olive groves and vineyards, Montalcino is a classic Tuscan hill town, drawing admiring crowds. It also attracts wine pilgrims, come to sample a glass or two of Brunello di Montalcino, one of Italy's most celebrated reds. But Montalcino is secure in its own identity and the tourist trade hasn't completely taken over.

Under Siena's rule in the 13th century, four families dominated the town's politics, and are represented today in Montalcino's four *contrade* (town quarters). Once known for its tanneries and leather, the town prospered in the Middle Ages – though the decline that followed didn't abate until the late 1970s and the town's grape-inspired renaissance.

All roads in Montalcino lead to piazza del Popolo, in the heart of town. Here you'll find the medieval Palazzo Comunale, studded with shields of the dominant ruling families and modelled after Siena's Palazzo Pubblico. Almost hidden beneath

On the wine (t)rail

It would be remiss, nay, foolish, to tour this area, home of two of Italy's great DOCG wines, without indulging in some serious vineyard visits. Not only are the wines likely to be cheaper, but, having seen the slopes, felt the sun and the wind on the face and talked with the proprietor, you will gain a personal understanding of provenance that will go straight to your palate.

Most wineries are happy to show visitors around, but few are equipped with the staff and tasting rooms for proper tours. Tastings – sometimes given for free if you look likely to purchase – are more likely to take place among the wines or in atmospheric vaults of oak barrels. Local tourist and Strada Vino (www.stradavinonobile.it) offices will be able to give you lists of wineries: it's always a good idea to call ahead.

If you're here, you've probably got a car. But if you're based in Siena, you should book yourself on to a day trip on the Treno Del Vino wine train (0577/835702, www.winestation.it; pictured). Departing from Siena every Saturday (spring to autumn), this dinky 150-seater takes you through the beautiful countryside of the Val d'Orcia to Montalcino. En route, you will be plied with wine and sweetmeats; on arrival, you are offered tours and tastings. The day includes lunch at the restored station's wine bar and shop, BinarioZero, which is open year round for drinks, snacks and live music at weekends.

For visits under your own steam, some of south Tuscany's more prominent and worthwhile wineries are listed below.

BRUNELLO DI MONTALCINO

Fattoria dei Barbi
Montalcino *Podere Novi village 170 (0577 841 111/www.fattoriadeibarbi.it). Open 10am-1pm, 2.30-6pm Mon-Fri; 2.30-6pm Sat, Sun.*
Dei Barbi has some fine old cellars selling a variety of wines.

Fattoria del Casato
Località Podere Casato 17 (0577 849 421/ www.cinellicolombini.it). Open 9am-1pm, 3-6pm Mon-Fri; Sat, Sun by appointment.
Donatella Cinelli Colombini's tour is fun and instructive, and the wines promising.

Further information
Montalcino *Consorzio del Vino Brunello di Montalcino Costa del Municipio 1 (0577 848 246/www.consorzio brunellodimontalcino.it).*

VINO NOBILE DI MONTEPULCIANO

Avignonesi
Valiano di Montepulciano *Via Colonica 1 (0578 724 304/www.avignonesi.it). Open 9am-6pm Mon-Fri.*
Approximately 23km (14 miles) outside Montepulciano, Avignonesi has tastings and tours on weekdays.

Poliziano
Montepulciano *Via Fontago 1 (0578 738 171/www.carlettipoliziano.it). Open 8.30am-12.30pm, 2.30-6pm Mon-Fri. Closed Aug & 2wks Dec.*
Three types of Vino Nobile are produced here, two of which are single-vineyard crus.

Further information
Montepulciano *Consorzio del Vino Nobile di Montepulciano Piazza Grande 7 (0578 757 812/www.vinonobiledimontepulciano.it).*

it stands a statue of Montalcino's 16th-century conqueror, the Florentine Cosimo I de' Medici.

The best of the piazza's restaurants and bars is Caffè Fiaschetteria Italiana at no.6 (0577 849 043, www.fiaschetteriaitaliana.it, open summer 7.30am-midnight, winter 7.30am-9.30pm). It was founded in 1888 by winemaker Feruccio Biondi Santi – creator of the famous Brunello wine. A few doors down, Pasticceria Mariuccia (piazza del Popolo 29, 0577 849 319, open 8.30am-9pm daily) is another local institution. Its delicacies include crunchy *cavallucci* and *panforte*; the rich hazelnut and chocolate torta Marita was created in honour of the pastry chef's daughter.

From the piazza, stroll up to the impressive Museo Civico e Diocesano (via Ricasoli 31, 0577 846 014, www.museisenesi.org, closed Mon, admission €4.50). Its collection includes works by Simone Martini, a brilliant altarpiece by Bartolo di Fredi and a worthy exhibit of early ceramics. Next door is the Church of Sant'Agostino, built in 1360 and boasting superb frescoes by Bartolo di Fredi (under restoration at time of going to press).

Abbazia di Sant'Antimo

Montalcino Castelnuovo dell'Abate (www.antimo.it).
Open 10.15am-12.30pm, 3-6.30pm Mon-Fri;
9.15-10.45am, 3-6pm Sun. Admission free.
The lovely Benedictine abbey of Sant'Antimo lies quietly in a valley beneath the hamlet of Castelnuovo dell'Abate. Its founding is attributed to Charlemagne in 781, though what remains largely dates to the 12th century. The Romanesque interiors feature finely carved capitals, including one portraying Daniel in the lion's den (second column from the right of the nave). A group of French Premonstratensian monks (Cistercian branch) moved here in 1979 and salvaged it from decline. The supremely peaceful sound of Gregorian chant accompanies many of the day's religious observations, drawing audiences and pilgrims from far and wide. Entrance is free and the church is open 6am-9pm.

Fortezza

0577 849 211. Open 9am-6pm Mon-Fri; 9am-8pm Sat;
9am-9pm Sun Admission €4.
Dominating the entrace to the town, the Fortezza was built by the Sienese in 1362 and in 1555 became the last (and short-lived) stronghold of the Sienese Republic. Under siege many times but never stormed, its battlements remain wonderfully intact and offer a splendid view of the surrounding countryside. It's a great place to bring children, and also to buy wine: there's a wine shop in the keep.

SAN QUIRICO D'ORCIA & BAGNO VIGNONI

San Quirico d'Orcia is one of the lesser known treasures of Siena province. Still perfectly preserved within its ancient walls, the town was an important stopping point on the via Francigena pilgrimage route in the Middle Ages. Today it's a peaceful spot – especially at lunchtime, when the townspeople stop for a siesta and the streets become eerily quiet.

The village's main square is piazza della Libertà. Here you can sample the local semifreddo from the classic Bar Central (no.6, 0577 897583). Afterwards, stroll through the Horti Leonini formal gardens, which date from the 16th century; the rose garden is particularly lovely. A short walk away is the village's 12th-century Romanesque church, the Collegiata. Lions and dragons adorn its stone portals, while inside there is an impressive altarpiece by Sano di Pietro. Next door is the splendid 17th-century Palazzo Chigi, now the seat of local government.

Like many towns in the area, San Quirico has its own traditional olive press, which becomes the focal point of the annual Festa dell'Olio (held around 10 December). It's a convivial, somewhat bibulous opportunity for gorging on bruschetta, soaked in the superb, freshly pressed oil.

Just south of San Quirico is the tiny hamlet of Bagno Vignoni, known for its ancient thermal baths. Piazza delle Sorgenti, the main square, has a large Roman pool at its centre, flanked by houses and a low Renaissance loggia; St Catherine of Siena was brought here by her mother to dissuade her from a life of piety and, later, Lorenzo de' Medici sought a cure for the gout that was to cut short his life. Though you're no longer allowed to swim in the historic baths you can soak blissfully in the Piscina val di Sole public baths (www.piscinavaldisole.it) for €12 a day (bathing caps must be worn). Several hotels also offer treatments, massage, saunas and Turkish baths.

PIENZA

Originally called Corsignano, this tiny town was reborn during the early Renaissance in an extraordinary transformation that took just three years. The town took its current name – which means Pius's town – from the man who remodelled it between 1459 and 1462: native son Aeneas Silvius Piccolomini, who became Pope Pius II in 1458.

The 'Humanist Pope', as he was later called, was a close friend of Renaissance genius Leon Battista Alberti, the designer of the façade of Santa Maria Novella in Florence and author of the *Treatise of Architecture*. Bernardo Rossellino, Alberti's main assistant, designed Pienza's makeover, creating a central square flanked by the cathedral, town hall and papal palace. Standing in piazza Pio II, you'll notice recurring decorative themes (such as the garland) that lend a sense of unity to the different buildings and materials used.

The body of the Duomo is in tufa stone and, at the rear, deliberately Gothic in design, as if to fit into the existing urban context. The travertine façade, by contrast, is Renaissance in style – at the time, a bold declaration of modernity.

Pienza is home to one of the great cheeses of Italy, pecorino di Pienza, and many *alimentari* have lavish displays of the red-skinned or ash-covered wheels in their windows. Try it *fresco* (fresh and slightly buttery), *semistagionata* or *stagionata* (seasoned, crumbly and more strongly flavoured); *foglie di noce* cheese has been wrapped in walnut leaves and left to mature in earthenware pots.

Also in Pienza is Enoteca di Ghino (via delle Mura 8, 0578 748 057, 9.30am-9pm daily), an excellent wine shop with keenly priced bottles from Tuscany and beyond.

"Pienza is home to one of the great cheeses of Italy, pecorino di Pienza, and many grocers have lavish displays of the red-skinned or ash-covered wheels in their windows."

Museo Diocesano

corso Rossellino 30 (0578 749905). Open 10am-1pm, 2.30-6.30pm Mon, Wed-Sun. Admission €8.
The Diocesan Museum is on the top floor of two adjoining buildings. The name of one – Palazzo Borgia – might give a clue as to its original owner. Yes, Alexander VI, the Borgia pope, was once resident here. However, much of the art on display was actually commissioned by Pienza's patronal son, Pius II. The sections devoted to medieval and early Renaissance art are particularly striking. Highlights include an exceptionally tender depiction of Madonna with Child by Pietro Lorenzetti, a wooden statue by Dei Cori of St Regolo holding his own head and the magnificent cope of Pius II, embroidered in England.

Palazzo Piccolomini

Piazza Pio II (0577 286 300/www.palazzopiccolomini pienza.it). Open 16 Oct-14 Mar 10am-4.30pm Tue-Sun. 15 Mar-15 Oct 10am-6.30pm Tue-Sun. Closed 15 Feb-28 Feb. Admission €7.
The residence of Pope Pius II, to the right of the Duomo, was modelled after Alberti's Palazzo Rucellai in Florence, and is one of the highlights of any visit to Pienza. You enter a sublimely harmonious inner courtyard with ground floor rooms exhibiting Pius II's ambitious humanist project for the ideal city. The lavish *appartamento nobile*, private

apartments, on the first floor include the dining room, music room, study, weapons room, library and several bedrooms, including that of Pius himself. The opulent splendour of this room alone makes the tour worthwhile. There is a delightful hanging garden overlooking the Val d'Orcia that was probably the first garden since antiquity deliberately designed for aesthetic pleasure.

MONTEPULCIANO

Montepulciano is a town of greater substance than others south of Siena. Its fine buildings speak for the influence of Florentine architects, which is hardly surprising since the town read the writing on the wall earlier than most and in 1511 swore allegiance to Florence to defend itself from Sienese and Perugian expansion. Among the eminent architects of the time brought in to rework the town's medieval fabric were Antonio da Sangallo the Elder and Vignola.

It was also well ahead of the game in the wine stakes. In 1685 a poem entitled 'Bacco in Toscana' declared that 'Montepulciano of all wine is sovereign'; in 1966 Vino Nobile di Montepulciano was one of the first wines to be given Denominazione di Origine Controllata (DOC) recognition and subsequently became first to receive the even more prestigious Denominazione di Origine Controllata e Garantita (DOCG).

The best way to see the town is by tackling the steep Via di Gracciano del Corso, which starts near Montepulciano's northern entrance, Porta al Prato. Along the way, note the Roman and Etruscan marble plaques cemented into the base of Palazzo Bucelli at no.73: they were gathered by Pietro Bucelli, an 18th-century collector who supplied the Museo Civico with some of its finest items. A bit further up, on Piazza Michelozzo, is the towering Torre di Pulcinella, a clock tower topped by a mechanical figure typical of the Neapolitan Commedia dell'Arte. It was given to the town by a nostalgic priest from Naples who was a long time resident in Montepulciano.

Your efforts will eventually be rewarded when you reach Piazza Grande, the town's highest and most beautiful point. The spacious square paved with chunky stones is reminiscent of Pienza's 'ideal city' layout. The Duomo was never given a proper façade; the rough brick front belies the treasures of the interior: the fine Gothic *Assumption* by Taddeo di Bartolo (1401) above the altar; the *Madonna and Child* by Sano di Pietro towards the top of the left of the nave; the marble ciborium sculpted by Vecchietta; and the delicately carved tomb of humanist Aragazzi (1428) by Michelozzo.

Also in the square are Sangallo's Palazzo Tarugi, with loggia; the 13th-century Palazzo Comunale, which deliberately echoes the Palazzo Vecchio in Florence (visits to the roof €1.50); and Palazzo Contucci, which has been continually in

Top: Castello di Velona.
Bottom: La Bandita.

Val d'Orcia, near Pienza.

the same family since it was built by Antonio da Sangallo il Vecchio. Palazzo Contucci contains a family-owned and beautifully frescoed enoteca and restaurant (entrance Via del Teatro). Finally, the Griffin and Lion well (1520) has two stone lions, the symbol of Florence, flanked by griffins, the symbol of Montepulciano.

Around 20 minutes' walk to the west of the town from Porta al Prato is the pilgrimage church of San Biagio. Designed by Sangallo and built between 1518 and 1545, this Bramante-influenced study in proportion is a jewel of the High Renaissance.

If you're around on the last Sunday of August, watch out for the fabulous Bravìo delle Botti Race (www.braviodellebotti.it). This is an ancient race between the eight *contrada* of Montepulciano, which compete to roll barrels (weighing a hefty 80 kilogrammes) up the precipitous hill, amid much flag waving and pageantry.

If you are wine touring, keep an eye out for the helpful Strada Vino ('wine route'; www.stradavino nobile.it) offices.

La Foce
Strada della Vittoria 61, Chianciano Terme (057 869 101/www.lafoce.com). Open hourly guided tours Apr-Sept 3-7pm Wed; Oct-Mar 3-5pm Wed. Admission by donation.

The family home of the Origo family for more than 80 years is situated on the crossroads between Montepulciano, San Quirico d'Orcia and Chianciano. Anglo-American biographer and historian Iris Origo (1902-1988) bought the 15th-century inn in 1924; she and her husband Antonio dedicated their lives to restoring the property and its estate. Along the way, they worked on philanthropic projects in the then-impoverished local area and, during World War II, gave a home to refugee children and sheltered escaped Allied prisoners as they tried to return home after Italy's surrender. Origo described her experiences in her two autobiographical books, *Images and Shadows* and *War in Val d'Orcia*. The gardens were designed between 1924 and 1939 under the supervision of English architect Cecil Pinsent who also enlarged the house. The property is now a hotel and cultural venue; the gardens are open to the public on Wednesday afternoons.

Museo Civico
Palazzo Neri Orselli, via Ricci 10 (0578 717 300). Open 10am-7pm Tue-Sun. Admission €4.

This palazzo, a typical example of 13th-century Sienese civic architecture, houses the town's art collection. The archaeology section is especially strong with Etruscan funerary urns and Roman artefacts from the collection of Polizian noble Pietro Bucelli. On the upper floor watch out for the 15th-century masterpieces in glazed terracotta by Andrea della Robbia. There is also a gallery of paintings and some architectural marbles.

Factfile

When to go
Choosing when to visit is a question of balancing coping with crowds against coping with the heat. Spring has ideal weather – the wheat fields are an almost iridescent green – but is starting to get crowded. Summer is hot – with ripe fields of golden wheat – and packed. Autumn sees the crops harvested, the weather cooler and the tourists fewer in number. Of course, winter is quiet, but as a result some restaurants and museums cut back their opening hours or close completely. The weather? Well, you take your chances: it can be glorious or dreary.

Getting there
Perugia Airport is at St Egidio, 76km from Montepulciano (075 592 141/www. airport.umbria.it).
Florence Airport is 110km from Montepulciano (055 306 1300/www.aeroporto.firenze.it).
Pisa Airport is 197km from Montalcino (050 849 300/www.aeroportodipisa.com).

Getting around
Bus and train connections are minimal, so driving is the only realistic option. Rent a car from your

arrival airport. Parking can be problematic in the narrow streets of the walled cities; bear this in mind when choosing hotels.

Tourist information
Ufficio Informazioni Costa del Municipio, Montalcino (0577 849 331/www.proloco montalcino.it). Open 10am-1pm, 2-5.50pm daily. Closed Mon in winter.
Ufficio Informazioni, Piazza Dante Alighieri 18, Pienza (0578 749 071/www.ufficioturistico dipienza.it). Open 9.30am-1pm, 3-6.30pm daily.
Pro Loco, via del Corso 59A, Montepulciano (0578 757 341/www.prolocomontepulciano.it). Open Summer 9.30am-12.30pm, 3-8pm Mon-Sat; 10am-12.30pm Sun. Winter 9.30am-12.30pm, 3-6pm Mon-Sat; 10am-12.30pm Sun.
Strada da Vino Nobile, Piazza Grande 7, Montepulciano (0578 717 484, www.stradavino nobile.it). Open 10am-1pm, 3-7.30pm Mon-Sat.

Internet
IT.Point Via di Gracciano nel Corso 26, Montepulciano (0578 717 253/www.internet train.it). Open 10am-11pm Mon-Fri, 10am-10pm Sat, noon-midnight Sun.

Clockwise from top left:
Piazza San Silvestro;
Benozzo Gozzoli; Bevagna
frescoes, Montefalco;
religious souvenir; statue
of St Francis, Assisi;
Duomo, Orvieto; Assisi (2).

Umbria

Home to some of the most bewitching rural landscapes in the country, Umbria is known as *il cuore verde dell'Italia* (Italy's green heart). The only landlocked region on the Italian peninsula, its attractive unspoiled medieval towns and villages are close enough to each other to be explored together, even on a relatively short break.

Many of these medieval towns were actually autonomous city-states until well into the 16th century, and all of them are spectacularly beautiful. Most famous of all, perhaps, is Assisi, where St Francis founded his order in 1209, though it is rivalled for religious significance by Orvieto, with its astonishing cathedral. The lovely hilltop town of Todi also has an impressive cathedral and a stunning setting overlooking the surrounding countryside.

Some of the smaller towns and villages are often neglected by tourists – unfairly. Spello, for instance, is a delightful medieval town on the lower slopes of Monte Subasio, famous for its olive production. Montefalco, east of Todi, which enjoys remarkable views extending as far as Assisi and Spoleto, is a centre of the regional wine trade.

Umbria is so packed with things to see and do that it would be impossible to include them all – so we have chosen a selection of destinations towards the centre of the region that includes a bit of everything. If you want to cover the lot, start in either Assisi or Orvieto and spend a week exploring.

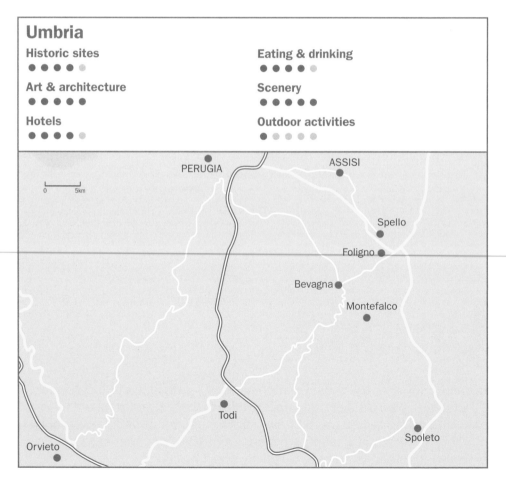

Umbria

Historic sites
● ● ● ● ○

Art & architecture
● ● ● ● ●

Hotels
● ● ● ● ○

Eating & drinking
● ● ● ● ○

Scenery
● ● ● ● ●

Outdoor activities
● ○ ○ ○ ○

PERUGIA

ASSISI

Spello

Foligno

Bevagna

Montefalco

Todi

Spoleto

Orvieto

0   5km

Stay

B&B Valentina
Orvieto *Via Vivaria 5 (076 334 1607). €.*
Occupying the top two floors of her home, Valentina's friendly B&B is just off piazza del Popolo. The six comfy bedrooms and self-catering apartment are prettily furnished with lots of personal touches, and all have private bathrooms. The biggest and best room has a 'kitchen corner' and a tiny terrace. Family groups will appreciate the flat at the top, with its attic ceilings, kitchen and working fireplace. Breakfast is laid out on the landing for guests to take back to their rooms on trays – breakfast in bed, if you fancy, at no extra charge.

Il Chiostro di Bevagna
Bevagna *Corso Matteotti 197 (074 236 1987/ www.ilchiostrodibevagna.com). €.*
The entrance to this hotel is through the lovely former cloister of San Domenico church, just off piazza San Silvestro. The 14 sunny bedrooms above the cloister were once part of a convent, and are a good budget option. With white walls, cool, tiled floors and rustic dark wood furniture, they are quite spartan, but all have private bathrooms and great views of the rooftops and surrounding country. In warm weather, breakfast is served overlooking the cloister.

Fattoria di Vibio
20kms from Todi *Località Buchella 9, Doglio, Montecastello di Vibio (075 874 9607/www.fatt oriadivibio.com). €€.*
High in rolling hills and olive groves about 20km north-west of Todi, the Saladini family's *agriturismo* is a comfortable base for explorations. The 13 pleasant, rustic bedrooms and four self-catering apartments are located in what were farm buildings, with communal spaces in the old farmhouse. Food is important at Vibio: meals served on a big summer veranda or in the glassed-in restaurant use olive oil, meat, veg and fruit produced on site. There's a good wine list too. A small spa and indoor infinity pool have recently been added to the outdoor pool, tennis, bikes and horse riding.

La Fortezza
Assisi *Piazza del Comune (075 812 418/ www.lafortezzahotel.com). €.*
The Chioccechetti family runs this budget hotel and adjacent restaurant up a steep hill from piazza del Comune. The seven rooms are simple, but comfortable and spotlessly clean; all have private baths and a ceiling fan. Those at the top have roof-top views and are sunnier; book well in advance for no.44, which has a small private terrace. No breakfast is provided, but you can get lunch or dinner at the family's rustic restaurant, serving Umbrian specialities such as guinea fowl with truffles *in crosta* (in pastry).

Hotel Posta
Orvieto *Via Luca Signorelli 18 (076 334 1909). €.*
This town-centre budget hotel was undergoing a much-needed refit when we visited. Housed in a once-grand medieval palazzo, it has been a hotel since 1812. All 20 rooms should now have been given a lick of paint, new light fittings and brand new bathrooms, but the pleasantly dated atmosphere remains; rooms are furnished with period and modern pieces, and many have marble floors. Those at the top of the house are smaller but sunnier, and have great views. There's a reading/TV room with a fireplace and a lovely shady garden. Not all bedrooms have private baths.

L'Orto degli Angeli
Bevagna *Via Dante Alighieri 1 (074 236 0130/ www.ortoangeli.it). €€€-€€€€.*
The ancestral home of the aristocratic Antonini dei Conti Angeli Nieri Mongalli family is in the centre of medieval Bevagna. The 14 gorgeous rooms combine discreet luxury with the atmosphere of a private residence. Communal areas and bedrooms are housed in two wings of the hotel, which face each other across a delightful hanging garden, an idyllic retreat in good weather. All rooms are filled with family antiques and pictures; the grander, first-floor rooms have original frescoes. Uniquely, the house incorporates part of a Roman amphitheatre, and the elegant Redibis restaurant occupies a section of the curved ambulacrum.

"Lucio Sforza uses recipes from Umbria and ancient Etruria, often offering unusual taste combinations."

San Crispino
Assisi *Via Sant'Agnese 11 (075 815 5124/ www.sancrispinoresidence.com). €€€.*
Assisi's mass tourism-orientated accommodation scene was given an upmarket boost by this attractive, suite-only hotel. In a medieval mansion not far from the church of Santa Chiara, the seven suites are loosely themed around St Francis's 'Canticle of the Creatures'. Frate Sole is a two-bedroom, two-bathroom suite with working fireplace and terrace; Sora Luna e Stelle has a midnight-blue vaulted ceiling and private garden; Madre Terra is a sunny room, done out in earthy colours, with fabulous views. Each suite has a kitchenette where you could make a basic breakfast.

San Lorenzo 3
Todi *Via San Lorenzo 3 (075 894 4555). €.*
Seven generations of the Pellegrini family have lived in this tall townhouse just off piazza del Duomo, and the top floor guesthouse Signora Morena runs is packed with mementos. The vaulted entrance hall is rather gloomy, but once inside you'll find parquet floors, painted ceilings, antiques, marble washstands, chandeliers, faded family photos, musty books and exquisite old bed linens. There are neither TVs nor phones in the six bedrooms to break the spell. In winter, fires are lit in the sitting room and in the huge, beamed room where breakfast is served at a communal table. There's a shady garden for hot weather.

L'Orto degli Angeli.

Villa Pambuffetti
Montefalco, 6km from Foligno *Viale della Vittoria 20 (074 237 9417/www.villapambuffetti.com). €€-€€€.*
This pink-hued villa is set in a huge, cool garden just outside the walls of Montefalco. The Pambuffetti family started taking in paying guests in the early 1900s (Gabriele d'Annunzio was a regular visitor), and the atmosphere is redolent of those days despite the addition of modern comforts. There are 11 comfortable bedrooms; if you want a view, splash out on the tower room which has 360° windows. There's a big pool for summer; in winter, a bright fire warms the sitting room. The restaurant serves excellent local cuisine – Alessandra Pambufetti, the present owner, gives cooking courses.

Eat

Umbria's native cooking is essentially rustic and wholesome, drawing on the fruits of its fertile, varied land; tangy green olive oil from the Valle Umbra, pork (fresh or cured) and truffles from the hills around Norcia, pulses from remote, mountain-bound Castelluccio, wines bold and red from Montefalco or fresh and white from Orvieto. Restaurants range from simple, family-run trattorias to fancy, white-linen restaurants, but the best in all categories source top-notch local ingredients.

L'Alchemista
Montefalco, 6km from Foligno *Piazza del Comune 14 (074 237 8558). Open 12.30-5pm, 7-10pm Mon, Wed-Sun. €-€€. Enoteca.*
This 'wine and olive oil bar' sits on a circular piazza, with tables out front in warm weather. The upstairs shop sells wine and local products, and meals are served in the cosy basement. You can order just a plate of cheeses or cured meats and a glass of full-bodied Sagrantino, or try something more substantial: perhaps *zuppa di roveja'* (made with dried peas), *zuppa di risina* (tiny dried beans from Lake Trasimeno), *bruschetta* with black truffles and *filetto al Sagrantino*. With only a 10% mark-up on wine compared to upstairs, it's worth trying something a little extravagant.

L'Asino d'Oro
Orvieto *Vivolo del Popolo 9 (076 334 4406). Open 12.30-2.30pm, 7.30-9.30pm Wed-Sun. Closed 15 Jan-15 Feb. €€. Trattoria.*
Lucio Sforza's trattoria is hidden down an alleyway just off piazza del Popolo. Inside, it's austere (bare wood tables are laid in two small, white-tiled rooms with few adornments), which means there's little to distract you from superb food that is all about seasonal availability of local ingredients. Sforza uses recipes from Umbria and ancient Etruria, often offering unusual taste combinations; *budino* (a kind of deconstructed flan) of sweet red peppers and plums, *lombrichelli* with broccoli and almond pesto, and pork ribs in an intense sweet-and-sour citrus sauce. This is also a great place at which to sample Umbrian wines.

La Bastiglia
Spello *Via dei Molini 7 (074 265 1277/www.labastiglia.com). Open 1-2.30pm, 8-10.30pm Mon, Tue, Fri-Sun; 8-10.30pm Thur. €€€€. Modern Italian.*
This converted flour mill is one of Umbria's gastronomic highlights. The Michelin-starred Bastiglia has a huge panoramic terrace for summer meals and a sober, warmly lit interior brightened by contemporary paintings. Marco Gubbiotti sources his mostly local ingredients carefully and works them into imaginative dishes such as farro flour papardelle with wild boar and fennel and the trademark *Chianina in tre livelli di cottura*, a three-way working of Chianina beef. There are fish choices too, and three set menus (including one for vegetarians). The wine list has 900 labels at more reasonable prices than you might expect.

Enoteca Oberdan
Todi *Via Ciuffelli 22 (075 894 5409). Open noon-midnight Mon, Wed-Sun. €-€€. Enoteca.*
Near San Fortunato, this little wine-bar-cum-restaurant is a great place for either a snack with wine or a full meal. Low beamed ceilings, rustic tables and chairs, background jazz and friendly young owners set the scene for a short menu of daily specials and a wide choice of carefully sourced *salumi* and cheeses, served with pickles and chutneys. Local specialities include own-made tagliatelle with truffles, rabbit *alla cacciatore* (with capers and black olives) and the classic *coratella di agnello* (lamb innards in a spicy sauce). The wine list favours Umbria, by the glass or the bottle.

"This *enoteca* gives serious wine buffs a run for their money."

Enoteca Properzio
Spello *Piazza Matteotti 8 (074 230 1521). Open 10am-10pm daily. €-€€. Enoteca.*
Recently voted one of Italy's top ten wine shops by an Italian wine magazine, this *enoteca* gives serious wine buffs a run for their money. Presided over by the enthusiastic Angelini brothers, it stocks some 2,200 global wines, including a vast selection from Umbria. You can also eat here, choosing from a menu that features soups and salads, crostini with truffle paste, and a great selection of local cheeses and cured meats. Some 20 wines are available by the glass, and there are bottles to suit every pocket. The *enoteca* occupies part of Palazzo dei Canonici, its sleek contemporary styling encased in ancient brick vaults. Dinner must be booked in advance.

Pallotta
Assisi *Via Volta Pinta 2 (075 812 649). Open 12.15-2.15pm, 7.15-9.30pm Mon, Wed-Sun. €€. Trattoria.*
Duck under an archway decorated with *grottesche* frescoes off piazza del Comune and down a steep stairway to find this busy, pleasantly old-fashioned and rather genteel trattoria, popular with locals and visitors. There's always a choice of seasonal specialities alongside the regular menu.

An autumnal meal might start with duck and pumpkin strudel or an earthy soup of rare Trasimeno beans and porcini. Follow this with the house *strangozzi* (eggless pasta) with porcini and sausages cooked with white grapes. This is good place at which to try *torta al testo*, a local flat, round bread – made here with a little cheese.

La Palomba
Orvieto *Via Manente 16 (076 334 3395).*
Open 12.30-2.30pm, 7.30-10.30pm Mon,
Tue, Thur-Sun. €€. Trattoria.
Located on a characteristic cobbled lane off piazza della Repubblica, the rustic, family-run Palomba is a good place for no-nonsense local fare. Tables are set in two dark wood-panelled rooms, brightened by cheerful flowers and checked tablecloths. Start with *bruschetta* drizzled with local olive oil that has fresh truffle grated on top at the table. Pasta dishes include *tagliatelle al cinghiale* (with wild boar) and *umbrichelli* with truffles or *alla matriciana* (pancetta and tomato sauce). For *secondo*, choose pigeon, lamb or wild boar, or splash out on *filetto al tartufo*. Own-made desserts include walnut tart and *panna cotta* with blackcurrants.

"Its superb frescoes positively glow in their bright colours, perfectly displayed in the simple, Gothic space."

Pianegiani
Todi *Corso Cavour 40 (075 894 2376).*
Open 6.40am-8pm daily. €. Bar/gelateria.
Unexciting modern-ish decor, harsh lighting, old timers playing cards and slurping coffee and grappa: a typical Italian small-town bar, in other words, except that it sells the best *gelato* in Umbria. The ice-cream is made with proper seasonal ingredients: in autumn, try *pinoli e crema* (pinenut and cream), walnut and fig, and bright green pistachio; for summer, flavours are fruit-based. There's no atmosphere in the bar, but it has a nice terrace.

La Piazzetta delle Erbe
Assisi *Via San Gabriele dell'Addolorata*
15B (075 815 352). Open 12.30-2.30pm,
7.30-10.30pm Tue-Sun. €€. Modern Umbrian.
Assisi is not blessed with particularly interesting restaurants, but this cheerful little *osteria*, on the site of a what was once a herb and vegetable market, is a cut above the rest. The short, seasonally based menu draws on local traditions but adds an inventive element, so you'll find unusual dishes such as pear and pecorino-stuffed ravioli or pan-fried guinea fowl breast with white grapes and blackcurrant conserve. The wine list is limited, but carefully chosen. In summer, tables are set out under the plane trees.

Explore

ASSISI
The medieval town of Assisi sits serene on its spur against a backdrop of Monte Subasio, a pale grey-pink slash visible for miles around, surrounded by silvery olives and undulating fields. At its feet is the monumental basilica of Santa Maria degli Angeli and the wide, flat expanse of the Umbra valley.

First settled in the Iron Age, the town has since become one of the world's great pilgrimage sites. Visitors come from all over the globe to pay homage to St Francis. High season is suffocatingly busy, but it's easy to escape the crowds by avoiding via San Francesco and corso Mazzini. There are plenty of quiet back streets to explore.

Via di San Francesco leads east from the basilica into the *centro storico* and piazza del Comune, passing handsome medieval palazzi and shop after shop selling religious paraphernalia and tourist tat. Look out for the delightful but easy-to-miss Oratorio dei Pellegrini at no.11 (for admission, ring at the convent, no.13), which is painted with 15th-century frescoes illustrating the lives of St James and St Anthony Abbot.

Piazza del Comune is the town's main gathering place, and is well endowed with bars and cafès. To the south-east lies the pink and white Gothic basilica of Santa Chiara (*see below*), supported by massive flying buttresses. This is the site of the earlier church of San Giorgio, where St Francis was originally buried and where his canonisation took place in 1228. The building you see today is a shrine to St Clare, companion of St Francis and founder of the order of the Poor Clares. Some 40 nuns still live in a closed order in the convent.

Via Sant'Agnese leads to the delightful, little-visited church of Santa Maria Maggiore. This was Assisi's first cathedral, built on top of a temple to Apollo, the remains of which can be seen in the crypt. Most people assume that San Francesco is Assisi's cathedral, and never bother with the beautiful Cattedrale di San Rufino (*see p84*), which is located in a quiet corner of the town.

Basilica di Santa Chiara
Piazza Santa Chiara (075 812 282). Open Nov-Mar
6.30am-noon, 2-6pm daily. Apr-Oct 6.30am-noon,
2-7pm daily. Admission free.
Santa Chiara's simple façade is adorned only by a splendid rose window and a portal decorated with fine reliefs. Inside, the church (built in 1257) is airy and simple, with a single nave and few embellishments. The faded frescoes in the transepts are by followers of Giotto, and the scenes from St Clare's life were painted by the Maestro di Santa Chiara. St Clare's remains lie in the neo-Gothic crypt.

L'Asino d'Oro.

Cattedrale di San Rufino & Museo Diocesano

Piazza San Rufino (075 816 016/www.assisimuseo cattedrale.com). Open Church Nov-Mar 8am-1pm, 2-6pm daily. Apr-Oct 8am-1pm, 3-7pm Mon-Fri; 7am-7pm Sat, Sun. Admission free. Museum Nov-Mar 10am-1pm, 2.30-5.30pm Mon, Tue, Thur-Sun. Apr-Oct 10am-1pm, 3-6pm Mon, Tue, Thur-Sun. Admission €3; €2.50 reductions.

The Duomo sits on what is believed to have been the Roman forum and the remains of a fifth-century chapel. Another church occupied the present piazza in the 11th century (only its bell tower and crypt survive), with the present church having been rebuilt in 1140. St Francis and St Clare were baptised in the font that stands near their statues.

Access to the Museo Diocesano is through the beautiful Romanesque crypt, where a Roman sarcophagus contains San Rufino's remains. The museum houses a mixed collection of paintings and frescoes from the Umbrian school and others, such as Dono Doni, Matteo da Gualdo and Filippo Lippi.

San Francesco

Piazza Inferiore di San Francesco (075 819 001/www. sanfrancescoassisi.org). Open Lower church Oct-Mar 6am-5.45pm Mon-Fri, 6am-7.15pm Sat-Sun. Apr-Oct 6am-6.45pm Mon-Fri, 6am-7.15pm Sat-Sun. Upper church Nov-Mar 8.30am-5.45pm Mon-Fri; 8.30am-6.45pm Sat, Sun. Apr-Oct 8.30am-6.45pm daily. Admission free.

Work on the basilica of San Francesco began in 1228, just two years after St Francis's death. The lower church was completed in record time, and in May 1230 St Francis's tomb was transferred here from San Giorgio (where Santa Chiara now stands). The upper church was consecrated in 1253.

From arcaded piazza Inferiore di San Francesco, the entrance to the lower church is through a grand Renaissance portico. It takes a while to adjust to the gloomy light in the dim interior, but in this vaulted space are some of Italy's most important 13th- and 14th-century frescoes. The oldest of them (by the Master of St Francis and dating from 1253) are in the nave; St Francis's life is depicted on the right wall. The Cappella di San Martino (the first chapel on the left) was painted by the great Simone Martini. Work on the Cappella della Maddalena at the end of the nave on the right is attributed to Giotto and assistants, while a pupil of Giotto painted the celebrated Quattro Vele frescoes on the cross vault over the high altar. Pietro Lorenzetti painted the moving cycle illustrating the Passion in the left transept; the right transept has frescoes by Giotto, Martini, Lorenzetti and Cimabue.

The airy, light interior of the upper church, now fully restored after the 1997 earthquake, is a complete contrast to the gloom below. Its superb frescoes positively glow in their bright colours, perfectly displayed in the simple, Gothic space. Two narrative bands, painted between about 1277 and 1300 by the likes of Giotto and Cimabue, run the length of the nave and back, remarkable for their vividness. The lower register, illustrating famous scenes from the life of St Francis, is generally thought to be by the young Giotto

and his assistants; it begins with the painting to the right of the altar. The upper frescoes are much harder to see (binoculars help) and some are badly damaged, but they depict scenes from the Old and New Testament and are attributed to followers of Cimabue.

SPELLO

Spello is a delightful little medieval town on the lower slopes of Monte Subasio, across the Valle Umbra from Montefalco and Bevagna. It is particularly interesting for its ancient history and Roman remains. Spello boasts the ruins of an amphitheatre and no fewer than three Roman gates. Monumental Porta Venere, flanked by two cylindrical towers, is the best preserved, but triple-arched Porta Consolare is the main entrance into town.

The most important buildings are mainly situated in or around piazza Matteotti and piazza della Repubblica. Palazzo dei Canonici houses the Pinacoteca Civica, where you can see an interesting collection of mainly Umbrian art dating from the 13th to 16th centuries. Next door is the church of Santa Maria Maggiore (*see p84*). The church of San Lorenzo has an unusual façade incorporating bits and pieces from Roman and medieval buildings.

Each year the manufacture of olive oil in the area is celebrated in the *Festa dell'Olivo e Sagra della Bruschetta,* held the weekend before Martedì Grasso (Shrove Tuesday).

"Often described as 'Italy's ideal town', this triangle of buildings does indeed enjoy an idyllic setting on a steep hill."

Santa Maria Maggiore

Piazza Matteotti 18 (074 230 1792). Open 9am-noon, 2.30-6pm daily. Admission free.

The baroque interior, with its grandiose side altars and carved baldacchino, mostly dates from the 17th century, but the Cappella Baglioni was commissioned from Pinturicchio in 1500. Come here for Pinturicchio's wonderfully vivid, brightly coloured frescoes illustrating the Nativity and Annunciation; in the top left corner, the old bearded man who appears to be floating on a cloud is a self-portrait. The church also guards a Roman treasure; the stoup on the right of the main door is a superb example of Roman carving, in the form of the funerary altar of Caio Titieno (60AD).

BEVAGNA & MONTEFALCO

In magnificent hilly countryside (the 'Monti Martani') east of Todi is an area that is becoming increasingly famous for its production of good quality, full-bodied red wine made from the Sagrantino grape, which is unique to the area. From late October to early November, the hillsides are ablaze with bright red vine leaves. Shops and *enoteche* in the local towns provide plenty of opportunity for buying and tasting, but if you're touring by car, it's a lot more fun to visit the wineries themselves.

The delightful medieval walled town of Bevagna is built on the site of the Roman settlement of Mevania. Remains of an amphitheatre are incorporated into the property that now houses the Orto degli Angeli hotel (*see p79*), and at the southern end of piazza Garibaldi, you can see the columns of a Roman temple, later re-built as a church. Via Porta Guelfa leads to the entrance of the Roman thermal baths (open 10.30am-1pm, 2.30-6pm Tue-Sun).

A short drive away, across vineyards and olive groves, lies another medieval gem. Montefalco is known as the *Ringhiera d'Umbria* ('Umbria's Balcony'), thanks to its dominant position. All roads lead to circular piazza del Comune, the town's highest point. The local wine consortium, Strada del Sagrantino, has its office on the square (0742 378 490, www.stradadels agrantino.com); it supplies information about the wineries in the area and can arrange cellar tours. Montefalco's cultural claim to fame is the superb fresco cycle by Benozzo Gozzoli in the Museo Civico di San Francesco, down a steep hill off the piazza.

Museo Civico di San Francesco

Montefalco, 6km from Foligno *Via Ringhiera Umbra 1 (074 237 9598/www.montefalcodoc.it). Open June, July 10.30am-1pm, 2.30-7pm daily. Aug 10.30am-1pm, 2.30-7.30pm daily. Mar-May, Sept, Oct 10.30am-1pm, 2.30-6pm daily. Nov-Feb 10.30am-1pm, 2.30-6pm Tue-Sun. Admission €4; €2 reductions.*
In the deconsecrated church of San Francesco is Montefalco's great pride and joy. Here Benozzo Gozzoli (best known for his work on the Cappella dei Magi in Florence) spent 1450-52 painting the apse with lively scenes from the life of St Francis; look out for the views of Arezzo and Montefalco itself. Gozzoli also painted the first chapel; others are by the 15th- and 16th-century Umbrian school.

TODI

Sophisticated little Todi was founded by the ancient Umbri, then seized by the Etruscans, before prospering under the Romans as the colony of Tuder (the locals still call themselves 'Tuderti'). Often described as 'Italy's ideal town', this triangle of buildings does indeed enjoy an idyllic setting on a steep hill, surrounded by picturesque countryside. Each year in July, the town plays host to nine days of music, poetry, dance and more at the Todi Arte Festival (www.todiartefestival.it).

Elegant Piazza del Popolo sits at the top of the town, at the heart of a dense maze of medieval lanes. Among its impressive grey stone Gothic buildings is the Palazzo del Capitano del Popolo, Todi's original town hall, which was built in 1213. It's one of the oldest buildings of its kind in Italy, and today houses the Museo Civico and an excellent Pinacoteca, laid out in a series of grand rooms. At the north end of the piazza stands the squared-off Duomo.

The church of San Fortunato (*see below*) lies above via Ciuffelli. From here you can walk down the hill to the remarkable 16th-century church of Santa Maria della Consolazione, an isolated landmark built on a Greek cross plan; it's a masterpiece of the Renaissance.

Duomo

Piazza del Popolo (075 894 3041). Open Apr-Oct 8.30am-12.30pm, 3-6.30pm Mon-Sat. Nov-Mar 8.30am-4.30pm Mon-Sat; 8.30am-12.30pm, 3-5.30pm Sun. Admission free.
Work on Todi's cathedral was begun in the 12th century and finished some 200 years later. Set at the top of a wide flight of steps, the façade sports three rose windows and an intricately carved portal, and the beautiful interior has an unusual fourth aisle, flanked by a Gothic arcade. Don't miss the superb Corinthian capitals, the fine wooden intarsia choir stalls and the beautiful 1507 baptismal font.

San Fortunato

Piazza Umberto I (075 895 6227). Open Apr-mid Oct 9am-1pm, 3-7pm Tue-Sun. Mid-Oct-Mar 9.30am-12.30pm, 3-5pm Tue-Sun. Admission free.
Dedicated to the town's patron saint and located at the top of a steep flight of steps, this church was built in 1292. The beautifully carved central portal is set in an unfinished façade, and the wide, luminous interior has a fresco of the Madonna and Child by Masolino and fine choir stalls. Todi's famous son, medieval poet and mystic Jacopone dei Benedetti (aka Jacopone da Todi), is entombed in the crypt.

ORVIETO

Perched dramatically on a 315-metre outcrop of dark golden volcanic tufa stone, Orvieto is one of Umbria's essential destinations. The town was incorporated into the Etruscan Confederation in the ninth century BC, and today is famous for the crisp, white wine produced in the vineyards that spread across the flat volcanic plain below. With its cafés and highly rated restaurants, bookshops and theatre, Orvieto is a civilised place in which to spend a couple of days.

Any visit here should start in piazza del Duomo, where the glorious, zebra-striped cathedral, with

Clockwise from top left:
Breakfast in Perugia;
Assisi; fountains,
Bevagna; Sagrantino
vineyard; Assisi.

its wedding cake façade, is simply breathtaking. To the right of the cathedral stands the impressive 13th-century Palazzo Papale, a complex of three Gothic papal palaces that was home to no fewer than 33 pontiffs.

Corso Cavour, the main drag, slices east to west through the town. Piazza del Popolo hosts a market on Saturday and Thursday mornings, and piazza della Repubblica sits on the site of the Etruscan and Roman forums.

West of here lies a network of Orvieto's oldest – and most picturesque – cobbled streets. Via Malabranca leads to one of the town's hidden gems, the beautiful little church of San Giovenale, the interior of which boasts faded frescoes and some superb stone carving. At the other end of town, be sure to allow time for one of Orvieto's more curious sights, the 63-metre-deep Pozzo di San Patrizio (see right).

Duomo

Piazza del Duomo (076 334 1167/www.opsm.it). Open Apr-Sept 7.30am-12.45pm, 2.30-7.15pm daily. Mar, Oct 7.30am-12.45pm, 2.30-6.15pm daily. Nov-Feb 7.30am-12.45pm, 2.30-5.15pm daily. Admission free (Cappella della Madonna €3).

The monumental Duomo was built by Pope Urban IV to house a miraculously blood-stained piece of linen, an altar cloth that convinced a doubting priest of the reality of transubstantiation just in time for Urban's visit. The foundation stone was laid in 1290, but the cathedral took another three centuries to be completed. It is built in alternating bands of pale travertine and grey basalt, with an intricate façade that towers above the piazza. You need to get up close to truly appreciate the wonderfully detailed 14th-century bas-reliefs on the lower pilasters, which run through key Old Testament moments from the Creation on the left to the Last Judgement, in full gory detail, on the far right.

Bathed in mellow, sepia-toned light filtered through alabaster windows, the vast interior is pleasingly uncluttered. Look out for Gentile da Fabriano's Madonna and Child by the left door and, next to it, an elaborately carved font. Left of the high altar, the Cappella del Corporale (built to house that blood-stained relic) is entirely covered in frescoes. The huge, gilded organ above the entrance is the second largest in Italy.

The Cappella della Madonna di San Brizio houses one of the region's most important works of art: a celebrated Renaissance fresco cycle by Luca Signorelli, whose richly coloured, dynamic images are said to have deeply influenced Michelangelo's work on the Sistine Chapel.

Pozzo di San Patrizio

Viale Sangallo (076 334 3768/www.bellaumbria.net). Open Nov, Feb 10am-5pm daily. Mar, Apr, Sept, Oct 9am-7pm daily. May-Aug 9am-8pm daily. Admission €4.50; €3.50 reductions. No credit cards.

In the mid 16th century, Pope Clement VII commissioned Antonio da Sangallo the Younger to build this remarkable well to guarantee the city's water supply in the event of a siege. Sangallo dug down 63m to access a spring, then encircled the 13m-wide hole with two spiral ramps, so that teams of donkeys could haul up the water.

Factfile

When to go

As in the rest of Italy, the hottest time of the year in Umbria is mid July to late August; but, avoiding this period, the best months in which to visit are May to October. Winters can be very cold and damp, and rural accommodation tends to shut down off-season. Umbria doesn't suffer from mass tourism the same way that Tuscany does, but Assisi and Orvieto can be very crowded at weekends in high season.

Getting there & around

Buses run regularly between Perugia's small Sant'Egidio airport (075 592 141, www.airport. umbria.it) and Perugia station. There you can catch a train to Assisi or Orvieto (via Terontola; see www.trenitalia.it for details). Alternatively, fly into Florence (055 306 1300, www.aeroporto. firenze.it) or Rome (Fiumicino: 06 65951, www.adr.it; Ciampino: 06 65951, www.adr.it).

Undoubtedly, the best way to explore is by car; car hire companies have offices at Perugia airport and in all the major towns. If you do need to use local transport, local tourist offices have details of bus routes; train timetables and routes are available on the Trenitalia website (www.trenitalia.it).

Tourist information

Information on Umbrian towns can be found on the regional tourist board's website (www.umbria2000.it). For tourist offices: Piazza del Comune, Assisi (075 812 534/ www.assisi.umbria2000.it). Open 8am-2pm, 3-6pm daily. Piazza del Duomo 24, Orvieto (076 334 1772/ www.orvieto.umbria2000.it). Open 8am-2pm, 3-6pm daily. Piazza del Popolo 38, Todi (075 894 5416/www. todi.umbria2000.it). Open 8am-2pm, 3-6pm daily.

Internet access

Most of Umbria's larger towns have some kind of public internet point, and many hotels offer guests access to the internet, which may be free of charge.

Urbino & around

Italy has so many glorious towns, it can be difficult to choose between them. So how about one that sits on top of a hill surrounded by miles of glorious countryside, whose entire centre is a World Heritage Site, and whose palace is decorated with works by Raphael and Piero della Francesca? If Urbino doesn't have enough allure, there are further glorious medieval sites nearby, such as Pésaro and Fano, and one of Europe's main pilgrimage destinations at Loreto. And to top everything off, although tourism is on the increase along Le Marche's coast, the ancient hill towns and rugged rural hinterland still feel gloriously undiscovered.

Top: Ancona; Pésaro; Fano. Middle: Urbino. Bottom: Museo della Citta, Urbino; Pésaro sweet; Café news.

Piceni tribes, Greeks and Romans have all ruled over Le Marche's fertile soils, and the Lombards and Byzantines moved in after the fall of the Roman Empire. But it was during the Renaissance that the region came to the fore – with Urbino as its glittering centrepiece, shaped by the wealthiest mercenary (or *condottiere*) of the time, Duke Federico da Montefeltre. His court became a magnet for the finest intellectual and artistic talents of the day, from Raphael, a native of the town, to Botticelli and Piero della Francesca. The Montefeltres were one of a number of rival aristocratic families who battled for supremacy in Le Marche – though over the centuries, the Papacy gradually laid claim to the region. Finally, in 1860, the region was annexed to the Kingdom of Italy.

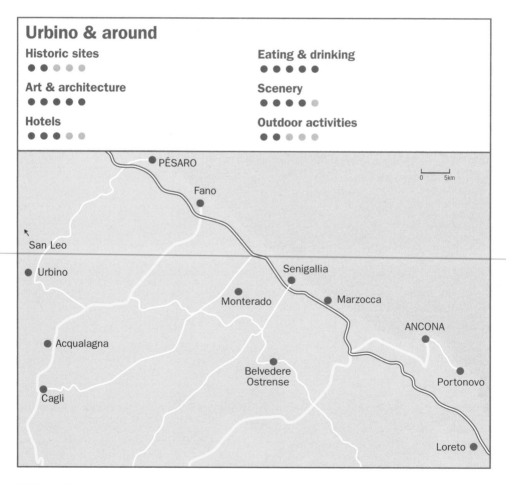

Urbino & around

Historic sites
● ● ● ● ●

Art & architecture
● ● ● ● ●

Hotels
● ● ● ● ●

Eating & drinking
● ● ● ● ●

Scenery
● ● ● ● ●

Outdoor activities
● ● ● ● ●

PÉSARO
Fano
San Leo
Urbino
Senigallia
Monterado
Marzocca
ANCONA
Acqualagna
Belvedere Ostrense
Portonovo
Cagli
Loreto

0   5km

Stay

Albergo Raffaello
Urbino *Vicolino S Margherita 40 (072 24784/*
www.albergoraffaello.com). €.
Set in a former seminary in the heart of the *centro storico*, just a short walk from the Piazza Repubblica, the Albergo Raffaelo is a real find. Bedrooms are quite simple but comfortable, many with excellent views over Urbino's old rooftops and the Ducale Palace; some have french windows. Prices are reasonable, and the Pecci family are impeccably friendly hosts.

Albergo Ristorante Villa Serena
6km south of Pésaro *Via San Nicola 6/3 (072 155 211/www.villa-serena.it). €€.*
Idyllically positioned in the rolling countryside between Fano and Pésaro, this noble 18th-century palazzo is run by aristocratic chef Count Renato Pinto de Franca y Vargas. Popular for wedding receptions and with visiting maestros, divos and divas performing in the Rossini Festival, it's furnished with antiques and has a lovely pool and sunny gardens. The restaurant is a romantic spot for a candlelit dinner, and the food's top-notch.

"There's a fine restaurant, pretty gardens, plenty of sun-kissed terraces and a beach spa."

Casa Ercole
Belvedere Otrense *Via Gavigliano 11 (073 162 206/UK 020 7700 7718/ www.ercolemoroni.com). €€€.*
This beautiful farmhouse was restored by top London florist Ercole Moroni, who was born in Le Marche. Quietly luxurious and gorgeously decorated, the seven-bedroom house can be rented out in its entirety or by the room. It's set on a hill near the medieval town of Belvedere Ostrense, affording guests panoramic views from the pool and terrace. Don't leave without sampling the delicious local wine, Lacrima di Morro d'Alba.

Castello di Monterado
Monterado *(071 795 8395/339 826 3842 mobile/www.castellodimonterado.it). €€.*
Inland from Senigallia, perched atop one of the Le Marche's many hills, this beautiful 18th-century castle was built by the Bourbons' architect of choice, Luigi Vanvitelli. There are just four suites, all of which have fabulous 19th-century frescoes, as well as six simple modern apartments to rent in converted cottages in the village. Surrounded by woodland and tranquil gardens, it's a romantic spot.

Fortino Napoleonico
Portonovo *Via Poggio 166, Baia di Portonovo, Conero Peninsula (071 801 450/www.hotelfortino.it). €€€.*
Built to see off marauding English troops, this imposing Napoleonic fort has now been converted into a sumptuous 33-room hotel. The glorious location, on a white shingle beach in the spectacular cove of Portonovo, is ideal for a sophisticated beach holiday. There's a fine restaurant, pretty gardens, plenty of sun-kissed terraces and a beach spa. Take a boat to Le Due Sorelle, or stroll along the beach to the 11th-century church of Santa Maria.

Grand Hotel Passetto
Ancona *Via Thaon de Revel 1 (071 31307/www.hotelpassetto.it). €€.*
This modern hotel commands a panoramic position over the bay of Ancona, in a new district near the city's best beaches. It's beautifully decorated with a mixture of antiques and modern chic, and many of the bedrooms have sea views. There's a lovely pool, and one of Ancona's finest fish restaurants, Il Passetto, is right next door.

Hotel Bonconte
Urbino *Via delle Mura 28 (072 22463/www.viphotels.it). €.*
It's a steep walk down from the centro storico to this pretty villa, just behind the city walls – but the spectacular views from its geranium-filled terrace make it all worthwhile. The rather old-fashioned furniture in the public rooms and bizarre psychedelic breakfast room mural might not be to everyone's taste, but bedrooms are very comfortable and the little garden is a delight in summer. Staff are warm and friendly and make excellent coffee – not an easy thing to find in Italian hotels.

Hotel Vittoria
Pésaro *Piazzale della Libertà 2 (072 134 343/www.viphotels.it). €€.*
The Vittoria has a long and distinguished history. Over the years, it's been a private home, town casino and gentlemen's club, and has played host to everyone from Pirandello to Pavarotti. Perfectly placed to enjoy Pésaro's beach scene and centro storico, it has a pool and restaurant, a little terrace and its own beach huts and lido access. Bedrooms are elegant, with antiques and smart bathrooms, and the staff are charmingly old-fashioned.

Locanda Ca'Vernaccia
Urbino *Via Panoramica 10, Località Pallino (072 232 9824/ www.locandaurbino.com). €.*
Rustic charm abounds at this lovely little inn, just under three kilometres outside Urbino. A cluster of stone buildings, dating from 1700, house various apartments and rooms; dotted with antiques, with terracotta-tiled floors and beamed ceilings, they're unpretentious and inviting. The rooms all have independent entrances and ensuite bathrooms, and one of the apartments has been adapted to accommodate disabled guests. A little gem, Locanda Ca'Vernaccia offers remarkably good value.

Clockwise from top left:
Hotel Vittoria (2);
Casa Ercole (3).

Eat

Food in Le Marche offers the best of both worlds, with wonderful fish from the Adriatic and copious produce from the fertile countryside. Fish lovers should try the raw seafood antipasti or local fish soup, *brodetto*, seasoned with tomato and vinegar. Ancona is also famous for *stoccafisso*, a dried cod casserole with potatoes, tomatoes and marjoram.

Spelt (*farro*) and chickpeas (*ceci*) feature heavily on menus, and the bread here is delicious – best enjoyed dipped in the local olive oil. There's hidden treasure all around Acqualagna, one of the contenders for the crown of truffle capital of Italy (white and black), and game is frequent fare inland – especially rabbit. Cured meats (*salumi*) and own-made pastas are staples, often combined with local cheeses. Particularly good are *pecorino di fossa* and *casciotta di Urbino*, Michelangelo's favourite, which he tucked into while painting the Sistine Chapel.

Vincisgrassi is a rich, meaty lasagne, perfectly accompanied by a glass of one of the excellent local reds: Rosso di Conero, Lacrima di Morro d'Alba, Rosso Piceno, Vernaccia di Pergola or Sangiovese. Jesi, meanwhile, is renowned for its white Verdicchio dei Castelli wine. If you're feeling under the weather, ask for a *Moretta di Fano*. A fishermen's tipple, knocked back before heading to sea of a morning, it comprises hot, sweet coffee laced with aniseed, a slice of lemon peel and rum or brandy.

Antica Osteria La Guercia

Pésaro *Via Baviera 33, off piazza del Popolo (072 133 463). Open 12.30-2.30pm, 7.30-10.30pm Mon-Sat. €. Trattoria.*
This lovely old tavern is tucked down an alley off the piazza del Popolo. Eat outdoors on the terrace or retreat to the rustic dining room, with its old Renaissance fireplace, wooden tables and lovely 1940s frescoes by Werther Bettini, which feature women picking olives and making wine – and men drinking it. The simple menu features local *salumi* and pasta dishes such as gnocchi di bacco, served in a sauce of gorgonzola and Rosso Piceno wine, along with vegetables, pulses and game. Ask to see the Roman mosaic in the back room.

Antico Furlo

Acqualagna *Via Furlo 60 (072 170 0096/ www.anticofurlo.it). Open noon-2.30pm Mon; noon-2.30pm, 7.30-10pm Wed-Sun. €€€. Traditional Italian.*
Open since the 19th century, Antico Furio was popular with Mussolini, who used to take over the kitchen to make tagliatelle and omelettes adorned with the local truffles. Chef-owner Alberto Melegrana serves up a storm with delicious concoctions such as turkey 'petals' with

cauliflower in balsamic and olive oil, or risotto with pumpkin and truffle. Game is a typical main, and the rabbit or guinea fowl are especially good.

Bontà delle Marche

Ancona *Corso Mazzini 96 (071 53985/www.bonta dellemarche.it). Open 8am-8pm Mon-Sat; 8.30am-1.30pm Sun. Table service 11am-6pm Mon-Sat; 8.30am-1.30pm Sun. €. Enoteca.*
Bontà delle Marche is a friendly, family-run delicatessen that serves up tempting local delicacies to take away or eat in; during the summer, there's a sunny terrace. Seafood, charcuterie, salads and daily specials are accompanied by a wonderful selection of local wines.

Il Castiglione

Pésaro *Viale Trento 148 (072 164 934). Open noon-2pm, 7.30-10.30pm Tue-Sun. €€. Traditional Italian.*
Il Castiglione is the former home and workshop of brilliant local ceramicist Ferruccio Megaroni, who met a sorry end when, in 1925, he was crushed by the head of the Medusa that now hangs at the entrance to the ceramic museum. The building is a delightfully fanciful Stilo Liberty creation, incorporating a pretty ceramic façade and lovely courtyard. Try the seafood or game carpaccio to start, then own-made *mazzancolle* pasta with porcini or delicious fish dishes such as monktail in *porchetta* with wild fennel. The wine list is equally tantalising.

Enoteca Enopolis

Ancona *Corso Mazzini 7 (071 207 1505/ www.enopolis.net). Open 12.30-2.30pm, 7.30-11pm Mon, Wed-Sun; 7.30-11pm Tue. Closed mid Aug. €€. Enoteca/Modern Italian.*
Established by wine guru Giuseppe Bianchi, Enopolis is a wine bar, restaurant and tasting room set within the elegant 18th-century Palazzo Jona, near Trajan's Arch. Dine in the cool courtyard in summer, or take refuge in the maze of cosy rooms. The ever-changing menu offers a small but creative selection of fish and meat dishes: ricotta tart with crunchy spinach, or salt cod and broccoli salad, perhaps, followed by seafood pasta or steak. Prices are remarkably conservative and the wine list is a delight.

Madonnina del Pescatore

Marzocca *Lungomare Italia 11 (071 698 267/www.madonninadelpesacatore.it). Open noon-3pm, 8-11pm Tue-Sun. €€€€. Modern Italian.*
Now with two Michelin stars, chef Moreno Cedroni is known for his creativity and passion for fish. Two tasting menus showcase this, offering extraordinary combinations of immaculately sourced ingredients: cabbage and cuttlefish egg soup with sardine ice-cream, turbot fillet on a slice of white beer and herb bread with monkfish tripe, or tuna in *porchetta* with potatoes and beans, perhaps. If you're a lover of desserts, the plum cake with chocolate, *sagrantino*, black truffle and vanilla will hit the mark – and you're very welcome to slip in after 10pm just for coffee and cake.

La Perla

Fano *Viale Adriatico 60, Zona Porto (0721 825 631/www.laperlafano.it). Open 12.30-2pm, 7-10.30pm Tue-Sun. €€. Fish/Pizzeria.*
Down by Fano's bustling port, this spick and span eaterie is renowned for its frutti di mare. Vast sharing platters of crustaceans and raw fish are the speciality, along with handmade pasta served with seafood. If you're feeling indecisive, ask for the tris – a taster selection of three pastas. There's also a superb value meat or fish menu of the day (€20), and wallet-friendly wood-fired pizzas. Portions are generous, the fish is spectacularly fresh and the airy veranda and terrace are delightful on balmy evenings.

Polo

Pésaro *Viale Trieste 231 (072 137 5902). Open 7.30-11.00pm Tue-Sun. € Pizzeria, €€€. Traditional Italian.*
Close to the seafront, Polo is set in a turn-of-the-20th-century villa with a pretty terrace. There's a sizeable menu – if you don't want a full meal, you can tuck into oysters, salads or excellent pizzas. Try delicious fish antipasti followed by own-made or durum wheat pasta from Torre Annunziata (near Naples). Alternatively, turbot, seabass and monkfish are beautifully grilled, steamed or baked to order. A strong wine list adds to the appeal.

> # "This 16th-century palazzo is delightful, with a beamed ceiling and twinkling star-shaped lamps."

La Trattoria del Leone

Urbino *Via Cesare Battisti 5 (0722 329 894/347 980 3812/www.latrattoriadelleone.it). Open Aug-Oct 7.30-10.30pm Mon-Fri; 12.30-2.30pm, 7.30-10.30pm Sat, Sun. Nov-July 7.30-10.30pm Mon-Sun. €€. Trattoria.*
Book well ahead at this tiny trattoria on the corner of piazza della Repubblica, run by the charming Mauro Lucarini. The breadbasket alone is reason enough to eat here, and most of the produce is organic. Delicious starters include smoked goose carpaccio with tomato and grilled vegetables, followed by *porchetta*-wrapped roast rabbit or own-made ravioli. A fine list of wines is offered by the glass, and you won't want to miss the biscotti dipped in sweet cherry wine.

Vecchia Urbino

Urbino *Via Vasari 3/5 (072 24447/www.vecchia urbino.it). Open noon-3pm, 7-11pm Mon, Wed-Sun. €€€. Traditional Italian.*
A steep walk downhill from piazza Repubblica, this 16th-century palazzo is delightful, with a beamed ceiling and twinkling star-shaped lamps. The chef uses plenty of organic seasonal produce; to start, try the prosciutto with pear or truffle, celery and parmesan salad – or simply

sample a selection of fine olive oils and breads (the owner is an oil sommelier). Handmade pasta dishes include *strozzapreti* with radicchio and pecorino di Urbino, and ravioli filled with local casciotta cheese. The fixed menus (one vegetarian) offer good value.

Explore

URBINO

Perched high on a hilltop, Urbino is unmistakeable: Duke Federico's magnificent twin-towered Palazzo Ducale is visible from miles away. For superb views of the surrounding countryside, climb the town's steep, cobbled streets to the Rocca, a semi-ruined fortress, or the pretty botanical gardens tucked just off via Raffaelo. A short stroll away are the superb frescoes of the Oratory of San Giovanni, and the house where one of Italy's artistic greats was born, the Casa Natale di Raffaello (via Raffaello Sanzio 57, 0722 320 105).
A vision of Renaissance perfection, Urbino is a UNESCO World Heritage site – but it's not stuck in the past. The university's dramatic glass and brick buildings off via Saffi, designed by Team X architect Giancarlo de Carlo, see to that – as does a lively student presence around town.
To the north of the city lie the beautiful fortified hilltop towns of San Leo, Montegridolfo, Pennabili and Gradara – miraculous survivors of the never-ending tussles between the Montefeltre and the Malatesta of Rimini.

Duomo

Piazza Federico. Open 7.30am-1pm, 2-8pm daily. Admission free.
Almost destroyed in an earthquake in 1789, Federico's Renaissance cathedral was rebuilt by Giuseppe Valadier. The only original part to survive is the Chapel of the Sacrament, with a Last Supper by Federico Barocci. You'll find more of his work in the right nave: a sweet scene of St Cecilia with a host of angels, along with a Martyrdom of St Sebastian – the archer is leaning right in to guarantee a sure hit. Beside it hangs a work by Veronese, it depicts the Holy House flying into Loreto on the backs of angels (*see p99*).

Il Mondo di Tonino Guerra

Via dei Fossi 4, Pennabili (0541 928 846/ www.toninoguerra.org). Open 3-7pm Tue-Sat; 10am-noon, 3-7pm Sun & hols. Admission €1.
Set within a 14th-century oratory in Pennabili is an intriguing exhibition on local poet, artist and screenwriter Tonino Guerra, a favourite of Fellini. Born in 1920, the charismatic Guerra is an accomplished sculptor, multimedia artist and furniture maker. More of his colourful pieces are

Clockwise from top left:
Vecchia Urbino (2),
Polo (4)

Clockwise from top left: Fano (2); Pesaro (2); Urbino; Urbino, Museo della Citta.

on display at the outdoor Luoghi dell'Anima museum, also in the village (www.museialtavalmarecchia.it).

Museo della Città

Palazzo Odasi, via Valerio 1 (0722 309 270/ www.museodelmetauro.it). Open 10am-1pm, 3-6pm Mon, Wed-Sun. Admission free.
Opened in 2007, this intriguing new museum links Urbino's past with its present. Striking displays – some interactive – explore different aspects of Urbino's role in the Renaissance, and attempt to analyse what defines a city. In the basement are monumental bronze and steel models for sculptures donated to the city by Umberto Mastroianni.

Oratories of San Giovanni & San Giuseppe

Via Barocci (347 671 1181). Open 10am-12.30pm, 3-5.30pm Mon-Sat; 10am-12.30pm Sun. Admission €2.
San Giovanni is famed for its spirited cycle of frescoes (1416), the work of Lorenzo and Jacopo Salimbeni. The Crucifixion and Baptism of Christ are the highlights, along with a lovely image of San Giovanni baptising a queue of nobles in the River Jordan; stuffy-looking, tightly buttoned-up new converts gingerly stripping off, with silver fish swimming over to take a peek. Next door in San Giuseppe, look out for the beautifully-sculpted nativity (1545).

Palazzo Ducale

Piazza Ducale (0722 322 625/0722 2760/www. artibeniculturali.it). Open 8.30am-2pm (last entry 1pm) Mon; 8.30am-7.15pm (last entry 6.15pm) Tue-Sun. Admission €8; €4 reductions.
The Palace's maze of rooms, lavishly appointed with magnificent fireplaces, angelic friezes and the giant black eagle insignia of the Montefeltre, are now home to the prestigious Galleria Nazionale delle Marche. There's a wealth of Renaissance art, including Raphael's La Muta, Piero della Francesca's Flagellation and Madonna with Child, and Paolo Uccello's Profanation of the Host. Federico's studiolo (study) features exquisite marquetry and panels depicting great thinkers, but the library was his real passion. Sadly, it is now empty; Cesare Borgia, then Pope Alexander VII, stripped it bare in 1657, appropriating its contents for the Vatican.

PESARO

A pleasant little resort town with a long, sandy beach, Pésaro was famed for its ceramics during the Renaissance. These days, it's best known as the birthplace of Gioacchino Rossini. There's a museum and a jewel of a theatre named after him, as well as an opera festival in August.

Aside from its cathedral and Ceramic Museum, the town's lesser-known treasures include the 17th-century Spanish synagogue on via delle Scuole, the romantically overgrown Jewish cemetery on colle San Bartolo and the beautiful little church of Nome di Dio, its walls and ceiling covered with paintings by Giovan Giacomo Pandolfi. For contemporary art and photography exhibitions, head to the Centro Arti Visive

Pescheria (corso XI Settembre 184, 0721 387651), housed in the old fish market.

The town's centre is the piazza del Popolo, but come sundown, everyone descends on the port. Though much of the seafront was rebuilt after the war, a few Stilo Liberty buildings remain – notably the flamboyant Villino Ruggeri (1907). Here too is Arnaldo Pomodoro's bronze sphere fountain, mirroring the sea and sky.

Two kilometres west of town is the Villa Imperiale, with its lovely gardens and frescoes. Once home to the powerful Della Rovere and Gonzaga dynasties, it can be visited in summer on bus trips organised by Pésaro's tourist office (*see p99*). Close by are the nature reserve and beaches of the Colle San Bartolo, where Pavarotti had his summer retreat.

Cathedral of San Terenzio

Via Rossini 56 (072 130 043/www.pesaromosaici.it). Open 7am-noon, 3-8pm daily. Admission free.
The magnificent floor mosaic panels discovered in Pésaro's Romanesque cathedral suggest it was built on top of an early Christian basilica from the early fourth century. Some of the intricate mosaics are on display beneath a glass floor, featuring geometric patterns, animal images and human figures. Excavation work is still in progress, and a museum is planned to house the best finds; a few are currently in the Museo Diocesano opposite. To the right of the altar is a small fresco, the Madonna with Saints, recently attributed to what would have been a very young Raphael.

Ceramic Museum & Pinacoteca

Piazza Toschi Mosca 29 (0721 387 541). Open 9.30am-12.30pm Tue, Wed; 9.30am-12.30pm, 4-7pm Thur-Sun. Admission €4 (€7 with Casa Rossini); €2 reductions. Free under-14s.
The museum's rich collection of local ceramics spans several centuries: the loving cups, in particular, are exquisite. Presented by a suitor to his beloved, the long-necked cups portray the face of the recipient, with her name and the word 'bella'. Look out for work by Pésaro's brilliant Ferrucio Mengaroni (*see p93*), whose scary Medusa greets you as you enter the foyer.

The *pinacoteca* (art gallery) showcases many pieces from Pésaro's former monasteries, dissolved under Napoleon, as well as over 200 paintings from private collections. Don't miss Bellini's Crowning of the Virgin, Marco Zoppo's Head of John the Baptist, or Simone Cantarini's Mary Magdalene and the Saint. Works by Paolo Veneziano, Palma Il Giovane, Guido Reni and local artist Giannandrea Lazzarini complete the collection.

FANO

Just south of Pésaro, Fano was an important port in Roman times – hence the impressive Arco di Augusto. In the central piazza XX Settembre stands the bronze Fontana della Fortuna; just off the square, on via de Pili, the Church of Santa Maria Nuova is home to two works by Perugino –

an Annunciazione and a Madonna. Five minutes away are the town's port and blue flag beaches; covered in smooth, multicoloured chalky stones, the Spiaggia Sassonia is particularly lovely. At the port, drop into the fishermen's cooperative, Pesce Azzurro (www.pesceazzurro.com), to sample the bargain-price set menu.

The town's lively cultural scene encompasses its famous carnival, along with jazz, polyphonic singing and short film festivals: for details, check the tourist office website (*see p99*). Every second weekend of the month there's also an antiques fair in the *centro storico*.

Inland from Fano are pretty Fossimbrone, the beautiful gorge of the Gola del Furlo, Acqualagna (the truffle capital of Italy) and Urbania, feted for its fabulous ceramics.

"Ancona has charm in abundance – and some of the best seafood in Le Marche."

ANCONA

The capital of Le Marche, Ancona was settled and named by Greek exiles from Siracusa in 390BC; its name means elbow, after the shape of its bay. Despite suffering two earthquakes and bombing in the war, Ancona has charm in abundance – and some of the best seafood in Le Marche.

The Roman arch of Trajan leads the way in from the harbour in the west, matched by Pope Clement XII's Arco Clementino to the east (1738). The pretty piazza del Plebescito is not to be missed, and a wealth of museums showcase the best art in the region. Modern art lovers should make for the Galleria Comunale on via Pizzecolli (0712 225 041), and the Mole Vanvitelliana (Banchina Giovanni Da Chio 28, 071 207 2348), housed in an impressive fort on the seafront, hosts important international exhibitions.

A steep hill overlooks the port, home to the Archaeological Museum; further up, the twelve-sided copper dome of the city's Byzantine Romanesque cathedral, San Ciriaco, is one of the local landmarks.

The stone used to build the cathedral's dramatic red and white portal is from the beautiful Conero coastline, to the south. Stretching some 30 kilometres, it's now Le Marche's main attraction after Urbino. Portonovo is easily the most picturesque resort, though Sirolo and Numana to the south have their charms. For the finest beaches, head here and jump on a boat; the Sassi Bianchi and Due Sorelle are popular

with divers. Up on the clifftops, there's spendid walking and horse riding amid the flower-strewn pastures and vineyards, as well as a prestigious golf course.

West of Ancona, inland, is the capital of verdicchio wine, Jesi, and the pretty town of Pergola with its Roman bronzes. South-west of Jesi is Fabriano, the paper capital of Italy, and the incredible Grotte di Frasassi.

Archaeological Museum

Ancona *Palazzo Ferretti, via Ferretti 6 (071 202 602/071 207 390/www.archeomarche.it/museoanc.htm). Open 8.30am-7.30pm Tue-Sun. Admission €4; €2 reductions.*
This is unquestionably the finest archaeological collection in the region. Housed within a beautiful 16th-century palazzo are room after room of impressive relics from prehistory, from Palaeolithic times to the Bronze Age, and the proud Italic kingdom of Picenum, which flourished before the Romans wiped it out. The jewellery, bronze votive figures and the striking limestone head of the Warrior of Numana are of particular note.

Bronzes of Pergola

Pergola *Museo dei Bronzi Dorati, Largo San Giacomo (0721 734 090/www.bronzidorati.com). Open Jan-Mar, Nov, Dec 10am-12.30pm, 3.30-6pm Tue-Sun. Apr-June, Sept, Oct 10am-12.30pm, 3.30-6.30pm Tue-Sun. July, Aug 10am-12.30pm, 3.30-7pm daily. Admission €6; €3-€5 reductions; free under-6s.*
An extraordinary discovery, unearthed by chance in 1946 in a field in Cartoceto, the bronzes of Pergola represent the family of Germanicus, general and counsel to Emperor Tiberius. The four spectacular figures, two on horseback, date from AD 1. It's thought they were designed as statuary for a fountain or forum, but were stolen and buried en route to their final destination. They used to be housed in Ancona's archaeological museum, but Pergola demanded their return; when they were loaned for an exhibition, the curators sealed the gallery exit and, after a ministerial kerfuffle, there they remained.

Le Grotte di Frasassi

10km north of Fabriano *Genga-Uscita Grotte di Frasassi (0732 90090/www.frasassi.com/ www.parcogolarossa.it). Open Nov-Feb hours vary. Guaranteed entry Mar-July 11am & 3pm, Sept-Oct 9.30am, 11am, 12.30pm, 3pm, 4.30pm, 6pm, Aug 8am-6.30pm every 10 mins. Closed 10-30 Jan. Admission €15; €10-€13 reductions. No under-12s.*
In the Esino river valley is one of the most impressive cave complexes in the world. Stretching 30km and covering eight geological levels, it's set within the Gola della Rossa National Park. The stalactites, stalagmites and alabaster forms are eerily beautiful: the highlights are the Grotta del Grande Vento, Sala Bianca delle Colonne and Sala del Trono. Guided tours last an hour and are available in English from June to September. For those wanting to venture deeper, there are longer, more physically demanding trips (€35).

LORETO

The house of Mary of Nazareth in Loreto is one of Italy's major sites of pilgrimage – though how the Holy House came to be here is a matter of some debate. The first version of the story is that it flew from Nazareth, carried by a host of angels and landing amid a laurel wood (*loreti*); the second that it was dismantled and shipped over by Crusaders from Palestine in 1291. Whichever you believe, scientists have confirmed that the stones are indeed from Nazareth, perfectly matching what remains of Mary's house there.

Embellished over the centuries by prestigious artists, the town grew up around the sanctuary. Among the millions of pilgrims who are said to have visited are some unlikely names: Christopher Colombus, Galileo, Descartes, Casanova, Mozart, Stendhal and James Stuart the Old Pretender. Believers, many of them seriously ill, flock here at times of pilgrimage (including Easter and much of August and December).

Santuario & Museo
Pinacoteca della Santa Casa

Piazza della Madonna (071 974 7198/www.santuario loreto.it). Open Sanctuary Apr-Sept 6.15am-12.30pm, 2.30-8pm daily. Oct-Mar 6.45am-12.30pm, 2.30pm-7pm daily. Museum Apr-Oct 9am-1pm, 4-7pm Tue-Sun. Nov-Mar 10am-1pm, 3-5pm Sat, Sun. Admission free.

The Santa Casa (Holy House) humbles even the most cynical with its simplicity – despite its marble cladding by Bramante. Inside is the venerated Black Madonna of Loreto, the patron saint of aviators. Her image accompanied Charles Lindbergh on his transatlantic flight and Apollo 9 on its mission to the moon; look out for the recent American Chapel, dedicated to the aviators of the world. The finest art is in the Sagrestia di San Giovanni, with its beautiful paintings by Luca Signorelli, and the treasury was frescoed by Pomarancio.

The adjacent museum holds a priceless collection, including paintings by Tiepolo, Parmigianino, Palma Il Giovane and Lorenzo Lotto, tapestries designed by Raphael and a huge array of Renaissance majolica donated by the Duke of Urbino. Tragically, many of the sanctuary's treasures were lost in a robbery in 1974.

Factfile

When to go

There are countless festivals in Le Marche, many of which have foodie themes. Among the best are the National Truffle Fairs held in Acqualagna, with black truffles celebrated on the penultimate Sunday in February, and a two-week event in mid-October. Other key events in the region include Pésaro's Rossini Festival, celebrated in the last weeks of August (www.rossinioperafestival.it), La Festa della Duca in Urbino, held on the third weekend in August, and July's Antiques and International Busking Fair in Pennabili. In Loreto, La Venuta (the anniversary of the Holy House's arrival from Nazareth) takes place on the ninth to the tenth of December.

Getting there

Fly to Ancona Airport (071 28271, www.ancona-airport.it). Buses run from the airport to the town's train station on piazza Rosselli and the centre, or to Fabriano or Jesi. Alternatively, you can fly to Rimini Airport (0541 715 711, www.riminiairport.com). For Urbino, take the train to Pésaro (www.trenitalia.com), then the bus from outside the station to Urbino (Adriabus, 0722 376 711). It leaves hourly, and takes 45-55 minutes.

Getting around

The coastal railway line between Rimini and Ancona stops at Pésaro, Fano and Sengallia. Some trains stop at Loreto; otherwise, change at Ancona for Loreto. A bus runs from Loreto station to the centre.

Buses go from Ancona to the Conero: no.94, Ancona-Pietralacroce-Portonovo, runs from June to September, taking 30 minutes (071 280 2092, www.conerobus.it). The nearest train station to the Conero is Osimo (buses connect the two).

Getting anywhere inland requires taking buses, which often requires considerable patience; better to hire a car. To reach San Leo or San Marino, you'll need to go via Rimini and catch a bus from there.

Tourist information

General information on the region is available at www.le-marche.com or www.turismo.marche.it. IAT Ancona, Port (071 207 9029) & piazza Roma, summer only (071 320 0196 321, www.comune.ancona.it/turismo). IAT Conero, via Venezia 59, Numana (071 739 0521, www.rivieradelconero.info). IAT Fano, via C Bettasti 10, Fano (072 188 7314/072 180 3534, www.turismofano.com). IAT Pésaro, viale Trieste 164, Pésaro (0721 69341, www.turismo.pesaraurbino.it). IAT Urbino, Via San Domenico 1, Urbino (072 22631/072 230 9221/ www.urbinoculturaturismo.it).

Internet

2000Net, via Mazzini 17, Urbino (closed Sun). Internet Centre, corso Carlo Alberto 82/A, Ancona.

Cities

Clockwise from top left: Santa Maria Novella; San Lorenzo; Santa Croce; Duomo; Boboli Gardens.

Florence

Florence's place in art and history is unique. This is the city that gave birth to the Renaissance, where Brunelleschi built his dome: the new Athens for the new world. The exiled Dante spent his adult life mourning it; the Medici family covered it with the most glorious graffiti. If you've come to the city on the Arno in search of beauty you won't be disappointed: all you need do is keep your eyes open. It's hardly necessary to visit any of the attractions per se: Florence itself is one enormous museum and gallery, with more art treasures per square metre than any other town on the planet.

Florence may be *paradiso* for art lovers, but it's *purgatorio* for claustophobics. Every year, around six million visitors swamp the population of 400,000. Aim to come when the crowds are thinner, and in particular from January to March, and0 October to mid December, for space to wander the backstreets, soak up the sun in piazza della Signoria and get an unimpeded view of the masterpieces.

Julius Caesar established Florentia in 59 BC as a veterans' colony, which quickly grew into a flourishing commercial centre. Following the collapse of the Roman Empire, Florence was controlled by the Goths, the Lombards, and the Franks, before improving economic conditions enabled the city to stand on its own. By the 13th century, it had become a major player in the ongoing struggle between the papacy and the Holy Roman Empire. The Medici family, rulers of Florence for 300 years, did much to cement the city's place as a leading intellectual and artistic centre. Unfortunately, lavish spending left Florence virtually bankrupt. Thereafter, the city continued its slow economic decline, until the rise of tourism in the latter part of the 19th century century fuelled its revival. Two world wars, a major flood, even a Mafia bombing have done nothing to blunt the appeal of this timeless city.

Florence

Historic sites
● ● ● ● ○

Art & architecture
● ● ● ● ●

Hotels
● ● ● ○ ○

Eating & drinking
● ● ● ○ ○

Nightlife
● ● ○ ○ ○

Shopping
● ● ● ○ ○

Clockwise from top left:
Residenza del Moro (2);
Palazzo Galletti; Helvetia
& Bristol (2).

Stay

Unlike several other major Italian cities, Florence has a decent choice of good accommodation in all price brackets. High season for Florence's hotels runs roughly from Easter (the busiest weekend of the year) until late July, and from September until early November. Scheduled to open in spring 2008, just after this guide went to press, was the luxurious 116-room Four Seasons Hotel Firenze (www.fourseasons.com), housed in the historic Palazzo della Gherardesca.

Antica Dimora Johlea

San Lorenzo *Via San Gallo 72 (055 462 7296/ www.johanna.it). €€.*
The newest of the owners' mini chain of hotels, the Antica Dimora Johlea is a ten-minute walk north of the central market. The cosy bedrooms, all with four posters, are done out in strong colours, with bright kilims on marble or parquet floors, Indian print covers on the beds, and swathes of raw Thai silk. Defying the low rates, all have flat-screen TVs, DVD players, digital radios and electric kettles. Breakfast is served at the top of the house, where there's also a sitting room with an honesty bar; from here a wooden staircase leads up to a roof terrace with 360° views.

Cestelli

Duomo & Around *Borgo SS Apostoli 25 (055 214 213/www.hotelcestelli.com). €.*
The Cestelli is a thoughtful conversion of an old one-star hotel: super-friendly owners Alessandro and Asumi have done a wonderful job in maintaining an old-fashioned feel, while updating a formerly shabby property. It's one of the best deals in Florence for simple, pristine, generously sized rooms (even the singles are ample). Antique parquet floors have been scrubbed up to great effect, and the mix of antique and new furniture works well. All but three of the eight rooms have a private bathroom.

Gallery Hotel Art

Duomo & Around *Vicolo dell'Oro 5 (055 27263/ www.lungarnohotels.com). €€€€.*
Florence's original hip hotel opened in 1999, back when its East-meets-West design aesthetic was refreshingly different from the norm. It's still a firm favourite. Located in a tiny piazza near the Ponte Vecchio, the place has a cosy library with squashy sofas, thoughtfully supplied with cashmere throws and arty books. Also here is the stylish Fusion Bar, which serves *aperitivi*, and the public rooms on the ground floor double as show-space for artists and photographers. The bedrooms are super comfortable, the bathrooms a dream.

Helvetia & Bristol

Duomo & Around *Via dei Pescioni 2 (055 26651/ www.royaldemeure.com). €€€€.*
A new, energetic young management has been breathing fresh life into the venerable Helvetia & Bristol, which opened in the late 1800s. The hotel is filled with antiques, fine paintings and prints, but the historic feel has a decidedly hip edge to it nowadays. Oil paintings, velvet sofas and vast *pietra serena* fireplaces characterise the beautiful salon, and background sounds are likely to be jazz or something cool and contemporary. The atmospheric, belle époque Winter Garden conservatory is perfect for cool-weather breakfasts (served alfresco in summer), and in the bedrooms, fine fabrics and period furniture sit alongside flat-screen TVs and new 'old-fashioned' bathrooms.

Lungarno

Oltrarno *Borgo San Jacopo 14 (055 27261/ www.lungarnohotels.com). €€€€.*
The most coveted rooms in this stylish hotel, housed in a 1960s building incorporating a medieval tower, have terraces overlooking the Arno. However, even if you can't secure a river view, you can enjoy the waterside setting from the breakfast room and lounge/bar, or the outside seating area on the river. More classic in feel than other Ferragamo-owned hotels, the Lungarno has been decorated in a cream and navy blue colour scheme, but some lovely mahogany and cherrywood antique furniture, and a collection of fine prints and drawings, lends a reassuringly traditional touch. Bedrooms are stylish and comfy but, with the exception of a couple of spacious suites, not that big.

> ## "All the elements of a grand palazzo are here (weathered old floors, elegant paintwork, frescoes), but it's not at all pompous."

Palazzo Galletti

Santa Croce *Via Sant'Egidio 12 (055 390 5750/ www.palazzogalletti.it). €€.*
Offering excellent value and situated on a busy street a few minutes' walk east of the Duomo, Palazzo Galletti occupies the first floor of an 18th-century mansion built around an internal courtyard. All the elements of a grand palazzo are here (weathered old cotto floors, lofty arched ceilings, elegant paintwork in soothing pastels, frescoes, the odd chandelier), but it's not at all pompous, thanks to the addition of some carefully chosen contemporary design details. All but two of the nine lovely bedrooms face on to the quiet *cortile* (yard) and have a tiny terrace. There's also an on-site spa.

Relais Santa Croce

Santa Croce *Via Ghibellina 87 (055 234 2230/ www.relaisantacroce.com). €€€€.*
This hotel offers contemporary style and personalised service in the shell of grand, 18th-century Palazzo Ciofi-Jacometti. The public rooms on the first floor are suitably grandiose – especially the vast music room, with its lofty, frescoed ceilings, wonderful old parquet floor and stucco

panels. The bedrooms, meanwhile, have clean, modern lines with quirky design details. Rear-facing rooms on the upper floors have views over a jumble of red-tiled rooftops to the façade of the Santa Croce church. The Relais shares its entrance with the celebrated Enoteca Pinchiorri, but a more reasonably priced alternative is the hotel's own restaurant.

Residenza del Moro
Santa Maria Novella *Via del Moro 15 (055 264 8494/www.residenzadelmoro.com). €€€€.*
The splendid *piano nobile* of 16th-century Palazzo Niccolini-Bourbon has been exquisitely restored and now houses this luxurious *residenza* with 11 rooms and suites. You'll find elaborate stucco work, impressive frescoes and lofty, painted ceilings. The bedrooms vary enormously in shape and size (and, consequently, price), from the cosy and almost-affordable Biblioteca to the palatial, completely-out-of-our-range Marchese Suite; but all feature precious antiques, rich fabrics and canopied beds made up with fine linens and cashmere blankets. In fine weather, breakfast is served in the beautiful hanging garden.

Eat

In a city that is so geared towards tourists, standards are variable. Luckily, there are still some good, family-run *trattorie* and *osterie*, along with newer places where the chefs are adding a contemporary element to their cooking, and paying more attention to sourcing ingredients.

"Rivoire is Florence's best loved café. Its chocolates are divine – try the puffed rice and gianduja – and its own-brand coffee is among the best."

Wine bars in Florence come in various guises. Tiny street booths (known as *fiaschetteria, vineria* or *mescita*) with virtually no seating, serving basic Tuscan wines and rustic snacks, sit alongside comfortable, traditional drinking holes. New, upmarket *enoteche* offer a huge range of labels from all over Italy and beyond, and something more sophisticated in the way of food.

Caffellatte
San Marco *Via degli Alfani 39r (055 247 8878). Open 8am-midnight Tue-Sat; 9am-midnight Sun. No credit cards. Café.*

This small café, which used to be a dairy shop, is done out with rustic wooden tables and chairs. Its lattes are among the best in Florence, but if they're too dull for you, the *cappuccione* comes piping hot in a giant bowl with honey and Turkish cinnamon. The pastries and cakes are made in the café's organic bakery.

Caffè Rivoire
Duomo & Around *Piazza della Signoria 5r (055 214 412/www.rivoire.it). Open 8am-midnight Tue-Sun. Closed last 2wks Jan. Café.*
Founded in 1872 as a chocolate factory, Rivoire is the most famous and best loved of all Florentine cafés. Its chocolates are divine – try the puffed rice and *gianduja* (hazelnut and almond-flavoured chocolate) – and its own-brand coffee is among the best in the city. The outside tables have views of the Palazzo Vecchio and the Loggia dei Lanzi. One downside: your wallet will be hit hard for the privilege.

Coquinarius
Duomo & Around *Via delle Oche 15r (055 230 2153/www.coquinarius.com). Open 9am-11pm Mon-Sat; 9am-4pm Sun. Food served from noon Mon-Sat. Closed Aug. €€. Wine bar.*
A useful address in an area largely devoid of decent places to eat, this cosy little wine bar and café tucked away behind the Duomo is great for a quiet lunch or an informal evening meal: unusually, the full menu is available between noon and 11pm. Bare brick walls and soft jazz provide the background for good pastas (such as pecorino and pear ravioli), carpaccio, imaginative salads and platters of cheeses and meats. The own-made cakes are truly divine, but you could also pop across the road to Grom for some of the best ice-cream in town.

Enoteca Pinchiorri
Santa Croce *Via Ghibellina 87 (055 242 757/www.enotecapinchiorri.com). Open 7.30-10pm Tue; 12.30-2pm, 7.30-10pm Thur-Sat. Closed Aug. €€€€+. Modern Italian.*
Enoteca Pinchiorri is generally acknowledged by gourmets to be one of Italy's great temples to gastronomic excellence. After a slight blip, it rightfully won back its third Michelin star in 2004. Although chef Annie Féolde no longer does any cooking, she oversees the kitchen and runs the dining room, where the atmosphere is of the formal, old-fashioned kind. You can choose à la carte, but there are several set menus, each involving eight or nine tiny but superbly executed courses. Then there's the stellar cellar: Giorgio Pinchiorri has amassed a collection of wines that's second to none. Men are required to wear jackets.

Libreria Café La Cité
Oltrarno *Borgo San Frediano 20r (055 210 387/www.lacitelibreria.info). Open 10.30am-1am daily. No credit cards. Café.*
La Cité has given this part of the Oltrarno a true Left Bank feel. The mezzanine café area of this bookshop and cultural centre is in rustic reclaimed woods with metal bolts, and serves own-baked cakes, freshly made fruit and veg juices and Fairtrade coffees.

'And yet it moves'

The year 2009 has been declared the International Year of Astronomy – thanks in no small part to it being 400 years since **Galileo Galilei** made his first telescope, setting in motion an ongoing revolution in our understanding of the universe.

The telescope had been invented in 1608, but it was Galileo who set about improving its magnification, eventually producing a model that could enlarge objects 30 times. By late 1609 he had already produced a version with a 20-fold magnification. This set him off on a string of discoveries, including the satellites of Jupiter, mountains on the Moon and the phases of Venus, that convinced him of the truth of Copernicus's heliocentric theory. Unfortunately, Galileo's belief was not the same as proof – in fact, until Kepler suggested that planets move in ellipses rather than circles, the Ptolemaic, earth-centred system had a better correspondence to observations than the heliocentric. But Galileo's less than even-handed presentation of the two systems and his lampooning of the pope brought about his condemnation by the Inquisition and a sentence of house arrest, although legend has Galileo muttering, under his breath, 'E pur si muove' ('And yet it moves') after recanting. It took a while for things to relax after that; in fact, nearly 400 years passed before the late Pope John Paul II issued an apology for the Church's role in the affair. Galileo himself was not around to comment.

As part of the celebrations for the International Year of Astronomy, between March and September 2009 the Palazzo Strozzi will host 'Macrocosm: the Representation of the Universe from Antiquity to Galileo', an exhibition exploring the complex relationship between astrology and astronomy through history, and featuring the only two known surviving telescopes that belonged to Galileo.

The city's Institute & Museum of the History of Science (pictured, bottom right) is also undergoing a revamp in time for the celebrations and will re-open in August 2009 as the Museo Galileo, along with the brand new Museum of the Universe, which opens in the Torre del Gallo castle on the Arcetri Hill.

There are also exhibitions, talks and tours in Galileo's hometown of Pisa (where he studied and began his teaching career), focussing on his relationship with the arts through exhibitions of paintings, statues, etchings and scientific devices in the Palazzo Giuli. Pisa is

pairing with another historical centre of modern European progress, Krakow in Poland, for a joint tribute to Galileo and his biggest scientific influence, Nicolaus Copernicus.

Palazzo Strozzi
Piazza Strozzi (055 277 6461/
www.palazzostrozzi.org).

Institute & Museum of the History of Science
Piazza dei Giudici 1 (055 265 311/
www.imss.fi.it).

Da Mario

San Lorenzo *Via Rosina 2r (055 218 550). Open noon-3.30pm Mon-Sat. Closed 3wks Aug. €. No credit cards. €. Traditional Italian.*

Be prepared to queue for a table at this tiny, cramped restaurant, in which four generations of the Colsi family have reigned for 50 years. Your fellow lunchers (who might even be sharing your bare-wood table) will include stallholders, businessmen, students and tourists, an egalitarian mix all drawn by the prospect of excellent Florentine home cooking and cheap prices: try the earthy *zuppa di fagioli e cavolo nero* (bean and black cabbage soup), the terrific *bollito misto* (mixed boiled meats) served with *salsa verde,* and, for a supplement, the excellent *bistecca.*

"In season (October to December), truffles arrive daily at around 10am, filling the room with their soft, musty aroma."

Ora d'Aria

Santa Croce *Via Ghibellina 3Cr (055 200 1699/ www.oradariaristorante.com). Open 7.30-11.30pm Mon-Sat. €€€. Modern Italian.*

This cool, minimalist restaurant at the eastern end of via Ghibellina, opposite the old prison, is quietly but confidently making waves among in-the-know local foodies. Young Tuscan chef Marco Stabile has impeccable credentials, and his dishes are executed with real skill and flair. The menus, featuring sunny, Mediterranean flavours, are based on seasonal ingredients; own-made breads are delicious, and everything is beautifully presented. With an excellent wine list, this is arguably the best-value gourmet dining experience to be had in Florence.

Procacci

Duomo & Around *Via de' Tornabuoni 64r (055 211 656). Open 10.30am-8pm Mon-Sat. Closed Aug. Bar.*

One of the few traditional shops on this road to survive the onslaught of designer names, Procacci opened nearly 125 years ago, and remains a favourite with nostalgic Florentines. In season (Oct-Dec), truffles arrive daily at around 10am, filling the room with their soft, musty aroma. The speciality is melt-in-the-mouth truffle and butter brioche: order one at the small wood-lined bar to go with a glass of prosecco, then stock up on gourmet goodies before you leave.

Vivoli

Santa Croce *Via Isola delle Stinche 7r (055 292 334/ www.vivoli.it). Open Summer 7.30am-midnight Tue-Sun. Winter 7.30am-9pm Tue-Sun. Closed mid Aug. No credit cards. Gelateria*

In business since 1930, local institution Vivoli has clung on jealously to its long-standing but increasingly threatened reputation as the best *gelateria* in Florence. There are so many flavours it's hard to single any out, but the wickedly rich chocolate orange and divine *riso* (rice pudding) are still up there with the best; so too are its famous *semi freddi,* creamier and softer than *gelato.*

Le Volpi e l'Uva

Oltrarno *Piazza de' Rossi 1r (055 239 8132/www. levolpieluva.com). Open 11am-9pm Mon-Sat. Wine bar.*

In winter, the only seats at this squeeze of an *enoteca* are at the bar, where you'll probably find yourself in the company of local wine aficionados. In summer, there's much more room, thanks to the terrace. Much of what's on offer will be unfamiliar to all but the most clued-up oenophiles: owners Riccardo and Emilio search out small, little-known producers from all over Italy, with an eye on value for money. A limited but delicious selection of nibbles includes cheeses, cured meats, *panini tartufati* (stuffed with truffle cream) and rich pâtés.

Explore

With a historic centre roughly a fifth the size of Rome's, Florence is easily navigable. Most major sights are within walking distance of any other central point, and it's practically impossible to get lost, with the often-visible dome of the Duomo and the River Arno and its four central bridges acting as reference points.

It's wise to book the major museums, such as the Uffizi and Accademia, in advance; note that some are closed on Mondays.

DUOMO & AROUND

Home to the glorious Duomo, one of the most recognised landmarks in Europe, this is the geographic, religious and historic hub of the city. The cathedral itself is so enormous that there's no spot nearby from where you can see the whole thing, though a walk through the surrounding streets will be punctuated by glimpses of its red-tiled dome. Running down from the south-west corner of the Duomo's Baptistery is via Roma, which opens into the pompous piazza della Repubblica, an ungainly 19th-century square now flanked by pavement cafés. From the piazza, walk down via Calimala, then turn left along via Calimaruzza, which brings you to the 13th-century piazza della Signoria. Lined with tourist-trap restaurants and cafés, Florence's civic showpiece square is nevertheless delightful, especially in the early morning before the tourist groups arrive, or by the Loggia dei Lanzi late in the evening, where musicians perform nightly. The piazza is dominated by the Palazzo Vecchio, whose clock tower can be seen from almost any point of the city. Noteworthy sculptures on the piazza include a copy of Michelangelo's *David* and an equestrian bronze of *Cosimo I* by Giambologna.

Leading down to the river from piazza della Signoria, the daunting piazzale degli Uffizi is home to the world-renowned Galleria degli Uffizi. Just along the river to the right, on the narrowest point of the River Arno in Florence, is the landmark 14th-century Ponte Vecchio. Built by Taddeo Gaddi in 1345, it's now lined with high-quality jewellery shops.

The western edge of the Duomo area is marked by via de' Tornabuoni, known chiefly for its designer shops and the massive 15th-century Palazzo Strozzi. On the west side of the street is the church of Santa Trinità, notable for its Ghirlandaio frescoes. Linking the river with Oltrarno is Ponte Santa Trinità, (re)built by Ammannati in 1567, and considered by many to be the most beautiful bridge in the world.

"Designed by Giorgio Vasari in the mid 16th century as a public administration centre for Cosimo I (hence 'Uffizi', meaning 'offices'), the Uffizi is now arguably the greatest treasure trove of Renaissance art in the world."

Duomo

Piazza del Duomo (055 230 2885/www.duomofirenze.it). Open 10am-5pm Mon-Wed, Fri; 10am-4pm Thur; 10am-4.45pm Sat (except 1st Sat of mth, 10am-3.30pm); 1.30-4.45pm Sun. Admission free. No credit cards.

Florence's most important religious building, officially called Santa Maria del Fiore, is an awe-inspiring sight, with a rich exterior of white Carrara, green Prato and red Maremma marbles. Designed by sculptor Arnolfo di Cambio and begun in 1296, it was built on top of the 900-year-old Santa Reparata. Upon completion in 1436, the Duomo was the largest cathedral in Europe.

The highlight of the interior is undoubtedly Brunelleschi's spectacular, 37,000-tonne cupola. The inner dome boasts one of the largest frescoed surfaces in the world; the images were started by Giorgio Vasari, who died two years later, and completed by the less talented Federico Zuccari. From Monday to Saturday, a separate side entrance

gives access to the top of the dome (463 steps), which offers fantastic city views. More wonderful views are offered from the top of the three-floor, 414-step Campanile (bell tower). The tower was designed by Giotto in 1334, although his plans weren't followed faithfully.

In piazza San Giovanni, the octagonal Baptistery faces the main doors of the Duomo. Lorenzo Ghiberti's bronze doors for the Baptistery's north entrance, designed in 1400, feature 28 relief panels telling the story of Christ from the Annunciation to the Crucifixion. Ghiberti also made the east doors, known as the 'Gates of Paradise'; the originals are in the Museo dell'Opera del Duomo, but the casts are fine enough to appreciate the stunning work. There is an admission charge for entrance to the Baptistery.

Uffizi

Piazzale degli Uffizi 6 (055 238 8651/www.uffizi.firenze.it). Open 8.15am-6.50pm Tue-Sun. Admission €6.50; €3.25 reductions. Small extra charge for special exhibitions. Advance booking via Firenze Musei (055 294 883); booking charge €3. No credit cards.

Designed by Giorgio Vasari in the mid 16th century as a public administration centre for Cosimo I (hence 'Uffizi', meaning 'offices'), the Uffizi is now arguably the greatest treasure trove of Renaissance art in the world. Don't try the impossible feat of seeing everything in one visit; even the highlights are too numerous to mention here, but of the unmissables, we recommend the three *Maestàs* by Giotto, Cimabue and Duccio (Room 2); Botticelli's *Birth of Venus* and *Primavera*, or *Allegory of Spring* (Room 10); the paintings by Leonardo da Vinci in Room 15 (including *The Baptism of Christ*, a collaboration with his master Verrocchio, who was said to be so distraught at being unable to match the talent of Leonardo that he never painted again); Titian's masterpiece *Venus of Urbino* (Room 28); and Caravaggio's striking *Medusa* (Room 47). Plans to double the gallery's display space, allowing long-hidden works to come out of storage and into the public domain, are finally underway, with a design by Japanese architect Arata Isozaki for a new exit wing approved in 2007. In the meantime, the queues remain, and even booking in advance isn't foolproof: during peak times you need to reserve up to a couple of months in advance.

SANTA MARIA NOVELLA

Despite being home to the city's main train station, Santa Maria Novella is a tranquil area with some must-see art treasures. A short walk south of the station, Leon Battista Alberti's exquisite façade for the church of Santa Maria Novella looks out on to the grassy (but scruffy) piazza of the same name. An ongoing overhaul will brighten it up with flowerbeds, as well as creating a larger pedestrianised zone. By day the square is a bustling tourist hotspot, but the nights can be dodgier. Keep your wits about you and your possessions close to you here and in the area around the train and bus stations.

To the south, the triangle formed by via de' Fossi, via della Spada and via della Vigna Nuova is cluttered with antiques emporia, designer

From top: Libreria Café
La Cité; Ora d'Aria;
Le Volpi e l'Uva.

clothes shops, cafés and *trattorie*. If you head north-west from piazza Goldoni, meanwhile, Lungarno Vespucci and borgo Ognissanti open out into piazza Ognissanti, flanked by swanky hotels and topped by the church of Ognissanti, whose cloister houses Ghirlandaio's most famous *Last Supper* (1480).

Santa Maria Novella
Piazza Santa Maria Novella (055 264 5184/219 257/ www.smn.it). Open 9am-5pm daily. Admission €2.50. No credit cards.
The church dominates the piazza with its magnificent, geometric façade and its 'arms' encompassing the north-west corner. In 1465 Alberti incorporated the Romanesque lower storey into a refined Renaissance scheme, adding the triangular tympanum and the scrolls that mask the side nave exteriors in an exercise of consummate classical harmony. The interior houses Masaccio's *Trinità* (1427), which demonstrates the first ever application of Brunelleschi's mathematical rules of perspective to a painting, and, in the Cappella Tornabuoni, Ghirlandaio's frescoes of scenes from the life of John the Baptist.

> "The workaday market of San Lorenzo constitutes the hub of this particular district, spreading its tentacles over a swathe of piazzas."

SAN LORENZO
The workaday market of San Lorenzo constitutes the hub of this particular district, spreading its tentacles over a swathe of piazzas. The stalls all but conceal the entrance to the bustling covered *mercato centrale*, whose top floor is filled with a dazzling array of fruits, vegetables and spices; downstairs is packed with wonderfully aromatic kiosks selling all manner of meats, fresh fish, cheeses and baked goods. The area is also home to some of Florence's must-see sights. Next to San Lorenzo, and technically part of the same complex, is the Cappelle Medicee (closed some Mon & Sun). A mausoleum for the main members of the Medici family, it was Michelangelo's swansong to the city. At the southern end of via Cavour is the Palazzo Medici Riccardi, with its beautiful family chapel painted by Benozzo Gozzoli, a student of Fra Angelico.

San Lorenzo
Piazza San Lorenzo (055 264 5184). Open 10am-5.30pm Mon-Sat. Summer 10am-5.30pm Mon-Sat; 1.30-5.30pm Sun. Admission €2.50. No credit cards.
The huge church of San Lorenzo was built between 1419 and 1469 to a design by Brunelleschi, the first church to which the architect applied his theory of rational proportion. Despite the fortune spent on the place, the façade was never finished. Opening off the north transept is the Sagrestia Vecchia (Old Sacristy): another Brunelleschi design, it has a dome segmented like a tangerine, along with a fabulous painted tondo by Donatello. Reached via the door to the left of the façade is Michelangelo's architectural classic, the Biblioteca Mediceo-Laurenziana (Laurentian Library).

SAN MARCO
This visitor-friendly district may be home to a certain world-famous statue, but it's not just for the tourists. Crowds of university types from the nearby faculty buildings create a buzzy collegiate atmosphere, and it's still an active centre of religious worship too. Surrounded on three sides by delicate arcades, the piazza della Santissima Annunziata is dominated by the powerful equestrian statue of Grand Duke Ferdinando I by Giambologna. On the eastern side is the Spedale degli Innocenti. Opened in 1445 as the first foundling hospital in Europe, it was designed by Brunelleschi. On the western side of the square is upmarket hotel Loggiato dei Serviti; the church of Santissima Annunziata is to the north. The street between the two, via C Battisti, leads west into piazza San Marco, a hub for local buses and the site of the church and convent of San Marco. Beside San Marco is the Museo di San Marco (closed some Mon & Sun), largely dedicated to the ethereal paintings of Fra Angelico, and also home to a Ghirlandaio *Last Supper* (1479-80).

Galleria dell'Accademia
Via Ricasoli 58-60 (055 238 8609). Open 8.15am-6.50pm Tue-Sun. Admission €10; €13 with reservation. No credit cards.
Despite the fact that the Accademia contains a huge number of magnificent and historic works, the queue snaking around the corner from the museum down via degli Alfani is more than likely to be here for one reason above all: Michelangelo's monumental *David* (1501-4), carved from a five-metre slab of marble. The artist intended it to be placed high up on the Duomo, and gave the figure a top-heavy shape so it would look its best from the beholder's viewpoint a good distance beneath it. However, in 1873, when the statue was moved from piazza della Signoria (where a copy still stands) following acts of vandalism, the authorities decided to keep the plinth low so that visitors could witness its curves close-up. Other Michelangelo works line the walls of the David salon; among them are his *Slaves*, masterly but unfinished sculptures struggling to escape from marble prisons. The gallery also houses two of Botticelli's *Madonnas* and a collection of musical instruments on the ground floor.

SANTA CROCE

The largest of Florence's medieval parochial areas has, like much of the centre, a heady air of history and learning. But it also has some less lofty attractions. At the head of piazza Santa Croce, via de' Benci is dotted with crafts shops and Bohemian restaurants running down towards the Arno. Piazza dei Ciompi is taken over by a junk and antiques market during the week, and a huge, day-long flea market on the last Sunday of the month. Further east is piazza Ghiberti, home of the fruit and vegetable market of Sant'Ambrogio (Mon-Sat), the renowned Cibrèo restaurant, and the shops, bars, pizzerie and restaurants of borgo La Croce.

Bargello

Via del Proconsolo 4 (055 238 8606/www.sbas.firenze. it/bargello). Open 8.15am-1.50pm Tue-Sat, 1st, 3rd & 5th Mon of mth, 2nd & 4th Sun of mth. Admission €4. No credit cards.

Officially the Museo Nazionale del Bargello, this imposing fortified structure had many different purposes over the centuries before it opened as a museum in 1865. It now holds Florence's most eclectic and prestigious collection of sculpture, with treasures including Michelangelo's *Drunken Bacchus* and *Brutus* (the only bust he ever sculpted), Giambologna's fleet-footed *Mercury* and the *Davids* of Donatello (the more famous of which is undergoing on-site restoration until the end of 2008).

"It's a beguiling, contradictory world of ornate palazzi with splendid gardens, church squares and tumbledown artisan workshops."

Santa Croce

Piazza Santa Croce 16 (055 246 6105). Open 9.30am-5.30pm Mon-Sat; 1-5.30pm Sun. Admission €5 (incl museum & chapel). No credit cards.

Known locally as 'the Pantheon' because of its tombs of many of the city's most illustrious historical figures, Santa Croce (founded in 1228) remains the richest medieval church in the city. The coloured marble façade is impressive, but at first sight the interior seems big and gloomy. In the niche alongside Dante's is the tomb of Michelangelo, by Vasari. The artist had insisted on burial here when the time came, as he wanted 'a view towards the cupola of the Duomo for all eternity'. At the top of the left aisle is Galileo's tomb, a polychrome marble confection

created by Foggini more than a century after the astronomer's death, when the Church finally permitted him a Christian burial. At the eastern end of the church, the Bardi and Peruzzi chapels, which were completely frescoed by Giotto, are masterpieces, although the condition of the frescoes isn't marvellous. Opening on to the cloisters of the church is the Capella dei Pazzi, Brunelleschi's geometric tour de force. Across the courtyard is a small museum of church treasures.

OLTRARNO

A bustling area that spans the width of the city centre south of the river, the Oltrarno (which translates literally as, 'beyond the Arno') is Florence's equivalent of the Rive Gauche. It's a beguiling, contradictory world of ornate palazzi with splendid gardens, church squares and tumbledown artisan workshops. At its heart is the gargantuan, rusticated Palazzo Pitti, whose numerous museums contain the vast, opulent Medici collection; behind are the Boboli Gardens (the €6 entrance fee to this statue-studded oasis includes admission to three museums). The palazzo looms over via de' Guicciardini, with its expensive paper, crafts and jewellery shops. Borgo San Jacopo, which is an odd mix of medieval towers and palazzi, shops and postwar monstrosities, connects it with antiques hub via Maggio. To the west are the Bohemian neighbourhoods of Santo Spirito and San Frediano. Piazza Santo Spirito is a lively but low-key space that still belongs to the locals and has a morning market from Monday to Saturday. The church, whose simple façade has variously been described as the most beautiful in Florence and as plain as a slab of marzipan, is by Brunelleschi. The refectory houses Andrea Orcagna's 14th-century *Last Supper* fresco. On the far side of via dei Serragli, in San Frediano, is piazza del Carmine, home to the Santa Maria del Carmine church and the Brancacci Chapel, frescoed in the 15th century by Masaccio and Masolino (book ahead, 055 276 8224, closed Tue).

Shop

If you're aiming to pep up your wardrobe, Italian style, go to via de' Tornabuoni and via della Vigna Nuova, which boast the lion's share of the designer big guns; for independent boutiques, try via Porta Rossa, or over a bridge to borgo San Jacopo and the surrounding streets. Via Maggio and via dei Serragli are lined with wonderful antiques shops, as is via dei Fossi, which has also become the hub for contemporary interior-design studios. The streets around piazza Santo Spirito are home to what is left of a once-full well of artisan craftsmen.

Clockwise from top left:
Santa Maria Novella;
Boboli Gardens;
Santissima Annunziata;
Bargello; Michelangelo's
David; Santa Croce.

Clockwise from top:
Obsequium; Dolcissimo (3).

A Piedi Nudi nel Parco

Santa Croce *Borgo degli Albizi 46r (055 234 0768).*
Open noon-8pm Mon; 10am-8pm Tue-Sat.
This shop takes its name from the 1960s film *Barefoot in the Park*, but the style is more neo-1970s, with beautifully cut, long, fluid and asymmetrical styles with a decorative twist, in understated colours and high-quality fabrics.

Carte Etc

Duomo & Around *Via de' Cerchi 13r (055 268 302/ www.carteetc.it). Open 10am-7.30pm daily.*
Exquisite glass and stationery, unusual postcards of Florence and handmade greetings cards.

Dolcissimo

Oltrarno *Via Maggio 61r (055 239 6268/www. caffeitaliano.it). Open 8am-1pm, 2-8pm Tue-Sat; 9am-2pm Sun.*
A delightful shop from another age, where chocolates are displayed in gilded cabinets, and glass cake stands hold delicious-looking concoctions.

Madova

Oltrarno *Via de' Guicciardini 1r (055 239 6526/ www.madova.com). Open 9.30am-7pm Mon-Sat.*
Madova makes gloves in every imaginable style and colour but with one important, self-imposed restriction: they are all made of leather. The factory is just behind the tiny shop.

Obsequium

Oltrarno *Borgo San Jacopo 17 (055 216 849). Open 10.30am-7.30pm Mon-Sat.*
A treasure trove for wine lovers, set in a 12th-century tower, offers an incredible cellar of wines, spirits and liqueurs.

Officina Profumo-Farmaceutica di Santa Maria Novella

Santa Maria Novella *Via della Scala 16 (055 216 276/ www.smnovella.it). Open 9.30am-7.30pm Mon-Sat; 10.30am-6.30pm Sun. Closed Sun Feb & Nov, 2 wks Aug.*
One of the most beautiful shops in Florence, an ancient herbal pharmacy with a 13th-century frescoed chapel. The products include pomegranate perfume and lovely soap.

Olio e Convivium

Oltrarno *Via Santo Spirito 4 (055 265 8198/ www.conviviumfirenze.it). Open 10am-2.30pm Mon; 10am-2.30pm, 5.30-10.30pm Tue-Sat.*
A wonderful place for Tuscan olive oils and wines, sweet and savoury preserves and superlative treats.

Scuola del Cuoio

Santa Croce *Via San Giuseppe 5r (055 244 533/ www.leatherschool.com). Open 9.30am-6pm Mon-Sat; 10am-6pm Sun.*
At this leather school inside the cloisters of Santa Croce, you can watch the craftsmen making bags, accessories and gifts.

Factfile

When to go

Florence is best visited in spring and autumn when it's very warm and only occasionally rainy. Winters tend to be cold and humid, whereas summers see temperatures soar.

Getting there

Florence's airport is Amerigo Vespucci at Peretola (055 306 1300/www.aeroporto. firenze.it). The Volainbus bus shuttle service runs half-hourly from 6am to 11.30pm daily, costs €4.50 and stops in the SITA station (see below). A taxi to Florence costs from €20 and takes about 20 minutes. Santa Maria Novella, located in Piazza della Stazione, is Florence's main train station. Some services go to Campo di Marte station to the north-east of the city. Coaches arrive at one of two stations in Santa Maria Novella – SITA is on Via Santa Caterina da Siena and LAZZI on Piazza Adua.

Getting around

Walking is the quickest way to get around central Florence. While the new tram system is under construction, the city's only public transport is still the comprehensive ATAF bus network. It's cheaper to buy tickets before boarding buses, but you can now get tickets on board at €2 for 70mins or a multiple ticket (*biglietto multiplo*) €4.50 for four tickets, each valid for 70mins.

Tourist information

San Lorenzo Via Cavour 1r (055 290 832). Open 8.30am-6.30pm Mon-Sat; 8.30am-1.30pm Sun. Santa Croce, Borgo Santa Croce 29r (055 234 0444). Open Summer 9am-7pm Mon-Sat; 9am-2pm Sun. Winter 9am-5pm Mon-Sat, 9am-2pm Sun.
Santa Maria Novella, Piazza della Stazione 4A (055 212 245). Open 8.30am-7pm Mon-Sat; 8.30am-2pm Sun.
There is also an office in Florence airport.

Internet

There are internet points in all areas of the city centre; most charge around €5/hour. As we went to press, local government announced plans for free Wi-Fi hotspots in piazzas around town, due to be fully operative by the end of 2008.
Internet Train Via de' Benci 36r, Santa Croce (055 263 8555/www.internettrain.it). Open 10am-midnight Mon-Sat; 3-11pm Sun.
Intotheweb Via de' Conti 23r, San Lorenzo (055 264 5628). Open 10am-midnight daily.

Genoa

The capital of Liguria – birthplace of pesto, Christopher Columbus, Niccolò Paganini and Italian football (the Genoa club is the oldest in the country) – deserves to be much better known than it is. Once the equal of Venice, Genoa has a medieval old town to rival any in Europe, and, since its stint as European Capital of Culture in 2004, the city has undergone a dramatic renaissance – thanks in part to a major programme of restoration overseen by Genoa-born architectural superstar Renzo Piano.

Clockwise from top left:
Via Garibaldi; Genoa port;
Cattedrale di San
Lorenzo; Genoa port.

Perhaps it's the gritty atmosphere of this ancient and still functioning port that puts the tourists off (the harbour is dominated by warehouses and cranes); or maybe it's just that visitors to Italy are spoilt for choice. Whatever the reason, those who stay away are missing out on something special.

Over the centuries, the city, wedged between mountains and the sea, was attacked, destroyed and then rebuilt by a succession of invaders, including the Etruscans, Romans, Carthaginians, Goths, Byzantines, Arabs, Lombards and Saracens. By the sixth century AD, however, Genoa had established itself as one of Europe's most important ports, vying for pre-eminence with Pisa and Venice. The first banks opened here in the 15th century, and the city became a republic in 1522.

Genoa has had political influence too: Giuseppe Mazzini, who spearheaded the Risorgimento (the 19th-century movement for Italian unity) was born in the city. Later, in 1860, Garibaldi arrived here to campaign for southern Italy's freedom from foreign domination.

The city was also favoured by European aristocrats taking the Grand Tour, for whom several palazzi were built. Occupation by the Germans in World War II meant that Genoa was heavily bombed (there is still an unexploded British bomb in Cattedrale San Lorenzo).

Genoa

Historic sites
● ● ● ● ●

Art & architecture
● ● ● ● ●

Hotels
● ● ● ● ●

Eating & drinking
● ● ● ● ●

Nightlife
● ● ● ● ●

Shopping
● ● ● ● ●

Stay

There are many budget and mid-range hotels in the *centro storico* and around the Brignole station, but, as you might expect, these areas can be less salubrious late at night.

A B&B service is offered by Paola and Federica (via XX Settembre 26/5, 010 8692 029, www.columbusvillage.com, open 10am-5pm Mon-Fri), tailor-making your stay at a range of prices within private houses, self-contained flats and villas.

Agnello d'Oro

Centro *Via Monachette 6, off via Balbi (010 246 2084/www.hotelagnellodoro.it).* €€.
It may be a short way from busy Principe station, but its position down a small side street ensures that this converted 16th-century convent is quiet. Choose from the downstairs rooms that retain some of the building's original character (with high or vaulted ceilings), or more modern rooms upstairs (some with air-conditioning and balconies) and views over the Old Town and harbour (best from no.56).

Bentley Hotel

Centro *Via Corsica 4 (010 531 5111/ www.bentley.thi.it).* €€€€.
Opened in October 2007, Turin Hotels International's latest venture is the first five-star establishment in Genoa. Its position on via Corsica means that sea-facing rooms have a spectacular view. By retaining the impressive original structure, a converted industrial building, and adding chic interiors, THI has successfully combined the traditional with the contemporary. Rooms are large, luxurious and well-appointed – with especially comfortable beds.

Bristol Palace

Centro *Via XX Settembre 35 (010 592 541/www.hotelbristolpalace.it).* €€€-€€€€.
For many years, the Bristol was the swankiest stay in town, offering fin-de-siècle elegance. Set in a period palace – once the residence of a local aristocrat – the three-star Bristol offers spacious accommodation, antiques dotted around, courteous staff, and great breakfasts. Centrally located, it's a good bet for shoppers and culture vultures.

Hotel Metropoli

Centro *Piazza Fontane Marose (010 2468 888/www.bestwestern.it/metropoli_ge).* €€€.
This Best Western offers traditional comfort, is centrally located and surrounded by wonderful 16th-century buildings. It's also quiet and pretty good value. Rooms are tastefully furnished, and the lounges are elegant and enhanced by modern art.

Jolly Hotel Marina

Porto Antico *Molo Ponte Calvi 5 (010 25391/www.jollyhotels.it).* €€€€.
In the port area, facing the aquarium and overlooking the bay, the four-star Jolly Hotel offers plenty of accommodation

and some good-value weekend deals. It also has a rather stylish restaurant, Il Gozzo. The setting is wonderful, of course, and the food is typical Ligurian fare prepared by Luca Molteni. Sister hotel, Jolly Hotel Plaza (via Martin Piaggio 11, 010 83161) is located in the city's commercial centre, close to via Roma, the Doge's palace and the Carlo Felice opera house.

Locanda di Palazzo Cicala

Centro Storico *Piazza San Lorenzo 16 (010 251 8824/www.palazzocicala.it).* €€€-€€€€.
Occupying the first floor of historic palazzo Cicala (dating back to the 16th century), the boutique Locanda – with its vaulted ceilings and 18th-century plastered interiors – boasts six beautifully styled, minimalist rooms with lovely bathrooms. A spacious lounge looks over piazza San Lorenzo and offers guests an opportunity to sip an aperitif while taking in the Duomo.

Navettaetica

Porto Antico *Molo Ponte Morosini 21 (010 2511 386/www.navettaetica.it).* €€€€.
If B&B seems a little old hat, how about 'boat and breakfast' on a 1923s fishing boat that has been lovingly restored and converted into a motor yacht? It's available for charter, mini charter and Boat and Breakfast.

Eat

Genoa is the home of pesto, a sauce made with crushed basil leaves, parmesan and pine nuts, traditionally served with *trofie* (pasta curls) or gnocchi, and focaccia (flat, savoury bread made with olive oil sometimes flavoured with onion or rosemary). The seafood restaurants that ring the old port (many only open at lunchtime) are also a big draw.

Chichibio

Centro Storico *Via David Chiossone 20r (010 247 6191). Open noon-3pm, 7pm-1am Mon-Fri; 7pm-1am Sat.* €€€. *Modern Italian.*
This recently opened restaurant is an epicure's dream. The small interior is cool and stylish, with red walls, heavy drapes, and glass, wood and steel furnishings. The menu includes simple spaghetti with sweet garlic and prawns, a pricier pasta dish served with Ligurian truffles (at €80 per kilo you'll appreciate the fact that they weigh them out in front of you), and tuna sashimi with seafood, tomato, caper and olive sauce. Doubling as a bar, Chichibio also has the perfect wine to accompany every dish. A very stylish addition to Genoa's eating options.

Il Guscio

Centro *Via XII Ottobre (010 595 8496). Open noon-12.30am Mon-Sat.* €-€€. *Pizzeria.*
Opened in July 2007, this is the best of the Il Guscio mini-chain. It's a modern, spacious restaurant on two levels, and the menu covers the usual antipasti, *primi*, meat and fish

Locanda di Palazzo Cicala.

secondi, and desserts – all at reasonable prices. But the real speciality here is the *camicie* (similar to calzone), made entirely by hand and stuffed with a huge variety of fillings. The place is also open for aperitivi, and between 5pm and 9pm the cocktails and cold beers are served with a buffet (which is good news for those who want to save on dinner).

Maxelâ
Centro Storico *Vico Inferiore del Ferro 9/11 (010 247 4209/www.cucinagenovese.it). Open noon-4pm, 7.30-11pm Mon-Thur; noon-4pm, 7.30pm-midnight Fri, Sat. €-€€. Enoteca.*
Close to via Garibaldi, this trattoria – with its wonderful green majolica tiles – has been in business since 1790. These days it serves as a butcher's shop as well as a restaurant. The original marble-topped counter displays every kind of meat imaginable, and there are 100 different wines to choose from. Booking is essential on Friday and Saturday nights.

Ombre Rosse
Centro Storico *Vico Indoratori 20-22-24R (010 275 7608). Open noon-3pm; 6pm-midnight Mon-Fri; 6pm-midnight Sat. €€. Bar.*
A poster of the film (starring Jim Wayne and Claire Trevor) from which this lovely bar takes its name hangs in the entrance located in a quiet side street behind the Cattedrale di San Lorenzo. The friendly bar resembles someone's front parlour, with shelves filled with knick-knacks and reading material for customers to peruse. Take a seat inside or, in warm weather, nip across to the little garden opposite and settle yourself at one of the marble tables. The *piatto del giorno* – perhaps gnocchi with chestnut pesto, or pumpkin with leeks and gorgonzola filo tart – costs €8 (€15 including a glass of wine and a dessert).

Osteria Da Maria
Centro Storico *Vico Testadoro 14r, off via XXV Aprile (010 581 080). Open 11.45am-2.15pm, 5-11pm Mon-Sat. €. Traditional Italian.*
Close to piazza Fontane Marose, this popular local trattoria is famous as much for the food as for its legendary owner/chef Maria Mante. Busy and bustling and lots of fun, the two-floor restaurant hosts a mix of folk sitting side by side at long tables while staff serve up typical Genovese fare: minestrone, risotto, *pansotti* (ravioli in a walnut sauce), zuppe da pesce followed by simple mains, and wonderful own-made ice-cream. Friday is the day for a Genoese speciality *stoccafisso accommodato* – a fish dish with olives, pine nuts and potatoes. The fixed price menu is a must for budgeteers.

Ristorante Piedigrotta
Centro *Piazza Savonarola 27 (010 580 553/ www.ristorantepiedigrotta.it). Open noon-3pm; 7pm-12.30am daily. €€-€€€. Pizzeria.*
Just off the corsa Buenos Aires, this airy restaurant is a popular destination for families as well as those looking for cheap, but excellent, food. The menu is long and pizzas are the speciality here; toppings are generous and the crusts drooping over the side of the plate will sate the biggest appetites. On a recent visit, a party of six ate for under €80.

Taggiôu
Centro Storico *Vico Superiore del Ferro 8 (010 275 9225/www.cucinagenovese.it). Open 10.30am-3.30pm, 5.30-10.30pm Mon-Sat. €€. Bar.*
Taking its name from the wooden chopping boards that the specialist meats and cheeses are served on, Taggiôu is a lovely bar housed in what was once an old cellar. Close to Via Garibaldi, on a street where abattoirs and butcher's shops used to abound, the bar serves from a wine list of over 120 bottles. Drinks are accompanied by a pile of meats, cheeses and focaccia at the absurdly reasonable price of €8.

Da Vittorio
Porto Antico *Via Sottoripa 59r (010 254 2197). Open 7pm-midnight daily. €€-€€€. Fish.*
This simple trattoria down by the port (and almost opposite the aquarium) is easily one of the best fish restaurants in Genoa. The small window is filled with the daily catch, and the place is rightly famous for its lobster linguine and *stoccafisso*.

Zeffirino
Centro *Via degli Archi 2, off via XX Settembre (010 591 990). Open noon-midnight Mon-Sat. Closed Aug. €€€. Traditional Italian.*
Zefferino is Genoa's most famous restaurant. Established in 1939, its reputation hasn't suffered from the fact that it was once one of Frank Sinatra's favourites (he even has a pasta created for him called *paffutelle*). Pavarotti was also a fan. The food is upmarket classic Genoese cooking including a signature dish of black ravioli with cuttlefish, squid and lobster.

Explore

Genoa is home to over 600,000 people, and the city sprawls out along the coast and up the hillside from the port. The centre is much more manageable, however, running from Principe station in the west to Brignole station in the east. The medieval city centre leads down to the port and up the hill to Castelletto. As a general rule, if you're going downhill you're heading for the *porto antico*, whereas uphill routes will take you towards the heart of the city.

CENTRO & CENTRO STORICO
This part of the city includes the city's commerical centre, the shopping streets of via XX Settembre and via Roma, as well as the famous via Garibaldi. There are wonderful shops to nip into, bars and restaurants aplenty, and labyrinthine medieval streets (*caruggi*) to get lost in. The *caruggi* are pockmarked by treasure-filled churches, cafés and stylish boutiques.

Cattedrale di San Lorenzo
Piazza San Lorenzo (010 247 1831). Open 8am-noon, 3-7pm daily.

This gothic masterpiece, with its grey-and-white striped exterior, was begun in the ninth century, but has had a variety of styles added over the years. The medieval doors display Bible stories and the martyrdom of St Lawrence (one of the city's patron's saints) and the imposing interior houses the Cappella di San Giovanni Battista and the Museo del Tesoro (010 247 1831, closed Sun), which is filled with Byzantine trinkets and relics, including a silver urn of ashes said to be the remains of John the Baptist. Sunday mass is held at 10.30am.

> "It's now the city's national gallery, and houses a superb collection of paintings, including works by Antonello da Messina, Tintoretto and Rubens."

Galleria Nazionale di Palazzo Spinola
Piazza Pelliceria 1 (off via San Luca) (010 270 5300/ www.palazzospinola.it). Open 8.30am-7.30pm Tue-Sat; 1.30-7.30pm Sun. Admission €4; €2 reductions.
The 16th-century Palazzo Spinola is one of the city's finest – and a tribute to the Genoese nobility (Pallavicino, Doria and, finally, Spinola families) that lived here. The palace was occupied until 1958 when it was donated, along with its fabulous collections of furnishings (furniture, porcelain, textiles and silverware, as well as artwork) to the state. It's now the city's national gallery, and houses a superb collection of paintings, including works by Antonello da Messina, Tintoretto and Rubens. There are also stunning trompe l'oeil frescoes (a Genoese speciality) and a gallery of mirrors.

Musei di Strada Nuova
Via Garibaldi (010 247 6351/www.stradanuova.it). Open 9am-7pm Tue-Fri; 10am-7pm Sat, Sun. Admission €7; €5 reductions.
With a single ticket, it's possible to gain entry to three of the finest Renaissance palaces in Genoa. Today they are all on UNESCO's World Heritage list, but originally they were private residences owned by the city's aristocratic families. Peter Paul Rubens was so impressed by these architectural masterpieces that he made detailed drawings of them, which were later used to assist in the reconstruction of some of the palaces badly damaged during World War II. Palazzo Rosso (no. 18), Palazzo Bianco (no. 11) and Palazzo Tursi (no. 9) house works by Flemish and Italian artists, including van Dyck, Rubens, Cambiaso and Caravaggio, as well as being home to fine collections of porcelain and Albisola ceramics, ancient coins and exquisite furnishings. On the fifth floor at Palazzo Rosso, there's a collection of art and furniture put together by the museum's director, himself a collector.

Palazzo del Principe
Piazza del Principe (010 255 509/www.palazzo delprincipe.it). Open 10am-5pm Tue-Sun. Admission €7; €5.50 reductions.
Its proximity to bustling and, at times, insalubrious Principe station means that visitors to this fascinating palazzo need to keep their wits about them. Built in 1529 as the town house of Andrea Doria, Genoa's most influential ruler, it was originally set in its own parkland beyond the city walls, but this has long since disappeared. Inside the palace you'll find a cycle of frescoes and stucco work based on mythological themes by Perin del Vaga, one of Raphael's pupils. Other exquisitely furnished rooms hold works by Sebastiano del Piombo, Bronzino and Piola, as well as a wonderful collection of tapestries. The lovely Italian-style garden has been restored to its late-16th century layout.

Palazzo Ducale
Piazza Matteotti 9 (010 557 4000/www.palazzo ducale.genova.it). Open 9am-7pm Tue-Sun. Admission is charged for exhibitions.
Centre stage in piazza Matteotti is the imposing 16th-century Palazzo Ducale, once home to Genoa's ruler, the Doge. Now a buzzing arts centre, the Ducale houses an exhibition hall where recent expositions have included that of 15th century artist, Luca Cambiaso, 'Garibaldi – the Myth', as well as some contemporary photographic exhibitions. The atrium, with its lovely porticoed courtyards, is where the magistrates' courts were once held. The palazzo is also home to the Museo del Jazz (Jazz Museum), which charts the history of jazz and its leading exponents. An antiques market is held within the palazzo twice a month (at weekends).

PORTO ANTICO
The 'regenerated' port area now offers an ice rink, a cineplex, a vast aquarium, local boy Renzo Piano's 'Il Bigo' crane/elevator, which offers panoramic views over the city and sea beyond, as well as plenty of bars and restaurants.
   Take a wander aboard the *Neptune* galleon docked opposite the Jolly Hotel Marina (used as a set in Roman Polanski's film *Pirates*). Sun-bunnies who'd prefer swimming in (rather than just admiring) the sea can head for San Nazzari Bagni Communale on the corso Italia.

Acquario di Genova
Ponte Spinola (010 234 5678/248 1205/www. acquariodigenova.it). Open July-Aug 8.45am-11pm daily. Sept-June 9.30am-7.30pm Mon-Fri; 9.30am-8.30pm Sat, Sun. Admission €15; €9 reductions.
One of Italy's most visited attractions, Genoa's aquarium is a must-see for those with children (though avoid weekends and bank holidays, when the crowds are intolerable). Even the structure is worth a look: located in the old harbour (beside the pier), and designed by Renzo Piano, the aquarium incorporates a decommissioned ship within which over 50 marine environments can be found, including re-creations of Red Sea coral reefs, Amazon rainforest pools,

Arctic waters and Mediterranean tidal zones. You'll see seals, sharks, stingrays, jelly fish and dolphins. There's even a pool where you can pet rays. Most hotels will book tickets so you can avoid queuing.

Galata Museo del Mare
Calata de Mari, via Gramsci 1 (010 234 5655/ www.galatamuseodelmare.it). Open Mar-Oct 10am-7.30pm Tue-Sun. Nov-Feb 10am-6pm Tue-Fri, 10am-7.30pm Sat, Sun. Admission €10; €5 reductions.

Celebrating the city's sea-faring past, the largest maritime museum (5,850sqm) in the Mediterranean is housed within the old Galley's Arsenal. Inside, a 17th century Genoese galley has been faithfully reconstructed, thanks to much historical research. Visitors can learn the history of the port (and of Genoa's famous seafaring sons – Christopher Columbus and Andrea Doria), explore the Arsenal and, with the help of multimedia and interactive areas, witness galleys arriving from the Americas, leaf through ancient maps and even travel round Cape Horn, on a 19th-century Ligurian brig, during a storm.

SHOP
Via Roma offers shoppers plenty of opportunities to lighten their wallets: designers such as D&G, Versace and Vuitton are just for starters. Via XX Settembre is also a good place in which to find brands such as Max Mara and Sisley, as well as Zara and small Italian boutiques.

There's a wealth of shopping opportunities in the *caruggi* – from Hermès to charming, little shops selling hand-crafted shoes, antiques and wines. Stock up on porcini, anchovies in chilli oil, parmesan cheese and honey at piazza Matteotti's wonderful food market. The Oriental Market, located in a former cloister on via XX Settembre (open daily) sells a spectacular array of cheeses, fresh fish and meat, fruit and vegetables, and dried goods.

A regular antiques/bric-a-brac market is held in the piazza Verde (the square in front of Brignole station). At the end of corso Buenos Aires, the Monday market (piazza Palermo, until 1am) is a good place at which to pick up cheap leather shoes, women's clothing, lingerie and household goods.

NIGHTLIFE
Genoa is a university town so, not surprisingly, there are plenty of interesting bars and restaurants – particuarly within the *caruggi* – to keep the student population happy. Piazza delle Erbe is a notable hotspot.

For details of live music, see www.genova tune.net or www.zenazone.it.

Il Clan
Centro Storico *Salita Pallavicini 16r, off XXV Aprile (010 254 1098/www.ilclan.biz). Open 6.30pm-2am Tue-Sun. Admission free.*
This nightclub was opened four years ago by Luca and Roberto Bizzarri. As well as serving up a great range of wines, aperitifs and cool music, it also provides plenty of live entertainment and fashion shows, making use of the 'catwalk' that cuts across the 'swimming pool' basement. The swanky restaurant opposite – Le Mamme dei Clan – is also owned by the Bizzarri brothers.

Factfile

When to go
With its temperate climate, Genoa can be visited at any time, but the best times to visit 'La Superba' (as Petrarch called it) are in spring or autumn, when you can avoid the hot summer temperatures, take advantage of near-empty museums and galleries, and wander through deserted 16th-century *caruggi*.

Getting there & around
Genoa's Cristoforo Colombo airport (010 60151, www.airport.genova.it) is six kilometres west of the centre. Volabus No.100 (€4 from the machine beside the bus stop) runs every 30 minutes, and takes 25 minutes to get to the city centre, calling at Principe and Brignole train stations and piazza de Ferrari. A taxi should cost €14.

Public transport in Genoa (www.amt.genova.it) consists of buses, a metro, local trains, funiculars and lifts. Single tickets (€1.20, valid for 90 minutes once stamped on board) and day passes (€3.50) are available from *tabacchi*. Most people get around the city on foot. Car hire is expensive, but you'll find Avis, Europcar, Hertz and Maggiore at the airport.

Tourist information
Genovainforma Piazza Matteotti (010 868 7452). Open 9.30am-8pm daily.

Sistema Turistico Locale Genovesato, Cristoforo Colombo Airport (010 601 5247, www.stlgenovesato.it). Open 9am-1pm, 1.30-5.30pm daily.

Stazione Ferroviaria Principe (010 246 2633, www.stlgenovesato.it). Open 9am-6.30pm daily.

Internet
World Communications Via S Luca 64. You'll need to provide ID to use the internet.

Clockwise from top left: fashion central; Teatro alla Scala; Il Salvagente; door; Duomo.

Milan

A visitor's first impressions of Milan can be at odds with traditional notions of 'Bella Italia'. There are no olive groves or cypress trees here; no crumbling columns: instead, it's the traffic and the graffiti that newcomers usually notice first. And, although the Duomo and *The Last Supper* are both breathtaking, Milan isn't brimming with world-famous attractions. But this is a city for city-lovers. Its urban genetics make it first cousin to London and New York: it's a powerhouse of a metropolis, a melting pot of races and a capital of business, media and design. And business: the Milanese claim that their city has as many banks as the Vatican has churches.

Positioned strategically at the gateway to the Italian peninsula, Milan and the surrounding region of Lombardy have been the subject of constant disputes over the centuries. At one stage or another, Celts, Romans, Goths, Lombards, Spaniards and Austrians all ruled the city. Then there were the Viscontis and the Sforzas, the two powerful families that imposed themselves on Milan between the late 13th and early 16th centuries. And Napoleon eventually got in on the act, assuming the throne of the Kingdom of Italy in the Duomo in 1805.

For the most part, Milan has successfully weathered the changes that punctuated its history, and even profited from them. Thanks to its position at the forefront of the economic boom of the 1960s, '70s and '80s, the city eventually emerged as the undisputed economic powerhouse of a united Italy. And with this new-found financial strength came an improved standard of living for locals along with an increasingly appealing set of diversions for visitors.

Indeed, Milan is now arguably less famous for its history than for its contemporary luxury. The fashion crowd will find plenty to cherish: the range of designer togs on offer is virtually unmatched. But one night out in the packed bars and restaurants will tell you that this is a town that not only works hard but plays hard too. Spas, shopping, luxury hotels... Milan is paradise for the decadent. Not the sort of place to visit on a tight budget, perhaps, but a hugely enjoyable destination if you've got some slack on the credit card.

Milan

Historic sites
● ● ● ● ○

Art & architecture
● ● ● ○ ○

Hotels
● ● ● ● ○

Eating & drinking
● ● ● ● ●

Nightlife
● ● ● ● ●

Shopping
● ● ● ● ●

Milan

ITALY

Stay

Milan's status as a commercial centre (as opposed to an out-and-out tourist magnet) has translated into a preponderance of large hotels in the upper price brackets and a shortage of small, inexpensive addresses. However, because Milan hotels are at a premium from Monday to Friday, discounts are often offered at weekends.

Alle Meraviglie

Sforzesco & North *Via San Tomaso 8 (02 805 1023/ www.allemeraviglie.it). €€-€€€.*
The *meraviglie* (wonders) that await the guest at this lovely B&B, just off via Dante, are ten inviting rooms with bright white beds, lavish silk curtains and fresh-cut flowers. The bathrooms, by contrast, are run-of-the-mill, with basic showers and large bottles of everyday unctions. Despite being set in a converted townhouse with plenty of olde-worlde character, there are plenty of up-to-date touches, such as free Wi-Fi in every room.

Antica Locanda Leonardo

Sant'Ambrogio & West *Corso Magenta 78 (02 463 317/www.leoloc.com). €€-€€€.*
An immaculate little hotel set back from busy corso Magenta, Antica Locanda Leonardo is housed in a late 19th-century palazzo. The rooms are all tastefully decorated with modern or antique wood furniture; some have a Japanese feel, as a nod to one of the owners. There's also a cosy breakfast/bar area in which tea and cakes are served. The hotel has been managed by the same courteous family for more than 40 years; it shows in the attention to detail. Ask for a room overlooking the flower-filled courtyard.

Bulgari

Sforzesco & North *Via Privata Fratelli Gabba 7B (02 805 8051/www.bulgarihotels.com). €€€€.*
At the end of a private road behind the Pinacoteca di Brera's botanic gardens, the Bulgari oozes the same exclusivity and class as its fine jewellery, with due attention paid to precious materials. The neutral-toned bedrooms are understated yet luxurious, with capacious travertine and black marble bathrooms. Floor-to-ceiling windows open on to teak balconies overlooking the hotel's private gardens, parts of which date back to the 13th century. The spa is a study in contemporary calm, and the bar is a magnet for style-conscious locals and hotel guests. The place to stay in if someone else is paying the bill.

Four Seasons Hotel Milano

San Babila & East *Via Gesù 6/8 (02 770 8167/ www.fourseasons.com/milan). €€€€.*
It's no longer the most expensive hotel in Milan, but the Four Seasons continues to be a favourite with the visiting fashion and film crowd. No doubt they love the location, slap bang in the middle of the Quadrilatero della Moda. The hotel is housed in a 15th-century convent, but away from the cloistered courtyard (many rooms face on to it), you'd never guess that. Each of the spacious bedrooms is individually decorated with Fortuny fabrics and pear- and sycamore-wood furniture; some suites feature parts of the building's original frescoes. As you'd expect, the hotel also boasts a first-rate formal restaurant, Il Teatro.

Grand Hotel et de Milan

San Babila & East *Via Sandro Manzoni 29 (02 723 141/www.grandhoteletdemilan.it). €€€€.*
Housed in an elegant 19th-century palazzo, the five-star Grand is as sumptuous as it gets. The gorgeous suites are named after illustrious former guests such as Maria Callas and Giuseppe Verdi: the composer called the hotel home when staying in the city, and actually made his final curtain call here, dying at the hotel in 1901. Although the room prices seem shocking at first glance, it's worth asking about weekend rates: you may be pleasantly surprised. Gerry's Bar is a nice place for a drink; throughout the property, the efficient service is as discreet as it is friendly.

Park Hyatt Milan

Duomo & Centre *Via Tommaso Grossi 1 (02 8821 1234/www.milan.park.hyatt.com). €€€€.*
Carved out of an old bank building, the Park Hyatt is an exercise in serenity. It's the work of Ed Tuttle, an American architect who has designed resorts in Thailand and Morocco. The warm, light-coloured rooms are equipped with generously proportioned bathrooms and modern luxuries, such as plasma-screen TVs and complimentary internet access. Treatments are available in the small spa, which has separate steam rooms for men and women. The restaurant serves contemporary Mediterranean cuisine; the bar is favoured by fashionable Milanese.

Principe di Savoia

Sforzesco & North *Piazza della Repubblica 17 (02 62301/www.hotelprincipedisavoia.com). €€€€.*
This historic hotel, parts of which date back to 1927, prides itself on treating its clientele like royalty while remaining in tune with the times; such service is perhaps only to be expected from a hotel that was the first in Italy to install phones in all its rooms. Frank Sinatra, Robert de Niro and Madonna have all stayed in the presidential suite, which boasts its own pool. Although most of the other rooms are stately and traditional, there are also 48 others for guests who prefer a more contemporary style. The location isn't perfect, but it's an easy stroll from the centre.

3Rooms

Sforzesco & North *Corso Como 10 (02 626 163/ www.3rooms-10corsocomo.com). €€-€€€.*
You've browsed the boutique, gazed at the gallery and posed at the bar – and now you can spend the night at Milan's multi-purpose style emporium. Describing itself as as a 'bed and breakfast', 3Rooms is actually made up of three apartments, each consisting of (yes) three rooms: a bedroom, a bathroom and a living room (plus lots of cupboard space for all those changes of outfit you'll need). Each apartment occupies an entire floor, overlooking the internal courtyard and tea garden, and is decorated with designer furnishings. Be warned: there's no lift and the apartments are on the second, third and fourth floors. Book well in advance.

Clockwise from top left:
Alle Meraviglie (2); Four
Seasons Hotel Milano (2);
Town House Galleria (2).

Town House Galleria
Duomo & Centre *Via Silvio Pellico 8 (02 8905 8297/ www.townhousegalleria.it). €€€€.*
Billing itself as the first seven-star hotel in Europe, Town House Galleria opened in March 2007, and its location in an 1860s palazzo above a Prada store in the Galleria Vittorio Emanuele II is a clue to the opulence within. Each of the 24 rooms (mostly suites) comes with a personal butler, who'll get you tickets for La Scala and can even have your glad rags pressed for the occasion (at these prices, so he should). Named after famous musicians, the rooms are luxurious, with subtle colour schemes, designer furniture and Wi-Fi connections. Sheer luxury.

Eat

You'll eat very well in Milan. Succulent cuts of meat, especially veal, are transformed into regional specialities such as *ossobuco alla milanese* (braised veal shanks) and *cotoletta alla milanese* (breaded and fried veal chop), and Lombardy also produces some excellent cured meats. Risotto is more widely eaten than pasta in Milan, although *tortelli di zucca* (pumpkin-stuffed pasta) and *pizzoccheri* (with cheese, cabbage and potato) are both local specialities. Although it's land-locked, the region is a good place in which to eat freshwater fish and seafood, and lovers of cheese won't go hungry – local offerings range from sharp gorgonzola to oozing taleggio and spreadable stracchino.

Happy hours are hugely popular in Milan. They generally involve only a token drop in prices, but cheap booze isn't the point: they're more about the generous and imaginative buffets that can often serve as a meal in themselves. Oenophiles should note that the Franciacorta area between Bergamo and Brescia produces champagne-quality sparkling wines, and the range of Oltrepò wines from the hills on the far side of the Po river include some good-value reds and whites.

Armani/Nobu
Duomo & Centre *Via Pisoni 1 (02 6231 2645/www.armaninobu.com). Open noon-2.30pm, 7-11.30pm daily. €€ Bar. €€€€ Restaurant. Sushi.*
Raw fish doesn't get any more fashionable than at the Milan outpost of Nobuyuki Matsuhisa's global restaurant empire. Purists might say that the food isn't as good as at as his New York or London flagships, but people-watchers will tell you that a visit to Nobu's happy hour is an essential fixture if you want to have a chance of watching Milan's fashion world unwind. The lounge bar is at ground level, with the restaurant proper up on the first floor.

Caffè Miani (aka Zucca)
Duomo & Centre *Piazza Duomo 21, Galleria Vittorio Emanuele II (02 8646 4435/www.caffemiani.it). Open 7.30am-8.30pm Tue-Sun. Closed Aug. Café.*

Part of the Galleria arcade since it opened in 1867, and formerly frequented by Verdi and Toscanini, this place is a Milanese institution. The interior is spectacular, with an inlaid bar and mosaics by Angelo d'Andrea. Many customers order that most Milanese of aperitifs, the rhubarb-based Zucca. You might want to stand and drink at the bar: prices increase dramatically once you sit down and have a waiter come to your table.

Caffè Verdi
Duomo & Centre *Via Giuseppe Verdi 6 (02 863 880). Open 7am-9pm daily. Closed 3wks Aug. Café.*
This quietly dignified caffè is a must for opera fans: situated across the road from La Scala, it's a convenient coffee-break spot for company members. But even if you don't bump into Placido Domingo, it's fun to soak up the atmosphere, surrounded by busts and photos of composers, while unobtrusive classical music plays in the background. Cocktails bear such names as Callas, Verdiano and Mozart; the martinis, in particular, are excellent. Verdi also serves food, and is popular with bankers at lunchtime.

> "You'll eat very well in Milan. Succulent cuts of meat, especially veal, are transformed into regional specialities such as ossobuco alla milanese."

Cracco-Peck
Duomo & Centre *Via Victor Hugo 4 (02 876 774/ www.peck.it). Open 11.30-2.30pm, 7.30-10pm Mon-Fri; 7.30-10pm Sat. Closed 3wks Aug, 3wks Dec-Jan. €€€€. Modern Italian.*
Cracco-Peck's creative menu is custom-made for Milan's expense-account power brokers, and the two Michelin stars show the high esteem in which the food is held. The restaurant is a beacon of Italy's serious dining movement; compared with Paris or London, it can be considered good value, thanks to its relatively full portions and a wine list that doesn't require a banker's approval. If you want a taste of the magic without the formality, try the more casual Peck Italian Bar (via Cesare Cantù 3, 02 869 3017).

Da Giacomo
San Babila & East *Via Pasquale Sottocorno 6 (02 7602 3313/www.dagiacomoristorante.it). Open 12.30-2.30pm, 7.30-11.30pm daily. Closed 3wks Aug, 2wks Dec-Jan. €€€€. Trattoria.*
This anonymous trattoria on an equally anonymous street is one of Milan's most exclusive restaurants. In a series of bright and chatty rooms, major players from Milan's

Clockwise from top left:
Peck; 10 Corso Como;
Armani/Nobu; Joia.

fashion and business worlds jostle for elbow room. Service can be uncertain, and the competent Mediterranean cuisine, with the emphasis on fish, might not win any prizes. But this is just what the city's captains of industry want: colour and comfort food in a trattoria that's as difficult to infiltrate as the Ivy in London. Book well ahead.

Joia

San Babila & East *Via P Castaldi 18 (02 2952 2124/ www.joia.it). Open 12.30-3pm, 7.30-11pm Mon-Fri; 7.30-11pm Sat. Closed 3wks Aug, 2wks Dec-Jan. €€€€. Vegetarian.*
This calm and minimalist yet woody-warm space near the Giardini Pubblici is the domain of Swiss chef Pietro Leemann, whose often inspired and always creative cooking has earned him a Michelin star – an unusual accolade for a vegetarian chef. The oriental-influenced menus, which also include a few fish and vegan dishes, feature whimsically named concoctions characterised by contrasting colours, textures, shapes and flavours. There are several set menus, including a €15 lunch menu. The cheaper, more casual Joia Leggero is located in the Porta Romana area (Corso di Porta Ticinese 10, 02 8940 4134).

Da Leo

Sant'Ambrogio & West *Via Trivulzio 26 (02 4007 1445). Open 12.30-2.30pm, 7.30-10.30pm Tue-Sat; 12.30-2.30pm Sun. Closed 3wks Aug, 2wks Dec. €€€. No credit cards. Fish.*
Giuseppe Leo has been going to Milan's fish market at the crack of dawn for the past 30 years in order to select the freshest produce for his fish restaurant. The dishes served here are simple and wholesome: spaghetti (no other pasta is served) in bianco (without tomatoes) with tuna, clams, king prawns or calamari; and main course fish dishes. The interior is unpretentious, the service friendly and efficient, and the wine list extensive. Book ahead for dinner.

Explore

SIGHTS

Most of Milan's main attractions are grouped around the central piazza del Duomo, from where you can easily reach the other areas of interest. Large sections of the centre of the city have been given over to pedestrians in recent years, and cars are banned on many Sundays, when the council deems pollution levels to be too high. Note that many major museums and galleries are closed on Mondays.

THE DUOMO & CENTRAL MILAN

It's perhaps ironic that Milan, the spearhead of modern Italy's financial growth and closely associated with cutting-edge fashion, should centre on a building that took half a millennium to construct. The Duomo is Milan's jewel, and an essential stop on any visitor's itinerary. The square in front of it, the piazza del Duomo, remains the city's beating heart.

The piazza della Scala is home to the Teatro alla Scala, one of the most celebrated opera houses in the world.

Biblioteca & Pinacoteca Ambrosiana

Piazza Pio XI 2 (02 806 921/www.ambrosiana.it). Open Pinacoteca 10am-5.30pm Tue-Sun. Library open only for members. Admission €8; €4-€5 reductions.
Founded in 1618, the Pinacoteca was originally based on Cardinal Borromeo's private art collection, which included Titian's *Adoration of the Magi* and Caravaggio's *Basket of Fruit*. Over the centuries, the collection has grown to include further Renaissance masterpieces, such as Botticelli's *Madonna del Padiglione* and Leonardo's *Musician*, as well as later works by the likes of Reni, Tiepolo and Canova. Curiosities include the gloves Napoleon wore at Waterloo. The Biblioteca, which houses Leonardo's original Codex Atlanticus, is open only to scholars.

Duomo (Cathedral)

Piazza del Duomo (02 8646 3456). Open Church 7am-7pm daily. Treasury & crypt 9.30am-1.30pm, 2-6pm Mon-Fri; 9.30am-1.30pm, 2-5pm Sat; 1.30-3.30pm Sun. Baptistery & early Christian excavations 9.30am-5.15pm daily. Roof Nov-Feb 9am-4.45pm daily. Mar-Oct 9am-5.45pm daily. Admission free. Treasury & crypt €1. Baptistery & excavations €2. Roof €7 by lift; €5 on foot. No credit cards.
The Duomo is a joy to behold. Although construction began in 1386, it took the best part of 500 years to complete, and refinements continue even into the 21st century: in 2002, a five-year project to clean the façade (originally installed by Napoleon) was undertaken, returning the Duomo to its full mind-blowing beauty. A staggering 3,500 statues adorn the structure, roughly two-thirds of them on the exterior, along with 135 spires. To appreciate them fully, take the lift to the roof, from where, on clear days, you can see the Alps. A roof visit also brings you closer to the Madonnina (1774), the gilded copper figure dear to the hearts of the Milanese.

Inside the Duomo, the 52 pillars of the five-aisled design correspond to the weeks of the year. On their capitals, imposing statues of saints stretch up into the cross vaults of the ceiling, creating a vertiginous effect. Other highlights include the gruesomely lifelike statue of a flayed St Bartholomew (1562) by Marco d'Agrate.

Galleria Vittorio Emanuele II

Between piazza del Duomo & piazza della Scala. Open 24hrs daily.
One of the city's most impressive buildings, this magnificent, cross-shaped, glass-roofed arcade, 47m (157ft) in length, was inaugurated by the king himself in 1867. (The architect, Giuseppe Mengoni, didn't make the occasion, having fallen to his death from his own creation a few days earlier.) The interior is flanked by swanky clothes retailers, media entertainment stores and pricey cafés. It's known as 'Milan's living room' for good reason: most of the city seems to pass through it at some point during the day.

Clockwise from top left:
Brera; Duomo; Il Cenacolo
(The Last Supper); Brera.

CASTELLO SFORZESCO, BRERA & NORTHERN MILAN

Presiding over one end of a long pedestrian corridor that runs from via Dante through piazza del Duomo and all the way to piazza San Babila, the fairy-tale Castello Sforzesco lends an air of historic distinction to the slightly less sophisticated aspects of north-west Milan: the drinking holes, the fortune tellers and the touters of contraband designer gear.

Brera lures locals and tourists in equal measure, and no wonder: the Pinacoteca di Brera is one of Italy's most prestigious art collections, and the roads around it all but cry out to be explored. Here, antiques shops, jewellers, boutiques, snazzy bars, traditional cafés and contemporary art galleries alternate along the cobbled streets of this slightly down-at-heel but still quietly wealthy area.

Castello Sforzesco/ Civici Musei del Castello

Piazza Castello (02 8846 3700/www.milanocastello.it). Open Grounds 9am-6pm daily. Museums 9am-5.30pm Tue-Sun (last entry 5pm). Admission Grounds free. Museums €3. No credit cards.
A feast of crenellations, machicolations and watchtowers, the Castello Sforzesco was begun in 1368 by Galeazzo II Visconti as part of the city's fortifications, and was later transformed into a sumptuous ducal residence by Filippo Maria Visconti. The court gathered here by Ludovico 'il Moro' Sforza included Leonardo da Vinci, and was regarded as one of Europe's most refined. But when Ludovico was captured by the French in 1499, the castle fell into decline. After the castle's bulwarks were knocked down under French rule in the early 19th century, there was talk of demolishing the rest, but architect Luca Beltrami fought to preserve what remained. Today, the Castello's 12 high-quality museums and galleries cover everything from Renaissance masterpieces to mummies.

Pinacoteca di Brera

Via Brera 28 (02 722 631/reservations 02 8942 1146/ www.brera.beniculturali.it). Open 8.30am-7.30pm Tue-Sun (last entry 6.45pm). Admission €5; free-€2.50 reductions. No credit cards.
The Pinacoteca began life as a collection of paintings for students of the Accademia di Belle Arti in the same building. The collection, considered by many to be the best in Lombardy, is modest in breadth but exquisite in quality, covering major Italian artists from the 13th to the 20th centuries. Among the highlights are works by Piero della Francesca, Titian and Tintoretto, along with Caravaggio's atmospheric *Supper at Emmaus* and Bramante's disturbingly realistic *Christ at the Column*. If you're only going to visit one museum in Milan, make it this one.

SAN BABILA & EASTERN MILAN

The style and wealth of Milan's fashion quarter, the Quadrilatero della Moda, is awe-inspiring. No wonder this designer heaven, delineated by via Montenapoleone, via Sant'Andrea, via Manzoni and pedestrianised via della Spiga, is also known as the Quadrilatero d'Oro ('Golden Rectangle'). However, even visitors without gold cards will find this area worth a look: it's also home to the Museo Bagatti Valsecchi (Via Gesù 5, closed Mon & Aug), the Museo di Milano e Storia Contemporanea (via Sant'Andrea 6, closed Mon & Aug) and San Francesco di Paola (via Manzoni 3), one of Milan's prettiest churches.

If you need some breathing space from the glamour, cross attractive piazza Cavour to the Giardini Pubblici. In addition to providing a welcome swathe of greenery, the gardens are home to several museums.

Museo dell'Ottocento

Villa Belgiojoso Bonaparte, via Palestro 16 (02 7634 0809/www.villabelgiojosobonaparte.it). Open 9am-1pm, 2-5.30pm Tue-Sun. Admission free.
This restored neo-classical villa was built by the Austrian architect Leopold Pollack in 1790 for Count Ludovico Barbiano di Belgiojoso. Napoleon lived here in 1802; Austrian field marshal Count Joseph Radetzky followed in his footsteps. After unification, ownership passed to the Italian royal family, who gave the property to the city of Milan in 1921. Today, it's home to Milan's 35-room Museum of the 19th Century, which covers everything from neo-classical paintings, sculpture and bas-reliefs to paintings from the Romantic period and Divisionist and Futurist works. The Vismara collection features works by modern Italian and international masters.

PORTA ROMANA, THE NAVIGLI & SOUTHERN MILAN

The area stretching from via Larga to Porta Romana is largely student territory. The first sight of note, across via Larga in piazza Santo Stefano, is the church of San Bernardino alle Ossa (1695), which houses an ossuary. Via Chiaravalle leads to the church of Sant'Antonio Abate; from here, you can't miss the magnificent Ca' Granda ('big house'), which now houses the arts faculties of the Università degli Studi di Milano.

Museo Diocesano

Corso di Porta Ticinese 95 (02 8940 4714/ bookings 02 8942 0019/www.museodiocesano.it). Open 10am-6pm Tue-Sun. Admission €8; €5-€6 reductions. Combined ticket with Cappella Portinari at Sant'Eustorgio & Cappella di Sant'Aquilino at San Lorenzo €12; €8 reductions. No credit cards.
Spread over three floors of the former Dominican convent of Sant'Eustorgio, the Museo Diocesano (Diocesan Museum) contains a wonderful array of religious art treasures culled from churches and private collections throughout Lombardy. The bulk of the collections (and temporary exhibitions) are housed on the first floor: don't miss Tintoretto's *Christ and the Adulteress*. Ground-floor exhibits include select pieces from St Ambrose's time; the basement holds an array of liturgical furniture.

Chic at half the price

When in Milan, do as many of the trendiest Milanese do and seek out cut-price clothes to mix with the latest (full-price) catwalk looks. Here's a selection of some of the best discount boutiques and bargain basements in the city.

STOCK HOUSES

The best of the stock houses are treasure troves of designer goods filled with racks of end-of-season shop and warehouse returns, stock from closed-down boutiques, and some factory seconds. The prices are often vastly reduced, but even when factoring in discounts of 50 to 70 per cent, price tags can still elicit the occasional 'ouch!'

One of the best known and longest established of the stock houses is the aptly-named (at least for cash-poor fashion followers) Il Salvagente ('The Lifebelt'), which garners large piles of top stuff. Pick through an ever-changing kaleidoscope of designer goods for men and women; for children, there's a separate location called Salvagente Bimbi.

However, Il Salvagente is no longer the only hope for impoverished fashionistas who fear that their bank manager is about to throw them overboard. Determined shoppers have been finding equally worthwhile bargains at discount outlets with more convenient, central locations. Some of them, such as Dmagazine Outlet, are wedged between the full-priced stores on the smartest shopping streets; you'll find serious discounts on clothes by Miu Miu, Marc Jacobs, Marni and many more. Next, head for Basement, located in a cellar on via Senato, for price cuts of 50 to 70 per cent on brands including Dolce e Gabbana, Prada and YSL.

Serious bargain-hunters should make a pitstop at Outlet Matia's in Brera for dramatic discounts on classy labels such as Aspesi, Ermenegildo Zegna and MaxMara. Affordable cashmere knits in a rainbow of colours sometimes fill a boardroom-sized table. Down an alley off corso Vittorio Emanuele, DT Intrend also deals in the MaxMara brands, including Sportmax and Marella. And for last season's (unworn) women's shoes by such sought-after designers as René Caovilla, Gianni Barbato and Alessandro dell'Acqua, head to Le Vintage, in the increasingly trendy Isola area behind Garibaldi Station. Here, you'll also find a small but well chosen selection of 1960s and '70s vintage clothes.

Finally, fashion slaves on a budget shouldn't miss the 10 Corso Como Outlet, a slightly

shabbier version of the super-cool original store with endless racks of (mostly black) clothes by Helmut Lang, Chloé, Comme des Garçons et al. Don't gasp when you check the price tags: though unmarked, most have been slashed by a further 50 to 70 per cent.

10 Corso Como Outlet
Via Tazzoli 3, North (02 2900 2674). Open 1-7pm Fri; 11am-7pm Sat, Sun. Closed 2wks Aug.

Basement
Via Senato 15, Centre (02 7631 7913). Open 3-7pm Mon; 10am-7pm Tue-Sat. Closed Aug.

Dmagazine Outlet
Via Montenapoleone 26, Centre (02 7600 6027/www.dmagazine.it). Open 9.30am-7.45pm daily.

DT Intrend
Galleria San Carlo 6, Centre (02 7600 0829). Open 3.30-7.30pm Mon; 10am-7.30pm Tue-Sat.

Outlet Matia's
Piazza Mirabello 4, North (02 6269 4535). Open 10am-7pm Mon-Sat. Closed Aug.

Il Salvagente
Via Fratelli Bronzetti 16, East (02 7611 0328/ www.salvagentemilano.it). Open 3-7pm Mon; 10am-12.40pm, 3-7pm Tue, Thur, Fri; 10am-7pm Wed, Sat. Closed Aug. No credit cards.

Salvagente Bimbi
*Via Balzaretti 28, East (02 2668 0764/
www.salvagentemilano.it). Open 3-7pm Mon;
10am-1pm, 3-7pm Tue, Thur, Fri; 10am-7pm
Wed, Sat. Closed Aug. No credit cards.*

Le Vintage
*Via Garigliano 4, North (02 6931 1885). Open
3-8pm Mon; 11am-2pm, 3-8pm Tue-Fri; 11am-
1pm, 2-6pm Sat; 1-7pm Sun. Closed 3wks Aug.*

SECOND-HAND & VINTAGE

In this image-obsessed city, it's unsurprising
that many Milanese women (and men) have
wardrobes that are full to bursting point. The
canniest of them offload last season's clothes
to help make room for – and fund – the latest
designer looks. And their cast-offs help make
Milan a rich terrain for bargain-hunters.

Il Nuovo Guardaroba has an array of well
organised racks of classic women's second-
hand clothing and accessories, along with a
small selection of men's items. Nearby, a
separate shop, Il Guardarobino, caters for
children, stocking clothing and baby hardware
such as strollers and highchairs.

At L'Armadio di Laura, a sign reads 'Please
don't ask for further discounts', and for good
reason: the prices in this thrift store-like shop
are low enough already. For vintage clothing
from old hands in the business, try Cavalli e
Nastri. Each piece is in mint condition and
selected with a razor-sharp eye; obvious and
dowdy 'period' pieces have been weeded out,
leaving only the crème de la crème. If you're
looking for a Victorian gown or a 19th-century
smoking jacket, try its other, larger location,
at via de Amicis.

Passionate vintage fans should head for
Franco Jacassi, a treasure trove of antique
clothing, bags, shoes, hats, buttons, trimmings
and rare fashion publications. This is where
Milan's big-name designers come when they
need inspiration. And for fabulous '50s looks,
make for Miss Ghinting, run by two stylish
Milanese 'misses' in the Isola district. The
shop's stock is a well-edited mix of tailored
pieces from that era, plus some from the
1960s and '70s.

L'Armadio di Laura
*Via Voghera 25, South (02 836 0606/www.
armadiodilaura.it). Open Spring, summer 10am-
6pm Tue-Sat. Autumn, winter 10am-6pm Mon-
Sat. Closed late July-early Sept.*

Cavalli e Nastri
*Via Brera 2, North (02 7200 0449). Open 3.30-
7pm Mon; 10.30am-7pm Tue-Sat. Closed Aug.
Other locations: via de Amicis 9 (entrance in via
Arena), South (02 8940 9452).*

Franco Jacassi
*Via Sacchi 3, North (02 8646 2076). Open
10am-1pm, 2-7pm Mon-Fri. Closed Aug.*

Il Guardarobino
*Via Senofonte 9, West (02 4801 5802). Open
10am-1pm, 3-7pm Tue-Sat. Closed 2wks July,
Aug. No credit cards.*

Miss Ghinting
*Via Borsieri, opposite No.16, North (02 668
7112/www.missghinting.com). Open 10am-
1pm, 3-7.30pm Tue-Sat. Closed Aug.*

Il Nuovo Guardaroba
*Via Privata Asti 5a, West (02 4800 1678).
Open 10am-1.30pm, 3-6pm Tue-Fri; 10am-
6pm Sat. Closed 2wks July, 4wks Aug. No
credit cards.*

SANT'AMBROGIO & WESTERN MILAN

Via Meravigli and corso Magenta are a nice balance of active, bustling streetlife and olde worlde shops, among them antiques merchants and rare book dealers. Off corso Magenta, the church of Sant'Ambrogio dates back to Roman times; nine Italian kings were crowned at its altar. Every year on 7 December, the feast of Saint Ambrose, the square outside the church hosts the Oh Bej! Oh Bej! festival; the rest of the time, it's filled with students from the nearby Università Cattolica del Sacro Cuore.

Continuing westwards along corso Magenta, you'll come to Santa Maria delle Grazie and the refectory housing Milan's most precious work of art, *The Last Supper*.

> "Visitors aiming for the latest catwalk look will find no happier hunting ground than Milan's famed Quadrilatero della Moda, home to an A(rmani) to Z(egna) of designer stores."

Santa Maria delle Grazie & Il Cenacolo (The Last Supper)

Piazza Santa Maria delle Grazie (02 4676 111). Open 7.30am-noon, 3.30-7.15pm daily. Admission free. Refectory (for The Last Supper) (02 498 7588/ reservations 02 8942 1146/www.cenacolovinciano.it). Open 8.15am-7.45pm Tue-Sun. Guided tours in English 9.30am, 3.30pm. Admission €8; €1.50-€4.75 reductions. Guided tour €3.25.

Just two years after the church of Santa Maria delle Grazie was completed in the 1480s, Ludovico il Moro is said to have commissioned Donato Bramante to turn it into a family mausoleum reflecting the new Renaissance style. At the same time, the adjoining Dominican monastery was given the *chiostrino* (small cloister) and a new sacristy. The complex escaped meddling restoration until the late 19th century, when faux-Renaissance elements were added. World War II bombing destroyed the great cloister of the monastery, but spared the *chiostrino* and the refectory.

The latter is the main attraction. The reason? Leonardo da Vinci's *Last Supper*, arguably the greatest artwork of the Renaissance. Painted between 1495 and 1497, it depicts the moment immediately after Christ has revealed that one of his disciples will betray him. The artist portrays their expressions of shock, amazement and hostility with acute psychological probity. However, because Leonardo painted the mural on dry rather than wet plaster, it began to deteriorate within his lifetime, and has been more or less in *restauro* ever since. You have to reserve your (timed, 15-minute) visit; try to book one of the guided tours.

SHOP

Visitors aiming for the latest catwalk look will find no happier hunting ground than Milan's famed Quadrilatero della Moda, home to an A(rmani) to Z(egna) of designer stores. Anyone allergic to big brands should head to the smaller stores on corso di Porta Ticinese or in Brera; corso Vercelli (the western continuation of corso Magenta) and the Isola area are also worth a trawl. Another historic shopping spot is the Galleria Vittoria Emanuele II, the glass-roofed arcade near the Duomo.

Several of the city's best spas are found in major designers' stores, and they're surprisingly affordable. Many of the top hotels also have spas; the Bulgari's is especially luxurious.

10 Corso Como

Sforzesco & North *Corso Como 10 (02 2900 2674/ www.10corsocomo.it). Open 3-7.30pm Mon; 10.30am-7.30pm Tue, Fri-Sun; 10.30am-9pm Wed, Thur.*
Owned by the former editor of the Italian edition of *Vogue* Carla Sozzani, this place is a must-see for neophytes and seasoned fashionistas. The merchandise mix includes men's and women's fashions, accessories, shoes, bags, housewares, books and CDs; there's also a café/restaurant, a photography gallery and a posh B&B on site. The prices are not for the faint-hearted.

Anna Fabiano

Porta Romana & South *Corso di Porta Ticinese 40 (02 5811 2348). Open 3.30-7.30pm Mon; 10.30am-1.30pm, 2.30pm-7.30pm Tue-Sat. Closed 2-3wks Aug.*
This is the sole outlet for clothes and accessories by Fabiano, whose quirky items include hand-painted, full 1950s-style skirts and beautifully tailored jackets with patchwork inserts on the collar turn-ups. Step out in something by Fabiano, and you'll be amazed at how many people will notice and comment on it.

Antonioli

Porta Romana & South *Via Pasquale Paoli 1, at Porta Ticinese (02 3656 6494/www.antoniolishop.com). Open 3-7.30pm Mon; 11am-7.30pm Tue-Sun. Closed 3wks Aug.*
Antonioli is a hit with the international fashion crowd that regularly descends on the city. Most of the clothes for men and women are dark and deconstructed, and the decor in this former cinema (a distressed steel skateboard ramp, scraped-down walls) has been designed to match. Labels include Dries van Noten, Dsquared2, Rick Owens and Ring.

Biffi

Porta Romana & South *Corso Genova 6 (02 831 1601/www.biffi.com). Open 3-7.30pm Mon; 9.30am-1.30pm, 3-7.30pm Tue-Sat. Closed 2wks Aug.*

From top to bottom:
Quadrilatero della Moda
(2); Galleria Vittorio
Emanuele II; Quadrilatero
della Moda (2).

A Milanese institution for men's and women's classic designer labels, Biffi also stocks the mildly wild trend pieces of the season. Gucci, Fendi, Yohji Yamamoto, Marc Jacobs and John Galliano are among the designers showcased here.

Erboristeria Officinale Mediolanum
Sforzesco & North *Via Alessandro Volta 7 (02 6572 882/www.erboristeriamediolanum.it). Open 3.30-7.30pm Mon; 9.30am-1pm, 3.30-7.30pm Tue-Sat. Closed 2wks Aug.*
Expert Gabriella Fiumani presides over this intriguing herbalist, mixing tisanes, cosmetic remedies and medicinal concoctions from more than 400 herbs stored in drawers and cupboards at the back of the shop. The shop also stocks organic herbal cosmetics, as well as spices and seasonings displayed in huge glass jars.

Mauro
Porta Romana & South *Corso di Porta Ticinese 60 (02 8942 9167). Open 3-7.30pm Mon, Sun; 10am-7.30pm Tue-Sat. No credit cards.*
This tiny store is always packed with Milanese signoras and fashionistas fighting over the latest own-brand, made-in-Italy styles of footwear. You'll find everything from suede courts in purple and turquoise to basic black knee-high boots, all at good prices.

> # "Home to two of Italy's top teams, AC Milan and Inter Milan, San Siro is perhaps the most renowned stadium in the country."

Peck
Duomo & Centre *Via Spadari 9 (02 802 3161/ www.peck.it). Open 3.30-7.30pm Mon; 9.15am-7.30pm Tue-Fri; 8.45am-7.30pm Sat, last 2 Suns of Dec.*
Milan's world-renowned delicatessen is a temple of fine food and wine. It was founded in 1883 by a humble pork butcher, originally from Prague, named Franz Peck. These days, the main action is in the three-floor flagship shop on via Spadari, which has a butcher's, a bakery and a delicatessen, plus a vast selection of wines from all over the world, prepared foods, oils and bottled sauces. There's a delightful tearoom upstairs, and, at separate locations, a sit-down gourmet restaurant (Cracco-Peck) and a café (Peck Italian Bar).

Il Salumaio di Montenapoleone
Duomo & Centre *Via Montenapoleone 12 (02 7600 1123/www.ilsalumaiodimontenapoleone.it). Open 3.30-7pm Mon; 8.30am-1pm, 3.30-7pm Tue-Sat. Closed 3wks Aug.*

Wedged into an inner courtyard between Dior and Lorenz (watches), this shrine to all things edible is one of the last non-fashion stores holding out in the centre of Milan. The shelves and cabinets are lined with tempting arrays of freshly made pastas and biscuits, cured meats, 100-plus varieties of cheese, and bottles stuffed with olives, artichokes, peppers, porcini mushrooms and just about anything else you can fit in a jar. There's also a café-cum-restaurant (open noon-6.30pm) on site.

Valextra Outlet
Duomo & Centre *Via Cerva 11 (02 7600 3459/ www.valextra.it). Open 10am-7pm Tue-Sat. Closed 3wks Aug.*
Tucked behind piazza San Babila, Valextra Outlet stocks mouth-watering arrays of end-of-line wallets, handbags and luggage from the legendary leather brand, but for 40% less than the usually stratospheric prices. Although these bags are beloved of the jet set, their sleek lines aren't subject to the whims of fashion. Not convinced you've got a bargain? Visit the full-price boutique (via Manzoni 3, Duomo & Centre, 02 9978 6060) and compare.

ARTS

Stadio Giuseppe Meazza (San Siro)
Sant'Ambrogio & West *Via Piccolomini 5, San Siro (02 404 2432/02 4879 8253). Open 10am-5pm daily. Admission Museum €7, €5 reductions. Guided tour €12.50, €10 reductions.*
Home to two of Italy's top teams, AC Milan and Inter Milan, San Siro is perhaps the most renowned stadium in the country. The two teams face each other here twice a year: if you're lucky enough to secure a ticket, make sure you turn up a good hour ahead of time to claim your spot. Tickets to AC Milan home games are sold at Milan Point (via San Gottardo 2, entrance in piazza XXIV Maggio, Porta Romana & South, 02 8942 2711). For Inter, try any branch of Banca Popolare di Milano (in the city centre, there's one at via Meravigli 2, 02 8646 0598, www.bpm.it).

Teatro alla Scala & Museo Teatrale alla Scala
Duomo & Centre *Piazza della Scala (02 7200 3744/ www.teatroallascala.org). Open Museum 9am-12.30pm (last entry noon), 1.30-5.30pm daily (last entry 5pm). Admission Museum €5; €2.50-€4 reductions. Open only half-days for most of Dec.*
Opera lovers the world over travel to pay their respects at La Scala. When the season begins on 7 December (the feast of Sant'Ambrogio), paparazzi descend on the place to catch snaps of the glamorous attendees. But the real stuff happens on the stage, where a consistently excellent line-up of performers regularly raises the roof.

The opera house takes its name from Santa Maria della Scala, the 14th-century church that once stood on the site. The church was torn down in 1776 when the Palazzo Reale was damaged by a fire, leaving the city with no principal theatre. Giuseppe Piermarini was given the task of designing a replacement; his building opened in 1778 with an opera by Salieri, and went on to host premieres of operas by Puccini, Verdi, Bellini and others.

Destroyed by bombing in World War II, La Scala was swiftly rebuilt after the war and reopened in 1946. More recently, three years of refurbishments, which included the addition of a new and controversial 'fly tower' visible from piazza della Scala, were completed in time for opening night in December 2004. Daniel Barenboim was appointed as La Scala's principal guest conductor in 2006.

NIGHTLIFE

If Milan is just one stop on your tour of Italy, it's a good idea to get the partying out of your system here: you'll be hard pressed to find a better selection of clubs anywhere else. At most venues, if you make it past face control, you'll be given a ticket; each drink will be hole-punched into it and you pay as you leave.

Blue Note

Sforzesco & North *Via Borsieri Pietro 37 (02 6901 6888/www.bluenotemilano.com). Open 2-7pm Mon, 2pm-midnight Tue-Sat, 7-11pm Sun. Admission €20-€40. Membership €60-€220.*
Affiliated to the renowned New York club of the same name, this modern jazz joint mixes good local talent with

well-known, visiting performers from the UK and the US: Marcus Miller, Maceo Parker, Al Di Meola, Sarah Jane Morris and guitar wizard Charlie Hunter, and José James have all visited in the recent pas. Look out for the regular Sunday brunch events.

Plastic

San Babila & East *Viale Umbria 120 (02 733 996). Open midnight-5am Fri, Sat, occasional Thur; 8pm-2am Sun. Closed July, Aug. Admission €10-€20 incl 1 drink. No credit cards.*
At this enduringly trendy spot – possibly the best club in Milan – you can dance until late to an agreeable mix of sounds (electro, indie, rock, Italian trash, '80s pop). Although it draws a straight crowd, it's also a popular stop on Milan's gay scene, and a prime place at which to spot some of the city's loveliest drag queens. Dress to impress or you'll have no chance of making it past the bouncers.

Rocket

Porta Romana & South *Via Pezzotti 52 (02 8950 3509/www.therocket.it). Open 10pm-2.30am Tue-Sat. Closed Aug. Admission free. No credit cards.*
It's no longer the new kid on the block, but this DJ bar is still hot on everyone's lips. Its recipe for success is simple but surprisingly rare in Milan: entry is free, the mix of sounds is excellent, and the cocktails are top-notch.

Factfile

When to go
The low-lying Po valley is bound to the north by the Alps and to the south-west by the Appennines, which keeps all that moisture firmly where it is, right over Milan. This is the explanation for the notoriously thick fog banks that can bring traffic in the area around the city to a halt. Winter in many parts of Lombardy can be bitter, with winds zipping down from the Alps; Milan, though, is almost wind-free, which makes it feel milder. Snow is uncommon. Spring can be rainy but is quite short, quickly turning to summer, which tends to be muggy and mosquito-ridden. If you're coming in July or August, ensure your hotel has air-conditioning. September is a very pleasant month in Milan, but rain may intrude in late October and November.

Getting there & around
Aeroporto di Malpensa Somma Lombarda, 50km north-west of Milan (flight information 02 7485 2200/switchboard 02 74851/www.sea-aeroportimilano.it).

Aeroporto di Linate, Segrate, 7km east of Milan (flight information 02 7485 2200/switchboard 02 74851/www.sea-aeroportimilano.it)

From Malpensa Airport, the Malpensa Express train (199 151 152, 02 85111) runs at 27 and

57 minutes past each hour from 5.57am to 8.57pm (Sun 9.27pm) between the airport and Cadorna metro station.

The ATM bus 73 departs every 10 minutes from Linate Airport and San Babila metro station; travel time is 25 to 40 minutes, and tickets cost €1. Alternatively, Starfly (02 5858 7237) services leave every half-hour and link Linate airport and Stazione Centrale (5.05am-10.35pm from Linate; 5.35am-9.35pm from Stazione Centrale). Tickets cost €3.

Regular train services link Milan to major cities such as Venice, Turin and Bologna.

Tourist information
Via Marconi 1, Duomo & Centre (02 7252 4301/www.milanoinfo.eu). Open 9am-1pm, 2-6pm daily.

Milano Tourist, Piazza Duomo 19a, entrance via Silvio Pellico 6, Duomo & Centre (02 7740 4362). Open 9am-12.30pm, 1.30-6pm Mon-Sat; 9.30am-12.30pm, 1.30-4pm Sun.

Via Beltrami, at piazza Castello 1, Sforzesco & North (02 8058 0614/5). Open 9am-6pm Mon-Sat.

Internet
Internet points around town include FNAC (Via Torino, at via Palla 2, Duomo & Centre, 02 869 541).

Naples

For some, it's hard not to fall in love with Naples. It's ancient, yet somehow eternally youthful; tatty in places, even decrepit; stylish in others, without being austere or forbidding. Its inhabitants are among the warmest-hearted in Italy, its history is exciting, and as for the food – well, let's just say you won't go hungry.

Clockwise from the top:
View of Naples from
Castel Sant' Elmo;
Constantinopoli 104;
Duomo interior; Vespa on
Quartieri Spagnoli;
Constantinopoli 104.

Clockwise from the top:
View from Hotel Paradiso;
Constantinopoli 104 (3).

a sigh of relief that you're not caught up in it. The 74 rooms are airy and bright, many with a private terrace – the restaurant occupies a panoramic terrace of its own – and staff are welcoming and professional.

Hotel del Real Orto Botanico
Toledo & Sanita *Via Foria 192 (081 442 1528/ www.hotelrealortobotanico.it). €€€.*
As its name suggests, this hotel overlooks the botanical gardens, which means guests get to enjoy a fine view as well as valuable (and often rare) peace and quiet. It's a ten-minute walk from the Duomo, the Sanità and the Museo Archeologico Nazionale – on a rather chaotic (and sometimes hairy) road. Inside there's a relaxed atmosphere and nice touches like the lounge with its old-fashioned bar, all etched glass and dark wood panelling; the 36 rooms (of which four are equipped for visitors with disabilities) are coolly elegant and well-appointed. There are plenty of decent places to eat at in the vicinity.

Hotel Una
Port & University *Piazza Garibaldi 9/10 (081 563 6901/www.unahotels.it). €€€.*
The Una, part of a smart Florentine hotel chain, opened at the end of 2005 in a restored 19th-century building on the corner of piazza Garibaldi and corso Umberto I: it's an oasis of calm after the chaos outside, and decorated with light wood, lots of bare stone, pale green, Pompeiian red and Neapolitan motifs and prints. It's extremely comfortable and stylish, there's a lovely roof terrace on the sixth floor – enjoy the view of Vesuvius with your breakfast – and a bar-restaurant serves food all day. Service is polite and very friendly. This is a particularly welcome newcomer.

Miramare
Royal Naples *Via Nazario Sauro 24 (081 764 7589/ www.hotelmiramare.com). €€€€.*
The small, family-run Hotel Miramare was converted in 1944 from an aristocratic Liberty villa built in 1914. In the 1950s it sprang to fame when its restaurant and piano bar, the Shaker Club, drew top-name Italian and international singing stars for live performances. The place has a friendly, welcoming atmosphere and breakfast is served on a roof-garden terrace with breathtaking views over the bay – and hammocks. Rooms vary in size; it's worth investing in those with sea views. Guests get a 10% discount at nearby restaurants La Cantinella (see p150) and Il Posto Accanto.

Neapolis
Centro Storico *Via Francesco del Giudice 13 (081 442 0815/www.hotelneapolis.com). €€.*
Right in the heart of the Centro Storico, close to the buzz of piazza Bellini, this hotel has all the traditional services, plus a PC with free internet access in all 17 rooms. Staff are particularly friendly; room rates are competitive and guests have discounts at the adjoining restaurant, La Locanda del Grifo. What's more, three of the rooms – one double and two singles – can be used in conjunction as an independent flat. The windows here are soundproofed, which makes the hotel a welcome retreat, but its walls are a little on the thin side.

Eat

Food in Naples is pretty much sacred, with mealtimes thought and talked about for hours each and every week. Change the tried and trusted way of doing things at your peril – Neapolitans regard that as well-nigh a mortal sin. The good side of this culinary conservatism is that it's difficult to eat badly in this city (especially in comparison to, say, Rome or Venice), and the odds on eating fantastically well are good – though it's worth remembering that 'smart' is not always best: much of Naples's finest eating can be had in spit-and-sawdust *trattorie* and *osterie*.

> **"Food in Naples is pretty much sacred, with mealtimes thought and talked about for hours each and every week."**

Although a certain amount of contemporary and non-Italian cuisine is emerging in Naples, the traditional fare, as far as Neapolitans are concerned, still wins hands down. Local chefs have at their disposal a superb range of seasonal local ingredients, and the Slow Food movement and now even the Italian government promote independent, diverse, local food production. Specialities include the tiny, slightly pear-shaped tomato known as a *piénnolo* and the more famous San Marzano plum tomato called *pummarola*; some exquisite mozzarella; and, naturally, lemons, used in lemon-flower honey and limoncello.

The city is also renowned for its fish and its seafood: the local (as opposed to 'imported' from further along the coast) fresh clams, known as *vongole verace*, are only available in summer; this is also the season for *cozze* (mussels), and the most popular places to eat them are on piazza Sannazzaro in Mergellina or on via Colletta, near the law courts at Castel Capuano. Naples also credits itself as the birthplace of the pizza; certainly the city has developed pizza from the simplest food of the poor to a gourmet art form.

And then there's the liquid refreshment. In recent years, energetic young winemakers have been working wonders with grapes like Aglianico (a red that can hold its own with Piedmont's august Nebbiolo) and Falanghina (the most popular white), as well as rediscovering local varieties such as Piedirosso and Gragnano.

Antica Pizzeria Del Borgo Orefici

Port & University *Via Luigi Palmieri 13 (081 552 0996). Open noon-2.30pm, 7-10pm Mon-Sat. Closed Aug. €. No credit cards. Pizzeria.*

This simple pizzeria is tucked away on a side street in the old goldsmith's zone (now pedestrianised and gentrified) and opposite the imposing University building on the corner with via Mezzacannone. It serves excellent pizzas: try the *friarelli e salsiccia* (sausage and local greens) or something from the great range of fresh fish. Dishes are served at tables located outside and in.

La Bersagliera

Royal Naples *Borgo Marinaro 10-11 (081 764 6016/www.labersagliera.it). Open 12.30-2.30pm, 7.30pm-midnight Mon, Wed-Sun. Closed 2wks Jan. €€€. Traditional Italian.*

Founded in 1919, this is a little jewel of the Belle Epoque, filled with sepia photos of former employees and enjoying a fine view of the harbour; it attracts a sophisticated clientele. The fish-based cuisine is generally of a high standard: try their speciality mussel and clam soup, the *taglierini alla Bersagliera* (fine ribbon pasta with baby octopus, tomato and olives) or the *orata* (sea bream) baked in a salt crust.

"Donnanna is beside the ghostly Palazzo Sant'Anna, where it's rumoured Queen Joanna seduced muscle-bound fishermen and then drowned them.'

La Cantina di Sica

Vomero *Via Bernini 17 (081 556 7520). Open 12.30-3.30pm, 7.30pm-midnight Tue-Sun. Closed 2wks Aug. €€. Trattoria.*

Come here for good, traditional dishes such as *ziti alla genovese* (pasta with very oniony mince sauce) or *tubettoni con gamberi e zucchine* (pasta with prawns and courgettes), at slightly higher prices than the average trattoria. There's an interesting choice of fresh fish and meat and delicious *contorni*: try the *parmigiano di peperoni* (layers of cooked peppers and white sauce). The place has an upmarket feel, there's an excellent wine list, and the bar downstairs hosts jazz or Neapolitan folk music.

La Cantinella

Royal Naples *Via Cuma 42, Lungomare Santa Lucia (081 764 8684/www.lacantinella.it). Open 12.30-3pm, 7.30pm-midnight Mon-Sat. Closed 2wks Aug. €€€€. Traditional Italian.*

One of Naples's most renowned restaurants. The menu includes dishes such as *cannelloni con ricotta e ortiche servito su ragù* (ricotta and nettle canelloni with classic beef and tomato sauce) or *tagliolini al buon umore* (pasta with a sauce of crayfish, clam and 'good cheer'), as well as caviar, *bistecca alla fiorentina* (T-bone steaks) and lobster; the set menus are worth investigating. La Cantinella is a tad dated in its decor, but there's a cigar and piano bar alongside that stays open into the wee small hours.

Coco Loco

Chiaia to Posillipo *Piazza Giulio Rodinò 31 (081 415 482). Open 8-11pm Mon-Sat. €€€. Modern Italian.*

The innovative cuisine served here is about as far from mama's traditional cooking as Neapolitan restaurants are prepared to venture. With candlelit outdoor eating in a small pedestrianised square off via Filangieri, and convivial seating indoors, Coco Loco chiefly serves as an evening *ritrovo* (hangout) for discerning locals, who roll up any time after 9.30pm. The cuisine is subtle and innovative, including dishes like *aragosta e gamberi alla catalana* (lobster and prawn salad with a hint of citrus fruit), designed by master chef Diego Nuzzo to get the taste buds tingling with pleasure. Service is courteous and efficient without being oppressive.

Donnanna

Chiaia to Posillipo *Via Posillipo 16C, between Mergellina & Posillipo (081 769 0920/www.sire ricevimenti.it). Open 12.30-3pm Sun; 12.30-3pm, 7.30-11pm Tue-Sat. €€€. Modern Italian.*

This stylish, abundantly wood-panelled restaurant is situated on the beach by the Bagni Elena, with a view of mount Vesuvius and beside the ghostly Palazzo Sant'Anna, where it's rumoured Queen Joanna seduced muscle-bound fishermen and then drowned them. Local art students created the Tiepolo-inspired Pulcinella frescoes. The owners, events organisers Sire, are responsible for state banquets, so everything here is hushed and polished; ingredients are the finest money can buy – and organic. Typical fare is *tonarelli* pasta with *cicala di mare* (a crustacean), tomatoes and basil-scented oil or langoustines in *grano saraceno* (buckwheat) tempura. Desserts are exciting: Schweppes tonic and red wine sorbet and orange tart with chocolate mousse. Check ahead, as it's often closed for private functions.

Da Michele

Port & University *Via Sersale 1 (081 553 9204). Open 10am-midnight Mon-Sat. Closed 3wks Aug. €. No credit cards. Pizzeria.*

You don't get much more minimalist than this traditional pizzeria: just large marble tables, two types of pizza (margherita or marinara), and a drinks menu that has only beer, Coca-Cola and water. But boy, are the pizzas good – delicious, among the very best in Naples – and enormous, and unbelievably low priced. Service is friendly and fast; take a number at the door before joining the inevitable queue and marvel at the theatrical pizzaiolo, staff and punters while you wait.

Clockwise from top:
La Bersagliera;
Trattoria San
Ferdinando (3).

This is one of Italy's largest and most artistically rich museums. It's housed in an 18th-century palazzo that was variously a receptacle for the royal collections, the main seat of the court and a royal holiday home. Allow at least half a day to visit, for the walls display as fine a collection of paintings and sculpture as you could hope for; a veritable Who's Who of Italian art – Raphael, Masaccio, Botticelli, Titian, Bellini, Correggio, Caravaggio, Artemesia Gentileschi and more. It's more a case of who isn't here than who is. There's also a fine selection of works by non-Italian artists including El Greco, Brueghel and even Andy Warhol.

VOMERO

Look up from almost any vantage point in central Naples and you'll see two of the city's flagship monuments: the Castel Sant'Elmo and San Martino monastery, perched on Vomero hill. This area feels almost like a city in its own right – and, compared to central Naples, its streets are cleaner and a degree or two cooler. At the heart of the district is diamond-shaped piazza Vanvitelli, whose pavement cafés cater to well-heeled residents and epitomise Vomero's pan-European, middle-class character. If you fancy a taste of this high life, take the train: three of Naples's four funicular railways lead up here.

"For shoppers, Naples is a breath of fresh air. There's a fantastic selection of family-run shops selling clothes, shoes, leather goods and homeware."

Certosa-Museo di San Martino
Largo San Martino 5 (081 558 6408). Open 8.30am-7.30pm Mon, Tue, Thur-Sun (ticket office closes 1hr earlier). Admission (includes Castel Sant'Elmo) €6; audioguide €4. No credit cards.
This Carthusian monastery was founded in 1325, although its present appearance is the result of much reworking at the end of the 16th century. Thanks to its state-of-the art visitor facilities, pleasing exhibits in airy rooms and the added bonus of access to the monastery's terraced gardens with sweeping views over the Naples waterfront, the Certosa has leapt up the shortlist of must-visits. The church's interior contains an excellent (and well labelled) selection of Neapolitan painting and sculpture, and the Museo dell'Opera (art gallery) is beautifully laid out around the main cloister. There are splendid maps and landscape paintings, a section devoted to Nativity scenes, and displays on theatre, shipping and, in the former pharmacy, glassware and porcelain.

CHIAIA

When the 19th century's Romantic poets and grand tourists mentioned Naples, they weren't referring to the crowded, disease-ridden centre of the city. No, they usually meant Chiaia, which today as then is wealthier, quieter and more salubrious than the old town. From Chiaia, the city's topography can be seen to splendid effect: the great sweep of the bay, Capri reclining on the horizon, Vesuvius slumbering to the south. Mergellina harbour, to the west, still has a small fishing community among the smart yachts, and some of the narrowest and oldest *vicoli* (alleys) can be found between piazza Amedeo and the Villa Comunale, though they're filled today with designer boutiques. The long seafront stroll from Santa Lucia to Mergellina is a classic Sunday walk.

Grotta di Seiano
Dicesa Gaiola 36, Discesa Coroglio (081 230 1030). Open by reservation only 9.30-11.15am Mon-Sat. Closed Aug. Admission free.
This tunnel, which was the private entrance to the ornate Villa Pausilypon, was built in the first century AD. It was strengthened in 1840 by a series of load-bearing arches, and stretches for 770m along the coast. En route, galleries provide magnificent views over the small Trentaremi Bay, named after the rowing boats the Romans used to unload stores. The fragile cliff into which the tunnel was bored is prone to landslides, and over the years access to the Grotta has been irregular, but for now it is open regularly.

SHOP

For shoppers, Naples is a breath of fresh air. Yes, major brands have footholds here, but there's also a fantastic selection of family-run shops selling clothes, shoes, leather goods and homeware that you might not find in other parts of Italy. You'll get better value for money, and more choice, in smaller shops and markets than in the big department stores. For designer gear, go to Chiaia; if you're on a tight budget, via Toledo, corso Umberto or the Centro Storico are bursting with bargains, especially during the sales in January/February and in July/August; for old-world elegance, take a turn around the Galleria Umberto I, or head for via San Biagio dei Librai in the Port and University area, and the streets west of Chiaia's piazza dei Martiri; and for the famous *presepi*, traditional Neapolitan Christmas cribs, visit via San Gregorio Armeno in the Centro Storico in December or, in fact, throughout the year. The city's largely pedestrianised main street, Spaccanapoli, is packed with shops, including musical instrument stores and bookshops.

Unfortunatetly, Naples has a reputation for petty crime, so shoppers should take care of their personal belongings.

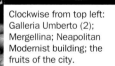

Clockwise from top left: Galleria Umberto (2); Mergellina; Neapolitan Modernist building; the fruits of the city.

Antiche Delizie

Via Toledo *Via Pasquale Scura 14 (081 551 3088).
Open 7am-9pm Mon-Sat; 7am-2pm Sun.*
Purveyor of the best mozzarella in town and a mouth-watering selection of meat, cheese and preserves. Try the aubergine antipasti, *caprignetti* (soft goat's cheese in herbs) and cheese with *tartufo* (truffles). There's also a range of local wines, and pasta dishes (made on the premises) to take away. It's not cheap, but it is friendly and well run.

Chi Cerca Trova

Chiaia *Via G Fiorelli 3 (081 764 7592). Open 4-8pm
Mon; 10am-2pm, 4-8pm Tue-Sat. Closed 3wks Aug.*
This Neapolitan institution is still going strong after two decades. The name roughly translates as 'seek and you'll find', which is what shopping here is all about. The racks in the basement seem to go on for miles, and you can rummage for hours. Prices start at €5. Eccentric owner Giuseppe Violante (who will probably be sitting behind the cash register) sometimes offers his clients coffees and rum baba.

Culti Spa Café

Chiaia *Via Carlo Poerio 47-47B (081 764 4619/
www.culti.it). Open 10am-10pm daily.*
Italians know that Naples is fast becoming the destination city of cool, and as if to reinforce the point, Alessandro Agrati, owner of Milan's concept store Habits Culti, has opened a second branch here. It stocks supremely swish interior design items and furnishings, as well as textiles, perfumery, art and flowers. There's also a sleek spa and a café-restaurant (Open 10am-1am daily).

Fratelli Tramontano

Royal Naples *Via Chiaia 142-143 (081 414 837/
www.aldotramontano.it). Open 10am-1.30pm, 4-8pm
Mon-Sat. Closed 2wks Aug.*
The legacy of more than a century of Neapolitan craftsmanship is to be found in the superb quality handmade leather goods displayed here: handbags and luggage, shoes, wallets, belts and other accessories. Marcello Mastroianni and Woody Allen are among the stars who have apparently bought items here.

Gambardella

Centro Storico *Largo Corpo di Napoli 3, nr via Nilo
(081 552 1333). Open 9am-7pm Mon-Fri; 9am-1.30pm
Sat. Closed 2wks Aug.*
This extravagant paper shop has to floor-to-ceiling displays of wrapping paper, boxes, cards, stationery and ribbons, mostly handmade. There are 500 paper creations, many of them made on site.

Gay Odin

Via Toledo *Via Toledo 214 (081 551 3491/www.gay-
odin.it). Open 9.30am-8pm Mon-Sat; 10am-2pm Sun.
Closed 2wks Aug.*
These shops are heaven for chocoholics, though they also sell a wide range of other confectionery. The small factory at via Vetriera 12 is kitted out with charming old chocolate-making equipment and is open to the public: the production line is something Willy Wonka would feel perfectly at home with.

Iermano Antiquities

Chiaia *Via Domenico Morelli 30 (081 764 3913).
Open 10am-1.30pm, 4-8pm Mon-Sat. Closed Aug &
Mon am in winter. No credit cards.*
The city seems to have antique shops around pretty well every corner, but many of the best known are to be found around piazza dei Martiri in Chiaia. Iermano has a wealth of local and European antiques, with a special emphasis on 18th- and 19th-century pieces.

Marinella

Chiaia *Riviera di Chiaia 287A (081 764 4214/
www.marinellanapoli.it). Open 7am-1.30pm, 3.30-
8pm Mon-Sat. Closed 2wks Aug.*
Although this shop is tiny, it's a Naples institution. It was founded in 1914 by Eugenio Marinella, and embodies his belief that 'it is the sum of all the small details that makes a gentleman elegant'. Mainly using British fabrics, the shop has been frequented over the years by the likes of Aristotle Onassis, Luchino Visconti and Giovanni Agnelli. Prince Charles apparently gets made-to-measure ties here.

Maxi Ho

Chiaia *Via Nisco 20 bis (081 414 721/www.maxiho.it).
Open 10am-1.30pm, 4.30-8pm Mon-Sat. Closed 2wks Aug.*
This unfortunately named shop is the Holy Grail for stylish Neapolitans: every well-dressed man and woman in the city loves it. Brands in stock include Marni, Fendi, Roberto Cavalli, D&G and Balenciaga. Both the men's and women's stores have recently been refurbished.

Merolla e del'Ero

Chiaia *Via Calabritto 20 (081 764 3012). Open 10am-
1.30pm, 4.30-8pm Mon-Sat. Closed Aug.*
It's a rare thing indeed to see a Neapolitan businessman who isn't wearing a gorgeous shirt. Many of those businessmen place their orders here, where they peruse a divine range of colours and diverse fabrics. There's also a large selection of buttons to choose from, running from the plain to the fancy (such as mother-of-pearl fastenings).

ARTS

Naples has a busy cultural calendar. Artists of all stripes come to perform or exhibit here, but there's also strong support for the local artforms, although painters complain that it's difficult to wean the locals from oil paintings of fishermen at Santa Lucia and sunsets over Capri. The 18th-century Teatro Mercadante has been revamped as the city's new showcase for traditional Neapolitan theatre and avant-garde productions, and in city-centre clubs, local musicians fuse the latest sounds with Neapolitan roots.

MADRe

Centro Storico *Via Settembrini 79 (081 1931
3016/www.museomadre.it). Open 10am-9pm Mon,
Wed, Thur, Sun; 10am-midnight Fri, Sat. (Ticket office
closes 1hr earlier.) Admission €7; Monday free. No
credit cards.*

The Museo d'Arte Contemporanea Donna Regina Napoli occupies a former public administration building, and is one of the city's hottest new art spaces. The permanent collection includes Damien Hirst, Jeff Koons, Anish Kapoor and Rebecca, as well as Italian artists such as Lucio Fontana and local-born Francesco Clemente. Upper floors are given over to temporary shows, there's a new bar/restaurant in one of the internal courtyards.

PAN

Centro Storico *Via dei Mille 60 (081 795 8605/ www.palazzoartinapoli.net). Open 9.30am-7.30pm Mon, Wed-Sat; 9.30am-2.30pm Sun. Admission €5. No credit cards.*
Like the MADRe (*see above*), the Palazzo dei Arti Napoli opened in 2005, but with a slightly different proposition: it has no permanent collection, but instead describes itself as a 'centre for arts and documentation'. An archive on the fourth floor has catalogues and pictures of contemporary art activity in Naples stretching back over the last few decades.. There are frequent new exhibitions (often drawn from the collection of other Neapolitan galleries), as well as film screenings, lectures and book presentations; exhibitors have included Peter Greenaway and Lou Reed.

Teatro San Carlo

Royal Naples *Via San Carlo 98F (081 797 2412/ www.teatrosancarlo.it). Open Box office 10am-7pm Tue-Sun; 1hr before performances. Guided tours 9am-7pm daily. Closed Aug.*
Second in prestige only to Milan's La Scala, the San Carlo is lavishly decorated, with acres of red velvet and intricate gilded stucco moulding, plus an unusual revolving clock in the vault of the proscenium arch. As well as opera, the San Carlo also has a ballet and an orchestral music season; in summer, the music and ballet move to outdoor venues.

NIGHTLIFE

The fun tends to start late in Naples, with venues filling up around midnight. In fact, you may not need to go to a club, as plenty of action goes on in the open squares and alleyways, with groups gathering in the Centro Storico's piazza Santa Maria La Nova, piazza Bellini and via Cisterna Dell'Olio to enjoy a beer. The trendiest clubs are around posh Chiaia and Mergellina, whose narrow streets become catwalks of fashion and style.

Farinella

Chiaia *Via Alabardieri 10 (081 423 8455). Open 1pm-1am daily. Closed 2 wks Aug.*
One of the newer spots is Farinella – a restaurant and wine bar combo in a large former cinema. The after-dark noise from the overspill of patrons into the street prompted authorities to shut it down for a few weeks at the end of 2005 (along with nearby Bar 66 and Chandelier), but it's now back in business, with DJs spinning the coolest sounds in town and occasional live music performances.

S'move

Chiaia *Vico dei Sospiri 10 (081 764 5813/www.smove-lab.net. Open last 2wks June, July 8pm-4am daily. Sept-mid June noon-2am Mon-Sat. Closed Aug.*
The smartest place in this part of town, S'move boasts upmarket decor (it's a bit like walking into an extremely posh furniture shop) and a buzzy, friendly atmosphere. The area's beautiful things make up most of the clientele, but it somehow manages to be refreshingly unsnobbish. There's no dancefloor as such, but the careful selection of music – from Latin to house to techno – encourages even the glacially cool to shake a limb or two. The management also runs the super-cool Nabilah beach venue in the summer.

Factfile

When to go
The Maggio dei Monumenti open house season (which runs from late April to early June; www.comune.napoli.it) is such a treat, you should seriously consider visiting at this time. Weather-wise, July and August can be oppressively hot and humid; most pleasant are March, April and September.

Getting there
Aereoporto Internazionale di Napoli (Capodichino) is 7km or 10mins from Stazione Centrale rail station. From the airport, Alibus runs a direct bus to Stazione Centrale and piazza Municipio (near the ferry port). Tickets cost €3.

Getting around
A single ticket, allowing up to three trips on all metropolitan transport – including one trip only on the underground and funiculars – costs €1 and is valid for 90 minutes. A 24hr ticket for unlimited travel on all metropolitan public transport costs €3 Mon-Fri and €2.50 Sat and Sun. Tickets must be bought at a newsstand, *tabacchi* or ticket machine before boarding any transport.

Tourist information
Azienda Autonoma di Soggiorno Cura e Turismo di Napoli Via San Carlo 9, Royal Naples (081 402 394/www.inaples.it). Open Apr-Oct 9.30am-2pm, 3-7pm Mon-Sat; 9am-2pm Sun. Nov-Mar 9am-1.30pm, 4.30-6.30pm Mon-Sat; 9am-1.30pm Sun.

Internet
Internet Bar Piazza Bellini 74, Centro Storico (081 295 237). Open 10am-2am daily. Rates €3/hr.

Clockwise from top left:
Teatro Massimo; mosaic
of Neptune; Cattedrale
di Palermo; back-street
Palermo; Cattedrale
di Palermo.

Palermo

As vital and intense as any Coppola epic, the capital of Sicily makes
other Italian cities feel positively sleepy. Its vibrancy lies in a collision
of people and ideas spanning 3,000 years: everyone from marauding
Vandals to Romans and Normans have left their mark here. But, while
the past is celebrated, there's a modern edginess too – so if you're
keen to mix opera with late-night gigs, or Palatine churches with
cutting-edge art, you've picked the right place.

Neve all'Alloro, 091 616 0796, www.parco
tomasi.it), a bar, library and cultural centre that's
dedicated to the city's most famous author.

Addaura Reef

Addaura 10km N of Palermo *Lungomare
Cristoforo Colombo 3021/3043 (091 684
0171/www.addaurareef.it). Open Beach
9am-6pm. Bar June-Sept 7pm-late. €€. Bar.*
Cool cocktails meet macho diving at this coastal diving bar,
2km from Mondello. By day, its bronzed clientele dive,
snorkel or sprawl across the sundecks; by night, the place
transforms into an Ibiza-style bar with DJ sets, live concerts,
an azure swimming pool and candlelit corners. Thai
massage and shiatsu are also on offer.

Antica Focacceria San Francesco

La Kalsa *Via A Paternostro 58 (091 320 264/
www.afsf.it). Open 11am-11.30pm Mon, Wed-Sun.
€. Traditional Sicilian.*
This 19th-century institution is one of the city's best 'fast
food' outlets, serving low-cost street food including *arancine*
(stuffed rice balls) and *focaccia maritata* (bread with spleen
and fresh ricotta). The highlight is the art nouveau interior,
featuring burnt orange walls, retro photographs, huge
ovens and a wrought-iron balcony.

Bar Alba

Libertà, 2km N of Vucciria *Piazza Don Bosco 7
(091 130 9016/www.baralba.it). Open Summer 7am-
midnight Tue-Sun. Winter 7am-11pm Tue-Sun. €.
Pasticceria/rosticceria.*
This Aladdin's cave of Sicilian treats is an essential stop-
off if you're hitting the shops on nearby via Libertà. There's
a good savoury selection, but it's the sweet tooth that is best
catered for: shelves groan with *frutta martorana* (marzipan
shaped into fruit and veg) and the bar's trademark *cassata*
(sponge cake with ricotta, chocolate and candied fruit). A
great place to buy some gifts to take home.

Caffè del Kássaro

Albergheria *Via Vittorio Emanuele 390 (334 368
1260). Open noon-3pm. No credit cards. €. Trattoria.*
Tucked away down a quiet back street, this simple trattoria
is a real find for the cash-strapped diner. Students and arty
types savour tasty salads and pizza amid cool stone walls
and rickety tables. Dig into a plate of *spaghetti al pesce* and
repair to the bar for an espresso with the kick of a mule.

La Cuba

5km N of Quattro Canti *Viale Francesco Scaduto,
Villa Sperlinga (091 309 201/www.lacuba.com). Open
5pm-midnight Mon-Sat; noon-midnight Sun. €€€.
Brasserie/wine bar.*
Set in a leafy garden, this lounge bar is a magnet for the
city's beautiful people. The brasserie turns out decent
snacks and salads alongside ravioli, hamburgers and ribeye
steaks. Turn up at around 10pm, take a seat in the
glasshouse and watch stick-thin Palermitani pick at plates
of aperitivi until late. Tasty brunches are also on offer on
Sundays, and afternoon teas are available every day.

Ferro

Quattro Canti *Piazza San Onofrio 42 (091 586 049).
Open 8pm-midnight Mon-Sat. €€€. Modern Sicilian.*
Eating in this restaurant – essentially a bare, white box
illuminated by stark bulbs – is akin to dining inside a giant
piece of modern art. Given the decor it's no surprise that the
cuisine has a modern slant too: try the fillet of beef with figs
and prosciutto, or the *millefoglie* of swordfish and marrow.
Handily, you're just ten paces from Coso Café, a funky bar
with excellent live bands.

I Grilli

Vucciria *Largo Cavalieri di Malta 2 (091 334 130/
www.igrillirestaurant.it). Open 8-10.30pm Tue-Sun.
€€€. Traditional Sicilian.*
Ignore the square's touristy Nabucco restaurant and hunt
out the anonymous-looking door that leads to this first-floor
establishment. Behind it lies a beautiful eaterie, decorated
with candles and soothing hues. Flavours are fresh and
sharp, and the menu's highlights include grilled squid, fillet
of swordfish and own-made pasta: the black fettuccine with
pesto and crabmeat is a must. After dinner, step across the
square for a drink at the hip I Grilli Giù.

> "By day, the bronzed
> clientele dive, snorkel or
> sunbathe; by night, the
> place transforms into
> an Ibiza-style bar."

Kursaal Kalhesa

La Kalsa *Foro Umberto I 21 (091 616 7630/
www.kursaalkalhesa.it). Open 11.30am-1.30am
Tue-Sat; 11am-6pm Sun. Meals served summer
1-3.30pm, 8-11.30pm; winter 8.30pm-midnight.
€€€. Restaurant/bar.*
This mixed-used space is an excellent place in which to plan
your stay in Sicily. Hidden inside the medieval city wall, its
vaults host a horseshoe bar, bookshop, internet kiosk and
tourist information centre. The restaurant, situated in a
courtyard in summer, serves North African specialities such
as *brik tunisino* (ravioli) to a crowd of earnest cognoscenti.

Osteria dei Vespri

La Kalsa *Piazza Croce dei Vespri 6 (091 617 1631/
www.osteriadeivespri.it). Open 1-3.30pm, 8-11.30pm
Mon-Sat. €€€€. Modern Italian.*
Classic Sicilian cooking meets nouvelle cuisine at this
upmarket restaurant – an elegant spot in which to dine, with
its candlelit tables glimmering under the stars in a quiet
piazza. The menu is a tad pretentious, with traditional
dishes such as swordfish and braised beef accompanied by
such fripperies as scent of cedar and courgette mousse. The
ravenous should beware: dishes are super-stylish but barely
visible to the naked eye. Booking advised.

Top to bottom: Mercure; Grand Hotel et Des Palmes; Hotel Letizia.

Clockwise from top:
Antica Focacceria San
Francesco; *Cannoli
siciliani*; Vucciria market.

Panificio Graziano

Libertà, 2km from Vucciria *Via del Granatiere 11/13 (091 625 4800). Open 7am-9pm. €. No credit cards. Pizzeria.*
This tiny takeaway is a magnet for young Palermitani – and once you've sampled its excellent pizza rustica, *arancine con carne* (rice balls with meat) or tabouleh, you'll understand why. Inside is reassuringly frenetic, as cooks heft mattress-size slabs of pizza about the place at speed. A few doors up is its arty sister café, Caffeteria Graziano.

Trattoria Da Pino

Vucciria *Via Dello Spezio 6 (09 1867 2380). Open 12.30-3.30pm daily. €€. No credit cards. Osteria.*
If you're keen on having an authentic dining experience and can muster a few words of Italian, this is the place in which to take the plunge. This lively osteria feels more like a working men's club: you'll be sharing your table with jostling locals, and the service is gruff, but you'll emerge buoyed by a huge sense of achievement. Dishes are typical Sicilian and include spaghetti with anchovies and *spiedini alla siciliana* (skewers of marinated veal); wine is served from a bubbling water dispenser.

Zia Pina

Vucciria *Via Cassari 65 (333 138 1318). Open noon-3pm daily. €€. No credit cards. Trattoria.*
This rustic eaterie is nothing much to look at – a cantina-style tiled interior that sports fading Sicilian scenes – but the freshest grilled fish and buzzy street atmosphere make for an enticing combination. Grab a wonky table outside and choose from numerous *alla griglia* options, including kebabs, *gamberi*, calamari and tuna.

Explore

SIGHTS

Palermo was a highlight of the Grand Tour, as even the shortest stroll will attest. Its twin cultural peaks come courtesy of the Normans (who held sway from the 11th to the 13th century) and the rulers, aristocracy and religious orders of the 16th to 18th centuries, who ushered in Baroque churches, monasteries and the occasional racy statue.

Your best reference point when exploring Palermo is the Quattro Canti. The crossroads at the centre of the city, it sits amid the four quarters of Albergheria, Il Capo, Vucciria and La Kalsa – each of which has its own distinctive atmosphere. To the north, beyond the periphery of the *centro storico* and about a 15-minute walk from the Quattro Canti, is a distinctly more modern grid of streets, home to the shopping district and major theatres.

Most sights are within easy walking distance, but if the heat proves too much, City Sightseeing buses (all stopping at Teatro Politeama) take in suburban attractions such as the Castello della Zisa (a spectacular Norman summer residence) and the Catacombe dei Cappuccini.

QUATTRO CANTI

Make sure you look skywards at this 17th-century crossroads: towering sculptures on its four corners, designed by Giulio Lasso and Mariano Smiriglio, depict the four seasons, along with the city's sovereigns and saints. The must-see fountain in piazza Pretoria lies a few paces southeast: the work of Tuscan architects Camilliani and Naccherini, its naked pagan deities have earned it the nickname Fontana delle Vergogne (Fountain of Shame). Overlooking the fountain is the gleaming Palazzo Pretorio, the seat of the city council. Some rooms are open to the public, so do try to catch a glimpse of the assembly room's 16th-century frescoes if you get the chance.

San Cataldo

Piazza Bellini (091 616 1692). Open 9am-3.30pm Mon-Fri; 9am-12.30pm Sat; 9am-1pm hols. Admission €1.
If the splendour of La Martorana (*below*) proves too much, its neighbour offers a scrubbed down alternative. This 12th-century Norman chapel, built by the Grand Chancellor to William I, is completely unadorned barring a fine mosaic floor. A good crowd-free address.

Santa Maria dell'Ammiraglio (La Martorana)

Piazza Bellini (091 616 1692). Open Summer 8am-1pm, 3.30-5.30pm Mon-Sat; 8.30am-1pm Sun. Winter 8am-1pm, 3.30-5pm Mon-Sat; 8.30am-1pm Sun.
If you only set foot in one church in the city centre, make it this one. Overlooking piazza Bellini, Palermo's Greek Orthodox cathedral dates back to 1143. A glittering collection of 12th-century mosaics draws a steady stream of tourists, with the cupola's Jesus and four angels proving the biggest crowd-puller. A good place to ponder Palermo's bizarre melding of Baroque and Byzantine.

LA KALSA & AROUND

A short walk from the Stazione Centrale, and with the added incentive of there being plenty of good restaurants and bars close at hand, La Kalsa's attractions include the Villa Giulia, a beautiful park that's popular with amorous teenagers, and the Galleria Regionale della Sicilia (via Alloro 4), with paintings and sculptures from the 12th to 17th centuries. Works on display include a virgin and child triptych by Mabuse and an unnerving 15th-century fresco, the *Triumph of Death*. Other hidden gems include Palazzo Mirto on via Merlo, with its riot of 18th- and 19th-century furnishings, bequeathed by Palermo's aristocracy, and the Oratorio di San Lorenzo on via dell'Immacolatella, adorned with a Baroque frenzy of stuccoed scenes by Giacomo Serpotta.

Museo Internazionale delle Marionette Antonio Pasqualino – Opera dei Pupi

Via Butera 1 (091 132 8060/www.museomarionette palermo.it). Open 9am-1pm, 3.30-6.30pm Mon-Fri; 9am-1pm Sat, Sun. Admission €5, €3 reductions. No credit cards.

Forget Punch and Judy: this is a world of swashbuckling knights, fearsome dragons and gory crimes of passion. This excellent museum and theatre takes you from puppetry's Chinese and Indian origins to the modern day. You can also catch shows at Teatro Carlo Magno (via Collegio di Maria, www.mancusopupi.it) and Cuticchio Mimmo (via Bara all'Olivella, 95, www.figlidartecuticchio.com).

Orto Botanico

Via Abr. Lincoln (091 623 8241/www.ortobotanico. palermo.it). Open Apr-Oct 9am-6pm Mon-Sat. Nov-Mar 9am-5pm Mon-Sat; 9am-2pm Sun & hols. Admission €4; €2 reductions. No credit cards.

The botanic garden dates from the 19th century and boasts 25 acres of exotic species – from palms and water lilies to giant banyan trees. It's founded on ambitious principles: zones are laid out according to Linnaean and Engler taxonomy systems, but poor labelling makes it difficult to distinguish your succulents from your rusty figs. Man-made elements such as the neoclassical gymnasium and well-tended glasshouses are saving graces.

Lo Spasimo

Via dello Spasimo 35 (091 616 1486). Open 9am-11pm daily. Admission free.

An edifying programme of cinema, exhibitions, classical music and jazz is on offer at this restored church complex. The roofless 16th-century Santa Maria dello Spasimo forms the hub, creating an atmospheric performance space complete with a huge tree where the pews once stood. There's a tranquil garden too.

VUCCIRIA & AROUND

Labyrinthine alleys and a smattering of ruined buildings – the still lingering relics of the Allied bombing campaign of 1943 – help to make this Palermo's most atmospheric quarter. The small market, centring on piazza Caracciolo, dates back to the 12th century and is the best-known in the city. Don't miss the witty graffiti in piazza del Garrafello, where crumbling façades have been spray painted with logos, the Baroque Chiesa di San Domenico (piazza San Domenico) and Serpotta's outstanding stuccoes in the Oratorio del Rosario on via dei Bambinai.

Museo Archeologico

Piazza Olivella 24 (091 611 6805). Open 8.30am-6.45pm Mon-Sat; 8.30am-1.45pm Sun & hols. Admission €4.50; €2 reductions. No credit cards.

Travel from ancient Egypt to the dog days of the Roman Empire at this well-stocked museum, which explores art and civilisation in western Sicily through sarcophagi, ceramics, tiny bronze animals and suits of armour. The

16th-century building, formerly a convent, is a marvel in itself: designed by Antonio Muttone, it features two leafy cloisters dotted with anchors and Hellenistic sculpture. Don't miss the Roman mosaics on the second floor.

ALBERGHERIA & AROUND

Home to the university, this student quarter has drawn immigrant communities for centuries, and is popular with Africans, Bangladeshis and Sri Lankans today. The main attraction is Ballarò market: arguably the liveliest in town, it packs the streets around piazza Ballarò with baskets of snails, vats of anchovies and sardines and acres of fruit and veg. Those seeking better-than-average holiday snaps should seek out the rooftop of Torre di San Nicolò (via N Nasi) or the bell tower at La Chiesa Parrocchia San Giuseppe Cafasso (via Benedettini). And for a petrifying vision of hell, check out the nave fresco in Chiesa del Gesù (piazza Casa Professa): the first Jesuit-built church in Sicily boasts a depiction of eternal damnation that would give James Joyce a run for his money.

Chiesa e Chiostro di San Giovanni degli Eremiti

Via dei Benedettini (091 651 5019). Open 9am-7pm Mon-Sat; 9am-1pm Sun & hols. Admission €6; €3 reductions. No credit cards.

This site's numerous occupants have included a mosque, a Benedictine monastery and, finally, a 12th-century church – sporting five distinctive if incongruous red Arabian domes. The garden is the highlight; a verdant enclave of lemon trees and jasmine blossom.

Palazzo dei Normanni & Palatine Chapel

Piazza del Parlamento (091 626 2833/www.ars.sicilia. it). Open 8.30am-5pm Mon-Sat; 8.30am-12.30pm Sun & hols. Admission €6; €4 reductions. No credit cards.

This magnificent palace complex is the history of Palermo in a nutshell. It started life as a Punic fortress – you can still visit the subterranean blocks of a fifth-century city wall – before successive occupations by Byzantines, Arabs, Normans and Bourbons. The 12th-century Palatine Chapel remains the undisputed star, thanks to its dazzling gilded interior and exquisite mosaics depicting Christ and scenes from the Old Testament. The palace itself is now the seat of Sicily's regional assembly.

IL CAPO & AROUND

Aside from the bustling market on via Beati Paoli and via Porta Carini, this is the most sedate *centro storico* quarter. The leafy piazza del Monte is a good place to relax in.

Cattedrale di Palermo

Corso Vittorio Emanuele (091 334 373/www.cattedrale. palermo.it). Open 7am-7pm daily. Admission free.

This 12th-century Norman cathedral presents a jarring amalgam of features: the exterior sprouted a Baroque dome in the 18th century, and a vigorous recasting added chapels and barrel vaulting to the interior. Look out for four giant silver urns on the north side, containing relics of Palermo's four patron saints, and the Egyptian sarcophagi containing the bones of Henry VI and Frederick II.

Teatro Massimo
Piazza G Verdi (06 4807 8400/www.teatro massimo.it. Open Guided tours 10am-3pm Tue-Sun. Admission Guided tours €5; €3 reductions.
Designed by Giovan Battista Basile, this refurbished 19th-century opera house boasts one of the largest stages in Europe and is one of the cultural gems on the island. Fans of Francis Ford Coppola will recognise the neoclassical exterior from *Godfather III*, and the Liberty-style auditorium is quite extraordinary, from its rich red seats and gilded boxes up to Rocco Lentini's painted cupola of *putti* (cupids) winging towards the heavens. Don't forget to test the eerie acoustics of the Pompeian Room on the guided tour. In summer, certain performances are held at the Teatro di Verdura (viale del Fante 70b, 091 605 3353).

BEYOND THE CENTRE

If you're heading north out of the city, stop by the Albero Falcone on via Notarbartolo. The tree stands outside the former home of Giovanni Falcone, a crusading investigative magistrate blown up by a Mafia bomb in 1992 along with his wife and three bodyguards. It's now an anti-Mafia shrine, festooned with scribbled hopes and dreams. Two nearby parks are also worth a look: the peaceful Giardino Inglese, laid out in an informal English style, and Villa Trabia, home to an impressive 18th-century country house.

Elsewhere, the Catacombe dei Cappuccini, to the west of the city, have become a rather macabre highlight of the tourist trail (via Cappuccini 1, 091 212 117, closed Sun). The vaults beneath this 17th-century monastery house the mummified remains of some 8,000 clergymen and monied citizens – many still sporting their best outfits in readiness for the afterlife. Not one for the squeamish.

The best way to explore areas further afield is by barrelling along on the back of a Vespa. Failing that, AMAT buses run the 11km to Mondello – a sandy beach resort packed with beautiful people – and to Monreale, 8km southwest of the city. As if breathtaking views down the valley weren't enough, Monreale's prime draw is its Norman cathedral, boasting the world's largest complete cycle of Byzantine mosaics.

ARTS

From classical concerts at Teatro Politeama (piazza Ruggero Settimo, 091 605 3421) to unplugged pavement gigs at Spirito dVino (via Principe di Belmonte, 05 3747 0827), Palermo offers a mix of the performing arts. Some venues relocate outside the city during the summer.

I Candelai
Il Capo *Via Candelai 65 (091 327 151/www. candelai.it). Open Sept-June 8pm-3am Wed-Sat. Admission €5-€7.*
If you're sniffing out the artistic zeitgeist, this is the best place to start. Formerly a brothel, this venue now hosts appropriately off-the-wall artistic 'happenings', along with theatre, tango, rock and jazz. If it all gets too much, repair to the balcony for a bird's-eye view of the madness below.

"The tree stands outside the former home of Giovanni Falcone, an investigative magistrate blown up by a Mafia bomb in 1992."

Expa Galleria di Architettura
La Kalsa *Scuderie Palazzo Cafalà, Via Alloro 97 (091 617 0319/www.expa.org). Open 7pm-late Tue-Sun. €€.*
This gallery, café, bar and small bookshop is one of Palermo's hidden treasures. Opened in a former stables by architects Tiziano Di Cara and Giuseppe Romano, Expa hosts an ambitious programme of exhibitions, workshops, festivals and live debates, exploring everything from architecture and design to cinema and wine. The highlight is the roof terrace – an open-air ruin littered with bomb-blown walls and funky furniture.

Galleria d'Arte Moderna
La Kalsa *Via Sant'Anna 21(199 199 111/ www.galleriadartemodernapalermo.it). Open 9.30 am-6.30pm Tue-Sun. Admission €7; €5 reductions. No credit cards.*
The complete antithesis of a dusty old museum, the restored Sant'Anna complex provides a bright and airy setting for a good collection of 19th- and 20th-century painting and sculpture. The ground floor features rippling torsos and judiciously placed fig leaves courtesy of Giuseppe Patania and other Romantics, and the two upper floors are given over to Realism and Modernism; Franz von Stuck's masterpiece, *Il Peccato*, is a major coup. A trendy café serves up drinks and snacks.

Kursaal Tonnara
6km north of Vucciria *Via Bordonaro 9, Arenella (091 637 2267/www.kursaaltonnara.it). Open 7.30pm-1am daily. Admission free.*
Perched on a rocky outcrop overlooking the Mediterranean, this 15th-century complex boasts one of Palermo's most picturesque performance spaces. During its long history the Kursaal Tonnara was a dock and a gunnery placement. It now hosts two bars, terrace and courtyard restaurants, and

Clockwise from top:
Kursaal Kalhesa (2);
Palermo street market.

a 400-seater open-air theatre. Performances (7.30-11.30pm, summer only) range from jazz and classical concerts to plays and films. Worth the ten-minute taxi hop from the city centre.

SHOP

Palermo musters a good clutch of independents, particularly around via Magliocco and via Ruggero Settimo, while via della Libertà is a haven for label-lovers. Most smaller shops are closed on Monday mornings and on the first Sunday of the month during the winter.

Casa & Putia

Libertà, 2km from Vucciria *Via Gaetano Daita 21a (091 320 101/www.casaeputia.com). Open 9.30am-7pm Tue-Sat.*
Putia (it means 'shop' in Sicilian) peddles a spirited brand of hippy chic courtesy of designer Massimo Ardizzone. The collection is all very Hansel and Gretel, full of pastel chiffon dresses, chunky belts, bodices and pillow lace, and the interior is a fairytale combination of artfully-distressed plasterwork and dreamy colours.

La Coppola Storta

Il Capo *Via del'Orologio 25 (091 743 4745/www. lacoppola.com). Open 10.30am-7.30pm Tue-Sat.*
Popular across Sicily from the 19th century, the *coppola* (flat cap) became synonymous with the Cosa Nostra – *coppola storta*, literally 'twisted cap', is one of the nicknames for the Mafia. But in 2000, models, politicians and intellectuals all sported the beret in a bid to turn it around and make it into an anti-Mafia symbol. This artisan outlet produces a huge selection of coppole, mixing traditional designs with new and funkier finishes such as leopard print.

Francocuoio

Libertà, 2km from Vucciria *Via V di Marco 27 (091 301 550/www.francocuoio.it). Open 9am-6pm Tue-Sat.*
Handbags or briefcases, belts or modernist chairs – if it incorporates leather, you'll find it here. Owner Francesco La Russa clearly has a motorbike obsession: his range of saddlebags is as long as an *autostrada*, and he does a good line in python skin and crocodile-print crash helmets.

Giglio In

Libertà, 2km from Vucciria *Via della Libertà 44 (091 625 7727/www.giglio.com). Open 10am-7pm daily.*
This New York-style store is a magnet for hip Palermitani, stocking D&G, Prada, Fendi and more. The art nouveau building is a triumph too: completely redesigned by architects Magnoli and Carmellini, it boasts an open-air bar and some impressive Valentino Vago frescoes.

Link 02

Libertà, 2km from Vucciria *Via Gaetano Daita 55-57 (091 580 582). Open 10am-8pm Tue-Sat.*
This boutique caters for the fashion-conscious party animal, but also offers an understated collection of jeans, tops and accessories for those less smitten with spangly clubwear.

Spazio Deep

Libertà, 2km from Vucciria *Via Rosolino Pilo 21-23 (091 321 090/www.spaziodeep.it). Open 4.30-8pm Mon; 10am-1pm, 4.30-8pm Tue-Sat.*
From futuristic lighting to cutting-edge bathroom accessories, you'll find it all in this funky interiors outlet. This place namechecks just about every hip designer out there, but primarily it's a love-in for david+pulvirenti, the young duo responsible for Woodesign's Eros bed.

Factfile

When to go

Visit Palermo all year round, with one important proviso: don't go in August. The weather is sweltering, many of the locals are away, and there's precious little to do since many bars, restaurants and shops are closed. You'll catch the best outdoor performances over the summer.

Getting there & around

Falcone Borsellino Airport (Punta Raisi) is 30km from the city centre (091 702 0273, www.gesap.it).
Buses stop outside the terminal building, running between 5am and noon. Tickets cost €5; journey time 30-50 minutes.
The train station is a short walk from the terminal. Services run hourly 5am-10.40pm. Journey time is 45 minutes, and tickets are €5.
Fast trains run from Paris and major Italian cities, including Naples, Rome and Milan.

For those wanting to make a nautical exit, there are direct ferry connections to Tunisia, Naples, Cagliari, Genova, Livorno, Civitavecchia and Salerno (www.directferries.co.uk) as well as to Ústica and the Aeolian and Égadi islands.

Tourist Information

Libertà, 2km from Vucciria Piazza Piazza Castelnuovo 35 (091 605 8111/www.palermo tourism.com). Open Sept-June 8.30am-2pm, 3-6pm Mon-Fri. July-Aug 8.30am-2pm, 3-6pm Mon-Fri; 9am-1pm Sat.

Internet access

Web access is hard to find outside of the top-of-the-range hotels. Try Centro Phone (Corso Vittorio Emanuele 11, Villabate) or Kursaal Kalhesa, La Kalsa, on Foro Umberto I 21 (091 616 7630/www.kursaalkalhesa.it; open 11.30am-1.30am Tue-Sat; 11am-6pm Sun).

Rome

There's a reason the Romans are so passionate about their city. History has left them a lot to be proud of, not least the vestiges of 500 years as *caput mundi*, hub of the ancient world's greatest empire. Considering the ravages that followed the fall of the Roman Empire, it's a miracle that anything remains, let alone monuments of the magnificence of the Colosseum or Pantheon.

Clockwise from top left: Appian Way; statue of Emperor Constantine; Swiss Guard; Santa Prassede; St Peter's; Campo de' Fiori; peppers; Museo dell'Ara Pacis.

Today the Eternal City is gleaming after a millennium spruce-up, and tourism is booming. And if some of the exciting new projects planned for the early years of the 21st century are dragging their heels – the Zaha Hadid-designed MAXXI art museum is a case in point – others, such as Renzo Piano's Auditorium and Richard Meier's striking container for the Ara Pacis, have been unveiled to much acclaim (and controversy, in the case of the latter). The pace of development and modernisation may worry those who love the city's ramshackle loveliness and enduring crankiness, but for the casual visitor, Rome has never looked so good.

ITALY

● Rome

Rome

Historic sites
● ● ● ● ●

Art & architecture
● ● ● ● ●

Hotels
● ● ● ● ○

Eating & drinking
● ● ● ● ○

Nightlife
● ● ● ○ ○

Shopping
● ● ● ● ○

Stay

Rome is one of the most-visited cities on the planet, so it's essential to book accommodation during peak times – which now means most of the year, with lulls during winter (January to March) and in the dog days of August.

Beehive

Termini *Via Marghera 8 (06 4470 4553/www.the-beehive.com). €.*
American owners Steve and Linda Brenner mix their penchant for designer furnishings (check out the Philippe Starck patio furniture) with reasonable rates and basic amenities to create a 'youth hostel meets boutique hotel' vibe. There's a sunny garden, and services include a free in-house guidebook to the city, complimentary internet access and a lounge café for guests. Breakfast isn't included, but can be provided in the Beehive's café for an extra fee. Proof that going budget needn't entail slumming it.

Buonanotte Garibaldi

Trastevere *Via Garibaldi 83 (06 5833 0733/ www.buonanottegaribaldi.com). €€-€€€.*
Hidden behind a gated entrance in a peaceful part of the Trastevere neighbourhood, this ex-convent is no ordinary B&B. Fashion designer-turned-artist Luisa Longo's three rooms – arranged around a spectacular courtyard garden – act as a showcase for her distinctive creations: wall panels, bedcovers and curtains in hand-painted silk, organza and velvet. Longo's atelier, in a corner of the courtyard, is open to guests curious to watch the artist at work, and all designs in the house are for sale. Guests are greeted after a long day's sightseeing with a restorative glass of wine.

Casa Howard

Tridente *Via Capo le Case 18 & via Sistina 149 (06 6992 4555/www.casahoward.com). €€.*
Casa Howard (Howard's End) offers beautifully decorated residenza accommodation in two locations a stone's throw from the Spanish Steps, with all rooms individually designed. All of the newer (and slightly more expensive) rooms in via Sistina have en suite bathrooms; in via Capo le Case, you may have to go along the hall to your (private) bathroom. Details such as fresh flowers in the rooms, a mini-Turkish bath, kimonos and slippers for every guest, and a sumptuous breakfast served on fine porcelain, make a stay memorable. There is no reception; guests are given keys.

Daphne Trevi

Trevi *Via degli Avignonesi 20 (06 8745 0087/ www.daphne-rome.com). €€.*
Owned by Italo-American couple Elyssa and Alessandro, Daphne sets the standard for inexpensive but stylish accommodation in Rome. The hotel – in two central locations (the other one's in the Veneto) – is decorated in modern, earthy tones, and the tasteful bedrooms have high ceilings, terracotta or parquet floors and decent-sized bathrooms (some with bathtubs). Guests are lent a mobile phone for their stay, and staff are endlessly helpful. All rooms are no-smoking.

Hassler Villa Medici

Veneto & Borghese *Piazza Trinità dei Monti 6 (06 699 340/www.hotelhasslerroma.com). €€€€.*
Looking down imperiously from its dominating position at the top of the Spanish Steps, the Hassler remains the grande dame of the city's deluxe hotels. With acres of polished marble and abundant chandeliers, the luxury may make your head spin, but it's the attentiveness of the staff that really distinguishes this place from the impersonal service often found at Rome's top chain hotels. The penthouse suite, with its antique Venetian mirrors and Louis XV chairs, obviously appealed to Tom Cruise and Katie Holmes, who checked in here before their wedding.

Inn at the Roman Forum

Monti *Via degli Ibernesi 30 (06 6919 0970/ www.theinnattheromanforum.com). €€€-€€€€.*
Opened in 2006, this boutique hotel is located near the Forum but it's set on a picturesque street that lies comfortably off the tourist trail. The rooms themselves are an elegant mix of rich fabrics and antiques; the spacious deluxe double rooms – some with their own fireplace – have canopied beds and marble bathrooms. Breakfast is served on the roof terrace or in a cosy room with open fire in the winter. Archaeology buffs can get a fix of ancient Rome on the ground floor, where a crypt featuring part of Trajan's markets is being excavated.

Portrait Suites

Tridente *Via Bocca di Leone 23 (06 6938 0742/ reservations 055 2726 4000/www.lungarnohotels.com). €€€€.*
Opened in 2006, Portrait Suites is the latest in a growing portfolio of luxury boutique hotels owned by Salvatore Ferragamo. Though black and white photos and memorabilia from the designer's archives decorate the hallways, the rooms themselves show little sign of the hotel's fashion pedigree. A somewhat predictable black-and-slate colour scheme is offset with touches of pink and lime, with spacious marble bathrooms, walk-in wardrobes and – ta dah! – a glamorous kitchenette. Breakfast is served in the rooms or outside on the spectacular terrace.

St Regis Grand

Esquilino *Via Vittorio Emanuele Orlando 3 (06 47091/www.starwood.com/stregis). €€€€.*
Founded in 1894 by Caesar Ritz, the father of luxury hotels, the St Regis was treated to a staggering $35-million makeover in 1999. Thanks to that, and its commitment to high standards of service, it remains a bastion of old-style luxury and puts the recent flood of five-star arrivistes in the shade. The original chandeliers hang in massive reception rooms with acres of marble and opulent gold, beige and red furnishings. Rooms have been individually designed and are filled with a mix of Empire, Regency and Louis XV-style furnishings. There are butler (suites and imperial rooms only) and limousine services, and a sauna.

Villa Laetitia

Prati *Lungotevere delle Armi 22/23 (06 322 6776/ www.villalaetitia.com). €€-€€€.*

Clockwise from top left:
Inn at the Roman Forum;
Buonanotte Garibaldi;
Antico Arco; Freni e
Frizioni; Remo (2).

The location may not be the most central, but this secluded bolthole makes a welcome addition to Rome's overpriced accommodation. The 15 rooms and suites, set in the annex of the villa itself, are stylish and funky – as they would be, given that Anna Fendi Venturini (of Fendi fashion fame) has designed them. Original art deco features combine with modern design and furniture to dramatic effect. Each has a kitchenette, and almost all of them have either a private terrace or access to the gorgeous gardens. Welcome touches include free internet connection

Eat

Rome takes food seriously, and today, with the rise of the new-school trattoria, even €25-a-head places point out the provenance of ingredients. Traditional Roman dishes include *spaghetti all'amatriciana* (with tomato, chilli, onion and sausage) and *saltimbocca* (veal strips with ham). Local eateries tend to get creative with offal.

Gelaterie (ice-cream bars) are worth seeking out for their home-made ice-creams (*produzione artigianale*); there's also *sorbetto* and the rougher *granita* and *grattachecca* (water ices).

Happy hour is becoming popular in Rome, with generous buffets laid out from 7.30pm onwards.

Agata e Romeo
Esquilino *via Carlo Alberto 45 (06 446 6115/ www.agataeromeo.it). Meals served 12.30-3pm, 7.30-10.30pm Mon-Fri. Closed 2wks Jan & 2wks Aug. €€€€. Traditional Italian.*
'Agata' is Agata Parisella – a talented chef who was one of the first to demonstrate that Roman cuisine could be refined without sacrificing its flavoursome roots in mamma's home cooking. Among the primi, the cannelloni filled with a white duck ragù are memorable. Agata's husband, Romeo Caraccio, presides over the dining room and extensive wine list, while their daughter Mariantonietta is fast becoming one of Rome's most exciting pastry chefs. The service is professional, and the decor elegant but welcoming.

Antico Arco
Gianicolo *Piazzale Aurelio 7 (06 581 5274). Open 6pm-midnight Mon-Sat. Closed 1wk Aug. €€€€. Modern Italian.*
On a busy corner behind Porta San Pancrazio, this restaurant, helmed by chef Patrizia Mattei, was one of the first of the new wave of creative Roman diners in the 1990s, and it can still be highly recommended. The menu is strong on all fronts, from the antipasti to the primi, and the excellent secondi cover the board from meat to fish to game. The wine list is extensive and well priced. Book in advance.

Bar Sant'Eustachio
Pantheon & Navona *Piazza Sant'Eustachio 82 (06 6880 2048/www.santeustachioilcaffe.it). Open 8.30am-1am Mon-Thur, Sun; 8.30am-1.30am Fri; 8.30am-2am Sat. No credit cards. €€. Bar.*

This is one of the city's most famous coffee bars, and its walls are plastered with celebrity testimonials. The coffee is quite extraordinary, albeit pricier than elsewhere; the barmen turn their backs while whipping up a cup so as not to let the secret out (though a pinch of bi-carbonate of soda is rumoured to give it its froth). Try the gran caffè: the schiuma (froth) can be slurped out afterwards with spoon or fingers. Unless you specify (amaro means 'no sugar'; poco zucchero means 'a little sugar'), it comes very sweet.

Freni e Frizioni
Trastevere *Via del Politeama 4-6 (06 5833 4210/ www.freniefrizioni.com). Open 10am-2am daily. €. Bar.*
Unlikely ex-garage surroundings – the name means 'brakes and clutches' – form Rome's hippest early evening spot, frequented by arty types and a creative, studenty crowd. A grand buffet is laid out on a white tablecloth decorated with long-stemmed roses and candles. There are baskets of focaccia, ceramic bowls of couscous and pasta, guacamole and raw vegetables: help yourself while you sip a cocktail, a beer, or a glass of well-priced wine.

Il Gelato di San Crispino
Trevi & Quirinale *Via della Panetteria 42 (06 679 3924/www.ilgelatodisancrispino.com). Open 11am-12.30am Mon-Thur, Sun; 11am-1.30am Fri, Sat. Closed mid Jan-mid Feb. €. No credit cards. Gelateria.*
This place serves what many consider to be the best ice-cream in Rome. In fact, some would go further, claiming it to be the best in the world. The flavours change according to what's in season – in summer the lampone (raspberry) and susine (yellow plum) are fabulous. Cones would interfere with the purity of the product: only tubs are allowed. Exquisite Jamaican coffee is also served.

Remo
Testaccio *Piazza Santa Maria Liberatrice 44 (06 574 6270). Meals served 7pm-1am Mon-Sat. Closed 3wks Aug. €. No credit cards. Pizzeria.*
The best place in town for authentic pizza romana, (thinner and flatter than other varieties), Remo is a Testaccio institution, with a prime location on the district's main piazza. You can sit at wonky tables balanced on the pavement, or in the cavernous interior, hung with Lazio team photos. The bruschette al pomodoro are the finest in Rome. A park with swings right across the road makes this a great place in which to eat with children.

Sora Margherita
Ghetto & Campo *Piazza delle Cinque Scole 30 (06 687 4216). Meals served Sept-May 12.30-3pm Mon-Thur; 12.30-3pm, 8-11.30pm Fri. June-July 12.30-3pm Tue-Thur; 12.30-3pm, 8-11.30pm Fri, Sat. Closed Aug. €€. No credit cards. Trattoria.*
This spit-and-sawdust, hole-in-the-wall trattoria offers one of Rome's best (and best-value) local dining experiences. Inside, wooden tables are crammed into a couple of narrow rooms, and the volume is matched only by the friendliness of the welcome. Local licensing laws mean that if you come for dinner on a Friday or Saturday evening, you'll need to fill out a (free) membership card. It's worth it.

TRASTEVERE & THE GIANICOLO

Trastevere, which is a corruption of the phrase *trans tiberim*, meaning 'across the Tiber', looks very much like the idyllic image of 'typical Rome': peeling palazzi, dark wine cellars and unspoilt trattorias. Many foreigners develop a love affair with the quarter, the wealthier ones to the point of acquiring a pied-à-terre, thus pushing prices up and locals out. Nonetheless, Trastevere retains much of its slightly louche charm.

Up above Trastevere, the Gianicolo is Rome's highest hill – though not one of the official seven. This luxuriously verdant hilltop neighbourhood is one of Rome's most beautiful.

THE AVENTINE & TESTACCIO

Though first inhabited by King Ancius Marcius in the seventh century BC, the Aventine was later colonised by sailors, merchants and undesirables who crept up the hill from the port below. In the fifth century BC, the plebeians, as they were called, forced the ruling patricians to grant them a say in the running of the Republic, and in 456 BC the whole area was earmarked for plebeians. As they found succes, so their villas became gentrified. Today it is still an exclusive area.

Across busy viale Aventino is the similarly well-heeled San Saba district, and, beyond, the giant Terme di Caracalla (Baths of Caracalla), built between AD 213 and 216.

Tucked below the quiet heights of the Aventine is bustling, noisy Testaccio, where longtime residents are stridently Roman. The produce market in piazza Testaccio (closed Sun) is arguably Rome's best.

CELIO & SAN GIOVANNI

If you're after a glimpse of what ancient, early Christian and medieval Rome were like, the Celio is where you'll find it. Here, what's underground is as important as what's above. From the remains of ancient aqueducts near the verdant and lovely Villa Celimontana park to frescoes by Masolino in the church of San Clemente, this area has a bit of everything.

To the east is San Giovanni, where, amid the traffic, smog and drab apartment buildings, are some of Christianity's most important churches. In 313 Emperor Constantine built San Giovanni in Laterano, the first Christian basilica, in this (then) far-from-central spot. It stands on the square of the same name, as does the Scala Santa (Holy Stairs), said to be the steps Jesus climbed in the house of Pontius Pilate before being sent to his crucifixion, and the adjoining Sancta Sanctorum, the pope's private chapel.

MONTI & ESQUILINO

When Rome became Italy's capital in the 1870s, this was an area of gardens, vineyards and ruins. But the country's new administrators were in need of offices and homes, and by 1890 a district of solid, soulless palazzi had sprung up.

The area of Monti that was the Suburra (the city's worst slum) – north-east of the Forum, between vie Nazionale and Cavour – is just as noisy, cosmopolitan and full of life today as it was 2,000 years ago. Via Nazionale, meanwhile is a traffic artery lined by identikit high-street shops.

The area around the Termini railway station may come as a shock: Esquilino's grimy palazzi and questionable after-dark denizens might not be what you expected of the Eternal City. Don't despair: there are attractions such as the vast basilica of Santa Maria Maggiore and nearby Santa Prassede, and top restaurants and hotels.

THE VATICAN

In the first century BC, the Campus vaticanus was just marshland by the Tiber, across the river from the city centre and known mainly for its poor-quality wine.

Emperor Nero built a circus here in AD 54 and added a bridge to the other bank. In the summer of AD 64, a fire destroyed two-thirds of Rome. When Romans blamed Nero, he looked for a suitable scapegoat and blamed the Christians. Thus the persecution of this troublesome new cult began in earnest. The apostle Peter is believed to have been crucified here – upside down at his own request – and buried close by on the spot where, in AD 326, Emperor Constantine built the first church of St Peter. Not all the following 264 popes have resided here but over the centuries, pilgrims have continued to visit the tomb of the Apostle.

The Vatican City is the smallest state in the world, but despite having fewer than 800 residents, it has its own diplomatic service, postal service, army (the Swiss Guard), railway station, and radio and TV stations. It also issues its own stamps and currency.

Outside in Borgo, salt-of-the-earth Romans mingle with off-duty Swiss Guards and immaculately robed priests from the Vatican.

St Peter's

Piazza San Pietro (06 6988 1662). No credit cards. Basilica: Open Apr-Sept 7am-7pm daily. Oct-Mar 7am-6pm daily. Admission free.
Dome: Open Apr-Sept 8am-5.45pm daily. Oct-Mar 8am-4.45pm daily. Admission €4; with lift €7. Note: there are 320 steps to climb after the lift has taken you to the first level.
Grottoes: Open Apr-Sept 9am-6pm daily. Oct-Mar 9am-5pm daily. Admission free.
Necropolis: Apply at the Uffizio degli Scavi (06 6988 5318). Open Guided tours 9am-5pm Mon-Sat. Admission €10.
Treasury Museum: Open Apr-Sept 9am-6.15pm daily. Oct-Mar 9am-5.15pm daily. Admission €6; €4 reductions.

Clockwise from top left:
Il Colosseo (Colosseum);
piazza Navona; St Peter's;
Villa Borghese.

St Peter's was consecrated by Urban VIII on 18 November 1626 – exactly 1,300 years after the consecration of the first basilica on the site. It was Pope Julius II and his pet architect Donato Bramante who began work on the current structure, in 1506. Bramante was followed by Raphael, and then by Michelangelo, who died in 1564, aged 87, but not before coming up with a plan for a massive dome and the necessary supporting drum. This was completed in 1590, the largest brick dome ever constructed, and still the tallest point of any building in Rome.

Outside the church a major highlight is Bernini's elliptical piazza (1656-67), the site of many papal events. The oval measures 340 by 240 metres, and is punctuated by the central Egyptian obelisk (1586) and two symmetrical fountains. The 284-column, 88-pillar colonnade is topped by 140 statues of saints.

Inside the church are more Bernini masterpieces: his vast baldacchino (1633), hovering over the high altar and Peter's tomb, and his Throne of St Peter (1665), at the far end of the nave beyond the high altar. On the pillars supporting the main dome are much-venerated relics, including a chip from the True Cross above the statue of St Helena.

Pilgrims head for the last pilaster on the right before the main altar to kiss the big toe of Arnolfo da Cambio's brass statue of St Peter (c1296); tourists, on the other hand, make a beeline for the first chapel on the right, where Michelangelo's Pietà (1499) is found, safe behind glass.

Beneath the basilica are the Vatican Grottoes – Renaissance crypts containing papal tombs. The Necropolis, where St Peter is said to be buried, lies under the grottoes. The dome, reached via hundreds of steps, offers views of the Vatican gardens.

Vatican Museums (Musei vaticani)

Viale del Vaticano (06 6988 3333/mv.vatican.va). Open (last entry 1hr15mins before closing) Mar-Oct 10am-4.45pm Mon-Fri; 10am-2.45pm Sat. Nov-Feb 10am-1.45pm Mon-Sat. Year-round last Sun of mth 9am-1.45pm. Closed Catholic holidays. Admission €13; €8 reductions; free to all last Sun of mth. No credit cards.

Begun by Pope Julius II in 1503, this immense collection represents the accumulated fancies and obsessions of a long line of strong, often contradictory, personalities. Major highlights include the Borgia Rooms, decorated by Pinturicchio with frescoes; the Museo Pio-Clementino, the world's largest collection of classical statues; and the Pinacoteca (picture gallery), which holds many of the works that the Vatican managed to recover from France after Napoleon stole them in the early 19th century.

No visit would be complete without a look at the Sistine Chapel (Cappella Sistina), built by Sixtus IV in 1473-84. In 1508 Michelangelo was commissioned to paint something undemanding on the ceiling. He chose instead to depict the Creation, and spent the next four years on the project, standing on 18m-high (60ft) scaffolding. In 1535, aged 60, the artist returned to paint the Last Judgment on the wall behind the altar (look out for Michelangelo's self portrait in the flayed skin that St Bartholomew is holding). In the 1980s and '90s, the frescoes were subjected to a highly controversial restoration job that revealed bright, almost luminous colours beneath centuries of grime. Equally unmissable are the Raphael Rooms; highlights include the School of Athens fresco in the Study (Stanza della Segnatura; 1508-11) and the Chapel of Nicholas V, with scenes painted by Fra Angelico.

Tips: wear sensible shoes, bring water and binoculars (for the Sistine Chapel), and buy an audio guide or book. Most importantly, don't wear shorts, mini skirts, or have bare midriffs or shoulders: you won't get in.

FURTHER AFIELD

Two brand new art galleries will soon open in Rome's northern suburbs: Odile Decq's MACRO (Museo d'Arte Contemporaneo di Roma) is due in Nomentano in summer 2008, and Zaha Hadid's MAXXI (Museo delle arti del XXI secolo), in Flaminio, is scheduled for early 2009. At the other extreme, the Appian Way is worth visiting.

SHOP

The emporia of the big guns of Italian fashion jostle for space on and around via Condotti, at the bottom of the Spanish Steps. When the glamour gets too much for you, nip down via Maria de' Fiori or via Bocca di Leone, where some great unfamous names survive, or along hip via del Babuino. Note that most non-food shops are closed on Monday mornings.

Antica Erboristeria Romana

Pantheon & Navona *Via di Torre Argentina 15 (06 687 9493/www.anticaerboristeriaromana.com). Open 8.30am-7.30pm Mon-Fri; 9am-7.30pm Sat. Closed 1wk Aug.*

Visit this charming 18th-century apothecary-style shop if only to admire the carved wood ceilings and banks of tiny wooden drawers – some etched with skull and crossbones – in which herbal remedies are hidden safely away.

Arsenale

Pantheon & Navona *Via del Governo Vecchio 64 (06 686 1380). Open 3.30-7.30pm Mon; 10am-7.30pm Tue-Sat. Closed 2wks Aug.*

Patrizia Pieroni's wonderful designs make for great window displays – not to mention successful party conversation pieces – and have been going down well with the Roman boho-chic luvvy crowd for a fair few years.

Borini

Ghetto & Campo *Via dei Pettinari 86/87 (06 687 5670). Open 3.30-7.30pm Mon; 9.30am-1pm, 3.30-7.30pm Tue-Sat. Closed 3wks Aug.*

Franco Borini's shop is busily chaotic, packed with clued-up shoe lovers. His elegant but durable shoes follow fashion trends religiously, and prices are fair.

Borsalino

Tridente *Via di Campo Marzio 72A (06 679 6120). Open 3-7.30pm Mon; 9.30am-1.30pm, 3-7.30pm Tue-Sat. Open Sun in Dec. Closed 3wks Aug.*

A race of heroes

The Mille Miglia road race was, by common consent, the greatest contest of its kind: a punishing trans-Italian race between daredevil drivers, in all weathers, through sleepy villages and winding country roads. For its three decades, the Mille Miglia was a powerful cocktail of skill, speed and a dash of danger.

The route from Brescia to Rome and back was finessed from year to year, but nearly always ran in a figure of eight of roughly 1,500 kilometres – the thousand miles of the name. The course went through Lombardy, Veneto, Le Marche, Umbria and Lazio on the outward leg, and Tuscany on the return trip. The first race, in 1927, was an all-Italian affair (and Italy dominated the event throughout its history) – but after just a few years, international interest was running high. Cars were fielded by Porsche, Mercedes, BMW and, subsequently, British marques like Jaguar, Aston Martin and Healey.

The 1930s were the Mille Miglia's golden age, when the sense of adventure was at its peak and the automobile was a powerful symbol of freedom. The race was a glorious epic of wire wheels, oily rags, steeply raked bonnets, rakish moustaches and the roar of colossal engines. Maseratis, Bugattis, Alfas and Lancias blurred around breakneck corners, chasing cars from now-extinct makers like Officine Meccaniche, Stanguellini and Cisitalia.

Cars were open-topped, had tiny windscreens and usually carried a co-pilot-cum-navigator along with the driver.

Accidents were common, and eventually killed the race. In 1938, a smash killed spectators lining the route and Mussolini had the race banned. In 1940 a surrogate was organised on a shorter route, a 100-kilometre circuit from Brescia to Cremona and Mantova (this was the event at which Ferrari made its racing debut, under the less evocative name of Auto Avio Costruzioni), but it was to be 1947 before the Mille Miglia ran again. Then, in 1957, another nasty accident shut the race down for good: a crash near the finishing line took the lives of the Spanish aristocrat driver Alfonso de Portago, his co-pilot and nine spectators.

Since 1977, the glory days have been remembered in the Mille Miglia Storica, a heritage rally held every year in mid May. The gorgeous cars that take part, all between 50 and 80 years old, are too valuable to be subjected to the rigours of the original event, but competitive speed trials and the incomparable noise of their engines give a feel for the way in which, as Enzo Ferrari put it, 'the Mille Miglia really did breed champions.'

Mille Miglia Storica
www.1000miglia.eu

Auditorium-Parco
della Musica.

Italian hat-maker Borsalino has been producing the world's most famous felt hat for over a century, plus assorted panamas and women's hats, and accessories.

Le Gallinelle
Monti *Via del Boschetto 76 (06 488 1017). Open 4-8pm Mon; 10am-2pm, 4-8pm Tue-Sat. Closed 2wks Aug.*
Vintage and ethnic garments are reworked by Wilma Silvestri and her daughter Giorgia in their funky shop. For those who shun the outlandish, there are classic linen suits for men and women.

Moriondo & Gariglio
Pantheon & Navona *Via del Piè di Marmo 21 (06 699 0856). Open 9am-7.30pm Mon-Sat. Closed Aug.*
This fairytale chocolate shop with beautiful gift-boxes is especially lovely at Christmas, when you'll have to fight to get your hands on the excellent marrons glacés. It usually closes on Saturday afternoons in summer.

Too Much
Pantheon & Navona *Via Santa Maria dell'Anima 29 (06 6830 1187/www.toomuch.it). Open noon-midnight Mon-Thur, Sun; noon-1am Fri-Sat.*
Lovers of kitsch need look no further: two storeys crammed floor-to-ceiling with gimmicky design and household objects, from retro T-shirts and badges to fuzzy dice, furry handcuffs and lava lamps.

Volpetti
Testaccio *Via Marmorata 47 (06 574 2352/ www.volpetti.com/www.fooditaly.com). Open 8am-2pm, 5-8.15pm Mon-Sat. July-Aug closed Tue pm.*
One of the best delis in Rome, with exceptional cheese, hams and salamis. It's hard to get away without one of the jolly assistants loading you with samples of their wares – pleasant, but painful on the wallet. If you can't get here, at least check the website: they ship all over the world.

ARTS
Thanks mainly to the activity of the Auditorium-Parco della Musica, Rome is back on the music-lovers' map of Europe.

Auditorium-Parco della Musica
Viale Pietro de Coubertin 15, north suburbs (06 80 242/06 8024 1281/box office 06 808 2058/www. auditorium.com). Admission free; guided tours €9, €5-€7 reductions.
This self-funding complex of concert and exhibition spaces, designed by Renzo Piano, entices Romans and visitors with a programme of extraordinary breadth – performances range from symphonies to soul, from jazz to jugglers. Guided tours cost €10 and take place at intervals throughout the day. Alternatively, wander in (open 10am-6pm daily, admission free) and have a look around.

Factfile

When to go
Spring and autumn are good for weather, bad for crowds. July and August are hot and humid, and the weather from November to February is unpredictable (but there are fewer tourists).

Getting there & around
Aeroporto Leonardo Da Vinci, Fiumicino, Via dell'Aeroporto di Fiumicino 320 (switchboard 06 65 951/information 06 6595 3640/www.adr.it).
There's an express rail service between Fiumicino airport and Termini railway station. It runs every 30mins from 6.37am until 11.37pm daily (5.52am-10.52pm to Fiumicino) and takes 31 minutes. The regular train service from Fiumicino takes 25-40 minutes. Trains leave about every 15 minutes (less often on Sun) between 5.57am and 11.27pm (5.06am-10.36pm to Fiumicino).
Terravision (06 6595 8646, www.terravision.it) runs a frequent coach service from Fiumicino to Termini (journey time: 70 minutes). Departures are about every two hours between 8.30am and 8.30pm daily. Coaches from Termini to Fiumicino leave via Marsala 7 from 6.30am to 6.30pm.
Aeroporto GB Pastine, Ciampino, via Appia Nuova 1650 (06 794 941/www.adr.it).

The most hassle-free way to get into town is to take the Terravision coach service (06 7949 4572, 06 7949 4621, www.terravision.it) to Termini station (journey time: 40 minutes). Buses from Termini to Ciampino leave from via Marsala 7. This is a dedicated service for the low-cost airlines, so you'll need to show your ticket or boarding pass.

Tourist information
APT (Azienda per il Turismo di Roma), via Parigi 5, Esquilino (06 4889 9200/infoline 06 8205 9127/www.romaturismo.com). Open Phoneline 9am-6pm daily. Office 9.30am-1pm, 2.30-4.30pm Mon, Thur.
PIT (Punti Informativi Turistici), piazza delle Cinque Lune, Pantheon & Navona (06 6880 9240). Open 9.15am-7pm.

Internet
Much of central Rome, plus the major parks and the Auditorium-Parco della Musica zone, is covered by Wi-Fi hotspots, which are sponsored by the city council.
EasyEverything, via Barberini 2/16, Trevi & Quirinale (www.easyeverything.com). Open 8am-2am daily. Rates €1-€3/hr. No credit cards.

Clockwise from top left:
Mole Antonelliana;
Palazzo Reale; Via Po;
Porta Palatina, near
Piazza Castello;
Piazza Carignano.

Turin

It's a credit to Turin's unpretentious nature that it doesn't have a chip on its shoulder. It's forever being unfavourably compared with Italy's older, warmer or less northern towns, rather than being assessed for what it is: a soberly beautiful city that has learned to revel in change, redefining its urban identity – often physically – with every twist of history.

Clockwise from top left:
Méridien Art+Tech (2);
Al Bicerin; Caffè San
Carlo; Mare Nostrum;
Hotel Victoria;
Hotel Boston.

The Duomo is Turin's only major example of Renaissance architecture. The very symmetrical 15th-century façade is decorated with bas-reliefs in white Chianocco marble, framing elegant 18th-century portals. Inside, an austere nave is flanked by two aisles that expand into chapels scooped out later from the thick lateral walls. At the far end stands Guarino Guarini's Holy Shroud chapel in black marble. It has been closed since a fire in 1997; there is a smaller copy on the north side of the Duomo and a full-size one in nearby San Lorenzo. It's due to reopen in 2009: there is speculation that the Shroud may once more be displayed.

Palazzo Madama & Museo Civico d'Arte Antica

Piazza Castello 1 (011 443 501/www.palazzo madamatorino.it). Open 10am-6pm Tue-Fri, Sun; 10am-8pm Sat. Admission €7.50; €6 reductions.
Palazzo Madama has seen a fair bit of action, from its early days as a 13th-century fortress to today's role as a museum of art, architecture and decorative arts. It has been variously a castle, the lodgings of Madama reale Marie Christine, who converted it into a palace in the 17th century, the residence of the Savoy dowagers and the home of the royal painting collection; and so has suffered from architectural agglomeration. However, it is well suited to its current purpose: the Museo Civico d'Arte Antica is a light and open space, grand but not oppressive. Collections include medieval stonework; art from the gothic to the baroque; and decorative arts, ceramics, textiles and cabinetry prominent among them. There's also a handful of pieces of world-class status, including *Portrait of a Man* by Antonello da Messina. At entry level, a glass floor gives views on to the Roman ruins below; the first floor café is a decorative joy.

Palazzo Reale

Piazzetta Reale 1 (011 436 1455/www.ambienteto. arti.beniculturali.it). Open 8.30am-7.30pm Tue-Sun. Ticket office closes 6.20pm. Admission Palazzo Reale €6.50; apartments €4; combined ticket €8.50; reductions vary. No credit cards.
The stern façade of Palazzo Reale contrasts with interiors rich with stucco, gilt, frescoes, tapestries and decor that make it one of the city's most impressive baroque monuments. Begun in the first half of the 17th century, the palace was the official Savoy residence. It was built over the existing Palazzo del Vescovo (bishop's palace), bits of which are still visible at the eastern end of the ground floor (near the lovely new café).

The first floor re-opens after refurbishments in summer 2008. It is rich with paintings, friezes, decorative works – and historic significance. Here you will see, among many other highlights, a 1558 frieze celebrating the Saxon origins of the Savoy family; fine 18th-century chinoiserie and Gobelin tapestries depicting scenes from the life of Don Quixote. On the second floor, the Sala degli Specchi (hall of mirrors) hides a private altar made for Carlo Emanuele III and his wife Anna Cristina di Baviera: their initials are on the tapestry. Vittorio Emanuele II's office and bedroom overlook the piazza and have access to a pretty terrace.

The Palazzo Reale can be visited only on half-hour guided tours in Italian, though the contents of each room are explained well on cards in English – if you're a quick reader. Note that the kitchens will open to the public for the first time in September 2008.

IL QUADRILATERO

North of the Duomo is Turin's least formal area, and its most bohemian. Round Porta Palazzo is a maze of magnificent churches and sprawling markets that is ballsy old Turin despite the inevitably encroaching gentrification. To the west of here, centring on piazza Emanuele Filiberto and via Sant'Agostino, is the area known as Il Quadrilatero Romano. This run-down area was once a ghetto for immigrants from southern Italy, but has now been transformed into the city's trendiest area: designer boutiques, galleries, restaurants and nightspots sprout regularly.

CITTADELLA

The area to the west of the baroque centre is a quieter and more staidly Torinese part of town, the result of a slum-clearance at the turn of the 20th century. The Crocetta district contains some of the city's most expensive real estate, including pretty art deco villas (and self important early 20th-century blocks of immense dullness).

Fondazione Merz

Via Limone 24 (011 1971 9437/www.fondazione merz.org). Open 11am-7pm Tue-Sun. Admission €5; €3.50 reductions; free under-10s, over 65s, 1st Sun of mth. No credit cards.
This converted Lancia heating plant was opened in 2005 as a tribute to the Arte Povera artist Mario Merz, who lived and worked in Turin. Arte Povera was an anti-elitist movement that favoured simple materials; Merz was fascinated by space, energy and light: the large spaces and slabbed surfaces of the former factory make a fitting background for his works. You can see an example of Merz's signature 'igloos' on Turin's Spina artery.

Galleria Civica d'Arte Moderna e Contemporanea (GAM)

Via Magenta 31 (011 442 9518/www.gamtorino.it). Open 10am-6pm Tue-Sun. Admission €7.50; €6 reductions; free 1st Tue of mth.
A low, grey, purpose-built 1950s structure houses a municipal collection numbering some 20,000 artworks from the 18th to 20th centuries, some 600 of which are usually on show. A core collection of Piedmontese pieces, including many from the 19th century, has been extended with acquisitions of international works. In the 20th-century collections, the works of avant-garde Torinese are pitted against the likes of Modigliani, Max Ernst and Paul Klee.

CENTRO

Piazza Castello might be the geographical heart of Turin, but the fulcrum of shopping, drinking, working and playing lies further south, along vias Roma and Po, with their sheltering arcades, and in the regular grid of streets sandwiched between.

MUSEO NAZIONALE DEL CINEMA
FONDAZIONE MARIA ADRIANA PROLO

**THE TEMPLE
OF CINEMA
IN THE HEART
OF TURIN**

Museo Nazionale del Cinema
Mole Antonelliana
Via Montebello 20, Torino, Italy
Tel. +39 011 8138.560/561

www.museocinema.it

Foto: Giovanni Fontana

Museo Egizio

*Via Accademia delle Scienze 6 (011 561 7776/www.
museoegizio.it). Open Sept-June 8.30am-7.30pm Tue-
Sun. June-Sept 9.30am-8.30pm Tue-Sun. Admission
€7.50; free-€3.50 reductions.*

The biggest collection of Egyptian artefacts this side of Cairo
is housed in what was built as a Jesuit-run school and has a
suitably boarding school air about its corridors and ex-
dormitories. Today the museum holds some 30,000 pieces,
a collection that was started by the Savoys in the 17th
century. It's fascinating for fans of the subject, but loses the
general audience with poor interpretation, an overwhelming
number of objects and an awkward route through the rooms.
An ongoing revamp means that not all areas may be open,
which will exacerbate the crowds – the Museo Egizio is very
popular locally, particularly with schools.

Museo Nazionale del Cinema

*Via Montebello 20 (011 813 8560/www.museo
nazionaledelcinema.it). Open 9am-7.15pm Tue-Fri,
Sun; 9am-10.45pm Sat. Admission Museum €6.50;
€5 reductions. Lift €4.50; €3.20 reductions. Combined
ticket €8; €6.50 reductions.*

The distinctive spire/dome that dominates Turin's skyline
is the Mole Antonelliana. The city's Jewish community
commissioned it from architect Alessandro Antonelli in the
mid 19th-century to mark liberalised discrimination laws.
It was a problematic building to complete and then to use,
but it found its vocation in 2000 as the home of Italy's
national cinema museum. Fitted with two giant screens and
a bank of red-upholstered recliners with built-in speakers,
the dome's vast, light-haunted interior could have been
made to evoke the spectacle of the medium, with extra
drama provided by the periodic passage of the tiny lift that
shoots up the centre on its way to the needle at the top. The
exhibits have similar chutzpah. You can create footage of
yourself flying on a bicycle, ET in your basket; watch
smutty films on the ceiling from a round, red bed; see a
series of exploding heads; or look at photos and props
including Fellini's hat and scarf, Lawrence of Arabia's
kaftan and *Alien*'s body suits. There's also a strong
exhibition of early 'moving picture' equipment, including a
camera obscura, and a snazzy aperitivo bar.

LINGOTTO

A few kilometres south of the city centre, the
Lingotto was the heart of Fiat's manufacturing
empire. The factories are now silent, but urban
blight is being fought off with a series of
redevelopments, notably a park and venues
originally built for the 2006 Winter Olympics and
the conversion of the Lingotto complex, a former
Fiat factory, into a US-style shopping mall.

Pinacoteca Giovanni e Marella Agnelli

*Lingotto Via Nizza 230 (011 006 2713/www.pina
coteca-agnelli.it). Open 10am-7pm Tue-Sun. Admission
€4; €2.50 reductions; combined entry with temporary
exhibitions €7; €6 reductions.*

The Pinacoteca (art gallery) sits in the square glass box on
top of the Lingotto's rooftop racetrack (to which your
admission ticket gives you access – take advantage, as both
the views and the track itself are fabulous). Inside, architect
Renzo Piano has given the gallery a minimalist treatment
in wood and glass, with the glass ceiling as the main light
source. The 25 pieces displayed here are taken from the
collection of Fiat's ruling family and includes some minor
gems, among them Giacomo Balla's *Velocità astratta* (1913),
Venetian landscapes by Canaletto, two landscapes of
Dresden by Bernardo Bellotto, *La Négresse* by Manet, *La
Baigneuse Blonde* by Renoir, six pictures by Matisse,
Picasso's *L'Hétaire* and a *Nue Couchée* by Modigliani.

OUTER TURIN

Santo Volto

*Spina 3, Via Val della Torre 11 (011 515 6480/www.
diocesi.torino.it). Open 8am-5pm daily; times may vary.*

This new church, which opened in 2007, is interesting as a
symbol of urban regeneration – the congregation is a new
one, from the perky apartment blocks that are springing up
in place of industrial buildings; and as a work of modern
religious architecture. It was a symbolic project and one on
which much money was lavished. The result is a stunning
interpretation of industrial materials, with a crown of thorns
motif evident in its circular form and a chimney re-used as
a spire, with a spiral of metal thorns.

La Venaria Reale

*Piazza della Repubblica 4, Venaria Reale (011 499 2300/
www.lavenaria.it). Bus 11, 72, then 1km walk. Open
9am-8pm Tue-Thur, Sat, Sun; 9am-5pm Fri. Ticket
office closes 90mins in advance. Admission Palace only
€10; €7 reductions. Palace & gardens) €12; €8
reductions (guide included). No credit cards.*

The Savoy's hunting estate at Venaria was commissioned
by Carlo Emanuele II in the mid 17th century. The palace,
its spectacular gardens and surrounding Mandria park were
designed by Amedeo di Castellamonte, who also ran up the
en suite *borgo* (hamlet) in just three years.

The vast palace is one of Italy's great sights. It is largely
unfurnished, and mercifully not populated by costumed
staff, other than the occasional flickering projections
provided by Peter Greenaway. Nor is it interpreted as a
historic piece (after an introductory exhibition): walking
through its rooms and galleries, with their exquisite
proportions, natural light and decorative features, is an
uplifting experience of architectural discovery.

SHOP

Turin has a good spread of shopping, from high-
end designer boutiques to sprawling fleamarkets.
Whatever you're looking for, piazza Castello is a
good point of departure. South along glittering via
Roma are bourgeois boutiques and celebrated
confectioners; west up via Garibaldi is the cheap
'n' cheerful buzz of Europe's longest pedestrian
precinct. Via Milano leads north from via Garibaldi
towards piazza della Repubblica; on side streets
such as via Bonelli and via delle Orfane are
clusters of artsy emporia. Parallel to via Garibaldi,

invito a corte

Opera

Take a plunge into history.

Spend a day immersed in architecture, art and nature.
Be amazed by the old and excited by what's new: the Royal Palace, the garden the old Town, and the Park.

Until 30 March 2008

La Reggia di Venaria e i Savoia
arte magnificenza e storia di una corte europea

The Reggia of Venaria and the Savoias
art, magnificence and history of a European court

An exhibition with over 400 works of art, includi paintings, tapestries, statues, furniture and weapons from the 16th to 18th century

"Peopling the Reggia"
life at court seen by Peter Greenaway

Information, reservations and guided tours tel.:
+39 011 4992333 - Email: prenotazioni@lavenariareale.it

Information and reservations of educational services tel.:
+39 011 4992355 - Email: prenotazioniservizieducativi@lavenariareale.it

Information: www.lavenariareale.it

Freephone number: from Italy: 800 329 329 - from EU: 800 111 333 00

Special GTT shuttle bus: Torino - La Venaria Reale

Ticket sales:
- www.lavenariareale.it
- Royal Palace Ticket office: Via Mensa, 34 – Venaria Reale
- Info Piemonte: Piazza Castello corner of Via Garibaldi – Torino
- TicketOne network
- Ticket office for Gardens only:
  Viale Carlo Emanuele – Venaria Reale

UNIONE EUROPEA   CITTA DI VENARIA REALE   REGIONE PIEMONTE

La Venaria Reale

via Barbaroux has antiques shops, home design, jewellers and candle shops. To the east of piazza Madama, via Po and piazza Vittorio have arcades to protect you from rain and sun as you browse through their eclectic mix of antiques, second-hand book stalls and fashion shops.

8 Gallery Lingotto
Lingotto *Centro Commerciale, via Nizza 230 (011 663 0768/www.8gallery.it). Open 2-10pm Mon; 10am-10pm Tue-Sun.*
This capacious mall in the old Fiat factory (check out the spiral ramp where the cars used to be driven up to the test track on the roof) houses 90 shops, including a decent supermarket, an 11-screen cinema and 16 bars and restaurants. The outlets are the usual chain fare but there's enough of them to satisfy most shopping needs, and at least the scale guarantees that it isn't claustrophobic.

"Nowadays it reflects the neighbourhood's rich ethnic mix and goes far beyond mere fruit and veg in a dazzling jumble of hues"

Borgiattino
Cittadella *Corso Vinzaglio 29 (011 562 9075). Open 8.30am-1pm, 4-7.30pm Mon, Tue, Thur-Sat. Closed Aug.*
The Borgiattino family has been selling fine cheeses from this shop since 1927. Dino, the friendly owner, always slices a sliver for you to sample. Try the toma or robiola cheeses from Piedmont's Alpine valleys.

Casa del Barolo
Centro *via Andrea Doria 7 (011 532 038/www.casadelbarolo.com). Open 3-7.30pm Mon; 9.30am-1pm, 3-7.30pm Tue, Wed; 10.30am-7.30pm Thur-Sat. Closed last 3wks Aug.*
Just off piazza San Carlo, Casa del Barolo is more a gourmet boutique than a wine shop, with its soft lighting and pale wooden shelves. Select a bottle of Barolo and a local gastronomic delight for reminiscing over your holiday when you get back home.

Eataly
Lingotto *via Nizza 230/14 (011 1950 6801/www.eatalytorino.it). Open 10am-10.30pm daily.*
The Slow Food movement (*see p302*) had its roots 20 years ago in the nearby Piedmont city of Bra. Now an organisation with global influence, it collaborated with commercial partners in 2007 to open Eataly, a temple to gastronomic antiglobalisation. Part shop, part education centre, part

restaurant complex, spread over 11,000 sqm of the old Carpano vermouth factory, it is an intense experience for anyone with a palate. Chilled rooms hold hams and enormous wheels of Gran Padano; wines and oils are dispensed from the barrel; a multiplicity of pastas fills the shelves and deli counters; fruit and veg cascade from mock market stalls; and a patisserie, *gelateria* and chocolate counter appease the sweet toothed. There are also books, kitchenware, a great range of beers and a bakery. Not least, you can walk up to food bars to sample cheese, meats cooked and cured, beers, ice cream, pizza and excellent pasta. Plus there's a gourmet restaurant, Guido per Eataly, and a museum dedicated to Carpano.

Il (Gran) Balon
Quadrilatero *Information 011 436 9741/www.balon.it). Open Flea market 8am-6pm Sat; Gran Balon 8am-6pm 2nd Sun of mth.*
This glorious flea market is a weekend must for visitors to Turin. It rambles through the streets (via Mameli, via Borgo Dora, via Lanino, via Andreis etc) north of piazza della Repubblica and west of corso Giulio Cesare towards the river Dora Riparia. There's a preponderance of cheap tat, and imitations are rife, but a patient rake may well turn up an authentic antique. Balon is mainly a second-hand and antique furniture market, but you'll also find stalls selling second-hand clothes, books, household goods, knick-knacks and memorabilia, along with the plain miscellaneous. Every second Sunday of the month it explodes into the Gran Balon, when 200 stall-holders from all over Piedmont and even from France descend on these streets selling pretty much everything in all states of repair.

Mercato di Porta Palazzo
Quadrilatero *Piazza della Repubblica. Open 7am-2pm Mon-Fri; 7am-7.30pm Sat.*
Straggling across the rather shabby baroque Piazza della Repubblica, Europe's largest open-air market is known locally as Porta Palazzo. It originally sold produce brought to town by local farmers; nowadays it reflects the neighbourhood's rich ethnic mix and goes far beyond mere fruit and veg in a dazzling jumble of hues, smells and wares that covers the square and extends into several side streets and three indoor markets.

San Carlo dal 1973
Centro *Piazza San Carlo 169 (womenswear) & 197 (menswear) (011 511 4111/www.sancarlo1973.it). Open 3.30-7.30pm Mon; 10am-7pm Tue-Sat (womenswear); 3.30-7.30pm Mon; 10.30am-7.30pm Tue-Sat (mens).*
Named after the year of its founding and the square on which the handsome building is located, this is Turin's most stylish fashion and interiors store. It carries all the big brands, and some more surprising ones, in six beautifully turned-out floors. Think Selfridges meets Barneys New York; look out for the famous Christmas display.

Stratta
Centro *Piazza San Carlo 191 (011 547 920/www.stratta1836.it). Open 3-7.30pm Mon; 10am-1pm, 3-7.30pm Tue-Sat.*

Top: Il Gran Balon;
Mercato di Porta Palazzo
(2); Middle: Museo del
Cinema (2); Lingotto;
Bottom: Via Po (2).

The beautiful shop windows of this old shop – it first opened in 1836 – reveal a fine display of candies, sweets, chocolates, pralines, *marrons glacés* and candied fruit set amidst precious crystal and wood. They taste as good as they look.

ARTS

Auditorium Giovanni Agnelli
Lingotto *Via Nizza 280 (011 631 1702/011 631 3721/ www.lingottomusica.it).*
Designed by Renzo Piano in the ex-Fiat Lingotto factory, this vast and handsome auditorium is renowned for its excellent acoustics. It regularly hosts major international conductors and orchestras, as well as the national Orchestra Sinfonica Nazionale della Rai, and is a main venue in Turin's September music festival.

Teatro Regio
Piazza Castello 215 (011 881 5241/www. teatroregio.torino.it).
This is Turin's main performing arts venue, hosting around 100 productions a year of opera, music and ballet, including an orchestral concert season from March to June. The 1930s modernist proscenium arch is faced by a half-shell seating area with icicle-like chandeliers and curvy white boxes that could have come straight out of *Barbarella*.

NIGHTLIFE

At the heart of Turin's nightlife are I Murazzi, clubs and bars built into the huge arches in the embankment along the west bank of the River Po from Ponte Umberto to Ponte Vittorio. Most are open year-round, but they come into their own in summer, when Torinese descend en masse to the waterfront. They open from around 7pm; many stay that way until dawn.

The traditional way to kick off an evening is with an *aperitivo*. Some nightlife venues extend this snack-buffet tradition later into the evening.

The Beach
Centro *Murazzi del Po 18-20-22 (011 888 777/www.thebeachtorino.it). Open Call for details.*
A beach indeed, with its deckchairs and umbrellas set out along the riverbank in summer: this is where smart Torinesi come to work on their tans while enjoying a great lunch menu and sipping a fresh mojito by day. By night, there's dancing, led by an ever-changing roster of guest DJs. The high arched brick interior contains clean contemporary furniture, light installations and video projections. Also a cultural centre, The Beach often hosts arts events.

Hiroshima Mon Amour
Lingotto *Via Bossoli 83 (011 317 6636/ www.hiroshimamonamour.org).*
One of Turin's historic *locali* and cultural centres, HMA started life in 1986 to promote Italian and international music and to stage comic and cabaret theatre. As well as clubbing on Saturday evenings (ska, reggae and pop), Hiroshima hosts concerts and theatre shows. It also works with city authorities to organise festivals and big events.

Palasport Olimpico
Lingotto *Via Filadelfia 82 (011 616 4963/327 9022/www.torinolympicpark.org).*
This dramatic metallic box hosted ice-hockey in the 2006 Winter Olympics; it's now a multipurpose venue that tends to be the Turin stopover for major touring acts.

Factfile

When to go
Turin is a year-round destination with a temperate climate. Summers are not too hot and winters only cold enough to appreciate the hot chocolate served in cafés.

Getting there & around
Aeroporto Internazionale Sandro Pertini (011 567 6361/www.turin-airport.com) is better known as Caselle. It's located 16 kilometres north of the city. It has a station, but the line doesn't go all the way into the centre of town; bus is the best way to do that: Sadem (www.sadem.it) runs services about every half an hour to Porta Nuova station. Buy tickets before you board, at the office in the airport or, on the return journey, bars around the stops served (see website for details, and arrive early as finding the exact stop can be confusing). Holders of a Torino + Piedmont card get a discount. Taxis cost €30-€40.

Most of Turin is easily explored on foot, though there is an efficient network of buses and trams, and a growing but as-yet not very visitor-relevant metro system. To get to the Lingotto from the city centre, take bus/tram number 1 or 35.

Tourist information
Turismo Torino e Provincia
(www.turismotorino.org) is efficient and friendly, with lots of good materials to give out. There are three offices, all open daily: at the airport (8am-11pm), on Piazza Castello (at via Garibaldi; 9am-7pm); and at Porta Nuova (9.30am-7pm) station. The number for telephone queries is 011 535 181 (9.30am-9.30pm).

Internet
Fnac Via Roma 56, Piazza Castello (011 551 6711). Open 9.30am-8pm Mon-Sat; 10am-8pm Sun.

Venice

Most visitors come to Venice with some idea of what to expect. The big surprise is that it's true – the streets are indeed full of water, and there is an otherworldly, fairy-tale quality to the place. It can sometimes seem as if the city exists solely for tourists, and offers little in the way of that heart-warming 'authenticity' found in other Italian destinations. But real, workaday Venice is there, beneath the surface, and it's well worth seeking out. Just be prepared to muster all your map-reading skills – and to get very, very lost.

Clockwise from top left: Hotel La Calcina; Piazza San Marco (2); Marina & Susanna Sent; Grand Canal; Piazza San Marco (Torre).

With a few exceptions, there's nothing cutting-edge – or even remotely modern – about the way Venice presents its immense cultural wealth. Indeed, were they to return today, the visitors who have flocked to La Serenissima since the 15th century would have no difficulty recognising the city they saw then. True, there are initiatives to bring Venice into the 21st century, with ambitious projects with prestigious names attached (Frank Gehry, Santiago Calatrava and David Chipperfield, to name but a few), but these are all lagging behind schedule.

Venice was founded in the fifth century AD, by refugees who fled to the islets of the lagoon in the aftermath of the falling Roman Empire. From this inauspicious beginning rose a city that would control eastern Mediterranean shipping for six centuries. The Venetian Republic lived for commerce, steadfastly maintaining political neutrality and focusing its geographic conquests on improving shipping routes. Such single-minded devotion to trade established Venice as the principle European source for luxury goods from the Middle and Far East – a happy state of affairs that ended in the 15th century, when the fall of Constantinople and rise of Portugal as a maritime rival severely damaged its monopoly. Worse, the city became embroiled in expensive wars in defence of its Adriatic possessions. By the 18th century, Venice was bankrupt, making it easy pickings for the Austrians (and, briefly, Napoleon), who quickly absorbed Venice into their empire. There it remained until 1866, when it became part of the newly united Kingdom of Italy.

Venice

Venice

ITALY

Venice

Historic sites

● ● ● ● ●

Art & architecture

● ● ● ● ●

Hotels

● ● ● ● ●

Eating & drinking

● ● ● ● ●

Nightlife

● ● ● ● ●

Shopping

● ● ● ● ●

Michelin man

The youngest chef ever to have attained three Michelin stars for his cooking lives not in France, but in Italy, in a suburb of Padua (50 kilometres from Venice, 35 kilometres from Vicenza). Massimiliano Alajmo took over his parents' one-star restaurant, Le Calandre, when he was only 19. Not only did he not lose that star – as sometimes happens when a new chef comes in – but three years later he was awarded a second, at a mere 22 years old. Unlike in France, where many restaurants have three stars, in Italy the Red Guide is parsimonious with its highest accolades: to date only a handful of restaurants have made it into the three-star culinary pantheon. So it caused a furore when, in 2004, aged 28, Alajmo took that accolade too. The softly spoken, gangly young man had become a star.

Le Calandre is on a busy road that leads into Padua from Verona, just a short drive from Soave and Valpolicella, an hour from Venice. The spare, colourful restaurant is run by Massimiliano and his older brother, Raffaele. It's flanked by the Alajmo's cosy Relais hotel and a large pasticceria-bar that faces the road where you can stop in for delicious pastries, light lunches or a drink any time of day – all prepared by the restaurant's kitchen. Raffaele is a sommelier and has hand-picked an exceptional wine list.

The hardest thing for a young chef to do is establish his own culinary trademark, especially in a country where the home-cooked food is so good. And so varied: each Italian region has its own palette of ingredients and dishes. Where does a chef with a modernist approach fit in? 'If you think about tradition, it's something that is handed down from generation to generation, unconsciously,' he says. 'For me, it's more the mood or feel of a dish than the specific ingredients that set the tone. I think traces of tradition can be found everywhere, which leaves lots of room for freedom of interpretation. What matters in a dish – just like in music – is its harmony.' Massimiliano Alajmo's dishes are full of surprises, yet they're still recognisably linked to the ingredients they're made from. His 'cappucino' of potato and squid is served in a squid-shaped glass. He puts an airy potato purée over ink-black chunks of tender squid which, when spooned up from the bottom, leave dark stains on the white froth. It's a sensual, playful dish, and one that characterises Alajmo's style. A layered 'sfoglia' of crisp pastry, saffron cream and Sicilian almonds is assembled at the

diner's table, like a magic trick. Another dessert is arranged on a child's wooden cart, a dozen little treats set out on building blocks.

'I started cooking as a child, and it's that trusting, open and sometimes playful curiosity I look for when I cook,' he says. 'There's a wonderful exchange between a child and its grandparent, where each turns to the other for inspiration. My way of moving forward is to dig back into the past.'

Alajmo's recent cookbook, *In.gredienti*, describes the young cook's adventures in the celebrated kitchens of Paul Bocuse, Gualtiero Marchesi and Michel Guérard. It presents his elegant recipes broken down into their elements: layers, textures, liquidity, expansion – dishes to be inspired by, but also to enjoy eating. And the latest recipe? 'It's a reinterpretation of the classic *spaghetti, aglio, olio e peperoncino* – spaghetti with garlic, oil and chilli pepper – that all-time Italian favourite.' Classic it may be, but cooked by Massimiliano Alajmo, you know it's going to take you back to the future.

Le Calandre
Via Liguria 1, Sarmeola, 35030 Rubano (PD), (049 630 303/www.calandre.com). Open noon-2pm, 8-10pm Tue-Sat. €€€-€€€€.

Stay

Venice has never had a shortage of places to stay at, but it's unwise to turn up without booking accommodation in advance. Prices are high, so it helps to visit off-season.

Al Ponte Mocenigo
Santa Croce *2063, fondamenta Rimpetto Mocenigo (041 524 4797/www.alpontemocenigo.com). €€.*
Located on a quiet canal near San Stae, this delightful hotel is one of Venice's best-value accommodation options. It boasts tastefully decorated mod-Venetian rooms and well-appointed bathrooms (plus Wi-Fi access throughout), and there's a pretty courtyard garden, a bar and Turkish bath. Laidback owners Walter and Sandro are genuinely charming.

B&B San Marco
Castello *3385L, fondamenta San Giorgio degli Schiavoni (041 522 7589/335 756 6555/www.realvenice.it/smarco). €.*
One of the few Venetian B&Bs that come close to the British concept of the genre, Marco Scurati's homely apartment lies just behind San Giorgio degli Schiavoni. Three cosy, antique-filled bedrooms share a bathroom; there's also an apartment which sleeps four. Breakfast is served in Marco's own kitchen and guests are treated as part of the family.

Bauer, Il Palazzo & Casa Nova
San Marco *1459, campo San Moisè (041 520 7022/www.bauerhotels.com). €€€€.*
This is a hotel with many guises. The five-star hotel that stands on campo San Moisè occupies an ugly '40s extension of the original 18th-century hotel building. More antique in style, and with Grand Canal frontage, is Il Palazzo, housed in the older building. Recently restored, it now offers even more luxurious accommodation than its younger sister. Adjacent to the Bauer, Casa Nova is a series of spacious, serviced apartments. The latest addition is Il Palladio, a hotel and spa on the Giudecca. Our opinion? Il Palazzo's discreet, sober opulence is the best bet.

Ca' Maria Adele
Dorsoduro *111, rio terà dei Catecumeni (041 520 3078/www.camariaadele.it). €€€.*
Eighteenth-century Venice meets modern design at this luxurious guesthouse, situated in the shadow of Santa Maria della Salute. Five of the 12 rooms are 'themed', including the ultra-sexy Sala Noire; others are more conventional. There's a cosy ground-floor sitting room (with chocolate-brown faux fur on the walls) and a Moroccan-style roof terrace for sultry evenings. Service is very professional and utterly charming.

Ca' Pisani
Dorsoduro *979A, rio Terà Foscarini (041 277 1478/www.capisanihotel.it). €€€€.*
Ca' Pisani's luxurious, designer-chic rooms in 1930s and 1940s style make a refreshing change from the usual glitz, gilt and Murano glass. This was the first hotel to throw off the yawn-making pan-Venetian style, and though it's no longer the only one, it's still one of the most effective. The striking, pink-painted, 16th-century palazzo is conveniently located behind the Accademia. Bedrooms are generously sized, and there's a restaurant, sauna and roof terrace.

La Calcina
Dorsoduro *780, fondamenta delle Zattere (041 520 6466/www.lacalcina.com). €€.*
The Redentore church and Giudecca canal provide the backdrop for meals taken on the terrace of this great-value hotel, a view shared by the bedrooms at the front of the building. There's an air of civilised calm about the place; rooms have dark parquet floors, classic 19th-century furniture and a refreshingly uncluttered feel, and suites and self-catering apartments are available in adjacent buildings.

Cipriani
Giudecca *10, fondamenta San Giovanni (041 520 7744/www.hotelcipriani.com). €€€€.*
Set on the eastern tip of the Giudecca island, the Cipriani has great facilities as well as a private harbour for your yacht and a higher-than-average chance of rubbing shoulders with a film star. Rooms are exquisitely decorated, many with marble bathrooms. If this seems too humdrum, take an apartment in the neighbouring 15th-century Palazzo Vendramin, complete with butler service and private garden. Facilities include tennis courts, a pool, sauna, spa and gym, and there's a motorboat to San Marco.

> "Of all the grand hotels that crowd this part of the riva, the Metropole is arguably the most characterful."

Excelsior
Lido *Lungomare Marconi 41 (041 526 0201/ www.starwoodhotels.com/westin). Closed Nov-mid March. €€€€.*
The early-1900s pseudo-Moorish Excelsior hosts hordes of celebrities when the Venice Film Festival swings into action each September (the festival headquarters is just over the road). Demand a sea-facing room for a view of beach happenings and the Adriatic beyond. The Excelsior's beach huts are the last word in luxury. There are tennis courts and a water taxi to San Marco.

Metropole
Castello *4149, riva degli Schiavoni (041 520 5044/www.hotelmetropole.com). €€€.*
Of all the grand hotels that crowd this part of the riva, the Metropole is arguably the most characterful. Owner-manager signor Beggiato is a passionate collector, and antiques and curios are dotted throughout the elegant

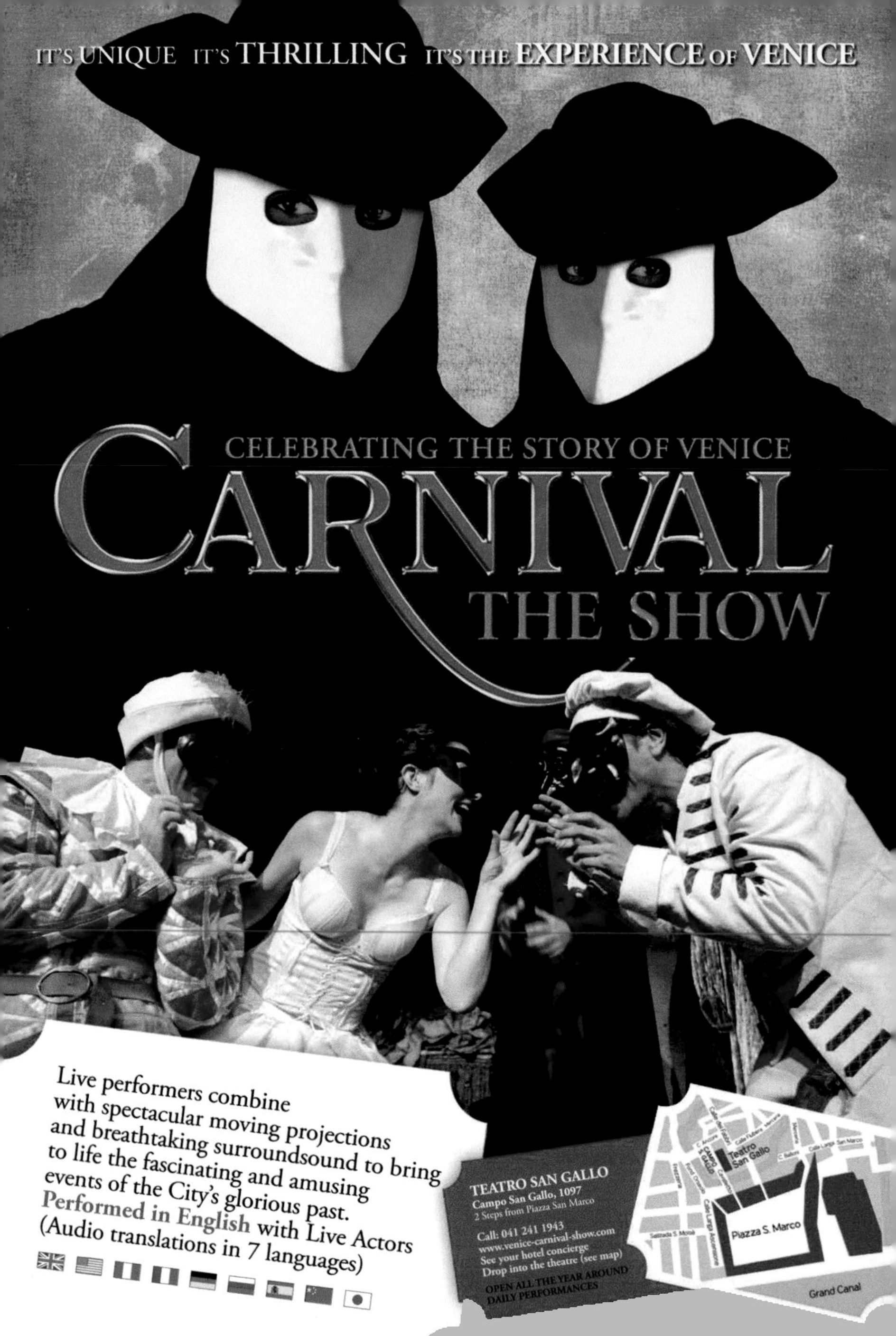
IT'S UNIQUE IT'S THRILLING IT'S THE EXPERIENCE OF VENICE
CELEBRATING THE STORY OF VENICE
CARNIVAL
THE SHOW
Live performers combine with spectacular moving projections and breathtaking surroundsound to bring to life the fascinating and amusing events of the City's glorious past.
Performed in English with Live Actors
(Audio translations in 7 languages)
TEATRO SAN GALLO
Campo San Gallo, 1097
2 Steps from Piazza San Marco
Call: 041 241 1943
www.venice-carnival-show.com
See your hotel concierge
Drop into the theatre (see map)
OPEN ALL THE YEAR AROUND
DAILY PERFORMANCES
Teatro San Gallo
Piazza S. Marco
Grand Canal

bedrooms and sumptuous public rooms. The velvet-draped salone comes into its own in winter, and in summer guests relax in the gorgeous garden. There are views over the lagoon (for a hefty supplement), the canal, or the garden.

Palazzo Abadessa
Cannaregio *4011, calle Priuli (041 241 3784/www.abadessa.com). €€.*
A beautiful, shady, walled garden is laid out in front of this privately owned 16th-century palazzo, which is filled with family antiques, paintings and silver. A magnificent double stone staircase leads to the 12 impressive rooms, some of which are truly vast. Beware, however; the low-ceilinged doubles on the mezzanine floor are rather cramped.

Eat

More and more, it's the humble neighbourhood *bacaro* (a sort of wine-oriented trattoria) that's the salvation of the Venetian dining scene. Here locals crowd the bar, downing a glass of wine (*un'ombra*) and taking the edge off their appetites with the *cicheti* (snacks) that line the counter. Indeed, there's something of the Spanish tapas mentality about the Venetian approach to eating: it's fine to order a few antipasti, then to follow with just pasta, a secondo, or dessert.

The wine-growing area that stretches from the Veneto north-east to Friuli is one of Italy's strongest, with good white wines like tocai and soave backed up by solid reds such as valpolicella and cabernet franc. Other popular drinks include a *spritz* (an aperitivo of white wine, Campari and a shot of selzer or sparkling water), grappa and, of course, coffee.

A double pricing policy applies in many local places, with one tariff for Venetians and another – the one on the menu – for tourists. There's not much you can do about this.

Ai Gondolieri
Dorsoduro *336, fondamenta Ospedaletto (041 528 6396/www.aigondolieri.com). Open noon-3pm, 7-10pm Mon, Wed-Sun. €€€€. Modern Italian.*
If you're looking to splash out, Ai Gondolieri offers a creative menu that belies its ultra-traditional decor and service. It's also, unusually for Venice, fish-free. Rooted in the culinary traditions of north-east Italy, the attractively presented dishes include a warm salad of venison with blueberries, panzerotti (pasta parcels) filled with topinambur (Jerusalem artichokes) in Montasio cheese sauce and rack of lamb with Barolo and radicchio. Truffles invade the menu in autumn. Owner Giovanni Trevisan also runs the bar-restaurant inside the nearby Peggy Guggenheim Collection.

Alle Testiere
Castello *5801, calle del Mondo Novo (041 522 7220). Open noon-2pm, 7-10.30pm Tue-Sat. Closed last wk Dec, 2wks Jan, last wk July, 3wks Aug. €€€€. Trattoria.*

One of the great success stories of recent years, this tiny restaurant is one of the hottest culinary tickets in Venice. With just 22 seats, there are two sittings each evening; the later one, at 9pm, is more relaxed. Bruno, the cook, offers creative variations on Venetian seafood; caparossoli (clams) sautéed in ginger, perhaps, or John Dory fillet with aromatic herbs in citrus sauce. Sommelier Luca guides diners around a small but well-chosen wine list and marvellous cheeseboard, and desserts are spectacular: don't miss the chocolate, pear and ricotta tart.

Busa alla Torre
Murano *campo Santo Stefano 3 (041 739 662). Open noon-3.30pm daily. €€€. Trattoria.*
This is Murano's ultimate gastronomic stop-off, and the perfect place for refuelling after resisting the hard sell at the island's glass workshops. In summer, tables spill out into a pretty square opposite the church of San Pietro Martire. The service is deft and professional; the fare is reliable, no-frills seafood. Excellent primi might include ravioli filled with branzino (bream) in a spider-crab sauce, or tagliatelle with canoce (mantis shrimps); note Busa alla Torre opens only for lunch.

> "Stepping into Florian, a mirrored, stuccoed and frescoed jewel of a café, sweeps you back to 18th-century Venice."

Caffè Florian
San Marco *56, piazza San Marco (041 520 5641/www.caffeflorian.com). Open May-Oct 10am-midnight daily. Nov-Apr 10am-midnight Mon, Tue, Thur-Sun. Closed early Dec-Christmas, 2wks Jan. Café.*
Stepping into Florian, a mirrored, stuccoed and frescoed jewel of a café, sweeps you back to 18th-century Venice. Founded in 1720, its present appearance dates from an 1859 remodelling. Rousseau, Goethe and Byron hung out here, but you pay for its illustrious pedigree: if you sit at one of the outside tables, nothing – not even a humble caffè – comes in at less than €10.

La Cantina
Cannaregio *3689, campo San Felice (041 522 8258). Open 11am-10pm Tue-Sat. Closed 2wks July-Aug, 2wks Jan. Wine bar.*
This is a wonderful place in which to enjoy your aperitivo, though the snack offerings are so substantial that a quick drink can easily turn into a full meal. Outside, tables set back from the strada Nuova are the perfect place from which to watch the world bustle by – assuming you can take your eyes off the mouth-watering crostini, made on the spot with whatever's in season at the local fish and produce markets. Some 30 wines are available by the glass.

Corte Sconta

Castello *3886, calle del Pestrin (041 522 7024).*
Open Feb-Dec 12.30-2.30pm, 7-10pm Tue-Sat.
Closed Jan, mid July-mid Aug. €€€€. Trattoria.
This trailblazing seafood restaurant is a firm favourite on
the well-informed tourist circuit, and best booked several
days in advance. The main act is an endless procession of
seafood antipasti, though the pasta is homemade and the
warm zabaione dessert is a delight. Decor is of the modern
Bohemian trattoria variety and the ambience is loud and
friendly. In summer, try to be seated at a table in the pretty,
vine-covered courtyard.

Da Fiore

San Polo *2202, calle del Scaleter (041 721 308).*
Open 12.30-2.30pm, 7.30-10.30pm Tue-Sat.
Closed Christmas-mid Jan, Aug. €€€€. Trattoria.
In the elegant, barge-like dining room of Michelin-starred
Da Fiore, owner Maurizio Martin treats his guests with
egalitarian courtesy, while his wife Mara concentrates on
getting the food right. Raw fish and seafood is a key feature
of the antipasti; primi are divided between pasta dishes and
risottos. Secondi bring out the flavour of the fish without
smothering it in sauce. There's an exceptional selection of
regional cheeses and a collection of decent desserts.

Dalla Marisa

Cannaregio *652B, fondamenta San Giobbe (041
720 211). Open noon-2.30pm Mon, Wed, Sun;
noon-2.30pm, 8-9.15pm Tue, Thur-Sat. Closed
Aug. €€. No credit cards. Traditional Italian.*
Signora Marisa, the proud descendant of a dynasty of
butchers, is a culinary legend in Venice, with locals calling
up days in advance to ask her to prepare ancient recipes
such as risotto con le secoe (risotto made with a special cut
of beef from around the spine). Pasta dishes include the
excellent tagliatelle con sugo di masaro (in duck sauce), and
secondi range from tripe to roast stuffed pheasant. In
summer tables spill out from the tiny interior on to the
fondamenta overlooking the busy Cannaregio canal. Book
well ahead, and note that serving times are rigid.

Harry's Bar

San Marco *1323, calle Vallaresso (041 528
5777/www.cipriani.com). Open 10.30am-11pm daily.
€€€€. International.*
This historic watering hole, founded by Giuseppe Cipriani
in 1931, is little changed since the days when Ernest
Hemingway came here to work on his next hangover –
except for the prices and the numbers of tourists. Despite
the pre-dinner crush and some offhand service, a Bellini at
the bar is as much a part of the Venetian experience as a
gondola ride (and at €14, far cheaper). At mealtimes, the
tables are reserved for diners who enjoy the Venetian-
themed international comfort food and are prepared to pay
very steep prices to be seen chez Harry.

Muro Vino e Cucina

San Polo *222, campo Cesare Battisti (041 523 7495).*
*Open noon-3pm, 7.30-11pm Mon-Sat; 5pm-2am Sun
(wine bar only). €€€. Modern Italian/wine bar.*

Muro is one of the city's most interesting new restaurants,
as German chef Jozef 'Beppe' Klostermaier plays fast and
loose with local traditions in dishes like caserecce
(homemade pasta) with radicchio di Treviso and pear in
gorgonzola sauce. There's a serious grill for fish or steak,
and the wine list's strong on the Veneto, Friuli and Alto
Adige. Dinner guests are offered a glass of prosecco, a small
starter and water free of charge. The lunch menu is
simpler and cheaper.

Explore

SIGHTS

Venice is divided into six *sestieri* (districts);
all addresses include the sestieri name.
    Among the various multi-entrance tickets are
the Venice Card (www.venicecard.it), which also
includes public transport, and the Rolling Venice
programme (details on the Venice Card site),
offering discounts around town. Ask at the tourist
office for information on museum passes.

THE GRAND CANAL

Whether you choose to take a leisurely (and
budget-breaking) gondola ride or squeeze on
to a packed *vaporetto*, this is the one trip you
can't omit. The canal may no longer be teeming
with merchandise-laden cargo boats, but it is
still Venice's main thoroughfare. Most of the
notable palazzi and buildings facing the canal
were built between the 12th and 18th centuries;
they include, near the covered fish market
(Pescaria), the Fabbriche Nuove (the longest
façade on the Grand Canal) and the huge
Palazzo Grimani – now being restored as a
museum. The interior was used in Nicolas
Roeg's 1973 classic *Don't Look Now*.

SAN MARCO

Napoleon referred to St Mark's Square as the
'drawing room of Europe', a description that
catches the quality of it: it may not be homely,
but it is a supremely civilised meeting place.
Here, Byzantine rubs shoulders with Gothic,
late Renaissance and neoclassical.
    Entering the square from the west, you
encounter one of the world's greatest views.
In the centre of the piazza is the *campanile*
(bell tower), the city's tallest building. At
the eastern end of the square are two world-
famous sights, the basilica di San Marco
and the Palazzo Ducale.
    Heading east from the piazzetta, between the
piazza and the lagoon, you cross the ponte della
Paglia (Bridge of Straw). If you can elbow your
way to the side of the bridge, there is a photo-op
view of the ponte dei Sospiri (Bridge of Sighs).

Clockwise from top left:
Hotel al Ponte Mocenigo
(3); Hotel La Calcina (2).

Basilica di San Marco

San Marco *piazza San Marco (041 522 5205/*
www.basilicasanmarco.it).
Basilica, Chancel & Pala d'Oro, Treasury Open
Apr-Sept 9.45am-5pm Mon-Sat; 2-5pm Sun. Oct-Mar
9.45am-4.45pm Mon-Sat; 1-4.45pm Sun. Admission
Basilica free. Chancel & Pala d'Oro €1.50; €1
reductions. Treasury €2; €1 reductions.
Loggia & Museo Marciano. Open Apr-Oct
9.45am-5pm daily. Nov-Mar 9.45am-4pm daily.
Admission €3; €1.50 reductions. No credit cards.
The present basilica, the third on the site, was built mainly
between 1063 and 1094, although its decoration continued
all the way through to the 16th century. The façade boasts
fantastic Gothic tracery, but its real treasures are the
sculptures, in particular the group of three carved arches
around the central portal, a Romanesque masterpiece.
Inside, the basilica is surmounted by five great 11th-century
domes and has more than four sq km of mosaics; the finest
pieces date from the 12th and 13th centuries. Look out too
for Christ Pantocrator, a 16th-century reproduction of a
Byzantine original, and the opulent Byzantine Pala d'Oro
(Gold altarpiece). The loggia provides marvellous views
over the square.

Palazzo Ducale (Doge's Palace)

San Marco *1, piazzetta San Marco (041 271*
5911/bookings 041 520 9070/www.museicivici
veneziani.it). Open Apr-Oct 9am-7pm daily (ticket
office closes 6pm). Nov-Mar 9am-5pm daily (ticket
office closes 4pm). Admission €12; €6.50 reductions
(for multi-entrance Musei di Piazza San Marco ticket).
No credit cards.
The Doge's Palace, home of Venice's rulers until 1797, has
occupied the same site since the ninth century, although the
current structure dates from the mid 1400s. Venice's great
Gothic building, the Palace is a treasure trove of painting
and sculpture by some of the greatest names of the
Renaissance, including Tintoretto, Titian, Veronese, Palma
il Vecchio and Bassano. It also houses an impressive array
of period weaponry, armour, ceramics and maps. A short
walk over the Bridge of Sighs (ponti di Sospiri) leads to the
palace's prison cells, apparently luxurious by 16th-century
standards. Frequent guided tours (€6) run from November
to March; call 041 520 9038 for information and bookings.

CASTELLO

Castello, the city's largest *sestiere*, takes
its name from the fortress that once stood
at the eastern end of the city, protecting it
from invasion by the sea.

At the heart of northern and western Castello
is the busy campo Santa Maria Formosa and, to
the north, campo Santi Giovanni e Paolo. Here,
the Gothic red brick of the Dominican church is
set off by the glistening marble façade of the
Scuola di San Marco (now a hospital), with its
magnificent trompe l'oeil panels.

The close-clustered buildings of working-class
eastern Castello housed the employees of the
Arsenale, Venice's dockland, much of which now

lies derelict. Further east, a lively market is
held in via Garibaldi (Mon-Sat). Close by, the
pleasantly leafy Giardini Pubblici give way to the
Giardini della Biennale, where pavilions come to
life for the annual arts (odd years) or architecture
(even years) festivals (www.labiennale.org).

CANNAREGIO

Few other cities offer newly arrived tourists
such a feast for the eyes: step out of the train
station and in front of you is the Grand Canal.
The quiet *calli* and *campi* immediately off the
heaving lista di Spagna conceal some great
churches and surprises, such as the original
Ghetto. Only around a dozen Jewish families
still live there, but it remains the centre of
spiritual, cultural and social life for the city's
Jewish community. The Jewish Museum
(Museo Ebraico) is at Cannaregio 2902B
(041 715 359, www.museoebraico.it).

The north-western areas of Cannaregio offer
respite from the crowds. Here, the Madonna
dell'Orto (campo Madonna dell'Orto, closed
Sun) is known as the 'Tintoretto church' for
the numerous works by the artist it contains.

SAN POLO & SANTA CROCE

Probably only postmen know where the boundary
lies between these two *sestieri*, the eastern
portion of which is the city's ancient heart.
The streets cluster around the Rialto market
(founded in 1097) and the famous Rialto bridge
(built in 1588-92 and until the 19th century the
only bridge over the Grand Canal). West of the
bridge lie campo San Polo – the biggest square
on this side of the Grand Canal – and Santa
Maria Gloriosa dei Frari (aka I Frari), with the
Tintoretto-filled Scuola Grande di San Rocco
(San Polo 3054, campo San Rocco, 041
523 4864, www.sanrocco.it) nearby.

The western part of the area, settled later,
has a slightly more spacious feel. Many of the
important sights face on to the Grand Canal,
including the Ca' Pesaro (Santa Croce 2076,
041 524 0695, www.museicivicineneziani.it),
home to the contemporary art museum and
oriental museum.

I Frari

San Polo, *campo dei Frari (041 522 2637/*
www.chorusvenezia.org). Open 9am-6pm Mon-Sat;
1-6pm Sun. Admission €2.50. No credit cards.
A gloomy Gothic barn, Santa Maria Gloriosa dei Frari is
one of the city's most significant artistic storehouses. The
sacristy houses one of Bellini's greatest paintings, the
Madonna and Child with Saints Nicholas, Peter, Benedict
and Mark (1488), and the high altar is dominated by Titian's
visionary Assumption. Another magnificent Titian, the
Madonna di Ca' Pesaro (1519), hangs to the right of the side
door in the left aisle. The artist is buried in the second bay
in the right aisle.

Caffè Florian.

DORSODURO

Dorsoduro – literally 'hard back' – is Venice's southern *sestiere* and stretches along Venice's southern flank, from the western docks to the magnificent church of the Salute. At its heart is the long campo Santa Margherita; the morning market (Mon-Sat) is enjoyably chaotic, and in the evenings the bars and cafés are packed out.

South of here are the picturesque rio di San Barnaba and the swaggering Ca' Rezzonico (Dorsoduro 3136, 041 241 0100, www.musei civiciveneziani.it), now a museum dedicated to 18th-century Venice. On the southern shore is the widest stretch of the Zattere; in good weather, the promenade fills with sun-worshipping locals.

Home to artists, writers and wealthy foreigners, the eastern reaches of Dorsoduro are elegantly prosperous. The Gallerie dell'Accademia and the Peggy Guggenheim Collection are based here, and plans are afoot to turn the huge 19th-century warehouses on the Punta della Dogana into a major contemporary art museum.

Gallerie dell'Accademia

Dorsoduro *1050, campo Carità (041 522 2247/ www.artive.arti.beniculturali.it). Open 8.15am-2pm Mon; 8.15am-7.15pm Tue-Sun. Admission €6.50; reductions €3.25; free under-18s. Audio guides: single €4, double €6. Video guides €6. No credit cards.*
The Accademia is the essential one-stop shop for Venetian painting up to the 18th century. The magnificent collection was made possible by Napoleon, who confiscated artworks from hundreds of suppressed churches and convents, and moved the city's fine arts school here. Highlights include three greats of 16th-century Venetian painting in Room 6 – Titian, Tintoretto and Veronese. In Room 10, Tintoretto's ghostly chiaroscuro Transport of the Body of St Mark vies for attention with Titian's moving Pietà – his last painting – and Veronese's huge Christ in the House of Levi. Room 11 has canvases by Tintoretto (the exquisite Madonna dei Camerlenghi), Bernardo Strozzi and Tiepolo. Carpaccio's Life of St Ursula cycle of frescoes in Room 21 is also not to be missed. Be aware that the layout may change in the wake of a massive restoration project, nearing completion at the time of writing.

Peggy Guggenheim Collection

Dorsoduro *701, fondamenta Venier dei Leoni (041 240 5411/www.guggenheim-venice.it). Open 10am-6pm Mon, Wed-Sun. Admission €10; €5-€8 reductions; free under-10s. No credit cards.*
The remarkable Peggy Guggenheim Collection is the third most visited museum in the city. Many big European names can be found here, including Picasso, Duchamp, Brancusi, Giacometti and Ernst, plus a few Americans such as Pollock. Key works include the beautifully enigmatic Empire of Light by Magritte and Giacometti's disturbing Woman with Her Throat Cut. Perhaps the most startling exhibit, though, is Marino Marini's Angel of the City out on the terrace, who thrusts his manhood towards passing vaporetti.

Santa Maria della Salute

Dorsoduro *campo della Salute (041 522 5558). Open 9am-noon, 3-5.30pm daily. Sacristy Admission €1.50.*
Queening it over the entrance of the Grand Canal, this magnificent Baroque church was built between 1631 and 1681 in thanksgiving for the end of Venice's last bout of plague. The three chapels on the right have paintings by Luca Giordano, while the high altar has a splendidly dynamic sculptural group by Giusto Le Corte. On the altar is a very early Titian representing Saints Mark, Sebastian, Roch, Cosmas and Damian, while three of his later works hang on the ceiling, depicting violent Old Testament scenes, such as the Sacrifice of Abraham, David Killing Goliath and Cain and Abel. The best paintings, including Tintoretto's Marriage at Cana (1551), can be found in the sacristy.

> ## "This unique spot cried out for a masterpiece, and Palladio provided it with his first complete solo church."

LA GIUDECCA & SAN GIORGIO

Immediately south of Venice 'proper', and divided from it by the Giudecca canal and the bacino di San Marco, the islands of San Giorgio and La Giudecca are quite different in feel.

The gondola-shaped La Giudecca has a residential but arty vibe. During the 19th century the city authorities converted some of its numerous abandoned convents and monasteries into prisons and factories. The latter are now being eyed up for redevelopment into housing and hotel complexes; in 2007, the massive Molino Stucky, an old flour mill, re-opened as a Hilton.

San Giorgio, meanwhile, realised its true potential under architect extraordinaire Andrea Palladio, whose church of San Giorgio Maggiore is one of Venice's most recognisable landmarks.

San Giorgio Maggiore

Isola San Giorgio Maggiore (041 522 7827). Open 9.30am-12.30pm, 2.30-6pm Mon-Sat; 2-6.30pm Sun. Admission Church free. Campanile €3; reductions €2. No credit cards.
This unique spot cried out for a masterpiece, and Palladio provided it with his first complete solo church. There are several notable works of art here, including two vast Tintorettos: a Last Supper and the Gathering of Manna. His last painting, a moving Entombment, hangs in the Cappella dei Morti. The view from the top of the campanile is truly extraordinary.

The Vetro Artistico® Murano
Murano trademark, a safeguard for Made in Italy.

Set up by the Veneto Region in 1994, the **Vetro Artistico® Murano trademark**, administered and regulated by the Promovetro Consortium, certifies the provenance of glass products made on the island of Murano. In addition, it guarantees the consumer's purchase as genuine and authentic. The seal is an essential safeguard of one of the symbols of Made in Italy and its efforts against counterfeiting. The VAM trademark guarantees the quality and originality of products which belong to an age-old and jealously preserved artisanal tradition.

 Since 2002, the trademark has been an integral part of artistic glass, respecting the specific characteristics of Murano's glassmaking traditions. It can only be used by Promovetro's member companies, who affix it directly onto the object. The mark represents the borsella, a traditional tool for shaping glass, and includes the manufacturing company's individual code. It prevents counterfeiting as it cannot be removed without breaking the seal itself.

Authorized Vetro Artistico® Murano trademark dealers, your added guarantee.

From this year, buying original Vetro Artistico di Murano glass in Venice will be even easier. Promovetro, the chief regulatory body and promoter of the Vetro Artistico® Murano trademark, has recently undertaken its usual series of thorough checks on all retailers selling Murano glass, and has selected a number of retailers able to guarantee customers total authenticity and security with their purchases. These retailers will display a window sticker like the one shown above, and all Murano glass objects will bear the standard anti-counterfeit mark, which will be clearly visible throughout the store in specially appointed display fixtures. They will also highlight each object's provenance, including those originating from other areas. This ensures that customers will be able to make an informed choice about their purchases, safe in the knowledge they are buying fully traceable, genuine Murano glass ∎

LIDO & LAGOON

The saltwater lagoon in which Venice sits is the world's biggest wetland, at 520 square kilometres. The lagoon is protected from the open sea by the two slender barriers of the Lido and Pellestrina. The former is a placidly residential suburb that perks up in summer, with an influx of city sunbathers and tourists staying in the Lido's overspill hotels. Things reach a head at the beginning of September, when the film festival rolls into town for two weeks.

Of the other 30-plus islands on the lagoon, many are uninhabited, but two stand out: Murano and Burano. In 1291, it was decided that all of Venice's glass furnaces should be transferred to Murano, for fear of fire in the main city. The pushy 'guides' and snipers' alley of shops selling glass knick-knacks along fondamenta dei Vetrai are offputting, but there are some serious glass makers on the island; look out for the Vetro Artistico™ Murano trademark.

Picturesque Burano is a magnet for tourists. Locals were traditionally either fishermen or lacemakers, though there are increasingly fewer of the latter. The street leading from the main quay throbs with shops selling lace – much of it machine-made in Taiwan (the authentic stuff is largely done on commission). But Burano is big enough for the visitor to meander through its quiet backstreets and avoid a lace overload.

SHOP

The Mercerie – the maze of crowded, narrow alleyways leading from piazza San Marco to the Rialto – and the streets known collectively as the Frezzeria, immediately to the west of St Mark's square, have been Venice's main retail areas for the past 600 years or so. The densest concentration of big-name fashion outlets (Prada, Fendi, Gucci et al) is around calle larga XXII Marxo. For fresh fruit, vegetables, fish and a taste of exuberant Venetian life, head to the open-air market at the north-west foot of the Rialto bridge (Mon-Sat mornings).

3856
Dorsoduro 3749, calle San Pantalon
(041 720 595). Open 10am-7.45pm Tue-Sat.
This shop is particularly popular with fashion-conscious students and, like Mary Poppins' bag, fits a lot into a small space. Jewellery, scarves and bags are tucked in alongside clothes and Georgina Goodman shoes.

Annelie
Dorsoduro 2748, calle lunga San Barnaba (041 520 3277). Open 9.30am-1pm, 4-7.30pm Mon-Sat.
There's a beautiful selection of sheets, tablecloths, curtains, shirts and baby clothes at Annelie, either fully embroidered or with lace detailing. Antique lace can also be had at reasonable prices.

Attombri
San Polo 74, sottoportego degli Orafi
(041 521 2524/www.attombri.com).
Open 9.30am-1pm, 2.30-7pm Mon-Sat.
Underneath the arches at the north-western foot of the Rialto, jeweller brothers Stefano and Daniele Attombri sell intricate, unique pieces that combine metal wire and delicate antique Venetian glass beads.

Gaggio
San Marco 3441-3451, calle delle Botteghe (041 522 8574/www.gaggio.it). Open 10.30am-1pm, 4-6.30pm Mon-Fri; 10.30am-1pm Sat.
Emma Gaggio is a legend among dressmakers, and her sumptuous, handprinted silk velvets (from €195 a metre) are used to make cushions and wall hangings as well as bags, hats, scarves and jackets.

> "You can watch chocolate being made while sipping an iced chocolate or nibbling on a spicy praline at this cornucopia of cocoa."

Marchini Pasticceria
San Marco 676, calle Spadaria (041 522 9109/www.golosessi.com). Open June-Sept 9am-8pm Mon, Wed-Sat. Oct-May 9am-10pm daily.
Probably Venice's most famous sweet shop, and certainly the most expensive, Marchini recently moved to new premises close to San Marco. Exquisite chocolates include Le Baute Veneziane – small chocolates in the form of Carnevale masks. Cakes can be ordered.

Marina & Susanna Sent
Dorsoduro 669, campo san Vio (041 520 8136).
Open 10am-6pm daily.
Venice's best contemporary glass jewellery is created by the Sent sisters. There's also a good selection of the work of the contemporary design house Arcade. The Sents also have a workshop on Murano (Fondamenta Serenella 20, 041 527 4665) – call ahead to make an appointment.

Pot-Pourri
San Marco 1810, ramo dei Fuseri (041 241 0990/www.potpourri.it). Open May-July, Sept-Oct 10am-1pm, 3.30-7.30pm daily. Nov-Apr, Aug 10am-1pm, 3.30-7.30pm Mon-Sat.
Walking into this shop is like stepping into an elegant friend's boudoir; clothes are draped over armchairs or hanging from wardrobe doors, and charming knick-knacks cover the dressing table. Designers include Cristina Effe and Marzi.

Visite guidate

Venice between contemporary and tradition

VISITS TO:
THE SYNAGOGUES, THE JEWISH MUSEUM AND CEMETERY
PALAZZO GRASSI AND ITS EXHIBITIONS,
ISLAND OF ST. GIORGIO AND ITS BASILICA,
ISLAND OF ST. SERVOLO
AND THE MUSEUM OF THE INSANE ASYLUM.
QUERINI STAMPALIA FOUNDATION AND ITS EXHIBITION
GIORGIO CINI'S ART GALLERY

**to book
info at
+39 041 5240119**

from Sunday to Thursday from 10 to 17
friday from 10 to 16

R O M A
I BARBARI
LA NASCITA DI UN NUOVO MONDO

VENEZIA
Corso del Popolo, 40
30172 Mestre
T. 041 0991100
F. 041 0991120

Campo San Polo, 2120
30125 Venezia
T. 041710200
041710091
F. 041717771
venezia@codesscultura.it

codess cultura

Palladian dream

The conveniently compact city of Padua (Padova; known to the Romans as Patavium) is just half an hour by train from Venice or Vicenza. The tourist office at the station (049 875 2077, www.turismopadova.it; open 9am-7pm Mon-Sat; 9.15am-noon Sun) will provide visitors with a map indicating the city's numerous attractions, including Giotto's must-see 1313 frescoes (it's essential to book in advance; www.cappelladegliscrovegni.it) in the Scrovegni Chapel, and the stunningly lavish Gothic basilica of St Anthony of Padua (known locally as il Santo; www.basilicadelsanto.org), which attracts thousands of pilgrims every day. But Padua also has some more idiosyncratic sites on offer.

Everybody in Vicenza knows the Gran Caffè Pedrocchi (via VIII Febbraio 15, 049 878 1231, www.caffepedrocchi.it); but tourists often just pop in to savour their speciality Pedrocchi coffee – a shot of espresso topped with choc-mint cream. Opened to the public in 1831, the café soon became known as 'the café without doors' because it never closed; other than the opening hours, little else has changed aside from extensive restorations completed in 1999. The café might appear to be much like any elegant 19th-century restaurant, but to really appreciate the results of Antonio Pedrocchi's determination to create 'the most beautiful [café] on the face of the Earth', a visit to the extraordinary chambers above the restaurant is essential (open 9.30am-12.30pm, 3.30-6pm Tue-Sun, admission €4, no credit cards). This magnificent upper floor, designed as a Ridotto (a club for gambling and dancing) and built by the great Venetian architect Giuseppe Jappelli, was opened in 1842 on the occasion of the IV Congress of Italian Scientists. The rooms unfold like a condensed tour of Western civilisation; charming Greek, Roman, Renaissance, Moorish and Egyptian-themed parlours surround a central ballroom, or Sala Grande. At twice the height of the other rooms, it features a balcony for performances and 11 inconspicuous internal windows, built because Pedrocchi is said to have enjoyed spying on cheats among the gambling nobles.

At the north end of the expansive Prato della Valle, which Paduans claim is the largest public square in Italy, stands a minute museum housing a number of optical curiosities lovingly amassed throughout the lifetime of collector Minici Zotti. In the days before film and cinema, many of the objects on display in the enchanting Museo del Precinema (Prato della Valle 1A, 049 876 3838, www.minicizotti.it, open mid June-mid Sept 4-10pm Mon, Wed-Sun, mid Sept-mid June 10am-4pm Mon, Wed-Sun, closed 2wks Aug) must have seemed wondrous; even magical. The museum has managed to retain an air of this mystique, with displays including a Javanese puppet theatre, a camera obscura, ghost lanterns and instruments of illusion – some of which can be handled by visitors. This delightfully quirky attraction is, in itself, worth a trip to Padua.

Clockwise from top left:
Grand Canal; Palazzo
Grassi; Piazza San
Marco; Piazza San Marco
(Torre); Marina & Susanna
Sent (4).

Tragicomica

San Polo *2800, calle dei Nomboli (041 721 102/www.tragicomica.it). Open 10am-7pm daily.*
A spellbinding collection of mythological masks, Harlequins, Columbines and Pantaloons, as well as 18th-century dandies and ladies. All the masks are painted by an artist trained at Venice's Accademia di Belle Arti.

VizioVirtù

San Polo *2898A, calle del Campaniel (041 275 0149/www.viziovirtu.com). Open 10am-7.30pm daily (with variations in July). Closed Aug.*
You can watch chocolate being made while sipping an iced chocolate or nibbling on a spicy praline at this cornucopia of cocoa. Unusual delights include cocoa tagliatelle (which the chef recommends be teamed with game sauces).

ARTS

For many visitors, experiencing Vivaldi in his hometown is a must. The Venice Baroque Orchestra is a global success story, and the orchestra of La Fenice one of the best in the Italy.

On Sundays, lovers of sacred music can catch the sung Mass at St Mark's (10.30am) and the Gregorian chant on the island of San Giorgio (11am). The city also has two resident gospel choirs, the Venice Gospel Ensemble (www.venicegospel.com) and the Joy Singers of Venice (www.joysingers.it).

Teatro La Fenice

San Marco *1983, campo San Fantin (041 2424/041 786 511/www.teatrolafenice.it).*
Venice's principal opera house, aptly named La Fenice ('the phoenix'), has a long history of fiery destruction and miraculous rebirth. The original theatre designed by Giannantonio Selva (1792) replaced the Teatro San Benedetto, which had burnt down in 1774. Selva's building was then destroyed in 1836, and rebuilt by the Meduna brothers. Roughly a century and a half later, in 1996, a massive blaze broke out, courtesy of two electricians. After years of legal wrangling, the theatre was rebuilt, and inaugurated in December 2003. As well as opera and ballet, La Fenice has at least two concert seasons a year. The guided tour (book ahead) lasts 45 minutes.

Factfile

When to go

In the still summer months, high humidity can make Venice stiflingly hot; the warm, southerly *scirocco* wind intensifies the heat. Autumn and spring are generally mild, with occasional pea-soup fog; November and March are the rainiest months. *Acqua alta* (high water) season is from September to April, but all that usually happens is that a couple of inches of water laps into the lowest parts of the city for an hour or two, then recedes. A damp chill often makes winter days seem colder than their average few degrees above zero. Strong north-easterlies have bone-chilling effects but make the weather crisp and clear.

Getting there

Closest to the city is Venice Marco Polo Airport – SAVE SpA (viale G Galilei 30/1, 041 260 9260, www.veniceairport.it).
Società Alilaguna's (041 523 5775, www.alilaguna.com) colour-coded services link Marco Polo airport to Venice. Most useful is the hourly Linea Rossa (Red line) service.
ATVO (0421 383 672, www.atvo.it) runs a frequent bus service (number 35) between the airport and piazzale Roma, taking 20 minutes; ACTV's number 5 buses (0421 383 672, www.actv.it) also run between piazzale Roma and the airport, with a 35-40 minute journey time.
You can also fly to Treviso Sant'Angelo Airport – Aer Tre SpA (via Noalese, Treviso (0422 315

111/www.trevisoairport.it), though it is further out. ATVO bus services (see above) run from piazzale Roma and back to coincide with flights.

Getting around

Public transport in Venice, including vaporetti and buses, is run by ACTV (www.actv.it). The website lists travelcard prices – much more economical than buying individual tickets, which cost a hefty €6 a throw.

Tourist information

Azienda di Promozione Turistica (APT) San Marco 71F, piazza San Marco (041 529 8740/www.turismovenezia.it). Open 9am-3.30pm daily.
Other locations: Palazzina Santi, San Marco 2, Giardinetti Reali (041 522 5150). Open 10am-6pm daily.
Autorimessa Comunale, Santa Croce 465B, piazzale Roma (041 529 8711). Open 9.30am-1pm, 1.30-4.30pm daily.

Internet

Venice lags behind in the Wi-Fi sector, with only unofficial hotspots (open private networks) to be found. You'll need to present ID in any of the city's internet cafés.
Internet Point Santo Stefano, San Marco 2958, campo Santo Stefano (041 894 6122, www.teleradiofuga.com). Open 10.15am-11pm daily. No credit cards.

Coast & Islands

Clockwise from top left:
Salina's promenade;
Lipari harbour; Casa
Mulina's mutt; Salina
beach; *Pane cunzato*
at D'Alfredo.

The Aeolian Islands

Astonishingly beautiful and extremely varied, the seven islands and various uninhabited islets of the Aeolian archipelago were designated a UNESCO World Heritage Site in 2000. Their volcanic origins left behind a dramatic legacy of black-sand beaches, smouldering craters and splintered, rocky coastlines. Island-hoppers can discover the individual charms of each one: from the spartan, conical Alicudi, where donkeys are the only form of land transport, to the international jet-set playground of Panarea.

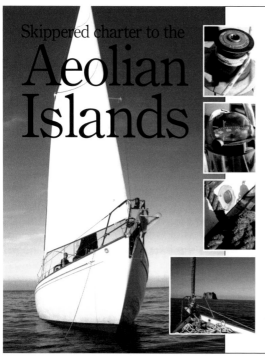

Raya

Panarea *Via San Pietro (090 983 013/ www.hotelraya.it). Closed Nov-Mar.* €€€€.
Opened in the 1960s and built entirely of natural materials, the Raya is the hotel that put Panarea on the international party map. Even today, it remains the hippest, sexiest and priciest hotel in the Aeolians; in-crowders will feel like they've died and gone to heaven, although outsiders may feel as though everyone but them has been invited to the party. The rooms (whitewashed walls, teak furniture, hand-batiked textiles, citronella candles) are built into the hillside at the back of the village, with great views to the sea over groves of olives, hibiscus and bougainvillea; the bar, club and restaurant are down above the harbour.

Sirenetta Park Hotel

Stromboli *Via Marina 33 (090 986 025/ www.lasirenetta.it). Closed Nov-Mar.* €€.
Founded by Domenico Russo in the wake of the craze for the island stimulated by Roberto Rossellini's 1949 film *Stromboli,* the Sirenetta sits outside town on the long black sand beach of Ficogrande, and is run with grace and imagination by the Russo family. With flat roofs and terraces, the whitewashed rooms are laid out in spacious, well-tended gardens that contain a saltwater pool. Yoga courses, massages, thalassotherapy and ayurvedic treatments are all available; there's also a diving centre, a tennis court and an amphitheatre in which concerts, plays, films and weddings are staged. On the beach across the road sits the chic La Tartana Club; in summer, the fashionable set gathers here for beachside cocktails, music and dinner.

Villa Meligunis

Lipari *Via Marte 7 (090 981 2426/ www.villameligunis.it).* €€-€€€.
Located in the old fisherman's quarter of alleyways and *piazzettas* behind the port of Marina Corta, the Villa Meligunis occupies an 18th-century palace once inhabited by the man who funded the first archaeological excavations of Lipari, and gave the island's museum many of its finest exhibits. The current owners continue the tradition of art patronage: paintings from their private collection of modern and contemporary Italian art hang in the public spaces. The 32 rooms have terracotta-tiled floors and heavy cream bed linen; the superior rooms have their own private terraces, and the nearby Residence Agave houses six self-contained apartments. However, the hotel's finest feature is its roof garden, complete with a pool, a bar, a restaurant, and some panoramic views over the island.

Eat

Aeolian cuisine revolves around a few key local ingredients – *pomodorini* (cherry tomatoes), capers, olives, anchovies, wild greens, fresh fish when available – and most restaurants at least nod towards tradition. However, it's true to say that most of the independent restaurants have yet to catch up with hotels in terms of style and service: the contemporary eating and drinking options are generally tied to the local hotels.

Eating choices on Alicudi are strictly limited; *agriturismo* Da Rosina Alla Mimosa (via Vallone 3, 090 988 9937, www.rosina-barbuto.it) is your best bet, offering meals made from ingredients grown on site alongside its simple rooms. Silvio and Gabriella Tanto also cook dinner for visitors at their home above the port (via Regina Elena, 090 988 9922).

> "Armani, Sean Connery and Dolce e Gabbana all send staff skimming over the sea in rubber boats from their yachts to bring back *granite* from Da Alfredo."

Da Adelina

Panarea *Via Comunale del Porto 28 (090 983 246). Open noon-3pm, 7-11pm daily. Closed Nov-mid Mar.* €€. *Trattoria.*
Mercurial young chef Giuseppe Taranto runs this cosy, relaxing candlelit restaurant overlooking Panarea's port. The menu is simple, with seasonal dishes such as *moscardini* (tiny octopus, cooked with tomato, capers, wild fennel and chilli) appearing alongside year-round recipes such as *pennette Adelina* (dressed with anchovies, aubergine, capers, olives, mint and basil). However, you can't really go wrong with the mixed fish of the day, either fried or grilled, served with a selection of vegetables.

Da Alfredo

Salina *Piazza Marina Garibaldi, Lingua (090 984 3075). Open 8.30am-late daily. Closed Nov-Mar.* €. *Café/gelateria.*
Armani, Sean Connery and Dolce e Gabbana all send staff skimming over the sea in rubber boats from their yachts to bring back *granite* from Da Alfredo. These sorbets of fresh fruit or ground nuts are made on the tiny premises by Alfredo and his sons; in season, the varieties are joined by fig and prickly pear. The café's terrace, which in summer takes up half the seafront piazza of Lingua, is the heart and soul of the village: during daylight hours, people hang out here between swimming and sunbathing, then come in the evenings for *aperitivi* or after-dinner *granite*. Da Alfredo is also famous for its gargantuan *pane cunzato*, a circle of grilled bread piled high with tomatoes, capers, roast aubergine, tuna, olives and ricotta that'll comfortably feed two. Around the corner at the elegant Alfredo in Cucina, eldest son Piero masterminds an inventive, daily-changing menu based around the day's fish catch.

Filippino

Lipari *Piazza Municipio (090 981 1002/www. filippino.it). Open Apr-Sept noon-3pm, 7pm-midnight daily. Oct-mid Nov, late Dec-Mar noon-3pm, 7pm-midnight Tue-Sun. Closed mid Nov-late Dec. €€€. Traditional Italian.*

With its plastic sign, green baize-carpeted terrace and wobbly white trellises of jasmine, this family-run, century-old fish specialist doesn't look like much, but it nonetheless attracts the likes of Naomi Campbell and Sting. The *menu degustazione* might include a translucent *bresaola di tonno* (sweet home-cured tuna) alongside original uses of typical Sicilian ingredients: a robust soup of beans, wild fennel and sardines, say, or a dessert of exotic *mousse di gelsomino* flavoured with jasmine flowers.

> "Chef Zurro started as a fisherman, but shocked his pals by tampering with traditional recipes; he eventually opened his restaurant to show them he was right."

Porto Bello

Salina *Via Bianchi 1, Santa Marina Salina (090 984 3125). Open noon-3pm, 7pm-midnight daily. Closed mid Nov-mid Mar. €€. Traditional Italian.*

Sitting right above the water at Salina's port, Porto Bello offers consistently excellent cooking. The menu is uniformly good, but look out in particular for the local prawns, served raw with a yoghurt dip, or the *spaghetti al fuoco*: invented by owner Teodoro d'Albora, it contains raw *pomodorini*, basil, chilli and *ricotta infornata* (baked ricotta, which takes on a nutty, caramelly taste). Mains depend on the catch of the day: if you're lucky, they'll have *scorfano* (scorpion fish), expertly hard-fried. Below the restaurant is Layla, Salina's coolest bar; owned by wine-maker Carlo Hauner, it offers a predictably great and extensive wine list, not to mention a pleasingly mellow soundtrack.

Signum

Salina *Signum Hotel, Via Scalo 15, Malfa (090 984 4222/www.hotelsignum.it). Open noon-3pm, 7-11pm daily. Closed mid Nov-Feb. €€€. Modern Italian.*

Attentive staff, a well-stocked cellar and great cooking ensure that a candlelit dinner at Signum is always a special experience. Signature dishes include a splendid *sformato* (a moulded savoury concoction) of raw prawns with pistachios; the crispest, lightest and most succulent fish *polpette* (fish cakes) imaginable; and own-made ravioli extravagantly stuffed with ricotta, orange and lemon zest. The fish of the day is also well worth investigating, as is

the excellent wine list; let the sommelier guide your choice. Hotel guests have priority until 4pm, after which bookings are taken from non-residents.

La Sirena

Filicudi *Via Pecorini Mare (090 988 9997/www. pensionelasirena.it). Open noon-3pm, 7.30-11pm daily. €€. Trattoria.*

Antonio, a former bank manager, might be a fierce defender of traditional Sicilian ingredients, but he's also an inventive cook. As such, although the food's local origins will be all too easy to detect, you'll find dishes on La Sirena's sea-view terrace that you won't get anywhere else. Spaghetti might arrive with a simple pesto of almonds or a *ragù* spiked with orange; the range of fish dishes could include a juicy, heartily spiced sausage of tuna, served with caramelised onion jam. If the service is sometimes a little too unhurried, the quality of the food and the friendliness of the service (from Alina, Antonio's gentle English wife) more than compensate. The couple also have several rooms and small houses around the village that are available to rent.

Da Zurro

Stromboli *Via Picone 18 (090 986 283). Open noon-4pm, 7pm-midnight daily. €€. Trattoria.*

With its startlingly bright lights and sliding aluminium framed windows, Da Zurro isn't exactly the most inviting environment. However, as the locals know, you'll eat extremely well here. Bearded, piratical chef Zurro started out as a fisherman, but shocked his pals by tampering with traditional recipes; he eventually opened his eponymous restaurant to show them he was right. The food is as flamboyant as Zurro himself: razor-thin slices of aubergine, flecked with chilli flakes and served with balsamic-dressed rocket and parmesan; *spaghetti alla strombolana*, with cherry tomatoes, anchovies, mint, chilli and garlic; and black ravioli stuffed with local fish *ricciola* and dressed with capers, cherry tomatoes and basil.

Explore

LIPARI

The largest of the Aeolian Islands, Lipari is also the only one with a sizeable town, a substantial year-round population and much in the way of industry. Pumice quarries have taken huge bites out of the mountains, although mining has recently been banned and there are plans to create a 'geo-park' with an eco-museum and thermal baths. That said, UNESCO is currently campaigning against a project to build a huge port capable of accommodating massive cruise ships.

Although the town has its attractions (the fortified acropolis, some flower-hung alleys, the pretty harbour of Marina Corta), it's not a very sophisticated place. Gaudy sarongs, mass-produced jewellery and overpriced tourist menus

Clockwise from top left:
Hotel Signum (2); Casa
Mulino (5); Hotel Signum.

Clockwise from top:
Da Alfredo; Zurro.

Solo
da Alfredo
Pane Cunzato

aprese: pomodoro, mozzarella

aprese + Tonno

oliano: pomodori, capperi, olive,
polla, acciughe, peperoncino

isto: pomodori, melanzane sott'olio,
pomodori secchi, capperi, olive, tonno,
mozzarella

alina: pesto di capperi e mandorle
pomodori, cucunci, melanzane
rigliate, ricotta infornata e menta
fresca

tto condito con: olio, sale, origano e basilico

ALFREDO
IN
CUCINA
RISTORANTE
PIZZERIA

compete for visitors' attention with hardware stores, chandleries and the archipelago's main supermarket, and the local boutiques cater only to the slightly tacky local tastes for sequinned T-shirts, tracksuits and stonewashed denim. The beach at Porticello is backed by ugly processing plants, but walk to the north and you'll find secluded niches lined with hunks of glimmering, glistening obsidian.

In Greek and Roman times, it was hot springs brought trade to the island. The Hotel Tritone (via Mendolita, 090 981 1595) is one of several businesses that are now reviving the spa tradition, but for a more authentically Roman experience, head to the Terme di San Calogero on the south-west side of the island: behind the long-defunct buildings of a 1950s spa lie the remains of Roman baths. The guide (tip expected) will take you into a steam room and then to a pool, where the water emerges at a fearsome 57°C. If the slimy bottom and the scum don't put you off, slither in and soak.

> "Vulcano offers the chance to wallow in warm mud baths and swim above bubbling mid-sea fumaroles. Not to mention a volcano."

The coast around here is wild and rocky and, best of all, undeveloped, with splintered rocks lying offshore and extraordinary views back on dry land. It's inaccessible by road; however, you can reach it on foot at Valle Muria, where there's a beach (and, in season, boats to and from the port), or at Punta delle Fontanelle.

For all that, the coastal highlight is the footpath that runs along the coast between the Terme di San Calogero and the kaolin quarry at Bagnosecco, where the surface of the creamy white kaolin has been stained indigo, violet, orange, mustard, blue and verdigris by emissions from steaming sulphurous fumaroles. Back in the third century BC, an unnamed Lipari painter made the pale-hued clay for pots by mixing this white kaolin with more pliable clay, and may also have sourced his pigments from the quarry. You can see examples of this work at the Museo Archeologico Regionale Eollano.

Museo Archeologico Regionale Eoliano
Via del Castello (090 988 0174). Open 9am-1.30pm, 3-7pm Mon, Tue, Fri-Sun; 9am-1.30pm, 3-10pm Wed, Thur. Admission €6; €3 reductions.

In the classical section of this imaginatively presented museum, stacks of amphorae salvaged from shipwrecks attest to the strength of Aeolian storms (as, for that matter, do the deaths of many of the archaeologists and looters who excavated them). Upstairs are Greek red-figure vases and, unique to the island, vases painted in delicate pastels on light clay dating back to the third century BC, attributed to an artist known simply as the Lipari Painter. Found in local graves, many of these vases depict beautiful young women preparing themselves for marriage, symbolising the union of the soul with the divine. The museum also holds the most complete collection of Greek theatre masks in existence, representing key characters from both tragedy and comedy. English captioning throughout the museum is a bonus.

VULCANO

Although it's awash with eminently marketable novelties (a constantly smouldering volcano, the chance to wallow in warm mud baths and swim above bubbling mid-sea fumaroles), Vulcano has been developed in careless fashion. The little town has the unfinished look of a Western film set, and the promontory of Vulcanello is studded with bland luxury hotels. There's also nowhere decent to eat, though this isn't necessarily a bad thing: the pervading rotten-egg stink of sulphur may already have killed your appetite.

The path up to the crater begins about a kilometre out of town on the road to Gelso, marked by a sign warning of the dangers of inhaling volcanic gases. The climb (access €3) will take less than an hour, though you'll need to wear hiking boots to combat the slitheriness of the ashy track. Also, be sure to follow the crater in an anticlockwise direction, so you're going downhill rather than up through the clouds of sulphurous emissions on the northern rim.

The Fanghi di Vulcano (or mud baths) and offshore fumaroles are a couple of minutes' walk from the port. In season, there's a small entrance fee. Don't wear contact lenses, don't let kids play in the mud, and don't be surprised if you stink of sulphur for a couple of days afterwards. Alternatively, you could head to the rather more genteel Oasi della Salute spa, which comes with three thermal hydromassage pools and a beauty centre (090 985 2093, closed Oct-Mar).

SALINA

Twin-peaked Salina is the greenest of the islands, famous for its starring role in the 1994 movie *Il Postino*. Santa Marina Salina, the main port, is notable mainly for its long, traffic-free main street, along which chic boutiques and down-to-earth food shops occupy the ground floors of the substantial 19th-century houses built by those who made their fortune selling *malvasia* (sweet wine) to the British. Most of the wine entrepreneurs lost their fortunes in 1890 when phylloxera destroyed 90 per cent of the vines and prompted a mass exodus to Australia (and the start of today's large wine industry Down Under), but viticulture in the area has since been wholly revitalised. Today, the local wines can be tasted at vineyards such as Fenech at Malfa (mobile 339 575 6155, www.fenech.it), Caravaglio at Capofaro (mobile 339 811 5953) and D'Amico at Leni (090 980 9123).

The story of the island and of the emigration are vividly evoked in two tiny folk museums, the Museum of Emigration at Malfa (090 984 4372) and the Ethnographic Museum at Lingua (090 984 3128). However, you're more likely to want to spend your time in Lingua lying on the stony beach or lingering over a *granita* at Da Alfredo. This is the focus of the Salina scene, attracting an eclectic, relaxed crowd of financiers, families, trendies and trekkers.

"The stranger got off the Naples ferry, walked on to the beach and asked the kids who were playing there where he could find a hotel. 'Hotel?' they replied. 'What's a hotel?'"

Spring and autumn are the best times to climb Monte Fossa delle Felci, the highest peak in the archipelago (summer being too hot and winter prone to sudden storms). There are a number of steep but well-marked paths that start from several points between Lingua and Santa Marina, although the easiest way up is to take the jeep track that kicks off from behind the church at Valdichiesa in the saddle between the two mountains. The best way to see the south side of the island, meanwhile, is to take a bus to the village of Leni and then follow a series of mule tracks down the mountain to Rinella, where there's good swimming from a black-sand beach.

If you can, try to be at Pollara, the setting for *Il Postino*, at sunset. A simple trattoria (Il Cappero) and a hotel (La Locanda del Postino) have recently opened here, but there are no shops or bars out of season, and the beach is officially closed due to the danger of erosion and falling rocks. On the first weekend in June, Pollara hosts the annual caper festival; the road into the village is lined with stalls selling dishes that utilise the ingredient in every conceivable way.

PANAREA

If you aren't a member of the rich and famous posse that hangs out at painfully cool Raya or takes its sunset *aperitivi* at the Bridge Sushi Bar in the port, Panarea in August is probably best avoided. But if you want to swim, walk or take boat trips around what's probably the most beautiful of the Aeolian Islands, come in spring or autumn; and if you want to party a little, come in June or July. The hotels are generally pretty expensive, but Pippo and Maria (mobile 368 781 5809 or 334 703 5010) have perfectly nice rooms to rent in a quiet part of the village.

Be sure to take the 40-minute walk to the dark gold sandy beach of Zammarà and the magnificent bay of Cala Junca beyond, set among jagged cliffs at the foot of a promontory topped by the oval foundations of Bronze Age huts. Taking a 20-minute walk to the other side of the village will lead you to the beach of Calcara; fumaroles steaming through sulphur-stained rocks here led ancient Panareans to believe it was an entrance to the underworld.

Taking a boat trip out to the offshore islets is another must. Each islet is the result of a specific vulcanological phenomenon, and the formation and colours of the rock on each is unique. Below Basiluzzo, when the sea is calm and clear, you can see the remains of a Roman port and clamber up to the ruins of a Roman villa; nearby, Lisca Bianca displays submarine fumaroles bubbling at the surface of the sea, little sandy beaches and cliffs that have been stained yellow.

STROMBOLI

The stranger got off the Naples ferry, walked on to the beach and asked the kids who were playing there where he could find a hotel. 'Hotel?' they replied. 'What's a hotel?'

Off they ran to get their teacher, Domenico Russo. 'I can find you a room for the night,' he offered, 'but there are no hotels on Stromboli.' Instead, he took the man to a family who had a spare room.

'This is fine for me,' said the man. 'However, I need to find somewhere for Ingrid Bergman, and she'll need her own bathroom.'

'If you bring Ingrid Bergman to Stromboli,' replied Russo, 'I'll give her a house for free.'

The stranger was Roberto Rossellini. He and Bergman became lovers after she wrote him one of movie history's most famous fan letters: 'Dear Mr Rossellini, I saw your films *Open City* and *Paisan*, and enjoyed them very much. If you need a Swedish actress who speaks English very well, who has not forgotten her German, who is not very understandable in French, and who in Italian knows only "ti amo", I am ready to come and make a film with you.'

Smooth sailing

The best way to explore the islands of the Aeolian archipelago is in a small sailing or cruising boat: you'll be able to anchor anywhere and thus access the many tiny coves and beaches as well as the islets. If you don't have your own boat, there's no need to worry: experienced sailors can hire boats and novices can charter a skippered yacht or motor cruiser.

Alessio Puglisi owns and captains the **Sikabau** (07831 113 725 UK mobile, 340 851 9213 Italian mobile), a classic 12.5-metre sailing boat from 1976 with teak decking and white-and-blue Bermudian sails. The boat sleeps four guests and can be booked for skippered trips lasting from one to ten days (May to November only), kicking off from its home port of Milazzo on the Sicilian mainland. Rates start from €200 per person for a day trip and from €3,500 per person for five days outside the peak July/August period; it sounds a lot, but it's actually pretty reasonable considering that the costs include breakfast, mooring costs and fuel. Puglisi, who speaks English, will give everyone the chance to get their hands on deck: raising the sails, pulling ropes and even taking a turn on the wheel. As he comes from a prominent Sicilian pasta-producing family, he's knowledgeable about local cuisine and can point you in the direction of the best restaurants on each island, or organise lunch on board. Transfers from the airport can be arranged for an extra charge.

Pajarita V and **Nassau** are two 13-metre classic wooden pilot boats that have been kitted out by English-speaking owner Marcello Grimaudo as miniature floating hotels (mobile 333 663 8666, www.orizzonterosso.com). There are three guest cabins and two bathrooms; snorkelling equipment is provided, and scuba diving with a professional is also available on request. The boat sleeps six, but groups of ten can fit comfortably aboard for a day trip. Day rates (€600-€1,000) are all-inclusive; the live-aboard rates run from €500 to €900 a day, excluding fuel, food, drink and berthing charges.

Skippered by RYA-licenced Italian Francesco Candiani and his Australian wife Melissa, and new to the Aeolian seas in 2008, the 16-metre catamaran **Ombre Blu** is more of a luxury craft (mobile 347 083 2995, www.ombreblu.com). Melissa is a massage therapist with a career background in five-star hotels and super-yachts (including Rupert Murdoch's), and Francesco is a diving instructor whose family operates a string of excellent restaurants. Your itinerary can be customised; as well as massage and scuba-diving, themes could include wellness, gastronomy (with a sommelier and chef on board the boat) and hiking and climbing the local volcanoes (with an onboard volcanologist to explain). Rates for six people, including airport transfers, all meals and an open bar, run from €15,600 to €21,000 a week.

Clockwise from top left:
Lipari; boats at Salina;
strolling in Salina; view to
Salina; smokin' Stromboli.

But in 1949, when they arrived on the island to shoot *Stromboli Terra di Dio*, this was all secret. True to his word, Russo gave Bergman a house in which to stay and even secured the house next door for Rossellini, so the two could meet without compromising their reputations. After the film was released and tourists began to visit Stromboli, Russo opened the island's first hotel.

These days, it's not Bergman but the volcano that attracts most of Stromboli's visitors, the vast majority of whom arrive brandishing alpenstocks and looking like hopefuls for the foreign legion. In fact, if you're in reasonably good shape, all you need to make the trek to the top are a pair of trekking boots, a torch, a warm jacket, some water and €30 for a place on a walk with an accredited guide. The climb takes two hours, and is timed so that your arrival on the summit coincides with sunset.

As for the rest of Stromboli, the best beaches are the cosy little coves of black sand tucked into lava crags along the coast at Piscità, from which there are fine views of the islet of Strombolicchio. Nightlife centres on the Tartara Club.

FILICUDI & ALICUDI

The tarmac road that connects the several small settlements on beautiful, understated Filicudi gives a false impression of the island. The villages that seem far apart are just a few minutes' walk from one another along one of the old mule tracks that cut down through the strata of terraces, and the island as a whole is best seen on foot or by boat. Outsiders who have villas on Filicudi tend to be a little reclusive: social life is largely confined to home entertaining.

With a sea bed that's home to scores of ancient shipwrecks, Filicudi offers some interesting diving. If you don't dive, take a boat trip around the island to see the hidden sea grotto, the scene of a candlelit festival every year on 15 September.

Even so, the port is the least attractive part of the island. Head, instead, for the tiny fishing port of Pecorini a Mare, where there's little to do except eat good food, beachcomb (Filicudi has some of the best shells in the archipelago), and walk slowly up the hill and out to the clifftop belvedere to watch the sun set over the mid-sea rock known as La Canna. We'd recommend taking a good bottle of wine along on the trip. For a taste of life before the onset of electricity made day master of the night, venture out to the abandoned village of Zucca Grande, where the current sole inhabitant has a couple of rooms and makes dinner for visitors (mobile 347 813 2579 or 368 407 544).

An uncompromising cone rising from the sea that can be scaled only by heaving yourself up steps a giant's stride high, Alicudi is an island that most visitors either love or hate. There are just 80 year-round inhabitants and, it's said, most of them loathe the sight of each other. Rumours, esoteric superstitions and ghost sightings abound, as does the conviction that some Alicudari are blessed with the magical power to divert cyclones.

Factfile

When to go
Spring and autumn are the best times to visit: it will be cool enough to walk in the mountains but warm enough to swim; and it's less crowded than in summer, so you won't have to book ahead for restaurants and boat trips. Many businesses close in winter, when there are frequent storms.

Getting there
The main port for ferries and hydrofoils to the Aeolian Islands is Milazzo on Sicily, but services are reduced outside the peak season. In summer, they also run to and from Messina and Palermo, and Reggio Calabria and Naples on the mainland. Most call at Lipari first, then continue on to the others. Contact Siremar (090 928 3242, www.siremar.it), Ustica Lines (090 928 7821, www.usticalines.it); or NGI (090 928 3415, www.ngi-spa.it).

On Sicily, buses run from Catania airport to Messina train station, a 15-minute walk to the hydrofoil port; in summer, there's also one bus a day to Milazzo port. There are more regular buses between Messina and Milazzo port; they leave from via Terrasini, a five-minute walk from the railway station.

Getting around
There are decent bus services all year round on Lipari and Salina. All islands except Alicudi have taxis; those on Panarea are electric.

Tourist office
Corso Vittorio Emanuele 202, Lipari (090 988 0095). Open 8.30am-1.30pm, 4.30-7.30pm Mon-Fri.

Internet
Salina Computer Via Risorgimento 110, Santa Marina Salina (090 984 3444). Open Summer 9am-1pm, 3-8pm daily. Winter 9am-1pm, 3-7pm Mon-Sat.

The Amalfi Coast & Capri

If your idea of heaven is gazing over peacock-blue water beneath an azure sky, with only the sound of a lone seagull to disturb your thoughts, you've come to the right part of Italy: the coast doesn't get more picturesque, nor more glamorous, than this. Between them, the Amalfi Coast and Capri have some of the most dramatic coastline in the world, but they have also long been millionaires' playgrounds, with swish shops, smart cafés and good restaurants in spades.

Clockwise from top left:
Amalfi's Duomo; Amalfi
beach; Padre Pio;
Limoncello (2); postcards;
fountain.

Villa Maria

Ravello *Via Santa Chiara 2 (089 857 255/ www.villamaria.it). €€€.*

The tables and chairs are arranged to make the most of the view across the spectacular Dragone valley in this converted villa's lovely shady garden. Most of the rooms are light and spacious, and all are furnished with brass bedsteads and antiques. Room three is a huge suite with a terrace and panoramic views. Friendly owner Vincenzo also runs the nearby Hotel Giordano (Via Santissima Trinità 14), a modern and less atmospheric (but cheaper) option. Guests at the Villa Maria can use the Giordano's free parking and pool.

Eat

The Campania region grows a superb range of seasonal ingredients, and its year-round staples – pasta di Gragnano, tomatoes and *mozzarella di bufala Campana* – can be found in abundance at the restaurants on Capri and the Amalfi coast. Unsurprisingly, you'll get some wonderful fish and seafood here; and the famous local speciality, lemon, is used in anything from lemon flower (*zagara*) honey to main courses to the potent liquor made from lemon rind, limoncello.

Of the local wines, keep an eye open for the Costa d'Amalfi Furore Rosso, a delicious, full-bodied blend of the Piedirosso and Aglianico grapes – the best label by far is Gran Furor (Marisa Cuomo); of the whites, Falanghina – the name means 'little stick' – is fresh, fruity and the most popular locally.

La Capannina

Capri *Via Le Botteghe 12 bis (081 837 0732/www. capannina-capri.com). Open May-Sept noon-3pm, 7.30-11.30pm daily. Mid Mar-Apr, Oct noon-3pm, 7.30-11.30pm Mon, Tue, Thur-Sun. Closed Nov-mid Mar. €€€.*

In the heart of the old town, this old-fashioned place is one of the most consistently good, and best known, restaurants on Capri. Opened in the 1930s, it's a celebrated celebrity haunt (come in the evening if you're a star-spotter) and the place for textbook renditions of Capri recipes: perfect *ravioli capresi, spaghetti alle vongole* and *linguine allo scorfano* (flat spaghetti with scorpion fish), the house speciality.

La Caravella

Amalfi *Via Matteo Camera 12 (089 871 029/www. ristorantelacaravella.it). Open noon-2.30pm, 7.30-10.30pm Mon, Wed-Sun. Closed mid Nov-Dec. €€€.*

Probably Amalfi's best restaurant (it was recently awarded a Michelin star), the Caravella ascends the culinary peaks. Sandwiched between the main road and the remains of the old Arsenale, the two-room restaurant has no view, but it offers excellent seafood, attentive service and an extensive wine list. Try the whole-grain *panzerotti* stuffed with lobster and ricotta and covered in prawns and sauce; pasta dishes such as *tagliata di pasta allo zafferano con zucca e crostacei*

(pasta strips served with saffron, marrow and crustaceans) are equally fine. Look out, too, for the day's catch grilled in lemon leaves.

Figli di Papà nel Palazzo della Marra

Ravello *Via della Marra 7-9 (089 858 302/ www.ristorantefiglidipapa.it). Open Apr-Sept 12.30-2.30pm, 7-10pm daily. Oct-Mar noon-3pm, 7-10pm Mon, Wed-Sun. Closed 2wks Nov, mid Jan-Feb. €€.*

Housed in a 12th-century palazzo, carefully restored to keep the original vaults and arches intact, the Palazzo produces creative Mediterranean cuisine. Some dishes don't quite hit the mark, but overall it makes a good (and fairly priced) attempt to go a little beyond the standard local seafood experience. They also operate a bed and breakfast called Palazzo della Marra (www.palazzodellamarra.com).

Da Gemma

Amalfi *Via Fra' Gerardo Sasso 10 (089 871 345). Open 12.30-2.30pm, 7.30-10.30pm Mon, Tue, Thur-Sun. Closed mid Jan-mid Feb. €€.*

The setting of this popular restaurant is hard to beat: there's a balcony terrace above the bustle of the main street, with views across to piazza del Duomo. Mario Grimaldi is continuing a tradition of good local cooking that was begun here by his mother Gemma; the menu looks mostly to the sea, but also includes a few dishes sourced from the hinterland, such as fettuccine *alla genovese* (fettuccine in a beef and onion sauce). Lovers of *zuppa di pesce* (fish soup) will find Gemma's version hard to beat. Book ahead in summer.

> ## "The Campania region grows a superb range of seasonal ingredients, and its year-round staples can be found in abundance on Capri and the Amalfi coast."

Da Gemma

Capri *Via Madre Serafina 6 (081 837 0461). Open Aug noon-3pm, 7pm-midnight daily. Mar-July, Sept, Oct noon-3pm, 7pm-midnight Tue-Sun. Closed Nov-Mar. €€.*

This Capri institution was novelist Graham Greene's favourite restaurant, and it remains in the same family to this day. The food is always reliable: fish is baked in an old bread oven, and good pasta and pizza are served too. It's worth trying the sausage and friarelli (pepper) pizza, which is especially popular with the locals. The place nestles snugly under the arches of the old town above Via Roma, which means there are lovely views outside. Inside the walls are covered with old black and white photos of famous punters.

Clockwise from top left: Villa Maria (2); Hotel Caruso (3); Villa Maria.

L'Olivo.

Le Grotelle
Capri *Via Arco Naturale (081 837 5719). Open Mar-June, Sept noon-2.30pm, 7pm-midnight Mon-Wed, Fri-Sun. July, Aug noon-3pm, 7pm-midnight. Oct noon-3pm Mon-Wed, Fri-Sun. Closed Nov-Feb. €€.*
On a clear night with full moon, Le Grotelle is hard to beat. On the path leading to the Arco Naturale, the restaurant is located half inside a cavern and half perched on a terrace overlooking a verdant slope and the sea. The food is earthy and reliable, but it's the sea view that makes this place so special. The kitchen turns out no-nonsense *primi* such as *scialatielli* with prawns and baby octopus or ravioli *capresi*, followed by grilled fish – *pezzogna* (bream) or *gallinella* (gurnard) – chicken or rabbit; finish with one of the best *torta caprese* (chocolate cake) you're likely to taste. Good local wine, too.

> ## "The famous local speciality, lemon, is used in anything from lemon flower honey to main courses to the liquor made from lemon rind."

Maccus
Amalfi *Largo Santa Maria Maggiore 1-3 (089 873 6385/www.maccusamalfi.it). Open noon-3pm, 7-11.30pm Tue-Sun. Closed mid-Nov-mid Dec, mid Jan-mid Mar. €€.*
It's worth exploring the quiet side streets that run parallel to Amalfi's touristy main drag. Not only do they reveal a lesser-known, more vernacular side of the town, they also harbour some unexpected surprises, such as this lovely little restaurant a stone's throw north of the Duomo. The courtyard dining area is usually packed, and most of the voices are Italian. The food is simple – mostly pasta and fish – but very nicely done, and strong on fine, local ingredients. Don't miss the *polpino* (octopus) salad.

L'Olivo
Anacapri *Capri Palace Hotel, via Capodimonte 2b (081 978 0111/www.capri-palace.com). Open noon-3pm, 7.30-10pm daily. Closed Nov-Mar. €€€€.*
Chef Oliver Glowig's restaurant L'Olivo deservedly won a Michelin star in 2004. It's set within one of the island's most prestigious and stylish hotels, the decor is as impressive as the service, and the outside terrace is a delight. Glowig uses local produce and blends ideas from humble *cucina povera* with those of haute cuisine. Typical fare includes sea bream with peach and fennel purée or a tortella of chick-peas with prawn and fried bone marrow. The breads and pastries are all freshly made on the premises, and the wine list is one of the island's best.

A Paranza
Atrani, 0.75km from Amalfi *Traversa Dragone 2 (089 871 840). Open July-mid Sept 12.30-3pm, 7.30pm-midnight daily. Mid Sept-June 12.30-3pm, 7.30pm-midnight Mon, Wed-Sun. Closed 3wks Dec. €€.*
The Proto brothers' friendly, relaxed seafood trattoria is located on the road that leads inland away from Atrani's pretty main square. Spread over two plain barrel-vaulted rooms, the place is done out in white and orange. Antipasti such as *alici marinati* (anchovies marinated in oil and lemon) are a prelude to delicious home-made pasta (the *scialatielli 'a paranza* – thick, hand-made spaghetti with seafood – is particularly good). Go for simple *secondi* like the *grigliata mista locale* (mixed seafood grill) or the grilled swordfish, which comes straight off the boat. Desserts are home-made, and the lemon sorbet is especially delicious.

Rossellinis
Ravello *Hotel Palazzo Sasso, via San Giovanni del Toro 28 (089 818 181/www.palazzosasso.com). Open 7.30-10.30pm daily. Closed Nov-mid Mar. €€€€.*
Ravello was a blank on the gourmet map of the Amalfi Coast until this restaurant opened in 1997. On a typical evening, the seasonally changing menu might include a starter of scallop carpaccio with caviar, sundried tomatoes, asparagus tips and lime ice, followed by tarragon-scented *garganelli* (a local pasta) tossed in a sauce of veal fillet, cannellino beans and crispy bacon. *Secondi* are evenly divided into fish and meat, and desserts are suitably theatrical. Add the charm of candlelit tables on the panoramic terrace, professional service and excellent wines, not to mention two Michelin stars, and you have a memorable meal.

Explore

AMALFI

Fringed by lemon trees, Amalfi is a very pretty tourist resort that spills over on to the coast and lines both sides of the steep and fertile Valle dei Mulini. Between the ninth and the 12th centuries, this was a glorious maritime republic; in its prime, Amalfi had 70,000 inhabitants. An earthquake in 1343 destroyed most of the old town, and Amalfi only recovered in the 19th century, when word of its spectacular setting and former glories began to reach literary and artistic travellers.

Amalfi's narrow, high-sided streets and alleyways mean it's always shady, even when the sun's at its fiercest. A map can be had from the tourist office, but you're as well just striking out up steps and side alleys to see what you find; it's amazing how quickly you can lose the crowds. On its coast side, the pretty, cream-coloured town makes a weak effort at bustling, as the port, bus terminus, bars and restaurants all jostle for elbow room on the tiny waterfront. To the east, the grey shingle beach is crowded in summer, although prettier water is tucked away in a series of coves to the west, served by a regular circular ferry service (marked 'spiagge') from the main quay.

Duomo di Amalfi (Cattedrale di Sant'Andrea)
Piazza del Duomo (089 871 324). Open Apr-June 9am-7pm daily. July-Sept 9am-8pm daily. Oct, Mar 9.30am-5.15pm daily. Nov-Feb 10am-3.30pm daily. Admission Cathedral free. Chiostro del Paradiso €2.50. No credit cards.

The town's central piazza is dominated by the colourful Duomo, reached by a long staircase. The lively façade is a doubtful 1860s reconstruction of the early 13th-century original; the pretty, free-standing campanile, from 1276, is authentic. Beneath a lofty porch, the central bronze doors of the Duomo were cast before 1066 in Syria; the inscription explains that they were donated to the republic by Pantaleone di Mauro Comite, head of the Amalfitan colony in Constantinople. The interior has recently been restored to remove some of its baroque excess. The delightful Chiostro del Paradiso is entered through a door at the left end of the porch in front of the Duomo; this cloister was built in 1266 as a burial ground for Amalfi's aristocracy. A door leads into the Cappella del Crocefisso, the only part of the church to have survived intact from the 12th century, where glass cases hold treasures including a lovely 15th-century marble bas-relief known as La Madonna della Neve, and a bejewelled mitre made for the Anjou court of Naples in 1297. From the chapel, stairs lead down to the crypt, dedicated to St Andrew, whose mortal remains were stolen from Constantinople in 1206. The sarcophagus that contains the saintly remains ooze a 'miraculous' fluid that the locals call *manna* (it's actually a plant extract).

"Amalfi's narrow, high-sided streets and alleyways mean it's always shady, even when the sun's at its fiercest."

Museo della Carta
Palazzo Pagliara, via delle Cartiere 24 (089 830 4561/ www.museodellacarta.it). Open Nov-Feb 10am-3.30pm Tue-Sun. Mar-Oct 10am-6.30pm daily. Admission €3.50 (incl guided tour in English). No credit cards.

To the north of the town is a deep valley – the Valle dei Mulini – that echoes to the sound of fast-flowing water, even at the height of summer. This was the site of some of Europe's first paper-making factories, all powered by a series of watermills; one, at Palazzo Pagliara on a quiet residential street, has been turned into the Museo della

Carta, with photos illustrating the history and techniques of this ancient industry. Downstairs, the original vats and machinery are preserved; the shop is full of beautiful gift ideas made from the local paper.

Pasticceria Andrea Pansa 1830
Piazza del Duomo 40 (089 871 065/www.pasticceria pansa.it). Open Apr-Oct 8.30am-1am Mon-Sat. Nov-Mar 8.30am-11pm Mon-Sat. Closed 3wks Jan-Feb. No credit cards.

This charming shop dishes up the famous local fruit in any number of inventive ways: candied lemon rind, *frolla* (a ricotta-filled pastry dome) and the sticky *delizia al limone* cakes are especially good. The same owners also run the lovely Cioccolateria (Piazza Municipio 12, 089 873 291, www.andreapansa.it, open 9am-1pm, 4-8pm, closed Tue and Jan).

ANACAPRI

Incredibly for such a small island, the first road linking Capri town and Anacapri was only built in 1872. Until then, and for the most part of their history, the two villages led different lives on the opposite sides of the seismic fracture and wall of cliffs that splits the island in two. If rural Anacapri today receives as many visitors as swish Capri town, it's largely thanks to Swedish society doctor Axel Munthe, whose book *The Story of San Michele* filled cold northerners with longing for the 'warm south'. Munthe was the first of a steady trickle of foreign residents who preferred Anacapri's quiet charm to the more glitzy delights of Capri: writers Compton Mackenzie and Graham Greene had houses here. Today the peace and quiet that attracted them is challenged by the busloads of tourists who come to visit the Villa San Michele and splash their euros in a thicket of tacky souvenir shops.

But away from this (thankfully limited) outbreak of bad taste, and out of season, Anacapri is a good place from which to see the other, more rural side of the island. Like most Italian islands, it has always looked more to the land than the sea for its sustenance – unlike the small Egyptian sphinx dating from the 11th century BC. Staring out to sea, the sphinx appears on innumerable postcards and posters, seeming to embody the elusive, almost mystical spirit of Capri.

Parco Filosofico
Via Migliara (www.philosophicalpark.org). Open 9am-1hr before sunset daily. Admission free. No credit cards.

This 'philosophical park' was set up in 2000 by Swedish intellectual and Capri resident Gunnar Adler-Karlsson. It's well worth a visit: wander through it and peruse the 60 quotations from western philosophers, from Plato and Aristotle to Wittgenstein and Mill – all written on little ceramic tiles in English and Italian. Each quote is categorised too, sometimes slightly eccentrically.

Clockwise from top:
Amalfi's coast; Andrea
Pansa; fruits of Amalfi;
taking the sun; Ravello.

Villa San Michele

Viale Axel Munthe 34 (081 837 1401/www.san michele.org). Open Mar 9am-4.30pm daily. Apr, Oct 9am-5pm daily. May-Sept 9am-6pm daily. Nov-Feb 9am-3.30pm daily. Admission €5. No credit cards.

Designed in a style that mixes Romanesque and Renaissance influences with Moorish trills, this villa and its trim gardens are studded with fragments of classical statuary. It was constructed for Swedish society doctor and psychiatrist Axel Munthe; the building clings to the edge of Anacapri cliff on the site of one of Tiberius's 12 Caprese villas. The gardens host delightful music concerts, some timed to make the most of the summer sunset; ask at the tourist office for information.

CAPRI

Traditionally, Capri town was regarded as chic and urbane in contrast to rugged Anacapri, and that's still largely true today. Most of the luxury hotels and villas cluster around Capri town; by day, the Piazzetta, Capri's heart and the world's most famous passeggiata, is a pedestrian log-jam. To properly appreciate the town's fascination, stay overnight; in the evening, as the late sunset sky darkens to cobalt and the last of the day-trippers drifts down to the port, the place reveals itself to be one of the Mediterranean's most elegant open-air living rooms. And just to be clear, the name is pronounced *Ca*-pree, not Ca-*pree*.

> "In the evening, as the late sunset sky darkens, Capri is revealed as one of the Mediterranean's most elegant open-air living rooms."

Blue Grotto

Open 9am-1hr before sunset daily. Admission €4 plus €4.50 rowing boat fee. Access by motor launch from Marina Grande is an additional €8-€10/person. Departs 9.30am-4pm daily. No credit cards.

The 'Grotta Azzurra' is Capri's most famous sight and an important local earner. Despite the costly palaver a visit entails, it's well worth seeing; the iridescent quality of the light inside is truly mesmerising. Known in Roman times, it subsequently became associated with evil spirits and was given a wide berth by locals. That all changed with its 'rediscovery' in 1826 by the German writer August Kopisch and his painter friend Ernst Fries. The remains of a Roman villa ('Villa di Gradola') stand just outside. To enter, you swap your motorboat for a rowing boat small enough to make it through the opening. The Grotto is also accessible on foot.

Villa Jovis

Viale Amadeo Maiuri, Via Tiberio (081 837 4549/ www.villajovis.it). Open 9am-1hr before sunset daily. Admission €2. No credit cards.

Not much is left of what must have been its decadent Roman splendour, and yet the Villa Jovis complex, the home of Emperor Tiberius, is still striking in its solitary glory. The most impressive remains are those of the huge cisterns in the centre and the long, straight loggia to the north, which ends in the 330m Salto di Tiberio, the precipice from which the emperor was supposed to have hurled those who annoyed him. The story may be pure fabrication, but the view across to Punta della Campanella on the mainland is real enough. The best time to visit is as soon as it opens, before the bulk of the day-trippers make their way up.

RAVELLO

Ravello is the aristocrat of the Amalfi Coast. Up here, high above the sea, all is shade, gardens and serenity. Even in high season it's easy to leave the coach parties behind: turn a corner in the old town, or visit the lovely gardens in the evening, and you can find yourself quite at peace.

Ravello's romantic ambience of faded, decaying nobility has always attracted writers, artists and musicians. Wagner stayed here, as did Liszt, Virginia Woolf and most of the other members of the Bloomsbury group. DH Lawrence wrote parts of *Lady Chatterley's Lover* in Ravallo and Graham Greene stayed here while writing *The Third Man*. Gore Vidal lived here for many years, sniping away in his sumptuous private villa, La Rondinaia. Staying overnight is the best way to tune in to Ravello's quiet, contemplative atmosphere, which is at its most limpid in the early morning or else at sunset. If you can avoid it, don't drive here. The main non-residents' car park, just beneath the Piazza del Duomo, is expensive. Instead, take one of the frequent buses from Amalfi; alternatively, Ravello is a long walk up quiet footpaths from Amalfi, Atrani or Minori.

Duomo di Ravello (Cattedrale di San Pantaleone)

Piazza del Duomo (089 858 311/089 857 160/ www.chiesaravello.com). Open Church 8.30am-1pm, 3-8pm daily. Museum Apr-Oct 9.30am-1pm, 3-7pm daily. Nov-Mar 9.30am-1pm, 3-7pm Sat, Sun. Admission €2. No credit cards.

The Duomo was founded in 1086, but little remains of its original façade, which was reworked in the 16th century. The central bronze doors are divided into 54 bas-relief panels that tell the stories of the saints and the Passion. The light-filled interior was re-done, Baroque style, in 1786; in the early 1980s, the courageous decision was taken to rip it all down and restore the church to something close to the state it would have reached by the late 13th century. Halfway down the central aisle, two exquisite pulpits are arranged face to face, as if for a preachers' duel. The *pergamo* (high pulpit) on the right was commissioned by a scion of the local Rufolo family in 1272; the simple *ambone* (low pulpit) opposite was donated by Costantino Rogadeo, the second bishop of Ravello, in 1130. To the left of the main altar is the chapel of San Pantaleone, Ravello's patron saint. It contains a phial of his blood, which is supposed to liquefy on 27 July each year and stay liquid until mid-September.

Villa Cimbrone

Via Santa Chiara 26 (089 857 459/www.villacimbrone. com). Open 9am-30mins before sunset daily. Admission €5. No credit cards.

Both Ravello's famous villas are historical assemblages, the work of Britons who came, saw, and did a bit of gardening. The Villa Cimbrone is a fair walk from the centre along via San Francesco, which climbs up past the reworked Gothic church and monastery of the same name. But it's an enchanting place, and well worth the trek – even though it's an out-and-out fake. The structure was built at the beginning of the 20th century by Lord Grimthorpe. In its 1920s heyday, it hosted most of the Bloomsbury group; later, Greta Garbo and conductor Leopold Stokowski used it as a love nest. To see inside the villa, you'll need to check in to the Hotel Villa Cimbrone, but the gardens can be admired by all. Roses, camellias and exotic plants line the lawns and walks, there's a pretty faux-Moorish tearoom, and the Belvedere Cimbrone, lined with classical busts, from where you can see along the coast for miles.

Villa Rufolo

Piazza del Duomo (089 857 657). Open Nov-Mar 9am-5pm daily. Apr, Oct 9am-6pm daily. May-Sept 9am-8pm daily (may close earlier on concert days). Admission €5. No credit cards.

The town's other garden estate, Villa Rufolo, entered via the 14th-century tower to the right of the Duomo, is named after its original 13th-century owners, the Rufolo family, who amassed a fortune as bankers; they're mentioned in Boccaccio's *Decameron*. By the time Scotsman Francis Reid bought the place in 1851, the villa and its surrounding garden were little more than tangled ruins. The house was reborn as an eclectic melange, although certain parts – especially the charming, double-tiered Moorish cloister – were not tampered with too much. But it's really the gardens that draw people, with their geometric flowerbeds amid Romantic ruins. When Wagner saw them in 1880, he knew he'd found the magic garden of Klingsor, the setting for the second act of *Parsifal*. In Wagner's honour, a world-class series of classical concerts is held here in the summer under the umbrella of the famous Festival di Ravello (089 858 360, www.ravellofestival.com). The Festival has been going since 1953, and in recent years has grown to embrace not just music but dance and the visual arts too. However, Villa Rufolo remains its central focus.

Factfile

When to go

The best time to visit is out of season (either in May or October), when the weather is cool enough that you can explore on foot, but still sufficiently warm for you to get a suntan. Between November and March, Capri closes down, more or less (Amalfi and Ravello pick up again in March); only a few hotels and restaurants stay open.

Getting there

The nearest airport is Aeroporto Internazionale di Napoli (081 789 6423, www.gesac.it).

Metro del Mare (199 600 700, www.metro delmare.com) runs ferry services from Molo Beverello in Naples to the islands and various points along the Amalfi coast.

For overland travel to the Amalfi coast, take the Curreri bus (081 801 5420, www.curreriviaggi.it) from Naples airport to Sorrento (six daily) and change for the SITA (199 730 749, www.sita-on-line.it) bus to Amalfi and Ravello. Alternatively, take the train from Naples to Salerno and continue by SITA bus.

Getting around

Amalfi's bus terminus is in piazza Gioia on the waterfront. Local services run to Ravello; bus is the easiest way to get there. Tickets can be bought from the SITA outlet in largo Scoppetta, next to the bus terminus.

Tourist information

Amalfi Tourist Office Corso delle Repubbliche Marinare 27 (089 871 107/www.amalfi touristoffice.it). Open May-Oct 8.30am-1.30pm, 3-8pm Mon-Sat; 8.30am-12.30pm Sun. Nov-Apr 8.30am-1.30pm, 3-5pm Mon-Fri; 8.30am-1pm Sat.
Anacapri Tourist Office, via G Orlandi 59 (081 837 1524/www.capritourism.com). Open 9am-3pm Mon-Sat.
Capri Tourist Office, piazza Umberto I (081 837 0686/www.capritourism.com). Open Apr-Oct 8.30am-8.30pm Mon-Sat. Nov-Mar 9am-1pm, 3.30-6.45pm Mon-Sat.
Ravello Tourist Office, via Roma 18/bis (089 857 096/www.ravellotime.it). Open May-Sept 8am-8pm Mon-Sat; 9am-7pm Sun. Oct-Apr 8am-7pm Mon-Sat; 9am-7pm Sun.

Internet

Internet cafés are not especially numerous in this part of Italy; ask at your hotel or the tourist office for directions to the nearest one.

Clockwise from top left:
Manorola; Vernazza (2);
San Remo (old town);
Portofino.

The Italian Riviera

Less glitzy than its brash French cousin, the Italian Riviera boasts a splendid coastline of relatively unspoiled small towns and villages. The mountainous strip of land that hugs the Mediterranean sea – or, to be more precise, the Mare Ligure – from France all the way down to Tuscany is covered in rocky wooded slopes stretching down to the sea. Sheltered coves and a near-perfect climate make this coast a holiday paradise.

The best guides
enjoying London

(but don't just take our word for it

'More than 700 places where you can eat out for less than £20 a head... a mass of useful information in a geuinely pocket–sized guide'

Mail on Sunday

'I'm always asked how I ke date with shopping and ser city as big as London.This the answer'

Red Magazine

'You will never again be stuck for interesting things to do and places to visit in the capital'

Independent on Sunday

Rated 'Best Restaurant Guide'

Sunday Times

Choose from over 15 London guides at
timeout.com/shop, from only £6.99

La Palma

Alassio *Via Cavour 5 (0182 640 314). Open 1-2pm, 8-9.45pm Mon, Tue, Thur-Sun. Closed Nov-5 Dec. Traditional Italian. €€€€.*

This small, Michelin-starred restaurant housed in an 18th-century palazzo in the old town, has been run by the same family since the early 1900s. The service is warm and attentive, with a chef who is always keen to talk customers through the menu. The cuisine is Ligurian-Provençal, and features some unusual combinations – squid stuffed with snails on a courgette purée being a notable example.

Pizzeria El Portico

Portofino *Via Roma 21 (0185 269 239). Open noon-2pm, 7-10.30pm Wed-Sun. €. Pizzeria/Trattoria.*

Well-heeled Portofino isn't the cheapest place in which to eat on the Riviera. However, down a cobbled street leading to the harbour, you'll find this unpretentious trattoria and pizzeria, all checked table cloths and rickety wooden chairs – and it's by no means a budget-buster. The pizza is good, but don't neglect the fresh fish and the pasta – and be sure to try one of the homemade desserts. Keep an eye open for the local pesto sauce too – it's served with the pizza and pasta dishes, as well as the gnocchi.

Polpo Mario

Sestri Levante *Via XXV Aprile 163 (0185 480 203/ www.polpomario.it). Open 12.15-2.30pm, 7.30-10.30pm Tue-Sun. €€. Traditional Italian.*

This small, family-run restaurant, located in the old town on the site of a tavern, isn't far from the Bay of Silence. It specialises in fish, much of which is caught by the restaurant's own fishing boat. Polpo Mario is very popular with the locals, and the menu includes such delights as octopus paté, fish pie and *misto all'antica*, a mix of cuttlefish, octopus, sea asparagus, prawns, olives and pine nuts.

Ristorante da U Tinola

Vernazza, Cinque Terre *Via Fieschi 31 (0187 821 200). Open 7pm-midnight Mon, Tue, Thur-Sun. Closed Jan-8 Mar. €€. Traditional Italian.*

Carlo Basso's stone-clad restaurant on the town's main square, one of the oldest in the Cinque Terre, was built in homage to his father, 'U Tinola', a well-known local wine producer. The emphasis here is on superb, traditional Ligurian cuisine: pasta with delicious fillings served with pesto sauce and fresh fish from one the local fishing ports are the specialities of the house. Choose one of the excellent locally-produced wines to accompany your meal.

Il Sommergibile

San Remo *Piazza Bresca 12 (0184 501 944/ www.ilsommergibile.com). Open Jan-June, Sept-Dec noon-2pm, 7-10.30pm Mon-Wed, Fri-Sun. July, Aug noon-2pm, 7-10.30pm daily. €€€. Traditional Italian.*

A great deal of thought has evidently gone into the design of this restaurant near San Remo's old port. Fish tanks arranged throughout the interior give diners the illusion of eating underwater – *sommergibile* in Italian means submarine. Needless to say, seafood is a speciality, and the proximity of France means that lobster and shellfish can be easily imported from Provence, Brittany and Normandy. Local produce is available too, such as olive oil from the Entroterra hills above Savona.

Trattoria di Mario

Rapallo *Piazza Garibaldi 23 (0185 51736). Open 12.30-2pm, 7.30-10pm Mon, Tue, Thur-Sun. Closed Nov, early Jan-early Mar. €€. Trattoria.*

Located in the historic arcades of the piazza Garibaldi, this delightful trattoria has been rustling up traditional Ligurian cuisine since 1963. Specialities include spaghetti with seafood and tomatoes and grilled fish. Be sure to leave room for the excellent Sabina cake, a confection of cream and hot chocolate named after the proprietor's mother. If you're visiting in summer, enjoy the terrace and perhaps leave time for a game of chess on the giant board in the square outside.

Explore

SAN REMO & AROUND

Perhaps the best known resort on the Riviera di Ponente, San Remo is renowned for its intensive cultivation of flowers. It has been popular as a holiday destination since the 19th century, when it first found favour with the English and Russians.

San Remo is divided into three districts: the shopping area round the corso Matteotti; the old town, La Pigna; and the formerly fashionable and still glamorous west end, with its splendid Belle Epoque Casino and onion-domed Russian Orthodox church. The Russian influence is still detectable in the corso Imperatrice, which was named after the wife of Tsar Alexander II. Today it's a favoured venue for that most Italian of activities, the *passeggiata* or evening stroll.

At the western end of the Riviera di Ponente is the magnificent botanical garden of Villa Hanbury. Nearby is Ventimiglia, so called because the town grew up alongside the twentieth milestone on the via Julia Augusta, the old Roman Road.

Inland is the village of Dolceacqua, just a few kilometres into the Val Nervia. Its graceful 15th-century Ponte Vecchio was painted by Monet, who called it 'a jewel of brightness'. The village may be known as 'sweet water', but it produces a much more potent tipple called Rossese, one of Italy's finest red wines and said to have been a favourite of Napoleon and Pope Julius III.

Giardini Hanbury, La Mortola Inferiore

Ventimiglia *(0184 229 507/www.amicihanbury.com). Open Mar-mid June, mid Sept-Oct 9.30am-6pm Mon, Tue, Thur-Sun. Mid June-mid Sept 9.30am-7pm Mon, Tue, Thur-Sun. Nov-Feb 9.30am-5pm Mon, Tue, Thur-Sun. Admission €7.50.*

These remarkable gardens were designed and planted in 1867 by an Englishman, Sir Thomas Hanbury, who, having amassed a fortune trading in the Far East, imported rare and exotic horticultural species from around the world. The recommended path winds down through the gardens to the Mediterranean and a pleasant café beside the sea.

Museo dell'Olivo

Imperia, 22km from Alassio *(0183 295 762/ www.museodellolivo.com). Open 9am-12.30pm, 3pm-6.30pm daily. Admission free.*
Housed in an impressive art nouveau building, this museum displays items relating to the 6,000-year history of olive cultivation and its crucial influence on Mediterranean civilisations. Vistors can, by appointment, also explore the adjacent Carli Oil Mill, which is open from December to March. The museum consists of 18 rooms, a library and cafeteria. Multi-lingual audio guides are available.

Russian Orthodox Church

San Remo *(0184 531 807). Open 9.30am-noon, 3.30-6pm daily. Admission free.*
This 'jewel box', begun in 1912 and consecrated in 1913, was built for San Remo's then sizeable and influential Russian community (which included the Tsarina). The onion domes and elaborate architecture bear more than a passing resemblance to St Basil's Cathedral in Moscow. Inside you will find the tombs of the royal house of Montenegro.

ALASSIO & AROUND

Alassio is the perfect place to relax in after the rigours of sightseeing. It has more than three kilometres of fine sandy beach sloping gently down to the sea, and has been a particular favourite of the English since the late 19th century, when the Hanbury family first spotted the potential of the place. Celebrities flocked here in the 1930s, and Ernest Hemingway started a tradition at the Caffè Roma when he left his signature on a ceramic plaque. These days, numerous clubs, bars and discos add a hedonistic edge to the resort.

In as stark a contrast as you could imagine to Alassio, near neighbour Albenga is a treasure trove of tower houses, piazzas, palazzi and churches, making it a prime destination for anyone interested in art and culture. The medieval centre still retains its Roman *castrum* layout, and the central main square, piazza San Michelle, overlooked by the west front of the cathedral, is magnificent and should not be missed. Look out also for the typical 13th-century brick towers displaying the wealth of local families, some of which lean drunkenly in Tower of Pisa fashion on the soft soil. The Palazzo Vescovile, with its black and white stripes, seems to echo the Pisan connection, and it's also worth taking a stroll down via Bernardo Ricci, once a Roman street and still lined with well-preserved medieval houses and a fifth-century baptistery.

GOLFO DI PARADISO & TIGULLIO

The eastern half of the Riviera, the Riviera di Levante, begins with the promise of the Gulf of Paradise. The mountains above the coast are where the Columbus family came from. Camogli, at the other end of the Gulf, is perhaps best known for the Sagra dei Pesce, which takes place on the second Sunday of May each year. The biggest frying pan in Italy, measuring about 4.25 metres across, cooks huge amounts of sardines which are then served to everyone in town.

From Comogli there is a pleasant (though strenuous) walk on to the peninsula of Portofino, where secluded coves await. However, the best way to reach Portofino is along the east side of the peninsula via the attractive resort of Santa Margherita Ligure.

"Portofino is one of those impossibly beautiful places."

Portofino itself is one of those impossibly beautiful places that people daydream about during dreary winters in more northerly climes. The pretty harbour, with its rows of colourful houses, is embraced by a rocky, villa-studded isthmus. The attractive Piazzetta provides an excellent venue in which to sip an espresso before a spot of window-shopping round some of the chic boutiques of the resort. Don't miss the yellow church of San Giorgio above the harbour, rebuilt four times during World War II. It's also worth taking a boat trip around the coast. Much of the area's beauty can only be seen from the sea.

Rapallo, once famed for its lace, enjoys a fine location at the top of the peninsula just where the Golfo del Tigullio begins to stretch away to the east. One of the best-known resorts on the Riviera, Rapallo first attracted visitors during the late 19th-century – as evidenced by the art nouveau cafés and the seafront Lungomare Vittorio Veneto. Nearby, Chiavari, with its busy morning market, sits cheek by jowl with Lavagna across the Entella torrent, spanned by the magnificent early 13th-century Ponte della Maddalena, constructed by Ugone Fieschi. The presence of the Fieschis can be felt even today, when every year the giant Torta dei Fieschi is consumed to celebrate a family wedding that took place back in 1230.

At the eastern end of the Golfo del Tigullio, Sestri Levante, one of the most lively of the resorts on the Riviera, is based round a peninsula known as Isola, which offers views of the sandy

Clockwise from the top: Royal Hotel (3); Hotel Splendido (3).

Clockwise from the top:
Il Sommergiblie (3);
food and drink in
Monterosso (3).

Panificio
da
FIORELLA

FOCACCIA

e olive, cipolle,
erdure, melanzane,
osmarino, salvia,
omodoo, pesto e
al formaggio

PIZZA

MERCE NON A SCOPO POL
THESE BOTTLES AREN'T A POLITIC
STATEMENT (DON'T BE IGNORAN

IL CHE
DER FÜHRER
Messaggero di Pace
REGGAE TH

il CASELLO
FOCACC
e
PANIN
E - MAIL
INTERNET SER
Ristoran
MUSICA dalN

Bay of Fairy Tales, named after the works of Hans Christian Andersen (who stayed here), and the idyllic little Baia del Silenzio (the Bay of Silence).

GOLFO DEI POETI & CINQUE TERRE

For visitors heading east from Genoa, Levanto is the gateway to the Cinque Terre, or 'five lands'. Today, Monterosso, Vernazza, Corniglia, Manarola and Riomaggiore, the five towns of the Cinque Terre, can all be reached by road – but a more convenient and less stressful way to get there is by train or boat.

One of the biggest draws of the area, and a good way to avoid the hordes, is the hiking. This 20-kilometre stretch of rugged coastline, with a hinterland carved out of the steep rock and used for the cultivation of olives and vines, is a National Park and UNESCO World Heritage site.

The coastal path, the Sentiero Azzurro ('Blue Path'), is a 12-kilometre walk from Riomaggiore to Monterosso al Mare. It's well worth the time and effort (the going is tough in places, although this ensures these sections are quieter) to see the extraordinary views of the coast that would otherwise be invisible. A longer (38-kilometre) ridge-top stretch from Portovenere to Levanto is the Sentiero Rosso, which could take anything from nine to 12 hours. The length of this walk deters many, leaving the spectacular views to the determined.

Vernazza is the prettiest of the Cinque Terre. Relaxing with a cold beer on the piazza Marconi is an opportunity to people-watch, as well as to appreciate the architecture of the Ligurian Gothic church of Santa Maria d'Antiochia, built on rocks leading down to the sea. If you can tear yourself away, visit Manarola, a port without a harbour where the anchovy fishing boats are parked up in the main street. Manarola is also famous for its wines, which have DOC status. The best known is the dessert wine Sciacchetrà, but the Cinque Terre white also slips down well with a plate of fried anchovies.

Riomaggiore is the quintessential Italian fishing village, with case torri tower houses in shades of red and yellow, grouped around the picturesque harbour. In the upper town, locals dub the steps between the houses 'stairways to heaven'.

The Riviera reaches a perfect conclusion at its eastern end, where the beautiful Gulf of Poets awaits. Writers seem to be particularly susceptible to its charms, with Shelley, Byron and DH Lawrence, among others, spending long periods here. On the western side of the Gulf, Portovenere stands proud on its promontory, dominated by its Doria castle and San Pietro. Also dominated by its castle, but on the eastern side of the Gulf, is Lerici, a sandy beach resort popular with those who favour marine pursuits, due to the protective rugged coastline.

San Pietro

Portovenere *(0187 790 691). Open Summer 7am-8pm daily. Winter 9am-5.30pm daily. Admission free.*
San Pietro was built between 1256 and 1277 on the ruins of an earlier Christian church, which itself reputedly stood on the site of a temple dedicated to Venus. Restored in the 1930s, this striped, Genoese-style church, dedicated to the patron saint of fishermen, stands proud with its loggia on a promontory overlooking the sea.

Factfile

When to go

Don't go in July and August. It's crowded and too hot to do anything other than languish in the shade. Spring and autumn are the best times to visit, with lots of sunshine, pleasant temperatures and fewer people. In winter, the crowds will certainly be absent, but the weather is uncertain and many places close.

Getting there & around

The main airport for the Riviera is Cristoforo Columbo at Genova-Sestri. There is a good, regular and inexpensive train service along the coast serving all the resorts on the Riviera (www.trenitalia.com).

Boats and ferries also offer a very practical and exceedingly pleasant way to get around and connect most resorts. Golfo Paradiso (www.golfoparadiso.it), Navigazione Golfo dei Poeti (www.navigazionegolfodeipoeti.it) and Servizio Marittimo del Tigullio (www.traghetti portofino.it) are the main operators. Tigullio Trasporti (www.tigulliotrasporti.it) operates buses on the Riviera di Levante only.

Tourist information

Piazza De Ferrari 1 Genova (010 54851/ www.turismoinliguria.it).
Largo Nuvoloni 1, San Remo, 0184 59059/ infosanremo@rivieradeifiori.org.
Via Mazzini 68, Alassio (0182 647 027/ alassio@inforiviera.it).
Via Roma 35, Portofino (0185 269 024/ www.apttigullio.liguria.it).

Internet

Most towns along the Italian Riviera have an internet café, and of course Genoa has many. En route, Albenga has Bar Internet, Caffè Di Croce Giacomo, Piazza Torlaro 5 (0182 50902).

Rimini

The tale of Rimini is a tale of two cities. The famous Riviera offers visitors a giddy whirl of sun-worshipping by day followed by full-on, fashion-happy clubbing into the night – a combination that draws summer-long crowds of pleasure-seekers. Yet a mere ten minutes away sits the beautiful *centro storico*, with Roman monuments and Renaissance architecture. People flock here simply to enjoy themselves, and many return year after year – not unlike the migrating flamingos further up the coast on the Po Delta.

Clockwise from top left: Rimini marina (2); Tempio Malatestiano; Rimini beach; Piazza Tre Martiri; street murals.

Osteria della Piazzetta

Vicolo Pescheria 5, Centro Storico (0541 783 986/
www.osteriadellapiazzetta.com) Open 11.30am-2.30am,
7pm-midnight daily. €. Trattoria.

Hidden down an alleyway not for from the beautifully
restored fishmarket in piazza Cavour, this popular little
osteria's outdoor tables are packed out in summer. Its
old town location is perfect for a spot of post-prandial
barhopping: plot your route as you feast on fragrant
pasta dishes, steaks or the daily specials. Service is good-
natured, prices are low and there's an impressive choice of
wines by the glass.

Papille

Viale Tiberio 11, San Giuliano (0541 53577).
Open 6pm-2am Mon, Wed-Sun. €. Enoteca.

More an *enoteca* than a restaurant, Papille offers good wine,
nibbles and some more substantial fare. The interior is
stylish but unstuffy; outdoor tables overlook the pretty
Roman bridge of Tiberius. A food and wine counter sells
excellent cured meats and local cheeses, as well as fresh
pasta and own-made desserts to take away.

Ristorante dallo Zio

Via Santa Chiara 16, Centro Storico (0541 786 747/
www.ristorantedallozio.it). Open noon-3pm,
8pm-midnight daily. Closed Aug. €€€.
Traditional Italian.

Open since 1965, this elegant restaurant was one of Fellini's
favourites, and remains one of the city's best known
eateries. The original Zio (uncle) is no more, but owner-chef
Giuliano Canzian serves *piatti di memoria* of the
restaurant's historic fish dishes (widow's risotto, cooked in
cuttlefish ink, say, or polenta with clams) as well as his own
creations made from the finest seasonal ingredients. One of
the three dining rooms has paintings by the celebrated
Tonino Guerra.

Rock Island

Piazzale Boscovich, Molo di Levante (0541 50178/
www.rockislandrimini.com). Open Summer 6.30pm-late
Tue-Sun. €€. Bar.

Located beyond the free beach and the harbour, this is the
best spot in town from which to see the sun set over the sea,
watch the moonlight dance on the water or catch fireworks
exploding over the beaches. A diverse crowd gathers to
party and dance from dusk to dawn during summer.

Sangiovesa al Mare

Lungomare Tintori 21, Marina Centro (0541 54237/
www.sangiovesa.it). Open 7.30pm-late Tue-Sat;
12.30-3pm Sun. €€. Trattoria.

This deservedly popular place on the seafront is an offshoot
of Sangiovesa, a renowned osteria in the enchanting hillside
town of Santarcangelo di Romagna (piazza Simone
Balacchi 14, 0541 620 854). Whereas the original is known
for its game, vegetables and own-made pastas, this outpost
also serves excellent fish and seafood. Sepia photos
of the hill town evoke the rustic spirit of the original; quirky
giant *piadine* wrapped around the pillars add the Rimini
fun factor.

Explore

SIGHTS

Start in Rimini's old town, at the piazza Tre
Martiri. West of here is the Arch of Augustus: built
in 27 BC, it marked the entrance to the city from
the via Flaminia, which led to Rome. South of
piazza stands the beautiful Tempio Malatestiano.
Piazza Cavour, the city's other main square, sits
along the Corso d'Augusto, its lovely renaissance
fountain facing the old fish market. North of here
stands the Castel Sismondo, once the pride and
joy of the ruling Malatestas but now used for
concerts and exhibitions. Following the Corso
d'Augusto towards the canal takes you past the
Cinema Fulgor at no.162 (a favourite with Fellini)
and on to the marble Tiberius Bridge. Across here
lies the tiny Borgo San Giuliano, once the town's
fishing quarter. Its narrow streets, daubed with
murals, are a pleasant place to wander.

The old town is also good for shopping, with an
abundance of designer boutiques on and off the
Corso d'Augusto. For big bargains, head out of
town to the outlets on via Cagnona Nuova.

The bus from Rimini station to the Lungomare
stops at piazzale Fellini, the heart of the resort,
and home to the Grand Hotel. Near the harbour
are Rimini's lidos and the free beach (*spiaggia
libera*). Many hotels have agreements with specific
bagni, some delightfully decadent; otherwise, two
beds and a parasol cost around €30 a day.

Galleria d'Arte Moderna

Villa Franceschi, Via Gorizia 2, Riccione (0541 693
3534, www.villafranceschi.it). Open July, Aug 8-11pm
Mon, Fri-Sun; 9am-noon Tue, Thur. Sept-June 9am-
noon, 4-7pm Mon, Wed; 9am-noon Tue, Thur, Sat,
Sun; 9am-noon Fri. Admission €2; €1 reductions.

This contemporary art gallery, a short walk from the station
in beachside Riccione, opened in 2005 in a beautifully
restored Stilo Liberty building. Most of the sculptures,
paintings and designs are by artists from Emilia-Romagna;
among the more notable examples are works by Alberto
Burri and early pieces by Forli artist Maceo Casadei.

Museo della Città

Via Tonini 1 (0541 21482). Open Mid June-mid Sept
10am-12.30pm, 4.30-7.30pm, 9-11pm Tue; 10am-
12.30pm, 4.30-7.30pm Wed-Sat; 4.30-7.30 Sun. Mid
Sept-mid June 8.30am-12.30pm, 5-7pm Tue-Sat; 4-7pm
Sun. Admission €4; €1.50 reductions; free to all Sun.

Currently being refurbished, the city museum is split into
archaeological and fine art sections. The former holds a
strong collection of late Roman relics, including a lovely
mosaic of a ship surounded by dancing dolphins. Next door,
in an old Jesuit hospital, are 36 rooms of 14th- to 19th-century
art, with works by Bellini, Ghirlandaio and painters of the
local school, Giovanni, Giuliano and Pietro da Rimini.

Club class

Time Out talks to Gilles Peterson, Radio 1's Worldwide DJ and the man behind the Talkin' Loud record label and Acid Jazz records, to find out what's so special about the Italian club scene.

Time Out: So, what is it about the Italian club scene that makes it so special?

Gilles Peterson: Cerrone was Italian... all Luther Vandross's early recordings were done in Italy... In its own way, Italy is the king of European clubbing. They don't follow the rest of Europe. It's about dancing, romancing and music – and they do it with aplomb. Italians are very confident about what they like... they have their own tempo.

TO: And where are the best clubs?

GP: In Naples, the **Nabilah** (via Spiaggia Romana 15, Bacoli, www.nabilah.it; pictured) is *the* club. It's on the beach and makes Miami look like Blackpool. When it comes to clubbing and vanity, Italy is *ichiban*! *Numero uno*! Nabilah is wall-to-wall beautiful people. Everyone is *cut*... sculpted! I've never felt so grey in all my life! The music policy is sexy Café de Flor... Charles Webster meets sexy house meets energetic bossas... very Latin.

TO: What about the rest of Italy? How are the clubs different?

GP: Club culture in Italy is diverse and sophisticated. On the one hand you get casual, swinging beach sessions like Ravenna's **Boca Barranca** (viale Italia 301, Marina Romea, Ravenna, 05 4444 7858, www.bocabarranca.it), which is popular with DJs like Domu, Far Out's Joe Davis, Mark De Clive Lowe and west London's broken beat crew, while down the coast in Locorotondo, **Mavú** (Contrada Mavugliola 22, Locorotondo, 393 021 3850, www.mavu.it) is held in a castle – the equivalent of an English stately home. People travel from all over Puglia for this session. You'll get early evening live performances – from local jazz outfits to very Italian cabaret – that eventually give way to the DJs. It will stay outdoors until 5am and then move inside for the more decadent vibe. The DJs who regularly play at Mavú include Louie Vega, Carl Craig and Jazzanova. Sophisticated, cultured clubbing.

TO: So much for the beach clubs, what about the big cities. Florence for instance?

GP: **Tenax** (via Pratese 46, 50127 Florence, 055 308 160, www.tenax.org) is *the* club in Florence; a super club; but the last time I was there I played at a new venue, called the **Viper Club** (corner of via Pistoiese & via Lombardia

le Piagge, 50145 Firenze, 055 318 231, www.viperclub.eu). Rome? It has to be **Goa** (via Libetta 13, 065 748 277) – it's always at the forefront of the scene in Italy. Proper clubbing. It's a kind of cross between Fabric and Pacha. The word is it's currently on a fashionista and electro vibe. Friday nights at Goa is couples night... girlfriend and boyfriend runnings. Saturday is flirting! The people are always *dressed*! Swanky!

TO: And Milan?

GP: They love their jazz in Milan. The **Blue Note** (via Borsieri Pietro 37, 899 700 022, www.bluenotemilano.com) is very cool with excellent programming.

TO: What was your last gig in Italy?

GP: Most recently I played at the **Borsa Club** in Mantova, 20km from Verona (via della Libertà 6, 03 7632 6016). It's a small bar, more of a drinking and chilling experience, but they splash out on the DJs. An Italian equivalent of Hoxton.

Clockwise from top left:
Grand Hotel (2);
DuoMo Hotel (3).

Museo Fellini

Via Oberdan 1 (0541 50085/www.federicofellini.it).
Open 4.30-7.30pm Tue-Fri; 10am-noon, 4.30-7.30pm
Sun. Admission free.
This museum pays homage to the local boy made good
with scripts, costumes, photos and memorabilia, as well as
some special exhibitions. True pilgrims can also watch
a film at Fellini's beloved Cinema Fulgor, meander around
the Borgo San Giuliano and peer through the gates at the
Grand Hotel, just as he did as a child.

Tempio Malatestiano

Via IV Novembre 35 (0541 439 098/
www.diocesi.rimini.it). Open 9am-12.30pm,
3.30-7pm daily. Admission free.
Renaissance pioneer Leon Battista Alberti designed this
intriguing cathedral at the behest of Sigismondo Malatesta,
who wanted to build a chapel dedicated to his beloved third
wife Isotta; you can see their entwined initials, S and I,
everywhere. It's a beautiful yet curious mixture of paganism
and Christianity, and features art by Piero della Francesco,
a crucifix taken from the site's earlier Gothic church by
Giotto and a host of enigmatic imagery. Make sure you
cover your shoulders or you won't be allowed in.

Clubs

Rimini and Riccione are paradise for clubbers. In
Ravenna, the beach at Boca Borranca (0544 447
858, www.bocabarranca.it) also hosts fine DJs.

Byblos

Piazza Castello 24, Misone Monte, Misano Adriatico
(0541 690 252/www.byblosclub.com). Open Mar-Oct
11.45pm-9am Fri-Sat. Admission €20-€25.
Perched in the hills near Riccione, this villa is good for dining
and poolside hanging-out, at least if you look fabulous in a
bikini or trunks. Byblos attracts Italian celebrity types; the
cosy dancefloor is so exclusive it can feel like a private party.

Coconuts

Via Lungomare Tintori 5 (335 561 2770/
www.coconuts.it). Open Summer 6.30pm-late daily.
Admission free.
This palm-clad disco-bar is on the main drag of Rimini's
Lungomare. Decked out in white and neon, with pumping
music and a Latino vibe, it's the most glamorous place on
the beach strip. Its Fly Bar is ideal for aperitifs at sundown;
the Street Bar booms out Italian house.

Cocorico

Via Chieti 44, Riccione (0541 605 183/www.cocorico.it).
Open Feb-Nov 10.30pm-late Sat. Admission €30-€35.
The place to come to for Italian techno and house on the
Romagnolo Riviera, this giant glass pyramid can hold a
couple of thousand ravers on a summer night. Along with
some of the best DJs in Italy, it attracts a stellar array of
international talent, such as Carl Cox and DJ Rush. There
are four additional spaces: Morphine, an ambient room; Il
Titilla, the private room; the gay-friendly Ciao Box, an
'ironic disco'; and Strix, a new club in the women's loos.

Paradiso

Via Covignano 260 (0541 751 132). Open Apr-Oct
11.30pm-late Fri, Sat. Admission €20-€25.
Located in the hills above Rimini, famously hedonistic
Paradiso lives up to its name with sea views and lush
gardens. It draws the most beautiful and/or beautifully
dressed people in town, so you'll need to look the part. The
huge dancefloor draws some of the best DJs around, with
Friday the top night, but there's also a lounging area with
massages and herbal teas.

Factfile

When to go
The Lungomare is quieter from Sept-May, but
many hotels stay open for conference delegates.

Getting there
Rimini has its own airport (0541 715 711,
www.riminiairport.com), eight kilometres outside
the city. Leaving every half-hour, bus 9 takes you
to the centre; a taxi costs €20. Ancona, Bologna
and Forlì airports are nearby; Rimini is well served
by the rail network (www.trenitalia.com).

Getting around
Public transport in Rimini is good, with buses
run by TRAM (0541 300 511, www.tram.rimini.it)
and plenty of taxis (0541 50020): there's a rank
outside the train station day and night. Note
that central Rimini is pedestrianised.

Tourist information
There's an information desk at Rimini airport,
and two offices in town: one by the station, one
by viale Vespucci. In summer (June-Sept), free
guided tours of the old centre run every Tuesday,
leaving at 9.30am from Corso d'Augusto 158.
IAT Rimini Marina Centro, Piazzale F Fellini 3
(0541 56902/www.riminiturismo.it). Open
May-Oct 8.30am-7pm Mon-Sat. Nov-Apr 9.30am-
12.30pm, 3.30-6.30pm Mon-Sat.
IAT Rimini Station, Piazzale C Battisti 1 (0541
51331).Open May-Oct 8.30am-7pm Mon-Sat. Nov-
Apr 9.30m-12.30pm, 3.30-6.30pm Mon-Sat.

Internet
Internet cafés dot the seafront and city centre;
viale Vespucci is a good bet. For a full list, ask at
the tourist office.

Clockwise from top left: Alghero lobster; Alghero's old town; Alghero fish market; the Maddalena archipelago; La Maddalena; Romazzino, Costa Smeralda.

Northern Sardinia

Sardinia's greatest asset is its spectacular coastline. There are more gorgeous beaches per kilometre here than in any other part of Italy, and the enviably temperate climate means that the island basks in the sun well into autumn. Centuries of invasion have left a rich architectural heritage scattered across the rugged interior, but the *cucina sarda* is just as much of a draw, from the little-known delights of *bottarga* (dried fish roe) to the celebrated *pecorino sardo*.

Up in the north-west, the quaint but bustling fishing port of Alghero is a good starting point for any exploration. The architecture is an interesting mix of Catalan and Italian, and a number of excellent seafood restaurants serve variations on the local speciality, lobster. What's more, there are cultural and coastal diversions aplenty from Alghero including the Grotta di Nettuno caves and the beach at La Pelosa, just north of Stintino.

No trip to northern Sardinia is complete without a peek at the playground of the rich and famous, the Costa Smeralda on the east coast, which provides a fairly pronounced contrast to Alghero. Although the low-rise architecture of the town, a pastiche of a Mediterranean idyll, isn't everyone's idea of good taste, few visitors would deny the beauty of the natural scenery. And if you've got the money it's worth exploring the five-star hotels, upmarket bars and designer shopping at its epicentre, the marina and town of Porto Cervo. When you tire of cocktails and window-shopping for Gucci, a few days on the tranquil, gorgeous island of La Maddalena is the perfect antidote. The beaches here are simply immaculate.

A full coast-to-coast tour is easily achievable in a week if you have a car, including slack for many diversions. Take time to stop off at some of the historic churches or to sample some of the island's top wines at the Sella & Mosca winery near Alghero.

Northern Sardinia

Historic sites
● ● ● ● ●

Eating & drinking
● ● ● ● ●

Art & architecture
● ● ● ● ●

Scenery
● ● ● ● ●

Hotels
● ● ● ● ●

Outdoor activities
● ● ● ● ●

0   10km

Santa Teresa
di Gallura ●

La Maddalena
●

Costa Smeralda
Baia Sardinia ● ●
Porto
Cervo

● Stintino

Ólbia ●

● SÁSSARI

●
Alghero

Stay

Accommodation in northern Sardinia ranges from top-end hotels with all mod cons to *agriturismi* with goats. Book well ahead for July and August. Useful websites include www.bebsardegna.it (in Italian only) or www.insardegnabb.it for B&Bs; www.agriturismodisardegna.it for farm holidays; and www.sleepinitaly.com and www.rent-sardinia.com for apartments.

El Balear

Alghero *Lungomare Dante 32 (079 975 229/ www.hotelelbalear.it). €€.*
Bag a room with a sea-facing balcony at El Balear, a short walk south of piazza Sulis. Decor-wise, it's stuck in the 1960s, but the beds are comfortable and the rooms are clean. The food is similarly mixed: breakfast is a limp affair that won't get you leaping out of bed, but the dinners are good value. There's a pleasant bar, an inner courtyard and a front terrace; the town beach is just across the promenade.

Carlos V (Carlos Quinto)

Alghero *Lungomare Valencia 24 (079 972 0600/ www.hotelcarlosv.it). €€€.*
A recent no-expense-spared makeover has given the Carlos V a posh but slightly corporate feel. The plushly carpeted rooms have been equipped with flat-screen TVs; the bathrooms are a vision in marble. You can quickly get into holiday mode by strolling around the gardens or lounging by the huge pool – the binoculars on the terrace mean you don't even have to step outside to get a close-up of the magnificent coastline.

La Coluccia

Santa Teresa di Gallura *Località Conca Verde (078 975 8004/www.mobyget.it/lacoluccia). €€€.*
The curvy architecture may nod to traditional Sardinian style, but this boutique hotel's bold looks are thoroughly 21st century. The design is matched by the stunning location on the north-east coast, with views across to the island of Spargi (part of the La Maddalena archipelago). From the elegant topiary to the chic sunbeds dotted around the sculptured pool, the public areas are super-smart; the bedrooms are equally sumptuous, with earthy, natural hues and sleek, dark wood furnishings. When you're not lazing on the private beach, head to the well-equipped gym and beauty centre.

Hotel Cala di Volpe

Porto Cervo *Località Cala di Volpe (078 997 6111/ www.hotelcaladivolpe.it). €€€€.*
Designed by Jacques Couëlle, this lavish Mediterranean-meets-Moorish classic overlooking the lovely Cala di Volpe bay is set in extensive grounds, complete with tennis courts and a saltwater pool by the sea. The rooms are luxuriously appointed, with colourful ceramic tiles, plush bedlinen and stunning private balconies. A choice of three bars means you won't get bored taking your evening *aperitivo*; for dinner, there's the Cala restaurant or a barbecue.

Hotel Capriccioli

Costa Smeralda *Punta Capriccioli (078 996 004/ www.residenzacapriccioli.com). €€.*
If the landmark Cala di Volpe (see above) is beyond your means, this family-run hotel is a more affordable option in the heart of Costa Smeralda. The rooms, furnished in typically Sardinian style, are simple and cool, and Capriccioli beach is just a short stroll away.

Hotel Miralonga

La Maddalena *Strada Panoramica, Via Don Vico (078 722 563/www.miralonga.it). €€.*
This modern addition to La Maddalena lacks character, but the sea views are stunning. The bedrooms are a good size and come with air-conditioning, satellite TV and, from the balconies, panoramic vistas. On the shore side, there's an ample-sized swimming pool in which novice divers can take lessons; the diving school can also organise excursions around the National Park. It's a shortish walk to the harbour at La Maddalena, but if you're feeling lazy, there's hearty fare available in the hotel restaurant.

> "The curvy architecture may nod to traditional Sardinian style, but this boutique hotel's bold looks are thoroughly 21st century."

Hotel La Rocca

Baia Sardinia *Località Pulicinu (078 993 3131/ www.hotellarocca.it). €€.*
This pastel-washed hotel complex is set amid tranquil, well-tended gardens. The generous bedrooms are tiled and furnished in simple Sardinian style, with air-conditioning and gleaming bathrooms. There's a daily minibus to the beach at Baia Sardinia, and the Costa Smeralda is a short drive away; that said, it's easy to spend a day basking by the attractive pool. La Rocca, its sister restaurant across the road, serves great seafood and local specialities such as culaurgiones, the Sardinian equivalent of ravioli.

Hotel San Francesco

Alghero *Via Ambrogio Machin 2 (079 980 330/ www.sanfrancescohotel.com). €.*
The San Francesco is the only hotel located in the heart of the old town. This place was once a convent: its rooms occupy the first floor of the cloisters attached to San Francesco church. The rooms may be pretty basic, and a few are on the small side, but the overall feel is atmospheric and cosy. Breakfast brings decent cappuccinos and pastries, served alfresco on a terrace festooned with pelargoniums. It's a nice spot for an aperitif, but you'll need to bring your own bottle of prosecco.

La Pelosetta Residence Hotel
Capo Falcone, Nr Stintino *(079 527 188/ www.lapelosetta.it). €€.*
It's an effortless five minutes from bed to beach at this complex, overlooking the turquoise sea and gleaming sands of La Pelosa. As a result, its ten rooms, all with balconies and beautiful sea views, invariably get booked up well in advance. The rooms are basic, with small bathrooms and showers; if you'd prefer more space and facilities, there are 70 self-catering apartments. La Pelosetta's other main selling point is a private, well-manicured lawn for the sole use of guests, not to be sniffed at during peak season.

Le Querce
Baia Sardinia *Via Vaddi di Jatta (078 999 248/ www.lequerce.com). €€.*
Get a taste of rural living within driving distance of the Costa Smeralda at this tucked-away collection of self-catering cottages. The cottages are tastefully decorated and peacefully located, with views of Baia Sardinia; the town and marina of Porto Cervo is a five-minute drive away. Two therapists offer health and beauty treatments; the enforced absence of under-12s should also aid relaxation.

> "Money buys you a private beach, saltwater pool, Michelin-starred restaurant, and the sound of the sea as you fall asleep."

Villa Las Tronas
Alghero *Lungomare Valencia 1 (079 981 818/ www.hvlt.com). €€€€.*
Occupying a private promontory with a commanding view of the bay, this turreted tower sits in splendid isolation. The interior is equally regal, with ornate chandeliers, high ceilings and miles of marble, and the bedrooms are lavishly dressed with expensive fabrics with antiques. Money buys you your own private beach, sunbathing by a glorious saltwater pool, a well-equipped gym, a Michelin-starred restaurant, and the sound of the sea as you fall asleep.

Eat

Seafood is the catch of the day in northern Sardinia; especially in Alghero, where lobster (*aragosta*) features on most menus and the city's cobbled streets are packed with reasonably priced eateries. In more rural areas, you'll find plenty of *agriturismos* with restaurants, serving the likes of traditional suckling pig spit-roasted

with myrtle. Booking is essential at the more upmarket restaurants: locals do cross the island to dine out at destination spots. Red wine, especially riserva cannonou, is the top tipple; the best whites are the dry, refreshing vermentinos.

Al Tuguri
Alghero *Via Maiorca 113 (079 976 772/ www.altuguri.it). Open noon-3pm, 6-10pm Mon-Sat. €€€. Traditional Italian.*
This small, charming restaurant concentrates on Catalan specialities, taking the strain out of choosing with its three set menus (fish, meat and vegetarian). Dishes such as boar carpaccio and mussels sautéed with local herbs show a pleasingly light touch, and the ingredients are sparklingly fresh. It gets packed, so book well ahead.

Andreini
Alghero *Via Ardoino 45 (079 982 098/ www.ristoranteandreini.it). Open 12.30-2.30pm, 7.30-10pm daily. €€€. Modern Italian.*
Run by two young brothers, the Andreini combines sleek decor with a cutting-edge menu, fusing traditional local ingredients with daring flavours. The six-course tasting menu (€60) is an imaginative tour de force, featuring amberjack carpaccio, red mullet millefeuille with vegetable caponata and tagliatelle with black truffle and squid, followed by peaches and Bombay gin. On balmy evenings, the plant-festooned terrace is a delight.

Cafè Latino
Alghero *Bastioni Magellano 10 (079 976 541/ www.miras.it). Open 9am-2am daily. €€. Café/Bar.*
Overlooking the harbour, the terrace at Latino is a prime spot from which to watch the world stroll by. Pull up one of the comfortable colonial-chic wicker chairs and settle in at sunset with a glass of sparkling torbato or a cocktail. Drinks arrive with bowls of crisps; if you're in need of something more substantial, there are *panini* and pizzas.

Fior Acqua Ristorante & Prince Café
Porto Cervo *Piazza del Principe (078 990 7021). Open 8.30-11am, noon-2.30pm, 6-10.30pm daily. €€-€€€. Café/bar/modern Italian.*
Open since 2007, this swish bar and restaurant is an ambitious venture. The design comes courtesy of Jean Claude le Suisse, who worked with the Aga Khan in the 1960s, while the summer chef is Michele Farru, star of La prova del cuoco (the Italian version of Ready, Steady, Cook). The day starts with speciality 'spa' breakfasts, before moving on to light lunches and then a heady dinner menu of decadent dishes such as risotto with wild baby lobster and champagne and ravioli with scorpion fish and chicory. If you can't stretch to dinner, come for a cocktail in the bar.

Il Gabbiano
Capo Falcone, Nr Stintino *Via Vigna Veccia (079 527 089). Open noon-3pm, 7-11pm daily. €€. Trattoria.*
A lively, informal outdoor beach restaurant, Il Gabbiano serves wonderfully hearty food at sensible prices. Watch in mouthwatering wonder as platters of grilled meats and fish

Clockwise from top left:
Hotel Cala di Volpe; La
Coluccia (2); Al Tuguri (2);
Villa Las Tronas; Hotel
San Francesco.

Clockwise from top left:
La Lépanto (2); fiore
sardo cheese (2);
La Casa del Formaggio;
pane carasau.

come flying out of the kitchen. The homemade culurgiones (stuffed pasta parcels) with tomatoes and basil and involtini di spada (rolled and stuffed swordfish) are a cut above; there are also mean selections of thin-crust pizzas and salads.

Grazia Deledda
Baia Sardinia *Strada per Baia Sardinia (078 998 990). Open Apr-mid Oct noon-2pm, 8pm-2am daily. Closed mid Oct-Mar. €€. Traditional.*
Set back off the Cannigione road, this homely B&B also dishes up authentic local cuisine. The restaurant has a typically 'antique' Sardinian look, but it's the warm welcome and the good food that stand out. Sample suckling pig cooked in myrtle leaves, Sardinian lamb with rosemary, local fish served hot off the charcoal grill, or malloredus (gnocchi-like pasta), served with a rich, spiced local cheese rather than the usual sausage.

La Lépanto
Alghero *Via Carlo Alberto 135 (079 979 116). Open 12.30-3pm, 7.30-midnight daily. €€€. Seafood.*
A seafood legend in its own lunchtime, the kitchen at La Lépanto can serve up to 100 lobsters a day. If you have the heart, visit the doomed crustaceans in the tank on the way into the restaurant. The most popular lobster options are Catalan-style with tomato and onion and Algherese-style with lemon and oil, but the menu also offers Catalan and Algherese seafood specials and great grilled meats.

La Pelosetta
Capo Falcone, Nr Stintino *Località La Pelosa, Sistino (079 527 140/www.ristorantelapelosetta.it). Open Apr-Oct 12.30-2.30pm, 7.30-10pm daily. Closed Nov-Mar. €€. Pizzeria.*
At first glance, this might appear to be just another beachside restaurant and snack bar. However, La Pelosetta takes its food a touch more seriously. Bypass the snack bar and order a proper pizza from the wood-fired oven in the main restaurant, or splash out and sample the Catalan and Sardinian specialities. Daily specials might include gnocchi with prawn sauce or ravioli with fish; spaghetti alla pelosetta, made with clams, is a perennial favourite.

Il Peperone
Porto Cervo *Via Sa Conca (078 990 7049/ www.ilpeperone.com). Open noon-3pm, 6pm-1am daily. €€. Pizzeria.*
Reasonable prices and a friendly buzz mean the turnover on Il Peperone's outdoor tables is brisk. Bargain-hunters should tuck into a pizza, but there are plenty of local specials to tempt those with a bigger budget: spaghetti with lobster, say, or platters of Sardinian cured meats.

Perla Blu
La Maddalena *Piazza Barone des Geneys (078 973 5373). Open noon-2pm, 6-11pm daily. €€. Seafood.*
If La Maddalena's restaurants seem uninspired, it's worth taking the short stroll up to the town's best place to eat. Whether you eat on the open terrace overlooking the harbour or in the more formal dining room, proceedings open with a complimentary *aperitivo*, usually a white wine

sangria with fresh peach. Seafood is the star turn, and you'll be spoilt for choice among the antipasti, carpaccio and fillets: try sea bass roasted with tomatoes and herb. If funds are running low, pick from a dozen or so pizzas.

Sa Mandra
Santa Maria la Palma, Nr Alghero *Strada Aereporto Civile 21a (079 999 150). Open 1-3pm Mon; 1-3pm, 8-11pm Tue-Sun. €. Traditional Italian.*
Housed in a typical Sardinian farmhouse, Sa Mandra is an unpretentious, family-run affair. Focusing on local recipes and homegrown produce, Rita Marrocu and her son Giuseppe are the main cooks; her other son Michele helps father Mario with the meats. The spit-roasted pork is a must, and so are the salamis with pecorino cheese, and the ravioli filled with fresh ricotta and herbs. It's worth the drive from Alghero; book well ahead.

> "A seafood legend in its own lunchtime, the kitchen at La Lépanto can serve up to 100 lobsters a day. If you have the heart, visit the doomed crustaceans in their tank on the way in."

Safina Lounge
Porto Cervo *Località Pevero, Porto Cervo Marina (0789 958 049/www.safina.it). Open 8pm-1am daily. €€€. Restaurant/bar.*
It's not often you get to lie by the pool at a bar, but Safina is an extravagant exception to the rule. Open during July and August, it's a magical place, best enjoyed after sunset when its Moroccan decor and candlelit lanterns conjure up a cosy atmosphere. Come here for champagne and cocktails; depending on the state of your finances, it may be prudent to head back into town for dinner.

Explore

ALGHERO

It's easy to be dazzled by the cluster of medieval domes and towers that rise out of the heart of bustling, harbourside Alghero. The appeal of the walled *centro storico* (old town), as suggested by its nickname of Barcelonetta, owes much to the conquering Catalans, who defeated the Genovese in the 14th century: they helped style the cobbled streets and palaces, built the city wall and its seven stone torres, and even left their mark on the local menus and dialect.

Signposted in Catalan and Italian, Alghero's golden grid of narrow streets is traffic-free. An ecclesiastical itinerary taking in the Cattedrale, the Chiesa di San Francesco and the distinctive ceramic-domed San Michele is easy, as they're all within five minutes' walk of each other. The city's shops are just as conveniently concentrated, along the pedestrianised via Carlo Alberto and its side streets.

From the harbour, follow the stairs up to Cafè Latino for a glass of sparkling white torbato from local vineyard Sella & Mosca; if you develop a taste for it, book a place on one of their daily tours (079 997 700, www.sellae mosca.com). Afterwards, stroll along the promenade to piazza Sulis and trawl the craft stalls set out in the early evening, or stop off at one of the small, lively bars. The tiny, rocky town beach is here, although the sandy, palm-lined beaches at Maria Pia are just a short bus ride from the Giardini Pubblici.

"Sacred treasures from the Cattedrale are housed here. The most chilling exhibit is a tiny skull, allegedly one of the newborn babies killed by Herod."

Cattedrale di Santa Maria
Piazzo Duomo (079 979 222). Open 7am-noon, 5-7.30pm daily. Admission free.
Work on the cathedral began in the 16th century but it wasn't consecrated until 1730, which explains the mish-mash of architectural styles. Some elements of the original design survive (most notably, the five Catalan-Gothic chapels); additions include a late Renaissance-style nave and four rather incongruous Doric columns by the main door on via Manno. The 18th-century main altar and the neoclassical mausoleum of Maurizio, Savoy Duke of Monferatto are two great marble pieces. There are free guided tours in Italian between 10am and 1pm. If you sneak in the side entrance on a summer Saturday, there's a good chance you'll catch a Sardinian wedding in full flow.

Chiesa di San Francesco
Via Carlo Umberto. Open 9.30am-noon, 5-7.30pm Mon-Sat; 5-7.30pm Sun. Admission free.

The beautifully restored church of San Francesco dates back to the 14th century, but in style terms, it has moved with the times. The result is a pleasing blend of Romanesque and Gothic styles, rounded off with a few late Renaissance flourishes. The main attractions are the marble altar and star-shaped ceiling above it, the elegant bell tower and the simple but atmospheric sandstone Roman cloisters, used as an open-air venue for classical concerts in summer.

Chiesa di San Michele
Via Carlo Umberto. Open 20mins before Mass at 7am, 10am & 7.30pm Mon-Sat; 7am, 9am & 7.30pm Sun. Admission free.
This colourful, ceramic-clad dome draws the eye from afar. However, although the tiles look ancient, they were actually fitted in the 1960s. Close up, this Jesuit church is more in the austere Baroque vein, but it's worth a visit to admire the carved wooden choir loft, burnished with gold leaf.

Grotti di Nettuno
Capo Caccia (079 994 6540). Open Apr-Sept 9am-7pm daily. Oct 9am-5pm daily. Jan-Mar, Nov, Dec 9am-4pm daily. Admission Boat trip €13; €7 reductions. Grotto €10; €5 reductions. No credit cards for grotto tour.
Guided tours of the grotto, with its otherworldly stalagmites and stalacites, set off on the hour. The 30-minute boat trip along the dramatic coastline to the caves at Capo Caccia is a delight in itself. If you're not sure of your sea legs, the bus from via Catalogna takes 50 minutes, then it's 654 calf-stretching steps down the aptly-named escala del cabriol (goat's steps) to the caves.

Mare Nostrum Aquarium
Via XX Settembre 1 (079 978 333/www.aquarium alghero.it). Open Apr, May 10am-1pm, 3-7pm daily. June, Oct 10am-1pm, 4-9pm daily. July, Sept 10am-1pm, 5-11pm daily. Aug 10am-1pm, 5pm-12.30am daily. Admission €8; €5 reductions.
The huge tanks at this subterranean water wonderland are inhabited by sea life from Sardinia and the Mediterranean. Spotted leopard sharks, poisonous stone fish, piranhas and giant sea turtles are among the residents.

Museo Diocesano
Via Maiorca, off Piazza Duomo (079 973 3041). Open Apr, May, Oct 10am-1pm, 5-8pm Mon, Tue, Thur-Sun. June, Sept 10am-1pm, 5-9pm. July 10am-1pm, 6-10pm. Aug 10am-1pm, 6-11pm. Admission €2.50; €1 reductions.
Various sacred treasures from the Cattedrale are housed here, from paintings to ornate ecclesiastical artefacts and crucifixes. The most chilling exhibit is a tiny skull, allegedly one of the newborn babies killed by Herod.

STINTINO

Stintino has a museum dedicated to its notable tuna-fishing industry, and no shortage of the fish on menus around town. But its more alluring claim to fame is as the gateway to La Pelosa, one of the island's most beautiful beaches.

Clockwise from top left: Alghero market; Alghero cathedral; traditional fans; the Maddalena archipelago; La Maddalena; La Pelosa; Porto Mannu; Costa Smeralda.

Small Gems

Bologna

Whether you come for *la Grassa* (the Fat), *la Dotta* (the Learned) or *la Rossa* (the Red), Bologna will not disappoint. The city's three nicknames sum up its obsessions with food, study and politics. The former is justly world famous, and the left-leaning nature of the latter is nationally notorious; the education, meanwhile, is taken care of at the oldest university in Europe, founded to unravel the muddles of Justinian Law and still as staunchly freethinking as ever. However, conspicuous consumerism also plays a part in this city's life: after all, this is the home of Ferrari, Lamborghini, Maserati and Ducati, as well as fashion brands Bruno Magli, Furla and La Perla.

Clockwise from top left:
Fontana di Nettuno;
Piazza Maggiore; Basilica
di San Petronio Ferrari;
Via Santa Stefano (2);
Padre Marella.

As a university town, Bologna has historically been a magnet for left-leaning thinkers. In the early 20th century, it gave birth to modern Italian socialist politics, and has retained its reputation as a hotbed of leftish political discourse even as the city, and the country, changed during the intervening 100 years. The election of centre-right politician Giorgio Guazzaloca as the city's mayor in 1999 stunned many, although old habits clearly die hard: five years later, Guazzaloca lost his bid for re-election, defeated at the polls by leftist Sergio Cofferati.

But for all the obvious seriousness and pervasive intellectualism of the city, it has another, rather more visceral side that brings together many segments of the population. If there's one thing that unites all Bolognese – rich or poor, left-wing or right-wing, religious or secular – it's their love of eating. Indeed, one of the subjects studied at the university is a course dedicated to Slow Food. The city's culinary riches draw any number of food tourists in what amount to modern-day pilgrimages. However, for travellers who simply come to unravel the secrets of this surprisingly little known city – alongside the Fat, Red and the Learned there are also some diverse and notable museums and interesting medieval architecture – the gourmet treats found within it are a bonus.

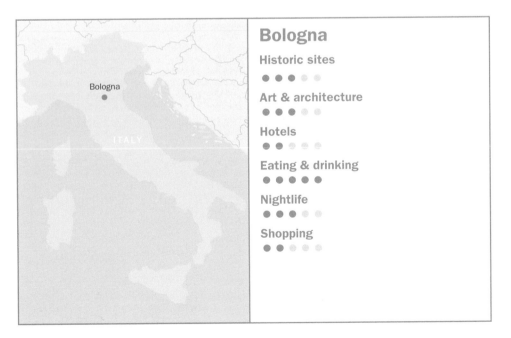

Bologna

Historic sites

● ● ● ○ ○

Art & architecture

● ● ● ○ ○

Hotels

● ● ○ ○ ○

Eating & drinking

● ● ● ● ●

Nightlife

● ● ● ○ ○

Shopping

● ● ○ ○ ○

Stay

Break 28
Via Marconi 28 (051 587 7814/www.break28.it). €.
Bologna's appetising range of B&Bs include former palaces, a former prison and this likeable operation in the Lancia Palace, an old Rationalist building from the 1930s with lovely views across the terracotta-tiled roofs of the old city centre. The rooms are tiny but nicely furnished, with Liberty style cherry-wood beds and satellite TVs.

Grand Baglioni
Via dell'Indipendenza 8 (051 225 445/www.baglionihotels.com). €€€€.
The Grand Baglioni oozes grace and charm. The lobby is hushed but not hallowed (this was once the Bishop's palace), the room keys are weighty and tasselled, and the corridors are wide enough to accommodate a U-turning Ferrari. Each room is unique; some of those on the fourth floor come with their own private terrace. The frescoes in the restaurant are by the Carracci school, but you'll have to beg your boss to hold a meeting in one of the wood-panelled conference rooms to see the pieces by the master himself.

Novecento
Piazza Galileo 4 (051 754 7311/www.art-hotel-novecento.it). €€€.
The latest addition to Bologna's small chain of Art Hotels (which also includes the Orologio and Commercianti), the hip, central Novecento takes its cue from the design style of the 1930s, all distinctive, angular lines, dark wood walls and leather furniture. The rooms are light, generously proportioned and fuss-free, and quirky design touches abound. The young staff are happy to offer tips on local restaurants and even loan out free bicycles.

Porto San Mamolo
Vicolo del Falcone 6/8 (051 583 056/www.hotel-portasanmamolo.it). €€.
A secret garden filled with pomegranate trees marks out this historic house as a special retreat for the romantically inclined. The 25 spacious bedrooms are softly furnished in pastel shades and equipped with modern comforts; those on the top floor have a terrace view across the city's red-tiled roofs. The friendly owner used to work at the Grand Baglioni; he clearly picked up a thing or two about service and attention to detail, but the room rates are far more palatable than at his former employer.

UNA
Via Pietramellara 41/42 (051 60801/www.unahotels.it). €€.
The location, right opposite the main railway station, is more convenient than salubrious, but the Marco Piva-designed UNA is a chic proposition as a place to stay. The style is uniquely contemporary – almost industrial, even – with 93 futuristically furnished rooms and six suites sitting behind the building's metallic skin. The lengthy mathematical equation that adorns the restaurant wall is a bit of a challenge, especially after an apertivo or two.

Views of Italy
Via Canonica (UK: 020 7096 1248/www.viewsofitaly.com). €€-€€€.
Housed in a 15th-century building on the edge of the Ghetto Ebraico (Jewish Ghetto), these apartments have been superbly renovated with antique furnishings and modern amenities. Those opting for the one-bedroom tower apartment on the top floor should note that there isn't a lift, although the climb is rewarded with what's probably the best view of the Due Torri in the city. Each apartment has its own well-equipped kitchen and welcoming picnic basket.

Eat

Back in the 14th century, Petrarch famously dubbed Bologna 'the Fat'; 500 years later, Paduan writer Ippolito Nievo suggested that it took the Bolognese a mere year to eat what Venetians would take two years to consume and what Romans would eke out over a three-year span. The abundance and variety of traditional dishes is well known, but the locals are keen to dispel some of the myths attached to Italian food: the meaty ragú that the rest of the world calls bolognese should be served not with spaghetti but yolk-yellow tagliatelle, and lasagna should be made only with green sheets of spinach pasta, not yellow. That said, it's not all pasta: boiled and roasted meats are popular, especially mortadella, the local cold-cut salami, and the surrounding fertile countryside produces plenty of vegetables and lambrusco wine (which, handily, is said to be good at dissolving fat).

When eating out, it's harder to go wrong than right, but don't be fooled by the pricey menus at the city's most lauded restaurants. Sure, they serve good food, but some of the finest food in the city is found in simple trattorie; there's a particularly good selection on via A Righi, the best of which are Il Portico (no.11) and the slightly more expensive Donatello (no.8).

AF Tamburini
Via Caprarie 1 (051 234 726). Open noon-2.30pm Mon-Fri. €. Traditional Italian.
Housed in a former butcher's shop in which pigs were once slaughtered (a row of hooks still hangs from the ceiling), Giovanni Tamburini's salumeria has been such a success that he's opened a branch in Japan. Over there, it may be a novelty; here, it's an institution. Don't be put off by the self-service style of the trattoria (or is it an osteria?): the only important labels are those stamped on the food crammed into the deli – everything from air-dried hams and 150 varieties of sausage to artisanal jars of anchovies and thick, syrupy balsamic vinegars.

Al Voltone
Piazza Re Enzo 1a (051 236 743). Open 8.30am-2am daily. €. Trattoria.

Clockwise from top:
Grand Baglioni (3);
Bolognese food.

www.treesforcities.org
Trees for Cities
Charity registration number 1032154
Travelling creates so many lasting memories.
Make your trip mean something for years to come - not just for you but for the environment and for people living in deprived urban areas.
Anyone can offset their flights, but when you plant trees with Trees for Cities, you'll help create a green space for an urban community that really needs it.
To find out more visit www.treesforcities.org
Leave Your Mark
Create a green future for cities.

Renato Lideo's trattoria might be a favoured meeting place among left-leaning artists, writers and academics, but you should be careful what you mutter: the restaurant is close to the whispering gallery of the Palazzo del Podestà. The local crescentine, a kind of half-boiled, half-fried doughy pancake, is a primo piatto speciality, served with truffles in season. Lideo also owns La Linea, the next-door tavern in which the same intellectual crowd gathers.

Café de Paris
Piazza del Francia 1c (051 234 980). Open 8am-1am Mon-Thur; 8am-late Fri, Sat. €€. Café/bar.
Bologna doesn't get much hipper than this achingly trendy café; indeed, were it not for the bar, you might think you'd stumbled into a Ligne Roset furniture showroom. The staff and clientele are effortlessly stylish and know it. But in a city where the bars can be stylistically conservative, Wallpaper* readers will break into a broad smile at the sight of the place. Complimentary nibbles (olives, crisps) are served at aperitivo hour; the lunchtime menu comprises plates of pasta and salads.

Cantina Bentivoglio
Via Mascarella 4b (051 265 416). Open Sept-May 8pm-2am daily. June-Aug 8pm-2am Mon-Sat. €€. Osteria.
Almost as much a Bologna icon as Neptune's rippling muscles, the cavernous cellars of the Palace Bentivoglio are where locals go for their jazz fix, and for freshly made pastas and large selections of wines and beer. The nightly programme often features artists of international repute, but homegrown talent is also given a fair shake. The music stops in July and August, when the cantina spills out onto Via Mascarella in the atmospheric Jewish quarter.

Diana
Via dell'Independenza 24 (051 231 302). Open 12.15-3pm, 7-10.30pm Tue-Sun. Closed Aug. €€€. Classic Italian.
Named after the goddess of the hunt, Diana is a gamy old bird that's barely changed its robes since opening in 1920. Some locals have suggested that it's past its prime, but they do so in hushed tones, as if afraid to offend a dependable dowager. Eating here is still a special event: when Italian dignitaries come to town, they almost invariably end up here. However, the staff seem no less attentive to the unknown as they are to the famous. Although game is still served in season, it's no longer the speciality; however, the creaky, antique dessert trolley remains very special indeed.

Franco Rossi
Via Goito 3 (051 238 818). Open noon-3pm, 8pm-midnight Mon-Sat. Closed July. €€€. Modern Italian.
Given that the menu is dedicated to John Grisham, you might expect this graceful restaurant to be a bit more cutthroat. However, owners Franco and Lino Rossi are merely returning the favour paid to them when the author name-checked the restaurant on several occasions in his novel The Broker, copies of which are on display in the window. Inside, Franco Rossi is romantic yet lively, with smartly-clad staff serving unexpected – and sometimes complimentary -– dishes in between the courses.

Nu Lounge Bar
Via dei Musei 6 (051 222 532). Open Restaurant noon-4pm, 8.30pm-1am Mon-Sat; 8pm-midnight Sun. Bar noon-2.30am daily. €€. Modern Italian/bar.
Located close to the book stalls of the Libreria A Nanni, this nu-jazz lounge bar is as chilled as a Balearic beach bar at lunchtime. By night, though, it gets as rowdy as a wedding banquet, thanks in part to its long martini menu. As well as pizzas and classic pastas, you'll find less conventional treats such as black ravioli with shrimp and saffron. The owners also run Pizz@s opposite, which shares the same outdoor space under frescoed porticoes.

Pappagallo
Piazza Mercanzia 3c (051 232 807). Open 12.30-2.30pm, 7.30-10.30pm Mon-Sat. Closed Aug. €€€. Traditional Bolognese.
Pappagallo's understated refinement is undeniable, its pedigree impeccable and its cuisine exemplary. Located in a 14th-century palazzo by La Due Torri, it's been serving superb traditional Bolognese fare to kings, presidents, artists and actors since 1917, and has rarely deviated from its roots. But as well as the usual tortellini in brood di carne and tagliatelle al ragú, you'll find more experimental dishes using ingredients such as sturgeon and guinea fowl. The menu changes with the seasons, but the sea of autographed photographs stays all year round, and is the only slightly jarring self-congratulatory note about the whole place.

Pizzerie Belle Arti
Via Belle Arti 14 (051 225 581). Open noon-2.30pm, 7-11.30pm Mon, Tue, Thur-Sun. €€. Pizzeria.
Located next to the graffiti-covered Odeon arthouse cinema, this pizzeria occupies a labyrinth of rooms, the last of which is accessed via a small bridge that straddles some Roman remains. The pizzas are thin, crisp, impossibly tasty and huge; however, the restaurant's close proximity to the university means the bill will be of an entirely manageable size. The restaurant actually doubles as a trattoria with fish as a speciality, but most Bolognese would advise you to stick to scoffing the finest pizza in town.

Explore

SIGHTS

Although Bologna has no single building that could be considered a staggering work of art, the city as a whole is an artistic masterpiece. The harmonious maze of streets dates back to the city's rapid expansion during the medieval era, but its foundations go back to Etruscan times. It's best seen by wandering aimlessly. Arrive with a fixed plan for exploration and it'll fall apart as soon as you turn a corner and stumble upon a hidden canal, a sleek shopping centre or one of 100 or so eccentric museums dedicated to anything from toy soldiers to beekeeping.

Clockwise from top left:
streets of Lucca (2);
Duomo di San Martino;
Piazza Napoleone.

Lucca

While Florence and Siena busy themselves capturing the crowds, nearby Lucca quietly goes about capturing the hearts of those who make the journey to see it. Visitors come here not to tick off the sights but simply to enjoy the city itself, fiercely independent for centuries and with its own distinct character. Civilised and charismatic, elegant and even a little eccentric, defined by its sumptuous architecture and its distinctive local cuisine, Lucca is urban Tuscany at its most beguiling.

On the whole, Lucca is spared the crowds that cram into Florence and Siena, although it's arguably more beautiful than either. Perhaps, like invaders of the past, they are deterred by the stern fortifications that encircle it. Visitors who do make their way inside enjoy the glorious churches and the unusual cathedral, the handsome, pedestrianised piazzas and the reserved, unhurried ambience. A conservative stronghold in left-leaning Tuscany, Lucca has changed precious little in centuries; most Lucchesi walk or pedal their way around their compact city. It's also one of the few cities left in western Europe whose relationship to its bountiful countryside remains that of a medieval city state: the former feeds the latter, imperious behind its imposing walls.

Lucca came of age as a Roman municipium in 89 BC, and its most striking sights remain the ornate white façades of its Romanesque churches. Chief among them is San Michele in Foro, which, as its name suggests, stands on the site of the old Roman forum, still the city's commercial centre. After Rome's fall, a short-lived heyday as the capital of a mini-empire in western Tuscany under the helm of the *condottiere* Castruccio Castracani (1320-28) soon gave way to a series of setbacks leading to domination by Pisa. In 1369, Lucca was granted autonomy and independence by Emperor Charles IV of Bohemia; it lasted, unbroken, until 1799.

In 1805, Lucca passed under the direct rule of Elisa Baciocchi, Napoleon's sister, who replenished the city architecturally and patronised a brief but intense period of artistic ferment. The town was ceded to the Grand Duchy of Tuscany just over four decades later and then joined a united Italy in 1860, since when it has maintained its prosperity amid an atmosphere of aristocratic aloofness that fosters a very different feel from Tuscany's other great cities.

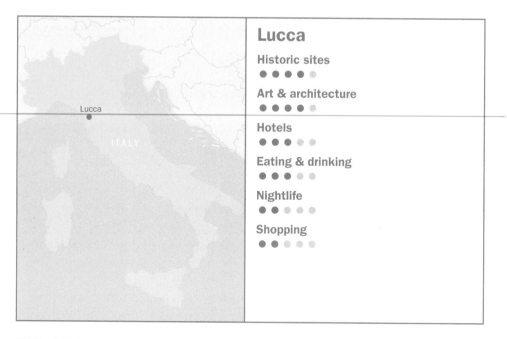

Lucca

Historic sites
● ● ● ● ○

Art & architecture
● ● ● ● ○

Hotels
● ● ● ○ ○

Eating & drinking
● ● ● ○ ○

Nightlife
● ● ○ ○ ○

Shopping
● ● ○ ○ ○

Stay

Affittacamere San Frediano
Via degli Angeli 19 (0583 469 630/
www.sanfrediano.com). €€.
This friendly B&B attracts many return customers for its reasonable rates and fine location (just off the top end of via Fillungo). The cosy rooms have iron bedsteads and satellite TV; the top floor of the building, which dates from the 16th century, was recently turned into a lounge for guests.

Alla Corte degli Angeli
Via degli Angeli 23 (0583 469 204/
www.allacortedegliangeli.com). €€€.
Some may find the rooms at Alla Corte degli Angeli, each named after a flower, offer a little too much of a good thing: many are embellished with wall murals and trompe l'oeil effects, and some retain original features such as ceiling beams. However, they're decorated to a high standard, with flat-screen TVs and Wi-Fi offsetting the antique furniture.

La Bohème
Via del Moro 2 (0583 462 404/www.boheme.it). €€€.
A rather grand B&B in the heart of town, this 17th-century building offers four spacious, high-ceilinged bedrooms, done up in rich colours with chandeliers and traditional, dark wood furniture; the suite has a four-poster bed. In true Italian style, you'll get a discount if you pay in cash.

"Fattoria Maionchi, a gorgeous 17th-century palazzo, comes complete with its own vineyards, olive groves and herb garden."

Fattoria Maionchi
Località Tofori, Camigliano (0583 978 194/
www.fattoriamaionchi.it). €€.
There's farmhouse and country house rental in the grounds of this gorgeous 17th-century palazzo, complete with its own vineyards, olive groves and herb garden in the hills overlooking Lucca. The rooms are discreet and spacious, decorated in traditional, slightly garish decor. The restaurant, which opens at weekends, has proven popular with the greats of the opera world: the food, which includes Tuscan black pudding and the fruits of the Maionchi's herb garden, is remarkable and very good value.

Hotel Noblesse
Via di Sant'Anastasio 23 (0583 440 275/
www.hotelnoblesse.it). €€€.
The first real boutique hotel to open within the city walls contains 13 rooms that come with LCD TVs and elaborate bathrooms. Yet, for all that, the decor remains crisp and surprisingly traditional despite glimpses of modernity.

Locanda L'Elisa
Via Nuova per Pisa 1952, Massa Pisana (0583 379 737/www.locandalelisa.com). €€€.
This elegant four-star hotel just south of Lucca is one of the area's best. The villa's current appearance dates back to 1805, when Elisa Baciocchi, Napoleon's sister and Lucca's ruler, had the interiors and gardens refashioned. The 18th-century furnishings are supplemented by revamped gardens and a large swimming pool, while the spacious, impeccable rooms come with period furniture.

Piccolo Hotel Puccini
Via di Poggio 9 (0583 55421/www.hotelpuccini. com). €€.
A baton's throw from Puccini's boyhood home, just around the corner from San Michele, this discreet, comfortable and fairly small hotel (hence the name) is excellent value for money. The decor is straightforward and the ambience is friendly; helpfully, the youthful staff speak English.

San Martino
Via della Dogana 9 (0583 469 181/
www.albergosanmartino.it). €€.
Converted from a 16th-century house, the San Martino is centrally located (within the city walls and near the cathedral) but nonetheless sits far enough away from the main drag that it maintains a tranquil ambience. The rooms are large and spacious with high ceilings; the hotel's two suites come with adjoining rooms and are perfect for families. Breakfast can be taken in the elegant courtyard

Eat

The Garfagnana valley contributes all the prime ingredients to Lucca's cuisine. Among them are chestnut flour, river trout, olive oil and, above all, *farro* (spelt grain), which pops up everywhere.

La Buca di Sant'Antonio
Via della Cervia 3 (0583 55881). Open 12.30-3pm, 7.30-10pm Tue-Sat; 12.30-3pm Sun. Closed 2wks Jan. €-€€. Traditional Italian.
La Buca might be the first stop on the tourist trail, but it's an undeniably fine hostelry nonetheless. The menu includes traditional Lucchese food, with the occasional innovative touch and an excellent cheese and dessert selection. Book ahead if possible; if it's full, try sister restaurant Il Giglio on piazza Napoleone (0583 494 058).

Caffè di Simo
Via Fillungo 58 (0583 496 234). Open Bar 7.30am-11pm Tue-Sun. Restaurant 12.30-2.30pm Mon, Tue, Thur-Sun. Summer also 7-10pm Thur-Sat. €€. Café.

Lucca's most celebrated belle époque café-pasticceria, a favourite of Puccini, is surprisingly unsnobby: workmen mix amiably with tourists and civil servants. Pastries, ice-creams and posh chocolates satisfy the sweet of tooth; more substantial dishes include the ubiquitous zuppa di farro.

Casali
Piazza San Michele 40 (0583 492 687). Open Apr-Oct 7am-midnight daily. Nov-Mar 7am-8.30pm Mon, Tue, Thur-Sun. Closed 2wks Jan-Feb. €. Bar.
Looking out on to the gigantic stone wedding cake that is San Michele, Casali is a great spot from which to get acclimatised to the slow pleasures of Lucca. The outdoor tables are the perfect spots from which to watch the crowds, with either an ice-cream or an aperitif in hand.

Da Guido
Via Cesare Battisti 28 (0583 467 219). Open noon-2.30pm, 7-10.30pm Mon-Sat. Closed 3wks Jan. €. Trattoria.
Don't be put off by the slightly down-at-heel appearance of this trattoria: once inside, you'll be treated to excellent home cooking by the friendly Guido and his family. The rich, thick zuppa di farro is literally a meal in itself, while the choice of main courses features simple roast meats, pastas and salads, and the own-made desserts might include crostate della casa (jam tarts) or panna cotta.

"In Lucca, nowhere is very far from anywhere else; it's a pleasure simply wandering through its streets."

Da Leo
Via Tegrimi 1 (0583 492 236). Open noon-2.30pm, 7.30-10.30pm daily. €. No credit cards. Traditional Italian.
Despite all the noise and bustle, with families straining to make themselves heard over bawling children and singing waiters, Da Leo is one of Lucca's most relaxed restaurants. You won't be hurried through your meal, which will be made up of hearty country dishes such as roast chicken, grilled steak and pappardelle broccoli e salsiccia.

Locanda di Bacco
Via San Giorgio 36 (0583 493 136). Open 12.30-2.30pm, 7.30-10.30pm Mon, Wed-Sun. Closed 2wks Feb, 2wks Nov. €€. Modern Italian.
A short walk north of piazza San Michele, this stylish, friendly restaurant quickly proved a hit with locals and visitors. Starters include crostini with melted gorgonzola and honey; pasta dishes might include pappardelle al cinghiale, and the own-made desserts are irresistible. The

extensive wine list includes a number of relatively rare northern Tuscan varieties. It's especially good at lunchtime, when the atmosphere is a little less frenetic.

Locanda Buatino
Borgo Giannotti 508, nr Piazzale Martiri della Libertà (0583 343 207). Open noon-2pm, 7.30-10pm Mon-Sat. Closed 2wks Aug. €€. Traditional Italian.
From the outside, Locanda Buatino looks like little more than a bar; the feel is low-key, with wooden tables, strings of garlic and rustic paintings. But the authentic food is perhaps the best in Lucca: typically Tuscan farro and beans, say, or cioncia, a fabulous stew made from a calf's head, chilli and olives. Jazz acts play on Monday nights from October to May (€25 including a meal with wine). There are basic rooms with shared bathrooms upstairs (€40).

Vineria I Santi
Via dell'Anfiteatro 29a (0583 496 124). Open 11am-3pm, 7pm-1.30am Mon, Tue, Thur, Fri, Sun; 11am-3pm, 7pm-2am Sat. €€. Modern Italian/wine bar.
From its modern rustic furniture and delicate light fittings to the discreet wine paraphernalia dotted around the walls, this little spot oozes character. The menu is short in length yet rich in imagination, with simpler dishes joined by the likes of smoked sea bass with marinated fennel, orange and pine nuts, but the extensive wine list is the real forte: look out, in particular, for the fine wines of the collini lucchese.

Explore

SIGHTS
In Lucca, nowhere is very far from anywhere else; it's a pleasure simply wandering or cycling through its streets. Most visitors enter through St Peter's Gate, at the south end of the city near the station. From there it's a relatively straightforward town in which to get your bearings. Walk straight up the central thoroughfare of via Vittorio Veneto, past the excellent tourist office and on through the main square of piazza Napoleone to your right. Further up via Veneto is piazza San Michele, the spiritual heart of Lucca; just opposite is the narrow street of via de Poggio, site of the Puccini Museum. Heading east from piazza San Michele, via Roma is the main shopping street; from piazza Bernardini, you can head south to the relatively isolated Duomo, or north to the Roman *anfiteatro* and the Torre Guinigi.

Lucchesi of all ages stroll, jog, picnic, cuddle and enjoy the views from *le nostre mura* ('our walls'). Built during the 16th and 17th centuries, Italy's best-preserved city fortifications stand 12 metres tall and run to a circumference of just over four kilometres. The walls are punctuated by 11 sturdy bastions that were designed to ward off

Caffè di Simo.

Parma

In a country famed for its love of eating, Parma is at the top of the food chain: this is the home of parma ham, parmigiano reggiano cheese and the mighty Barilla pasta company. And it's comparably rich in architecture and music. The Parmigiani are enthusiastic opera lovers – and the toughest audience in Italy, notorious for booing performances at the Teatro Regio. And while the city boasts splendid medieval and Renaissance architecture, contemporary pursuits are not ignored, with fervent shopping in the central design district and the modern Barilla Centre. That said, Parma should never be thought of as cutting-edge, and is far from a slave to fashion. The unhurried pace of life makes for an effortlessly lazy weekend, as do the compact, cobbled streets – best explored at a pleasantly contemplative pace.

Clockwise from top left: Duomo & Baptistery; Strada Cavour; Parco Ducale (2); Palazzo della Pilotta; Teatro Regio.

Colonised by the Romans in 183 BC, Parma soon become an important hub on the Via Emilia trading route. Its strategic position was fought over by warring factions, anxious to gain control of what had once been called Crisopoli (the Golden City). The town's position strengthened under the Lombards, when it became a stopping-off point for pilgrims heading south on the Via Francigena, the medieval route that stretched all the way from Canterbury to Rome.

A golden age of art and architecture began when the Farnese family took control in the mid 16th century. In 1731, after they died out, the Duchy was given to Charles of Bourbon. He left four years later to claim the Kingdom of Naples, with many of Parma's art collections tucked under his robes. After the Bourbons came Napoleonic rule, and Napoleon's estranged second wife Marie Louise (known locally as Maria Luigia) was installed as Duchess from 1815 to 1847. Under her benevolent rule, the city's cultural scene flourished – and the majestic Teatro Regio opera house (via Garibaldi 16, 0521 039 393, www.teatroregioparma.org) was built. The Bourbons returned briefly upon her death, but were sent packing once Parma joined the Kingdom of Italy in 1861.

Parma

Historic sites
● ● ● ● ○

Art & architecture
● ● ● ○ ○

Hotels
● ● ○ ○ ○

Eating & drinking
● ● ● ● ●

Nightlife
● ● ○ ○ ○

Shopping
● ● ● ○ ○

Parma

ITALY

Stay

Hotel Leon d'Or
Viale Fratti 4a (0521 773 182/
www.leondoroparma.com). €-€€.
A renovation in 2005 spruced this family-run hotel up, but left the rather ramshackle furnishings in place. Rooms are clean and simple, and although breakfast isn't provided, it's easily had on nearby strada Cavour or Garibaldi. The adjoining restaurant is owned by the same friendly family.

Hotel Verdi
Via Pasini 18 (0521 293 539/www.hotelverdi.it). €€.
In a city bereft of decent lodgings at the lower end of the price spectrum, the Hotel Verdi is a standard bearer for those on more modest budgets. But lower prices doesn't mean bland surroundings: the hotel is a handsome art nouveau villa, opposite the grounds of the Parco Ducale. Its 20 rooms, furnished in briarwood and with parquet flooring, are often full, and advance booking is essential. Warm evenings can be spent in the delightful inner courtyard, and the adjacent Santa Croce restaurant is well worth a visit.

Jolly Hotel Stendhal
Via Bodoni 3 (0521 208 057/www.hotelstendhal.it). €€.
Despite being acquired by the Jolly Hotel group, the Stendhal has managed to maintain a sense of individuality. Its 62 air-conditioned rooms are decorated in faux Marie Louise style (for those expecting lots of gaudy gilt and brocade, this is actually much more airy than it sounds), and though none are huge, some on the first floor have balconies overlooking the back of the Palazzo Pilotta. But the Stendhal's principle attraction is its location, a stone's throw from the central train station: you can stumble out of bed and be in the Galleria Nazionale within a minute.

Palace Hotel Maria Luigia
Viale Mentana 140 (0521 281 032/
www.palacemarialuigia.com). €€.
The rather morose exterior of the Maria Luigia (the local name for Napoleon's second wife, Marie Louise) hides a personable hotel, with spacious rooms and red and beige marble bathrooms; ask to stay on the top floor for impressive views across the city's cupolas. There's a quiet patio for an aperitivo just beyond the pink marble floors of the ground floor lobby. Although the restaurant is rather over-rated, it's just a few minutes' walk to the extraordinary Salumeria Garibaldi and two of Parma's finest places to eat, Il Trovatore on via Affo and La Greppia on Garibaldi.

Sofitel Grand Hotel de la Ville
Largo Piero Calamandrei 11, Barilla Centre
(0521 0304/www.grandhoteldelaville.it). €€€.
With input from celebrity architect Renzo Piano (co-creator of Paris's Centre Pompidou, and the man behind London's forthcoming Shard), the Grand Hotel de la Ville opened in 2003 in the modern Barilla complex as Parma's only five-star establishment. Its location is perfect for concerts at the Niccolò Paganini Auditorium, and the city centre is just a short walk away (bicycles are also available on request).

Beautifully furnished rooms feature lots of muted wood and all the amenities that you'd expect from a luxury chain (including WiFi), though some may find it all a tad too corporate for their tastes. There's a smart fitness centre and turkish bath on the rooftop terrace.

Starhotels du Parc
Viale Piacenza 12c (0521 292 929/
www.starhotels.it). €€€.
This Liberty-style hotel was artfully renovated from an old ice factory, and its 169 rooms include a wonderfully romantic, two-storey loft-style suite. Rooms are warm and sensuous, with rich, dark wood and brass accessories, and the overall ambience is of a casually genteel New York club. A cast iron bridge connects the hotel to the Parco Ducale, and the dramatic glass panels that adorn its neoclassical façade allow floods of light to filter into the lobby and bars.

Eat

The Parmigiani take their food extremely seriously; it does, after all, form the basis of the local economy. Here, the pig is king – and air-dried parma ham is just one example of a multitude of porcine treats; there's also *mortadella, salame felino* and the exquisite *culatello di zibello* to consider. Hands-on activities are many and varied, with trips to a prosciutto production plant or vinegar lofts in nearby Modena and three suggested food trails covering hams and wines, the black truffles of Fragno and Borgotaro's porcini mushrooms. Details and a map are available from the tourist office. There are also cookery courses at the Barilla Academy in the Barilla Centre (largo Piero Calamandrei 3/A, 0521 264 060, www.academiabarilla.com). Located in the old pasta factory, the centre, designed by Renzo Piano, also includes a boutique shopping mall, five-star hotel, numerous restaurants and the Paganini concert hall and conference centre.

Eating in Parma is more hit than miss, with a scene that barely changes from year to year. The Barilla Centre's offerings may include a sushi bar and a Mexican cantina, but Parma is so confident of its culinary traditions it feels little need to fall in with cosmopolitan fads. The best dishes of pumpkin-stuffed tortelloni, a local specialty, are often to be found at the most unprepossessing of trattorie. If you want to assemble a picnic, join the scrum at the daily market on piazza Ghiaia (Monday to Saturday, mornings).

Angiol d'Or
Vicolo Scutellari 1 (0521 282 632). Open 10am-midnight Tue-Sun. €€. Modern Italian.
If location is everything, the owners of this chic ristorante have hit the real estate jackpot. Overlooking the Duomo, it's predictably packed with opportunist tourists. However,

those worried about authenticity can rest easy in the knowledge that locals come here too, as much for the cool, cream decor, efficient service and relaxed ambience as for the food. After the obligatory antipasti plate of air-dried meats, mains include traditional Italian cuts (*costoletta di vitello alla Milanese*, *cima alla Genovese*), though vegetarians will breathe a sigh of relief at the *penne alle verdure* (pasta served with fresh peppers, courgettes and celery).

Canon d'Or
Via Nazario Sauro 2 (0521 221 350). Open noon-3pm, 8pm-1am Mon, Tue, Thur-Sun. €. Osteria.
The locals who gather outside this rough and ready osteria tell you why you should brave the lumpy whitewashed walls and jumble sale art: simply delicious food, exactly what you'd expect from a basic Italian kitchen. Fat, pumpkin-stuffed tortelloni and slow-cooked beef *strocatto* are best eaten with a glug of local Quercia wine. It's also one of the few places to stay open in August, should you be in town at the height of summer.

La Greppia
Via Garibaldi 39a (0521 233 686). Open 12.30-2.30pm, 8-10.30pm Wed-Sun. Closed Aug. €€€. Traditional Italian.
It may no longer be staffed exclusively by women, but the glass-fronted kitchen remains, and it's not La Greppia's only nod to modernity. Elegant without being stuffy, it continues to turn out accomplished traditional fare, based on locally-sourced produce. The antipasti are a delight to tongue and eye, as is the own-made pasta, with herbs pushed in at the rolling stage. But do save some room for dessert: tongue-tingling gelato and fresh seasonal fruit.

Non Solo Latte
Via Torelli 15 (0521 243 589). Open 7am-1am Mon-Thur, Sun; 7am-2am Fri, Sat. €. Café/Bar.
Sure enough, it's not just milk at the stylish Non Solo Latte, where live bands and DJ sets accompany video projections of an artistic bent seven nights a week. You can do the bossa nova on Thursday and Friday nights in the company of Parma's university students, who head here for some time away from their books. The complimentary sushi may also be an inducement. Trendy professionals have cottoned on as well, and now come for breakfast, lunch and dinner, or for an aperitif. There's a gelateria too.

Ombre Rosse
Borgo Giacomo Tommasini 18 (0521 289 575). Open 7.30pm-midnight Mon, Wed, Thur; 12.30-3pm Sun. €€€. Enoteca.
This veritable temple to wine (with over 1,500 varieties to choose from, some served in quarter- or half-litre carafes) does not thereby neglect its food. Meat, fish and pasta dishes all come artfully presented, though they are not always locally sourced. There's steak from Argentina, lamb from New Zealand and fresh or seawater fish from wherever they can find it, much of it served with New Age touches such as kataifa pasta or *aspargi di mare* (seaweed). The look is rustic and romantic, with sand-coloured rooms; the candlelit courtyard, with its rattan canopy, is a delight.

I Parizzi
Via Repubblica 71 (0521 285 027). Open 12.30-2.30pm, 7.30-10.30pm Tue-Sun. Closed Aug. €€€. Traditional Italian.
The redoubtable Parizzi family works on the floor and in the kitchen to keep this elegant eaterie at the top of Parma's hip list and hold on to their Michelin star. They have never rested on their laurels: expect classic Italian, with an innovative twist so subtle it won't offend traditionalists. The modern decor is now as good as the food, and the cellar contains a magnificent 800 – mostly Italian – wines.

Parma Rotta
Via Langhirano 158 (0521 966 738). Open noon-2.30pm, 8-10.30pm Tue-Sun. €€€. Traditional Italian.
It takes a brave soul to order seasoned lard with toasted polenta, but simple meats grilled on wood embers are the speciality here; you can also sample rabbit, snails or sautéed duck breast and foie gras. In winter, fare such as truffles and mushrooms take pride of place, and Cuban cigars and wee drams of Scotch are served up all year round. Save some space for the delicious own-made desserts, or ask if you can take some home.

Sorelle Picchi
Via Farini 27a (0521 233 528). Open noon-3pm Mon-Sat. Closed Aug. €€. Trattoria.
The Sorelle Picchi used to be a closely-guarded secret, tucked away at the back of a bustling *salumeria*, but the sheer volume of international press the Picchi sisters have garnered over recent times has made that a thing of the past. There are only 50 covers in one simple room, so get there early if you want to be sure of grabbing a seat. They are clearly doing something right, with home-cooked pasta (variously stuffed with pumpkin, ricotta or potatoes) being the speciality, and a lively, down-to-earth atmosphere.

La Table
Via Mistrali 3b (0521 289 536). Open 8am-1am daily. €. Enoteca.
This small wine bar/café, tucked down an alley off Borgo Venti Marzo, was pronounced the finest café in the city by national newspaper *Corriere della Sera*. It's open for breakfast, best taken in the semi-shaded courtyard, but also serves simple panini, salads and pastas for lunch. The neighbouring shopkeepers often pop out for a chat and espresso, though you might prefer the iced green tea on hot summer afternoons. At night, the long, thin bar is crammed with the after-work office crowd, who come for a glass of wine and end up staying the entire evening.

Al Tramezzo
Via Del Bono 5b (0521 487 906/www.altramezzo.it). Open noon-3pm, 7-11pm Mon-Sat. Closed Aug. €€€. Traditional Italian.
When Ugo Bertolotti renamed his Al Tramezzino sandwich bar Al Tramezzo in 1975, it lost a few letters but gained ambition, a cellar that stocks more than 1,000 local, national and international wines, and – eventually – the recognition of two Michelin stars. A small labyrinth of rooms makes the experience cosy, with aged *culatello*, prosciutto and

Slowly does it

Fast food is as addictive as heroin – and just as soul-destroying, according to scientists at Princeton University, who, in 2003, found that the consumption of fast food transformed the process of eating into an act of despondency. It was a conclusion that had already been reached by Italy's Slow Food movement back in the 1980s, when McDonald's attempted to open a branch by Rome's Spanish Steps. A group of left-leaning journalists, led by campaigner and writer Carlo Petrini, gathered at their neighbourhood *osteria* in the small Piedmont city of Bra to create a manifesto that celebrates conviviality, promotes local, seasonal ingredients, and counters 'the degrading effects of fast food'. Taking a snail as its insignia, the Slow Food movement was born. After a successful start at home, it went international in 1989 just as foodies sprouted organic consciences en masse. A dynamic non-profit organisation still based in Bra, it now has 83,000 members in 100 countries, and in 2004 opened a University of Gastronomic Sciences in Piedmont and Emilia-Romagna.

The Slow Food ethos is about the taste and enjoyment of food, but by necessity and design it is also about the ethics of provenance. Local networks promote and support small producers at grass-roots level, offering help with marketing and sales, and Petrini is vehemently opposed to agri-businesses. Naturally, he admits, the food costs more, but he argues for its superior quality and also suggests that by eating in moderation the consumer keeps obesity at bay. Critics have hinted at elitism, but Petrini and his colleagues work hard to offer more than just *tagliarini* tossed with trendy values.

In Italy, Slow Food is hard to miss. You can attend events all year round, visit the world's largest non-industrial food fair, the biennial Salone del Gusto in Turin (next held in 2009), or go to one of the 33 Città Slow cities applying Slow Food principles to the urban environment.

Nowadays you can also shop at a Slow Food supermarket: in 2007 Slow Food took the game to the enemy by collaborating with commercial partners to open Eataly in Turin. Eataly is a food education centre and bookshop, but more visibly a large and lovely food shop and restaurant complex packed with products given the Slow Food seal of approval. A mouthwatering experience all round, it was an instant success. A Milan branch has since opened (floor -1, inside COIN, piazza 5 Giornate), and more are planned throughout Italy and, in spring 2008, in midtown New York.

This is food as an expression of culture and identity: a sensory exploration that stimulates the mind and satisfies the stomach. At over 21 years old, the Slow Food movement may not be a new phenomenon, but it is one that will continue to grow – and not so slowly.

Slow Food
Via Mendicità Istruita 14, Bra (01 7241 9611/ www.slowfood.com). Open 2.30-6.30pm Mon; 8.30am-12.30pm, 2.30-6.30pm Tue-Sun.

Clockwise from top left:
Sofitel Grand Hotel de
la Ville; Hotel Verdi;
Salumeria Garibaldi;
Angiol d'Or; Hotel Verdi.

parmigiano as specialities. On warm evenings, try to grab a table on the tiny veranda and let the attentive staff guide you through a menu sourced from the best local producers.

Trattoria del Tribunale
Vicolo Politi 5 (0521 285 527). Open 12.30-2pm, 7.30-10pm Wed-Sun. €€. Traditional Italian.
Tucked away down an alley behind the city's courtrooms, this trattoria is extremely popular with those in the legal profession. If you've read Parma resident Tobias Jones's *The Dark Heart of Italy*, you'll have an inkling of the convoluted conversations going on all around you, but mercifully the food is much more simple: expect traditional Italian fare like *tagliolini al culatello*. High ceilings with exposed beams and a network of small rooms and alcoves add character to the busy atmosphere.

Explore

Although much of its notable architecture dates from the 11th and 12th centuries, when Antipope Honorius II started work on the Duomo, and from the great artistic renaissance of the Farnese dynasty, Parma's layout is firmly Roman. The via Emilia still cuts through its heart, crossing the Ponte di Mezzo at via d'Azegli and continuing down via Mazzini to piazza Garibaldi, where the surrounding narrow streets retain their original grid-like pattern.

Built on the site of the old Roman forum, piazza Garibaldi remains the political heart of the city, home to the city council and mayor's office. It's dominated on one side by the neoclassical, Parma-yellow façade of the Palazzo del Governatore and surrounded on all sides by alfresco restaurants. From here, it's a short walk to Parma's spiritual centre, along the pedestrianised strada Cavour to the piazza Duomo. The vast piazza is home to the Romanesque Duomo with its Gothic bell tower, pink Verona marble baptistery and rather stern medieval palazzo, now the Diocesan Museum (0521 208 699). Here, ancient paving stones and original mosaic floors from the early-Christian cathedral sit alongside items from the Farnese collection. But piazza Duomo is also an unofficial crossroads for the city's residents as they clatter across the cobblestones on their elderly bicycles, heading for the shops along via Nazario Sauro and via Farini (also worth a quick detour).

Behind the Duomo, the Baroque church of San Giovanni Evangelista is hardly less impressive, and next to the adjoining monastery is the Spezieria di San Giovanni, an apothecary that jealously guarded the secrets of ancient medicine for centuries.

A quick diversion south will take you to the restored Casa della Musica, which pays tribute to one of the city's favourite obsessions, music

– in particular the music of locally born *maestri* Giuseppe Verdi and Arturo Toscanini. For another cultural fix, head due west of piazza Duomo to piazza della Pilotta, overshadowed by a monumental and never-completed Farnese palace. Now home to the Museo Archeologico (no.5, 0521 233 718), the Biblioteca Palatina (no.3, 0521 220 411) and the Galleria Nazionale, the Palazzo Pilotta also contains the Teatro Farnese (0521 233 309), a tremendous wooden theatre that was completely rebuilt after its destruction during World War II.

In season, the audiences at the Teatro Regio (next to the Palazzo Pilotta) are formidably vocal in their enthusiasm and dissent, and across from the piazzale della Pace, the Museo Glauco-Lombardi (via Garibaldi 15, 0521 233 727, www.museolombardi.it) gives a glimpse into life during Marie Louise's reign. For respite from the culture trail, cross the stream-like River Parma at ponte Verdi and meander through the romantic gardens of the Palazzo Ducale.

"Music is one of the city's obsessions – in particular that of locally born *maestri*."

Casa della Musica
Piazzale San Francesco 1 (0521 031 170/www.lacasa dellamusica.it). Open 9am-6pm Tue-Sat; 9am-1pm Sun. Admission €2; €1 reductions. No credit cards.
Away from the cultural overload of the Palazzo Pilotta, the House of Music stands as a reminder that this is as much a city of music as of food or art. The Cusani Palace has been beautifully restored to house the National Institute of Verdi Studies, the Regio Theatre's Historical Archives and a small auditorium and concert hall, used for occasional performances. Instruments associated with Verdi and Toscanini complete the collection; there are also films, CDs and online resources in the museum and library.

Il Castello dei Burattini
Via Melloni 3a (0521 239 810/www.castello deiburattini.it). Open Mar-Oct 9am-7pm Tue-Sun. Nov-Feb 9am-5pm Tue-Sun. Admission €2.50; €1.50 reductions. No credit cards.
After popping into Camera di San Paolo, a trip to the neighbouring Puppet Museum provides some light relief. Culled from the collection of puppet master Giordano Ferrari, the exhibits are arranged in roughly chronological order, with pantaloons and harlequins from the Commedia dell'Arte leading to devils and death's heads among the *pupazzi da Pinocchio*. Most are colourful Italian creations, which makes Czech surrealist Jan Svankmajer's ghostly white *marionetta gestuale* all the more striking.

Petrolhead passions

The via Emilia, the long, straight and ancient road that links the cities of Bologna, Parma and Modena, is not the most alluring of drives. The countryside of Emilia-Romagna is table-top flat though very fertile, a place where abundance far outweighs aesthetics. But for those who love cars, this region of northern Italy is the centre of the world, home to two of the most famous marques in the business. Lamborghini and Ferrari.

A short drive from the city of Modena, the compact town of Maranello is given over entirely to the creation of some of the most famous supercars in the world. The enormous Ferrari factory and test track, adorned with the famous prancing stallion crest – 'Cavallino Rampante' – dominates the district, emitting the unmistakable growl of its creations. This is where Enzo Ferrari, the engineering genius trained at Alfa Romeo, turned a family affair into a global superbrand, celebrated at the ultra-modern Galleria Ferrari.

The museum is a petrolhead's delight, crammed with rarities such as the 125S of 1947, Enzo Ferrari's first creation, right up to modern-day Scagliettis, Spiders, 430s and Enzos. Formula One gets its own spectacular gallery – Ferrari has been world champion a record 18 times – complete with pits and track. Not surprisingly Michael Schumacher, Ferrari's greatest driver, takes pride of place. Films and hands-on installations explain the innovative technology that Ferrari has developed for over half a century: it somehow manages to make even the workings of a gearbox interesting. It's a class act and, like the cars, beautifully designed, let down only slightly by a gallery dedicated to celebrity owners – all very well at the beginning, when we see Steve McQueen in his open Spider, but the devaluing of celebrity is all too evident as we approach the present where C-listers such as Jay Kay grin down on us. Even so, the Galleria Ferrari serves its role well as keeper of the myth – even the gift shop avoids tat.

If Ferrari is the first family of Italian motoring, Lamborghini is its crazy cousin. Based just down the road near Bologna, at the village of Sant'Agata Bolognese, it was founded in 1963 by tractor manufacturer Ferrucio Lamborghini – inspired, allegedly, by an argument over clutches with Enzo Ferrari – who decided on the very fitting raging bull marque because he was born under Taurus. The company became famous for its striking, often utterly impractical, sometimes unreliable creations, such as the

Miura and, above all, the Countach – unbearably hot, noisy, poorly finished and utterly beautiful, which just about kept the troubled tractor maker solvent. When Ferrucio sold out to tend his vineyards, Chrysler and then Volkswagen, stepped in – with a very noticeable improvement in build quality and reliability of current models such as the wildly expensive, brutally fast Gallardo and Murciélago (Jeremy Clarkson has compared modern Lamborghinis to sturdy German-made hampers full of delicious Italian delicacies).

Located inside the factory itself, the Lamborghini Museum is, like the cars, very stylish and a little bit bonkers: the wonderfully hi-tech, gleaming production line is worth the journey alone, though it's best to phone ahead, the company being a little bit paranoid about visitors – especially as they are allowed to get right to the heart of the production process. Inside, you'll see all the classics – Diablos, Espadas, and the first ever Lambo, the 350GTV, as well as the massive V12 engines that power these beasts. Just don't do what we did: turn up in a rented Nissan Micra. The feeling of inadequacy is overwhelming.

Galleria Ferrari
Via Dino Ferrari 43, Maranello (0536 943 204/www.galleria.ferrari.com). Open 9.30am-6pm Tue-Sun.

Lamborghini Museum
Via Modena 12, Sant'Agata Bolognese (0516 817 613). Visits by appointment. Guided tour on request.

Duomo

*Piazza Duomo (0521 235 886/www.cattedrale.parma.it).
Open Church 9am-12.30pm, 3-7pm daily. Baptistery
& Museum 9am-12.30pm, 3-6.30pm daily. Admission
Church free. Baptistery €4; €2 reductions. Museum €3;
€1.50 reductions. No credit cards.*

It was the anti-Papal bishop Cadalo (later elected Antipope
Honorius II) who in 1059 ordered the building of Parma's
cathedral, finally consecrated by Pope Paschal II in 1106. A
catastrophic earthquake a century later damaged much of
the edifice, but more interesting than the original remains
is the cupola's swirling fresco, the work of Correggio.
Painted in 1534, its sea of angels were famously dismissed
by one contemporary as a 'hash of frogs legs'.

The octagonal Baptistery, carved from Verona marble,
is strikingly embellished with Antelami's mythological
friezes. Its sombre interior is brightened by a circle of
sculptures depicting the seasons and signs of the Zodiac,
and by shafts of light that filter through the loggia. A
combined ticket grants you access to the Diocesan Museum
in the old Bishop's Palace across the piazza.

Galleria Nazionale

*Palazzo della Pilotta, piazzale della Pace (0521 233 309/
www.gallerianazionaleparma.it). Open 8.30am-1.45pm
Tue-Sun. Admission €6 (inc Teatro Farnese); €3
reductions; free under 18 and over 65. No credit cards.*

The grassy piazzale della Pace may be where the locals
come to put the world to rights, but inside the Palazzo della
Pilotta complex is a plethora of art. The city's National
Gallery is the main attraction, with displays ranging from
primitive painting to the French Enlightenment. Access it
via the magical Farnese theatre, worth a lengthy linger.
Inaugurated to celebrate the marriage of Odoardo Farnese

to Margherita de' Medici, it was also intended to show the
'superior' Milanese a thing or two. In the gallery, the
Parmesan School get a wing to themselves, with major
works by Parmigianino and Correggio, and two huge
Roman statues depicting Bacchus and Hercules stand guard
over the main museum rooms, which house paintings by
Da Vinci and Canaletto.

Parco Ducale

*Entrance opposite Ponte G Verdi. Open Sept-Apr
7am-8pm; May-Aug 6am-midnight. Admission free.*

Parma is not blessed with green spaces, so the expansive
grounds of the Ducal Palace are worth seeking out. The
Palace itself is now predominantly occupied by – O, joy! –
the European Food and Safety Authority, but anyone can
wander the shaded paths and landscaped lawns outside. A
happy convergence of English romantic, classical French
and formal Italian influences, the gardens were first opened
up to the public by Marie Louise.

San Giovanni Evangelista

*1 Piazzale San Giovanni (Church 0521 234 937;
Apothecary 0521 508 532). Open Church 8am-noon,
3-7.45pm daily. Apothecary 8.30am-1.45pm Tue-Sun.
Admission Church free. Apothecary €2. No credit cards.*

Best seen as a prelude to the larger Duomo, the church of
St John the Evangelist is notable for its lovely frescoes (1522)
by a young Parmigianino, the best-known pupil of
Correggio (who himself daubed the magnificent *Vision of
St John* in the dome). The Baroque façade abuts a
monastery, which provides welcome shade under the
porticoes of its Renaissance cloisters. Close by on Borgo
Pipa, the 13th-century Spezieria apothecary contains
weights, majolica vases and pharmaceutical documents.

Factfile

When to go
A good time to visit Parma is late autumn,
especially during November, when many of the
food fairs take place. However, the city's generally
pleasant climate makes it an attractive place to
visit all year round, though high summer can be
uncomfortably hot and humid. The one month
we can definitely say you shouldn't go is August,
when the Parmigiani head out of town for their
summer retreats. While most of the major sights
and museums do remain open, some have
reduced hours; even worse, almost all the
restaurants and shops close for at least part,
if not the whole, of the month.

Getting there
Parma airport is the Aeroporto di Parma G
Verdi (0521 980 394, www.aeroportoparma.it).
Bus no.6 (0800 977 966) runs every hour to
the city centre, from 6.30am to 8pm, and takes
around 15 minutes.

Getting around
The train station is centrally located some 500
metres from piazzale della Pace on piazzale Carlo
Alberto dalla Chiesa. It's a convenient place to
catch taxis and local buses; an eight-journey
carnet on the latter costs €6. That said, buses
can't get down many of Parma's narrow streets,
and the compact city is best explored on foot.

Tourist Information
Via Melloni 1a (0521 234 735/www.turismo.
comune.parma.it). Open 9am-7pm Mon, Tue,
Thur-Sat; 9am-1pm, 3-7pm Wed; 9am-1pm Sun.

Internet
There is free Wi-Fi access in many public spaces
in Parma, but you'll need to get a password from
the Tourist Office. Internet cafés are relatively
scarce: the most central is Polidoroweb.
Polidoroweb Galleria Polidoro 6b (0521 200 864).
Open 10am-8pm Mon-Sat. €3.50/hr.

Clockwise from top left:
Ravenna street life;
Locanda del Melarancio;
Mausoleo di Galla
Placidia; Cappello hotel;
Locanda del Melarancio;
piazza del Popolo.

Ravenna

Ravenna is not a name that trips off the tongues of most visitors
to Italy – which is very much their loss. This little town boasts an
array of staggering Byzantine mosaics that is unmatched anywhere
else in the world. Although it may be off the beaten track these days,
Ravenna was once the hub of the ancient world.

In AD 402, Ravenna was declared the capital of the Western Roman Empire. The centuries that followed saw it become a stronghold for the Goths and then, in the sixth century, for the Byzantines – who transformed it into a glittering showcase made of their famously opulent palaces, churches and mosaics.

The city was a source of inspiration for two very different literary giants. Exiled from Florence in 1302, Dante chose it as his refuge, finishing *The Divine Comedy* here. After his death in 1321, Florence demanded the return of his body for burial in his native city; Ravenna stoutly refused, and Dante's tomb still stands just off piazza Garibaldi. Five centuries later, Lord Byron – another writer in exile – fell in love with the Countess Teresa Guicciolo and moved here to be with her. He considered his time in Ravenna one of the happiest periods of his life.

Modern Ravenna is a prosperous *città d'arte* and bustling commercial centre, with several beach resorts nearby. Not that the past has been forgotten: the long silted-up port at Classe, once home to the imperial fleet of Augustus, is currently being excavated, and plans are being hatched for a new archaeological museum to showcase the finds. And the mosaics aren't just a thing of the past – there's an active art school fostering new talent here, as well as perhaps the world's finest school for mosaic restorers. Several mosaic artists live in Ravenna; some of them offer summer courses for visitors.

Home nearby to another art form is the charming little town of Faenza, where a particular kind of majolica (faience) was born in the 16th century. It caught on like wildfire across Europe, and since then the craftsmen of the town have held the title *maestri del fuoco* ('masters of the kiln'). The Museo Internazionale delle Ceramiche is hugely impressive.

Ravenna

ITALY

Ravenna

Historic sites
● ● ● ● ●

Art & architecture
● ● ● ● ●

Hotels
● ● ● ● ●

Eating & drinking
● ● ● ● ●

Nightlife
● ● ● ● ●

Shopping
● ● ● ● ●

Stay

There are only a handful of hotels in central Ravenna so it pays to book in advance.

Azienda Vitivinicola e Agrituristica Trerè

Faenza, 30km from Ravenna *via Casale 19, Monte Coralli, nr Faenza (0546 47034/www.trere.com). €.*
Set amid groves of vines, this lovely, family-run agriturismo has a swimming pool and a fine restaurant (open Fri-Sun) that serves their own produce, accompanied by delicious house wines. It's an ideal place for those craving peace and quiet; borrow bikes from the farm or simply go for long rambles between forays to Faenza or Ravenna (both of which are within easy driving distance). The air-conditioned rooms are charming, with wooden beams and tasteful antiques; some have kitchenettes and mini gardens too.

Bed & Breakfast A Casa di Paola

Via Paola Costa 31 (0544 39425/www.acasadipaola.it). €.
Recently opened by Paola, its artist owner, this B&B has three stylish rooms, kitted out with TV/DVDs and air-conditioning, plus a small apartment for longer stays. Guests take breakfast on a sunny little terrace and have access to the pretty garden – which once belonged to San Nicandro, destroyed during the war. Tucked away near the Battistero degli Ariani, Paola's is tranquil yet conveniently close to the main sights.

Hotel Cappello

Via IV Novembre 41 (0544 219 813/ www.albergocappello.it). €€€.
Housed in a 14th-century palazzo, the Cappello is Ravenna's smartest option, hands down. With seven rooms (five of them suites), an upmarket restaurant and a friendly wine bar (see below), it's a cosy hideaway in the heart of town. Each antique-furnished room is different; most also have frescoes, beamed ceilings or period fireplaces. The Rose & Roses Suite faces the hotel's small garden and overlooks an old camellia tree – heavenly when in flower.

Hotel Centrale Byron

Via IV Novembre 14 (0544 33479/www.hotelbyron.com). €.
Smack in the centre of town, within easy walking distance of all the sights, this friendly hotel offers clean, well-kept rooms at reasonable prices. The decor is a tad functional, with slightly 1980s overtones, but all rooms have air-conditioning. The no-nonsense manageress runs a tight ship, and the rest of the family management team is all smiles.

Hotel Diana

Via Girolamo Rossi 47 (0544 39164/ www.hoteldiana.ra.it). €€.
In a quiet spot, a short stroll from San Vitale, the pretty Hotel Diana is housed in a sunny yellow 18th-century palazzo. Although all the rooms are nicely decorated and air-conditioned, superior rooms are larger and have better bathrooms. Deluxe or executive rooms have internet access, along with massage armchairs and tea and coffee facilities – almost unheard of in Italian hotels.

Hotel Vittoria

Faenza, 30km from Ravenna *Corso Garibaldi 23 (0546 21508/www.hotel-vittoria.com). €€.*
This charming period residence is in the heart of the pretty town of Faenza, a short walk from the ceramics museum and main square. Open since 1861, it has a Stilo Liberty façade and distinguished list of former guests. Some of the rooms have lovely frescoed ceilings; those in room 111 are attributed to Giani, who painted frescoes in the neoclassical Palazzo Milzetti, one of Ravenna's loveliest buildings.

Eat

Typical Romagna cuisine predominates in Ravenna: pasta, meat, cheese and the ubiquitous *piadina* (a thin flatbread), washed down with excellent local wines. Seafood is good too, particularly around Cervia, where 'sweet' sea salt is a key ingredient. (Try the salted chocolate, a local delicacy.) Head to Faenza to sample the much-praised sangiovese grape in situ – the countryside has abundant rustic spots where you can dine among the vines.

For a glass of wine and good nibbles, seek out the beautiful 16th-century Ca' dè Vèn (via C Ricci 24, 0544 30163); Corte Cavour (via Cavour 51, 0544 30154); hidden in a courtyard beside a tinkling fountain, is perfect for coffee and cakes.

Angusto & Bar Clandestino

Faenza, 30km from Ravenna *Viale Baccarini 21/a-b-c (0546 681 327). Open Restaurant noon-10pm Mon, Wed-Sat; noon-4pm Tue. Bar noon-1am Mon-Sat. Performances Mon, Tue, Thur-Sat. €. Bar/restaurant.*
Conveniently positioned between the ceramic museum and Faenza's *centro storico*, this stylish little restaurant and bar has outdoor tables in summer and a decidedly retro feel. Its promixity to the ceramic school means it attracts an arty clientele, drawn by the mellow, unpretentious vibe and value-for-money food (bar snacks and a daily menu are offered). There's also a wide-ranging international programme of live music all year round.

Boca Barranca

Viale Italia 301, Marina Romea (0544 447 858/ www.bocabarranca.it). Open Restaurant open noon-1am. Club Apr-Sept 11pm-3am. €€. Osteria/pizzeria.
An excellent *osteria*/pizzeria by day, Boca Barranca turns into a trendy outdoor club by night. Watch out for the Boca All Stars night, every fourth Saturday of the month, which hosts some of the best DJs on the Adriatic coast. And if the music doesn't do it for you, indulge in a frisbee party or learn how to surf between mojitos.

Cappello

Via IV Novembre 41 (0544 219 813). Open noon-2.30pm, 7-11pm daily. €-€€. Traditional Italian/wine bar.
Spilling on to outdoor tables, the friendly enoteca at the chic Hotel Cappello (see above) offers wine by the glass and a

choice of daily specials, as well as bruschette, salads and platters of cheese or cured meats. Next door, the hotel's elegant restaurant has a winter garden and serves a menu based solely on fish. Buttery salt cod on brioche with capers and tomatoes, potato gnocchi with peas, pork cheek and cuttlefish or John Dory in a creamy sweet pepper sauce are typical fare. There's also a good-value tasting menu.

Locanda del Melarancio

Via Mentana 33 (0544 215 258/www.locandadel melarancio.it). Open noon-3pm, 7.30-11pm Mon, Tue, Thur-Sun. €-€€. Osteria.
Set in a lovely Renaissance building in the heart of Ravenna, this local institution covers all bases. Downstairs is the cosy, candlelit osteria, where an excellent selection of wines is served by the glass with piadine, salads and daily specials. Upstairs there are four rooms you can stay in, and a smart restaurant that serves delicious combinations such as lasagna with radicchio, fonduta and pecorino cheeses or wood pigeon stuffed with chestnut and dried figs. Enthusiastic, efficient staff and a sweet little shop selling local crafts and produce complete the picture.

Locanda Salegrosso

Milano Marittima, Cervia, 25km from Ravenna
Viale 2 Giugno 15 (0544 971 538). Open June-Aug 7.30pm-1am daily; Sept-May 7.30pm-1am Tue-Sun. €€. Seafood.
South of Ravenna, the historic seaside town of Cervia is the perfect place to sample excellent seafood. Located by the port, the unpretentious Locanda Salegrosso serves only the freshest fish and seafood. The menu di degustazione (which might include octopus terrine with wild fennel, fish soup or stuffed calamari) is excellent, as are the daily specials. The Salegrosso's name harks back to the town's major claim to fame – its ancient sea salt industry.

Trattoria alla Strada

Via Colonna 7 (0544 33220). Open 12.30-3pm, 7-11pm Mon-Sat. €€. Trattoria.
Alla Strada is a pretty place, with hand-printed table linen, a cool interior and a couple of outdoor tables. The reasonably priced menu offers a decent array of meat and fish dishes; try the swordfish carpaccio with Tropea onion jam or a dish of own-made pasta – tagliolini with clams and cappelletti al ragù, perhaps – followed by perfectly cooked grilled tuna or steak fiorentina. The own-made desserts are the cherry on the cake.

Trattoria La Rustica

Via Alberoni 55, corner of viale Santi Baldini (0544 218 128). Open noon-2.30pm, 7-10.30pm Mon-Thur, Sat, Sun. €€. Trattoria.
Not far from the station, in a quiet spot close to the church of Sant'Apollinare Nuovo and the Pinacoteca Comunale, this charming little restaurant has a decidedly rustic feel. Copper pots hang on the walls and a pergola outside shelters alfresco diners. The menu includes such delicacies as squacquerone cheese and formaggio di fossa with caramelised figs, hand-made cappelletti pasta in brodo (broth) and steak cooked with bay leaves and juniper.

Explore

Ravenna's historic centre is compact – you could tear your way round the main sites, eat well and then vanish into the sunset. Alternatively, you could linger and let the sleepy atmosphere of the place seep in, delighting in the many mosaics and ancient remains.

The train station at piazza Farini is a ten-minute stroll from the centre down via Diaz, past Galla Placidia's first church, San Giovanni Evangelista. The fifth-century church lost its original mosaics in the Counter Reformation and was badly bombed in World War II; today, only fine fragments of medieval floor mosaics remain.

Beyond is the pretty piazza del Popolo, with its twin pedestals – one of which was once topped by the lion of the Venetian Republic. A Renaissance loggia opens on to via Ricci, which leads towards Dante's tomb. Via IV Novembre at the far end takes you to piazza Costa and its covered market. On the corner of via Costa and via Ferruzzi is the Torre Civica, a red-brick medieval tower; close by is the fifth century Arian Baptistery of King Theodoric, with its beautiful dome mosaic of the baptism of Christ and the apostles.

The main shopping thoroughfare, via Cavour, opens on to via Salara and the helpful tourist information centre, where you can hire bikes and audioguides. A little further south are the beautiful Basilica of San Vitale and Mausoleo di Galla Placidia, housing Ravenna's finest mosaics. Next door is the town's museum. A more recent find, the magnificent Domus dei Tappeti di Pietra, is on nearby via Barbiani, beneath the tiny church of Santa Eufemia.

The Neonian or Orthodox Baptistery, inside the cathedral on piazza Duomo, is Ravenna's oldest site, with mosaics in the late fourth century Hellenic-Roman style. Highlights at the adjacent Museo Arcivescovile include the ivory throne of Bishop Maximian and exquisite mosaics of the chapel of Sant'Andrea, due to reopen after several years of restoration work. On nearby via Rondinelli, prestigious exhibitions are held in the deconsecrated church of San Nicolò.

Basilica di Sant'Apollinare

Classe, 5km from Ravenna *Via Romea Sud (0544 473 569). Open 8.30am-7.30pm Mon-Sat; 1-7.30pm Sun. Admission €3.*
The basilica once enjoyed a sea view across the noble port of Classe – but the marshland shifted over time, and it now stands inland. Dedicated to the first bishop of Classe, St Apollinarus of Antioch, and bankrolled by a rich Greek silversmith, the church was consecrated in 549. Its nave is lined with 24 magnificent marble columns, leading to a breathtakingly iridescent mosaic depicting Christ as the Good Shepherd and filled with early Christian symbolism.

Basilica di Sant'Apollinare Nuovo
Via di Roma (0544 219 938). Open Apr-Sept 9am-7pm daily. Mar, Oct 9.30am-5.30pm daily. Nov-Feb 10am-5pm daily. Admission €7.50; €6.50 reductions; free under-10s.
Once gleaming with golden mosaics, the Basilica was built by Theodoric in the early sixth century. When the church in Classe came under threat from pirates in the ninth century, the relics of St Apollinarus were moved here – and the church was renamed. Though much of the mosaic decoration is lost, the left and right walls of the nave remain intact. The left wall depicts the procession of the 24 virgins and the three kings to the Madonna, and the right shows the procession of the 26 Martyrs to Christ. Rumour has it that Pope Gregory the Great had the glorious gold ceiling mosaics removed because they proved too distracting for the congregation.

Domus dei Tappeti di Pietra
Church of Santa Eufemia, via Barbiani (0544 32512). Open Summer 9am-11.30pm Mon-Fri. Winter 10am-6.30pm Mon-Fri; 10am-4.30pm Sat; 10am-6.30pm Sun. Admission €3.50; €2.50 reductions; free under-10s.
Lying three metres below street level, the remains of this sixth-century Byzantine villa were discovered in 1993, when a local began digging the foundations for a new garage. The site's name translates as 'the house of the stone carpets' – and the 14 floor mosaics, with their floral, figurative and geometric imagery, are exquisite. Highlights include the rare Dance of the Geniuses of the Seasons and the Good Shepherd.

Mausoleo di Galla Placidia & Basilica di San Vitale
Via Fiandrini Benedetto (0544 215 193). Open Mausoleo Apr-Sept 9am-7pm daily. Mar, Oct 9.30am-5.30pm daily. Nov-Feb 10am-5pm daily. Basilica 9.30am-5pm daily. Admission (combined ticket) €7.50; €6.50 reductions.
The mausoleum's simple brick barrel entrance belies the beauty that lies within, where you'll find Ravenna's oldest and most complete mosaics.
The eastern influences on the design of San Vitale next door are clear. The decoration is pure Byzantine, from the mosaics to the carved capitals and stucco work. Flowers, birds, trees and saints are depicted, along with key imperial figures: the Emperor Justinian is shown in the left apse, and his wife, the Empress Theodora, is in the right apse.

Museo Internazionale delle Ceramiche
Faenza, 30km from Ravenna *Viale Baccarini 19 (0546 697 311/www.micfaenza.org). Open Nov-Mar 9.30am-1.30pm Tue-Thur; 9.30-5.30pm Fri-Sun. Apr-Oct 9.30am-7pm Tue-Sun. Admission €6; €3 reductions; free under-11s. No credit cards.*
Faenza's vast ceramics museum, celebrating its centenary in 2008, is terribly under-visited. Whether you start amid faience-ware and Italian ceramics from the Middle Ages and the Renaissance, or begin with modern-day masterpieces, you're in for a treat. Other highlights include art nouveau and art deco ceramics and pieces by Chagall and Matisse.

Factfile

When to go
The third weekend of each month is the antiques market, but the biggest annual event is the Ravenna Festival, which runs from June to late July. It's also worth visiting between late June and early September, when the Mosaico di Notte takes place: this involves late-night openings of the town's mosaics, with floodlights revealing their full richness of colour.

Getting there
The nearest airports are Forlì (0543 474 990, www.forliairport.com), Rimini (0541 715 711, www.riminiairport.com) or Bologna (051 6479 615, www.bologna-airport.it). Regular airport buses connect with the railway station.

Getting around
Bologna and Rimini have good train links with Ravenna and Faenza. There is no direct rail service between Ravenna and Forlì, though, and trains connecting Ravenna and Faenza are infrequent, often replaced by a bus service. See the rail website (www.trenitalia.com) for up to date information. Buses for Classe leave from Ravenna station, with the lidos served by buses and trains.

Tourist information
IAT Cervia Viale dei Mille 65 (0544 993 435). Open Sept-May 10am-4pm Mon-Fri, 11am-5pm Sat, Sun. June-Aug 8.30am-7.30pm daily.
IAT Ravenna Via Salara 8/12 (0544 35404/ www.turismo.ravenna.it). Open Sept-May 8.30am-4pm Mon-Fri, 10am-4pm Sat, Sun. June-Aug 9am-6pm daily.
IAT Riolo Terme Corso Matteoti 40 (0546 444 912). Open Sept-May 9am-noon, 3-6pm Mon-Thur; 9am-noon Fri, Sat. June-Aug 9am-6pm daily.
Pro Loco Faenza Voltone della Molinella 2 (0546 25231/www.prolocofaenza.it). Open May-Sept 9.30am-12.30pm, 3.30-6.30pm Mon-Sat; 9.30am-12.30pm Sun. Oct-Apr 9am-12.30pm, 3.30-5.30pm Tue, Wed, Fri, Sat; 9am-12.30pm Thur.

Internet
G Spot Via Canal Grande 44/27 Faenza (0546 22795). Open 9.30am-12.30pm, 2.30-7.30pm Mon-Wed, Fri-Sun; 2.30-7.30pm Thur.
TerzaEra, Viale Titano 84, Pinarella di Cervia (0544 988 404). Open Sept-Apr 10am-noon, 4-7pm Mon-Wed, Fri, Sat. May-Aug 10am-noon, 4-7pm, 9-11.30pm Mon-Wed, Fri, Sat; 4-7pm, 9-11.30pm Sun.

Siena

The Sienese are fond of saying that theirs is the world's most perfect medieval city, and it's hard to disagree. Not only has Siena preserved its exquisite monuments, it has maintained its traditions and its passion for local cuisine. Yet the historical rival to Florence isn't some bloodless museum piece. Radiating out from one of Italy's most beautiful squares, Siena's historic *contrade* (neighbourhoods) pulsate with life, and its steep, winding alleys are a delight to explore. Smitten visitors return here year after year, but the city's well-trodden streets haven't lost their charm.

Clockwise from top left:
Siena views; Duomo
façade detail; Palazzo
Pubblico; Siena views;
Duomo.

All the pretty horses

Siena's Palio horse race is the explosive culmination of centuries-long neighbourhood rivalries, and the event that defines the social, cultural and political fabric of the city each year. There's a singular objective: to win at all costs. Cheating, biting and dosing opponents' mounts with laxatives have all been tried. No one seems to care very much when the hired bareback jockeys – often dismissed as mere mercenaries – fall off their horses. The horse, on the other hand, is adored, receiving special rites and banquets.

The *contrade* that contest the Palio are districts of Siena that trace their roots back to the 12th century and vaguely represent the military groups that once protected it. At the head of each was a mayor and a central governor (*podestá*) supported by councillors. Originally, the city was divided into 42 *contrade*, but the numbers shrank to the current 17 in 1729, and of these ten are selected to participate, always including the seven that missed out last time round.

The Palio takes place in piazza del Campo twice a year, commemorating the feast of the Virgin Mary on 2 July and the Assumption on 16 August. On the perimeter, there are balconies and stands for spectators (usually wealthy tourists) willing to shell out €300 to watch the race in comfort. Most Sienese – up to 30,000 of them – stand under the blazing sun in the centre of the square.

The Palio starts in the late afternoon with a parade of costumed drummers and flag carriers. The horses charge three times round the square; the first one over the line (with or without rider) wins the Palio and earns a banner of the Virgin Mary as a trophy – not to mention adulation from fans. The event is normally over in a startlingly brief 90 seconds, as riders spur on their steeds (and attack enemy riders) with their *nerbo*, a whip made of dried ox penis.

The reactions of the Sienese, depending on their allegiance, range from weeping and hair-tearing to rapturous embracing; second place is considered a far worse way to lose than last place. Banquets and festivities sponsored by the winning *contrada* last into September, and animosity between the first- and second-placed teams lasts until the following year.

The event is preceded by three days of trials, every day at around 9am and 7.30pm in the Campo, plus dress rehearsals, banquets and horse blessing.

Grand Hotel Continental
(3 top); Certosa di
Maggiano (3 bottom).

Eat

Many of the recipes from the Siena region have been around since medieval times, including *pici* (thick, irregular spaghetti) and *panzanella* (dried bread soaked in water and served in a salad with basil, onion and tomato). Popular desserts include *panforte* (delicious slabs of nuts, candied fruits and honey) and *ricciarelli* (almond biscuits).

On a summer night, piazza del Campo turns into one great eating bowl. There are a dozen or so establishments from *birrerie* to *pizzerie*, most are mediocre: the best bets are Al Mangia (no.43, 0577 281 121, www.almangia.it) and L'Osteria Bigelli (no.60, 0577 42772), which has an interesting menu. Wine bar Liberamente Osteria (no.27, 0577 274 733, www.liberamente osteria.it) has a short, appetising menu.

Buena Vista Social Pub
Via San Martino 31 (33 3659 8043).
Open 6pm-midnight daily. Bar. €.
Siena isn't known for its nightlife, but this little reggae bar in a quiet part of town is worth checking out. Set in a single vaulted chamber with posters pasted up, it's a great place for cocktails on the terrace on a warm summer evening.

Café Ortensia
Via Panteneto 95 (0577 40039). Open 8.30am-1.30am Mon-Fri; 5pm-midnight Sat, Sun. Café. €.
One of the few places that still stays open late after the Sienese authorities wound back the opening time of most bars due to noise complaints. This is a pleasant, old-fashioned place recalling a 1950s Paris café – all marble-topped tables and cane chairs – serving light snacks and drinks. The collection of books and board games reflects its popularity with students, and there's a lively scene later in the evening.

Cane e Gatto
Via Pagliarese 6 (0577 287 545). Open 8-10.30pm Mon, Wed-Sun. Traditional Italian. €€€.
Booking is highly recommended at this small family-run restaurant, as is a hearty appetite. The setting, with its fussy ornaments, is a bit like being in someone's dining room, but the food is top notch. Among the specialities are osso buco and pasta dishes based on the locally made *pici*, and there's a seasonal *degustazione* menu for €65; fine local wine is served with each course. Luxurious lunches for small groups can also be arranged.

Compagnia dei Vinattieri
Via delle Terme 79 or via di Pittori 1 (0577 236 568/ www.vinattieri.net). Open 11am-1am daily. Traditional Italian/wine bar. €€€.
This stylish *ristorante*-cum-*enoteca* has a brief to make wine more approachable. The 700-strong list covers Tuscany, other Italian regions and beyond. You can drop in at any time of day to sample typical tasting plates of

crostini, *salumi* (cured meats) or pecorino cheese alongside wine served by the glass. There are also excellent own-made sweets and breads. The restaurant menu changes on a monthly basis, but you might get to enjoy *tortini di verdure* (a kind of savoury pie containing onion reduced in balsamic vinegar) followed by more usual meat or fish dishes, or perhaps a variation on *pici* served with a sauce of dried tomatoes, capers from Pantelleria and oregano.

Grattacielo
Via Pontani 8, corner of via dei Termini (0577 289 326). Open noon-7pm Mon-Sat. Traditional Italian. €.
The Grattacielo ('skyscraper') is proof that the Sienese have a sense of humour, as anyone over six feet tall will have trouble standing up straight inside. Tiny it may be, but it's excellent value. Food is presented in the style of old-fashioned Italian *osterias*, where what you see in the window is what you get: hearty, wholesome fare such as ravioli, beans, artichokes and stuffed aubergines. Tables inside are inevitably to be shared with locals; outside, you can sit and observe the passing parade. The wine – a very drinkable rough red – should help the conversation, but some Italian is an advantage.

Hosteria Il Carroccio
Via del Casato di Sotto 32 (0577 41165). Open Summer noon-2.30pm, 7.30-10pm daily. Winter noon-2.30pm, 7.30-10pm Mon, Thur-Sun; noon-2.30pm Tue, Wed. Traditional Italian. €€.
A little *osteria* with a big menu, this family-run restaurant pretty much covers the spectrum of Sienese food and has a respectable wine list. The soups are good: the classical Tuscan vegetable *ribollita*, *cipollata* (onion) or *zuppa di cavoli* (cauliflower soup). Try the *tegamate di maiale* (pork cooked in a ceramic bowl), which is based on an ancient Sienese recipe, and interesting antipasti such as *lardo* (cured pork fat) with pear, honey and pepper sauce.

Medio Evo
Via dei Rossi 40 (0577 280 315). Open noon-3pm, 7pm-midnight Tue-Sun. Closed Jan. Traditional Italian. €€€.
Set in an imposing medieval cavern, Medio Evo is bedecked with Palio flags, marble plaques and paintings. Yet unlike any number of ersatz historical joints elsewhere in the world, it is still possible to get a good meal here. Try the *gnocchi al prato*, made with pesto and gorgonzola, fillet steak with a rich Chianti sauce, or the house special pasta, *tagliolini* with porcini. The wine list includes a good range of Chianti; the service is friendly and there's a jovial atmosphere.

Da Mugolone
Via dei Pellegrini 8 (0577 283 235). Open noon-1am Mon-Wed, Fri, Sat. Traditional Italian. €€€€.
Many residents consider this one of Siena's best eateries, and it attracts a well-heeled, mainly local clientele to its simple yet elegant premises. Da Mugolone serves largely meat-based dishes using local ingredients, cooked and presented to unfussy perfection. Typical fare includes *tagliata aglio e rosmarino* (sliced grilled veal steak with

garlic and rosemary), *capretto in umido* (stewed kid) and vegetable mousses. Truffles and porcini feature strongly when in season.

L'Osteria
Via de' Rossi 79 (0577 287 592). Open noon-3pm, 7-11pm Mon-Sat. Traditional Italian. €€.
This spot is renowned (especially among faculty members from the neighbouring university) for its unpretentious Tuscan fare, served in simple surroundings and at palatable prices. It's the perfect place in Siena at which to eat like the locals. *Pici* dishes, *ribollita*, *panzanella* and tripe are all usually available. Especially worth trying in winter is the wild boar in a sauce made with bitter cocoa, pine nuts, raisins, almonds and balsamic vinegar. The house wine is very basic.

Osteria le Logge
Via del Porrione 33 (0577 48013). Open noon-3pm, 7-10.30pm Mon-Sat. Modern Italian. €€€.
Just off the Campo, this popular spot is better for a fine dining rather than an *osteria* experience, providing a menu with a creative, contemporary edge. You might, for example, kick off with an antipasto of *ravaggiolo con insalata profumata alla menta* – a green salad with a light foam of cheese, its subtle mint flavour cool and refreshing on a hot day. Pastas are often prepared with ricotta to give them a lighter quality, but main courses can be substantial: perhaps *filetto di chianina* (a local breed of beef) *al porcino* or lamb cutlet in a pistachio crust. Gianni Brunelli, the owner, produces his own (very good) wine – a fine Brunello di Montalcino. There are also tables outside, pleasant in summer as they get some shade from the medieval buildings on either side.

La Torre
Via Salicotto 7 (0577 587 548). Open 12.45-2.45pm, 6.30-9.45pm Mon-Wed, Fri-Sun. Closed for 2wks following the Palio. Trattoria. €€.
This small, family-run trattoria, a few paces off the Campo in the little street that runs beside the great tower, is something of a legend in Siena. Favourably reviewed over the years, it attracts a constant stream of visitors eager for authentic Italian food. Incredibly, the place hasn't been spoiled by all this attention. The kitchen, in plain view of the dining room, provides constant entertainment, and the whole family pitches in, with the father acting as master of ceremonies. There's no menu; the limited choice of dishes might include *tagliatelle* with sage butter or *ragù*, or ravioli with spinach and ricotta, followed by wild boar, roast veal or duck, osso buco and sometimes fish. Everything is fresh with an own-made quality.

Trombicche
Via delle Terme 66 (0577 288 089). Open 10am-3pm, 5.30-10pm Mon-Sat. Bar. €.
This minuscule, friendly little spot is great for a quick snack or a glass of wine and plate of prosciutto and cheese. Students and locals pop in for a bite and a drink. The surroundings may be getting a little worn, but it is cheap and cheerful. Be prepared to share a table.

Explore

Built where three hills converged, Siena's undulating topography and twisting alleys can be confusing for visitors: even finding piazza del Campo is harder than you'd think.

Basilica di San Domenico
Piazza San Domenico (0577 280 893). Open Nov-Apr 9am-1pm, 3-6pm daily. May-Oct 7am-1pm, 3-6.30pm daily. Admission free.
This soaring brick edifice was one of the earliest Dominican monasteries in Tuscany. Although established in 1226, the building that remains today is mostly mid 20th-century restoration. That said, a few historic features have survived. At the end of the nave is a *Madonna Enthroned* attributed to Pietro Lorenzetti, while halfway down on the right is the restored chapel of Siena's patron saint, St Catherine. The chapel itself is beautiful, with trompe l'œil pilasters, marble floors and works by Sodoma, who also did the tabernacle. Inside the chapel, in a container, is the relic of the saint's head.

Battistero
Piazza San Giovanni (0577 283 048). Open Mid May-Aug 9.30am-8pm daily. Sept-mid Nov, Mar-mid May 9.30am-7pm daily. Mid Nov-Feb 10am-5pm daily. Admission €3. No credit cards.
Whereas most baptisteries are octagonal, Siena's is rectangular. Its unfinished Gothic façade has three arches, adorned with human and animal statues; inside is a riot of richly coloured frescoes (mainly by Vecchietta). The focal point, though, is the central font (1417-34). Designed by Jacopo della Quercia, it is considered one of the masterpieces of early Renaissance Tuscany and features gilded bronze bas-reliefs by Jacopo, Donatello and Lorenzo Ghiberti.

Complesso Museale di Santa Maria della Scala
Piazza del Duomo 2 (0577 224 811/www.santamaria dellascala.com). Open Mid Mar-early Nov 10.30am-6.30pm daily. Early Nov-mid Mar 10.30am-4.30pm daily. Admission €6; €3 reductions; free under-11s. No credit cards.
Founded in the ninth century and funded by donations from local noble families, Santa Maria was one of the earliest and finest hospitals in Europe. Having served as the city's main hospital until the 1980s, it is now a museum, encompassing the Museo Archeologico and spectacular temporary exhibitions such as Etruscan treasures from Palermo and a homage to fashion designer Pucci's Palio collection. The museum is entered through the cavernous Sala del Pellegrinaio (Pilgrim's Hall); originally a hospital ward, its walls are covered with elaborate frescoes depicting the history of the hospital, some by Domenico di Bartolo (1440-43). Underground, a labyrinth of corridors and chambers carved out of the tufa now house the Archaeological Museum, which exhibits ceramic sculptures and pottery from the region, as well as artefacts excavated from the site itself. Highly recommended for children.

Palazzo Ravizza (2 top);
market (3 bottom).

Duomo

Piazza del Duomo (0577 283 048). Open June-Aug 10am-8pm Mon-Sat; 1.30-8pm Sun. Sept, Oct, Mar-May 10.30am-7.30pm Mon-Sat; 1.30-8pm Sun. Nov-Feb 10.30am-6.30pm Mon-Sat; 1.30-8pm Sun. Admission €6 (mid Aug-Sept); €3 (Oct-mid Aug). Libreria Piccolomini €3. No credit cards.

Work on the Duomo began in 1150 and continued for nigh on two centuries – until the Black Death struck in 1348. The resulting structure, Gothic in style but Romanesque in spirit, is more modest than originally hoped, but it's still a hugely impressive achievement. Banded with black and white marble, the recently cleaned façade is an imposing sight.

Inside, the cathedral's polychrome floors are its most immediate attraction. Between 1369 and 1547, numerous artists contributed an intricately decorated panel or two, but their handiwork is generally only on show between mid August and the end of September; for the rest of the year, it languishes under protective planks.

Above a splendidly carved wooden choir in the apse is a glowing 13th-century rose window designed by Duccio di Buoninsegna, depicting the life of the Virgin. The tabernacle, meanwhile, contains Bernini's Maddalena and San Girolamo statues. The pulpit was completed in 1266 by Nicola Pisano, helped by his son Giovanni and Arnolfo di Cambio – who later made his name by designing the Duomo in Florence. The Piccolomini altar is decorated with four statues of saints by a young Michelangelo; the Madonna above it is attributed to Jacopo della Quercia. At the far end of the left aisle, a door leads to the Libreria Piccolomini, built in 1495 to house the library of Sienese nobleman Aeneas Silvius Piccolomini, the Renaissance humanist who became Pope Pius II. The vibrant frescoes that adorn the vaulted chamber depict ten scenes from Pius II's life, and were Pinturicchio's last work (1502-9) – assisted, it's said, by a young Raphael.

"The Duomo, Gothic in style but Romanesque in spirit, is more modest than originally hoped but still impressive."

Museo dell'Opera del Duomo

Piazza del Duomo 8 (0577 283 048). Open Mid Mar-Sept 9am-7.30pm daily. Oct 9am-6pm daily. Nov-mid Mar 9am-1.30pm daily. Admission €6; €5 reductions. No credit cards.

Occupying the never-completed nave of the Duomo, this museum displays works from the cathedral. On the ground floor is a large hall, bisected by a stunning 15th-century wrought-iron gate; here the walls are adorned with 12 magnificent marble statues (1285-97) by Giovanni Pisano, which once adorned the façade of the Duomo. In the centre of the room stands a bas-relief Madonna and Child with

St Anthony by Jacopo della Quercia, commissioned in 1437 and probably not quite completed when the artist died the following year. On the first floor is the Pala della Maestà (1308-11) by Duccio di Buoninsegna, used as the high altar of the Duomo until 1506. The front depicts the Madonna, and the reverse comprises 26 religious scenes, all in dazzling hues.

Palazzo Chigi Saracini Accademia Musicale Chigiana

Via di Città 89 (0577 22091/www.chigiana.it). Open Guided tours 10am-7.30pm Sat; 10am-1.30pm Sun. Admission €7.

This musical academy, founded in the 1930s, is housed in a beautiful Renaissance palazzo with its own rococo-style concert hall. It hosts a week of Sienese music in July, followed by a series of classical concerts, the Estate Musicale Chigiana, through to the end of August. The Palazzo's concert hall, art collection, displays of musical instruments and library are accessible only by guided tour.

Palazzo delle Papesse (Centro Arte Contemporanea)

Via di Città 126 (0577 22071/www.papesse.org). Open 11am-7pm Tue-Sun. Admission €5; €3.50 reductions; free under-11s. No credit cards.

Occupying an opulent palazzo built in 1460, Siena's centre for contemporary art offers a harmonious juxtaposition of ancient and modern. Exhibitions here provide intense, sometimes edgy pieces from an international roster of artists (Richard Wilson, Medhat Shafik, Elger Esser) – often in stark contrast to their delicately frescoed surrounds.

Palazzo Pubblico

Piazza del Campo 1 (council cultural office 0577 292 226/ticket office 0577 292 263). Open Museo Civico Mid Feb-mid Mar, Oct-late Nov 10am-6.30pm daily. Mid Mar-Oct 10am-7pm daily. Late Nov-mid Feb 10am-5.30pm daily. Admission €7. No credit cards.

Work on this elegant Gothic structure began in 1288, and it wasn't completed until 1342. A potent symbol of medieval Siena's mercantile wealth, the palazzo was the seat of the Council of Nine more than seven centuries ago. Still in use as the town hall, it's now also home to the Museo Civico. Gems include the Anticappella, decorated with frescoes by Taddeo di Bartolo (1362-1422); behind a screen is the altar of the Cappella del Consiglio and a lovely Madonna and Child with Saints by Sodoma. The Sala del Mappamondo, once Siena's law court, was named after its cosmological frescoes, which depict the universe and celestial spheres – now, alas, barely visible. It also houses one of the city's most cherished jewels: Simone Martini's Maestà fresco (1315). The equestrian Il Guidoriccio da Fogliano is also attributed to Martini, though this has been disputed in recent years. Finally, the Sala della Pace contains Lorenzetti's extraordinary but badly damaged fresco cycle, the *Allegory of Good and Effects of Bad Government* (1338-40). Commissioned to remind the Council of Nine of their responsibilities, its detailed depictions of medieval life in the city and countryside are fascinating.

Clockwise from top left:
Palazzo Pubblico (2);
piazza del Campo;
market.

Piazza del Campo

Completed in 1349, the shell-shaped piazza del Campo is one of Italy's most beautiful squares. The city's various quarters converge here, making it the physical and symbolic heart of Siena. Its nine sections represent the ruling Council of Nine and also the nine folds of the Madonna's cloak, protecting the townsfolk. The early 15th-century Fonte Gaia, designed by Jacopo della Quercia, sits on the north side of the piazza. Its seriously eroded marble panels were replaced by copies in 1868; what remains of the originals can be seen in Santa Maria della Scala (*see above*).

Pinacoteca Nazionale

Palazzo Buonsignori, via San Pietro 29 (0577 281 161). Open 8.30am-1.30pm Mon; 8.15am-7.15pm Tue-Sat; 8.15am-1.30pm Sun. Admission €4; €2 reductions. No credit cards.

One of Italy's foremost art collections, with over 1,500 works, the Pinacoteca is particularly renowned for its Sienese *fondi d'oro* (paintings with gilded backgrounds). The first floor houses works by the Sienese Mannerist school of the early 1500s, including Sodoma and Beccafumi, and the next floor is devoted to Sienese masters from the 12th to 15th centuries, including Guido da Siena and the Lorenzettis (don't miss *A City by the Sea*). The upper level holds the Spannocchi Collection, works by northern Italian and European artists of the 16th and 17th centuries.

Torre del Mangia

Palazzo Publico, piazza del Campo (0577 226 230). Open Mid Mar-June, Sept, Oct 10am-7pm daily. July, Aug 10am-11pm daily. Nov-mid Mar 10am-4pm daily. Admission €6 (from Museo Civico ticket office). No credit cards.

When completed in 1348, the Torre del Mangia, next to the Palazzo Pubblico, was Italy's tallest tower, measuring 102m and commanding magnificent views over the province. It is named after one of its first bell-ringers: the pot-bellied mangiaguadagni ('eat-profits'), who bulked up at the local trattoria despite a daily climb up the tower's 503 steps. These days only 15 visitors are allowed up at any one time, and tickets sell quickly. At the foot of the tower is the Gothic Cappella di Piazza, commemorating the end of the plague.

Factfile

When to go

Siena has year-round appeal, but in the weeks leading up to the Palio (which happens twice a year, on 2 July and 16 August), the city is packed and hotels are booked up far in advance.

Getting there

The nearest airport is Florence's Amerigo Vespucci (www.aeroporto.firenze.it), 85km away. Pisa's Galileo Galilei airport (www.aeroporto dipisa.com) is 170km away.

The *raccordo* dual carriageway links Florence and Siena, a journey that takes around 45mins. Alternatively, there's the SS2, which slowly weaves its way through the countryside (very slowly if you get stuck behind a tractor).

The historic centre of Siena is mainly traffic-free, so park on the outskirts and walk in; there are nine big car parks, including the Stadio Comunale, near the Fortezza Medicea, and the large, misleadingly named Il Campo, which is nowhere near the piazza (http://siena.parcheggi.it). Even these can fill rapidly on weekends and public holidays, and around the time of the Palio. To hire a car, try Avis (via Simone Martini 36, 0577 270 305) or Hertz (viale Sardegna 37, 0577 45085).

If you don't have a car, bus is the best option for getting to the city, especially if you're travelling from Florence. Siena's major bus terminal is at the edge of the historic centre at piazza Gramsci; the main ticket office (0577 204 225) is underground. Most buses leave from the adjacent viale Federico Tozzi or nearby piazza San Domenico. Tra-in (0577 204 225), the principal bus company serving Siena and beyond, has departures every 30 minutes for Florence (direct service takes 75 minutes), as well as services to Arezzo, Grosseto and most regional towns of interest. The excellent www.comune.siena.it/train gives full timetable information on all services.

There are some direct trains to and from Florence, but more often you'll have to change at Empoli (journey time up to two hours). For Pisa, change at Empoli. Siena's train station is at the bottom of the hill on the east side of the city (piazza Fratelli Rosselli, tickets 0577 280 115, national timetable information 892021, www.trenitalia.it). From here, a local bus makes the short journey up to piazza Gramsci.

Getting around

Call Radio Taxi (0577 49222) or go to one of the taxi ranks at piazza Stazione (0577 44504) or piazza Matteotti (0577 289 350).

For bike hire, contact DF Bike (via Massetana Romana 54, 0577 271 905). Mopeds are available for rent at Automotocicli Perozzi (via del Romitorio 5, 0577 223 157).

Tourist office

Centro Servizi Informazioni Turistiche Siena (APT), piazza del Campo 56 (0577 280 551/ www.terresiena.it). Open 9am-7pm daily.

Internet

There are IT.Siena internet points at via di Città 121, via Pantaneto 58 and via Pantaneto 54.

Clockwise from top left:
Arche Scaligere (2);
Sant'Anastasia (2); Arena;
Due Torri Hotel Baglioni.

Verona

The whole world knows Verona as a hotbed of adolescent lust: you only need to see the vast number of visitors standing below Juliet's ersatz balcony in the heart of the old town to realise that Shakespeare's play has romantic relevance four centuries after it was written. The citizens of 21st-century Verona might appear to care for nothing but art, architecture and economic well-being, but this fabled city remains an undeniably romantic place.

Despite the Mittel-European edge to the architecture, ancient Rome provides the guiding influence to the look of 21st-century Verona. Dominating the entrance to the thumb-shaped old town in piazza Bra, the Arena is the most obvious sign of the Romans' presence, but it's not the only surviving trace: the streets were laid out according to a grid devised by Emperor Augustus, and many of the buildings stand on Roman foundations or incorporate fragments of Roman marble-work. However, a number of the finest buildings went up several centuries later during the construction boom that followed the great north Italian earthquake of 1117. Among them is the Castelvecchio, which has since been given a Modernist revamp by Carlo Scarpa.

After it was colonised by the Romans in 89 BC, Verona became a frequent prize of conquest, as invaders from central Europe and avaricious families from Italy itself coveted the city's position at the mouth of the Adige river valley. In the late 13th century, the home-grown Della Scala family succeeded in taking control over a swathe of northern Italy, but they fell in 1387 during a fit of Montague and Capulet-style family feuding. They were replaced by Milan's Viscontis, who were superseded in turn by the Venetian Republic. Only in 1866 did Verona rid itself of foreign rulers, when it joined the newly united kingdom of Italy.

Unlike Venice, Verona has not been preserved in aspic. It remains a vivacious city: the economy isn't dependent on the heritage industry, and the spending power of the populace has helped make it the undisputed capital of Veneto. This economic energy has in turn contributed to the city's alluring street life. Along with its beautiful location on the River Adige beneath cypress-topped hills, Verona's compact, walkable centre makes the city an attractive destination for a weekend break.

The shopping is good, the culture respectable and the history tangible. And romance? Enjoy a sunset *aperitivo* in the shadow of the Arena or an evening stroll through the old town, both of which may lend your Veronese memories a sepia tint.

Verona

Verona

Verona
●

ITALY

Historic sites

● ● ● ● ●

Art & architecture

● ● ● ● ○

Hotels

● ● ● ○ ○

Eating & drinking

● ● ● ○ ○

Nightlife

● ● ○ ○ ○

Shopping

● ● ○ ○ ○

Stay

Hotels fill up during the opera season, so it's best to book in advance. CAV (via Patuzzi 5, 045 800 9844, www.cav.vr.it, open 10am-7pm Mon-Sat) operates a free hotel-booking bureau.

Appartimenti L'Ospite di Federica De Rossi
Via XX Settembre 3 (045 803 6994/www.lospite.com). €€-€€€.
Literally 'Federica de Rossi's hospitality apartments', this small, 19th-century building contains six pleasantly furnished, self-catering apartments, which come with sitting rooms and fully equipped kitchens. The studio flats are ideal for couples and although the two-room apartments only have one bedroom, the presence of pull-out beds means that there is room for up to four people. As well as meeting you upon your arrival, English-speaking Federica can direct you around the city on the map she thoughtfully provides.

Cà del Rocolo
Via Gaspari 3, Località Quinto (045 8700 0879/www.cadelrocolo.com). €€.
This lovely little *agriturismo* is housed in a 19th-century farmhouse overlooking Lessinia National Park, 11km from central Verona and perfect for visitors with a car who'd prefer to visit the city from a base in the quieter countryside. The simple rooms are large and rustic; breakfasts can be taken out on to the terrace. A kitchen and a small barbecue are available for guests, but you may also be given the chance to share in a vegetarian dinner.

Due Torri Hotel Baglioni
Piazza Sant'Anastasia 4 (045 595 044/ www.baglionihotels.com). €€€€.
Beethoven, Mozart and Goethe have all stayed at this celebrated hotel, which is widely considered to be the city's finest. Still, despite its reputation, some of the rooms are looking a little tired. A few rooms allow guests to go eyeball to eyeball with Gugliemo di Castelvarco, whose tomb tops the archway across from the hotel.

Hotel Accademia
Via Scala 12 (045 596 222/www.accademiavr.it). €€€-€€€€.
It might be set in a 16th-century stone building, but this hotel is as modern and comfortable as they come. Some rooms face on to an inner courtyard that offers a peaceful escape from the lively side street on which the hotel sits.

Hotel Aurora
Piazza delle Erbe (045 594 717/ www.hotelaurora.biz). €€€.
This simple but efficiently run hotel sits slap bang in the centre of Verona, just a short walk from Piazza Bra. The rooms are clean and air-conditioned; many come with their own balconies, to which you can take your continental-style breakfast. There's also a great communal terrace that overlooks the bustling piazza delle Erbe.

Residence Antico San Zeno
Via Rosmini 15 (045 800 3463/www.residenceanticosanzeno.it). €€€.
Just around the corner from the church of San Zeno, this quiet and beautifully restored hotel has enormous rooms and mini-apartments with room for up to five people; all the apartments have cooking facilities. During the opera season and important trade fairs, prices can almost double.

Eat

Verona's cuisine is an interesting combination of Italian tradition and Middle European heft. Boiled and roasted meats are served with *cren*, the local take on horseradish sauce, or *pearà*, a blend of bone marrow, bread and pepper; braised horse meat (*pastissada de caval*) is another speciality. However, vegetarians need not be deterred: *bigoli*, a sort of thick spaghetti, is often served with meat-free sauces, and the fertile farms to the south of the city yield excellent vegetables. The area around piazza dei Signori is home to a number of generally reliable pavement eateries.

Wine-wise, the vineyards around Verona are responsible for some of Italy's most recognisable wine exports: Soave, Bardolino and Valpolicella. The Vinitaly festival takes place in Verona's fairgrounds every spring (www.veronafiere.it), keeping the lightweight export names for everyday use and the better-kept secrets like Amarone and Valpolicella Classico for special occasions.

Antica Bottega del Vino
Via Scudo di Francia 3 (045 800 4535/www.bottegavini.it). Open 10.30am-3pm, 6pm-midnight Mon, Wed-Sun. €€€. Traditional.
Open the heavy wooden door and you'll find a bustling, flamboyantly decorated dining room. Excellent local dishes include traditional fare such as *sfilacci di cavallo* (sliced horse meat with oil and lemon) and *trippa alla parmigiana* (tripe with parmesan cheese); there's also an amazing selection of wines available.

Cappa Caffè
Piazzetta Bra Molinari 1a (corner of via Ponte Pietra) (045 800 4516/www.cappacafe.it). Open 9am-2am daily. €€-€€€. Traditional bar/café.
Cappa Caffè's terrace affords views of the ponte Pietra, across the Adige to the Teatro Romano and the cypress-clad hillside above. While you're taking in the sights or enjoying an early-evening drink, fill up on kitchen standards such as spaghetti *alla pomodoro*, lasagne alla bolognese or the ubiquitous *sfilacci di cavallo* (horse meat) with rocket and parmesan. Things liven up later.

Hostaria La Vecchia Fontanina
Piazzetta Chiavica 5 (045 591 159/www.vecchiafontanina.it). Open noon-2.30pm, 7-10.30pm Mon-Sat. €-€€. Traditional.

Not far from piazza delle Erbe and popular with savvy locals, this eaterie serves a varied menu that features creative versions of local specialities. Among the highlights are *bigoli* with nettles and smoked ricotta cheese, buffalo mozzarella, and plenty of lovely cooked or raw *contorni*.

Ostaria Sottoriva

Via Sottoriva 9A (045 801 4323). Open noon-2pm, 5-10.30pm Mon, Tue, Thur-Sun. €€. Bar/osteria.
Set under porticos on a picturesque street, this traditional, venerable Veronese *osteria* offers a simple and traditional menu, and a good selection of Venetian wines, many poured from the barrels in the cellar below. It's popular with locals.

Trattoria Tre Marchetti

Vicolo Tre Marchetti 19B (045 803 0463). Open Sept-June noon-3pm, 7-10.30pm daily. July-Aug noon-4am Tue-Sun. €€. Trattoria.
Meals have been served on this site since 1291, which just about qualifies Tre Marchetti as one of the most ancient eateries in Europe. Informal and crowded, the trattoria has lost none of its allure over the centuries, and booking is advisable. Specialities include *bigoli* with duck, *pastissada de caval* and *baccalà* (cod) *alla vicentina*.

Explore

SIGHTS

The atmospheric old town, nestling in the loops of the serpentine Adige River, stretches out from piazza Bra. Overshadowed by the magnificent Arena, this large square is home to a number of cafés and the Museo Lapidario (045 590 087, open 1.45pm-7.30pm Mon, 8.30am-2pm Tue-Sun, €3, €2 reductions), a small collection of Greek and Roman fragments.

The heart of the city is centred on the adjoining piazza delle Erbe and piazza dei Signori, a short walk north-east from piazza Bra. The *piazze* are linked by 12th-century Palazzo della Ragione which is dominated by the medieval Torre dei Lamberti. Once the site of the Roman forum, piazza delle Erbe today hosts a slightly tacky food and souvenir market every morning except Sunday. But try as it might, the market can't detract from the stunning buildings that surround the square. At the northern end stands the huge 14th-century Casa Mazzanti, complete with its splendid late Renaissance frescoes; the Palazzo Maffei, a highly ornamented structure; and the medieval Torre Gardello, Verona's first clock tower. The tall houses at the southern end once marked the edge of the Jewish ghetto.

South-east of the piazza delle Erbe, via Cappello leads to the Casa di Giulietta. Further down stands the Porta Leoni, a picturesque fragment of a Roman city gate that's now part of a medieval house; the Gothic church of San Fermo Maggiore stands where via Cappello meets the river. North of delle Erbe, the narrow streets are a captivating labyrinth dotted with medieval and Renaissance palazzi. From via Pigna, head north up via San Giacomo alla Pigna towards the Duomo, taking in Arche Scaligere, or south towards the imposing Sant'Anastasia.

The ponte Pietra leads across the river to some of Verona's most beautiful churches, including San Giorgio in Braida and Santa Maria in Organo, as well as the Museo Archeologico and the remains of the Teatro Romano. Head south-east from the bridge along regaste Redentore and its continuations in order to reach Giardino Giusti.

To the east, the Galleria Arcades mark the start of Verona's prime shopping territory. You'll find a number of boutiques here, most notably some designer shoe shops; further on, you'll hit the more plebeian drag of via Macelli, which links to the newer parts of town on the east side. Just before the main station sits the main city market, housed in an unprepossessing concrete shed and open on weekday mornings. You might find some bargains if you're after household goods or knock-off designer clothes.

If you're planning to visit a number of churches and museums, you can cut costs by purchasing a Verona Card (€8 for one day, €12 for three days), valid for all the sights that charge admission. Alternatively, the *itinerario completo* offers entrance to five of Verona's churches for €5.

Arena

Piazza Bra (045 800 5151/www.arena.it). Open 1.45-7.30pm Mon; 8.30am-7.30pm Tue-Sun (hrs vary during season). Admission €4; €3 reductions. No credit cards.
The largest Roman amphitheatre in northern Italy at 139m by 110m, Verona's Arena had room for the city's entire population of 20,000 when it was constructed in roughly AD 30 from pink marble quarried from nearby hills. Given its age and the fact that it's been in near-constant use throughout the centuries, it's in remarkably good shape: the 44 tiers of stone seats are virtually intact, as is the columned foyer. Try to catch a gig (anyone from Lou Reed to Enrique Iglesias), an opera (www.arena.it) or one of the dance or drama events held over summer during the Verona Festival.

Casa di Giulietta (Juliet's house)

Via Cappello 23 (045 803 4303). Open 1.30-7.30pm Mon; 9am-7pm Tue-Sun. Admission €4; €3 reductions. No credit cards.
The Montagues and Capulets may have been real, but the Capulets never lived in the so-called Casa di Giulietta. What's more, Juliet most certainly never stepped out on the balcony (a 1920s addition) in order to get Romeo's attention, but that hasn't stopped tourists from crowding underneath it for photo opportunities. The price of admission allows you inside to pen and post your own letter to Juliet, before taking a quick bow on the balcony.

To Sirmione, with love

Just 30 kilometres from Verona lie the shores of Italy's largest lake: Garda, 'beautiful as Paradise' according to DH Lawrence. The lake's jewel is the southern peninsula of Sirmione, with the 13th-century Scaligero castle standing guard. From here, narrow pedestrian streets lead past the Romanesque church of San Pietro in Mavino to the Grotte di Catullo, ruins of a well-to-do Roman resort (Catullus's family had a villa here). Behind this is the villa Maria Callas escaped to when the glam opera world became too oppressive.

From Sirmione, head through the fortress town of Peschiera and take the Gardesana Orientale road past Gardaland, Italy's biggest theme park, to the pretty port of Lazise. Enclosed in swallow-tailed castle walls, this was once Venice's main lake port; la Serenissima's customs house can still be seen by the harbour, next to the Romanesque church of San Nicolò, protector of fishermen.

An obligatory stop for oenophiles, especially during the annual 'grape cure' in September, is the next town up the coast, Bardolino. Visit the vineyards along the Bardolino wine road (SP31) out of Lazise via Calmasino and Cavaion, or follow the road hugging the lake, past the Museo dell'Olio d'Oliva (olive oil museum; 9am-12.30pm, 2.30-7pm Mon-Sat, 9am-12.30pm Sun), where you can taste the area's other main product, which gives this stretch its name, the Riviera degli Ulivi.

In Bardolino, the eighth-century San Zeno and 12th-century frescoes at San Severo both merit a visit before stopping off at the stylish Enoteca del Bardolino (piazza Principe Amedeo 3-4, 045 721 1585, www.enotecadelbardolino.it, open 3pm-2am Fri, 11-2am Sat, Sun) on the lakefront for lunch. Between the next resort towns of Garda and Torri del Benaco nestles the cypress-tipped promontory Punta di San Vigilio, with its gorgeous Renaissance villa by Sanmicheli. Park at the top, and head for the lakeside park of Baia delle Sirene ('mermaid bay', 045 725 5884, www.parcobaiadelle sirene.it, open May-Oct 9.30am-9pm, Nov-Apr 10am-7pm). For €10 a day or €2 an hour you get a sunlounger to set up on the pebble beach or the shady olive terraces. A cobbled street leads down to a hotel and taverna (045 7256 688, www.punta-sanvigilio.it, closed Nov-Mar, €€€), probably the most romantic (if pricey) meal on the lake.

Further north, before the Mediterranean landscape gives way to the sheer cliffs of the Trentino region is Malcesine, where narrow

medieval streets cling to the lakeside beneath a castle (closed Sun, admission €4). Climb to the top of the castle for breathtaking views over the lake. For even more dramatic views, a ten-minute cable car ride (045 740 0206, www.funiviedelbaldo.it, open Oct-Apr 8am-4.45pm, May-Sep 8am-6.45pm, departs every 30mins, €17 return) takes you up to the 1783-metre peak of Monte Baldo, from which walkers, mountain bikers, parascenders (and skiers in winter) all make their way down. Malcesine's lakeside bars and eateries offer the perfect place from which to watch the sun set before heading home. Alternatively, stay up for the night and take the car ferry in the morning across to Limone, unsurprisingly famous for its lemons but also for the population's total lack of heart disease.

From here you can take another day to explore the lake's western shore as you head back down south. Like Callas, you may already have begun to 'yearn for Sirmione'.

Top to bottom: Casa di Giulietta (Juliet's house); Verona's rooftops.

Castelvecchio
Corso Castelvecchio 2 (045 806 2611/www.comune. verona.it/castelvecchio/cvsito). Open 1.45-7.30pm Mon; 8.30am-7.30pm Tue-Sun. Admission €4; €3 reductions. No credit cards.
The various parts of the castle, stronghold of the Della Scala family, are linked by overhead walkways and passages, which offer superb views of the city and the surrounding hills. The museum itself contains important works by Mantegna, Veronese, Tintoretto and Canaletto among other masters, as well as a vast collection of pieces by local artists.

Duomo
Piazza Duomo (045 592 813/www.chieseverona.it). Open Mar-Oct 10am-5.30pm Mon-Sat; 1-5pm Sun. Nov-Feb 10am-5pm Tue-Sat; 1-5pm Sun. Admission €2.50. No credit cards.
Verona's cathedral is Romanesque downstairs, Gothic upstairs and Renaissance at the top half of the bell tower. Inside, the first chapel on the left has a magnificent Assumption by Titian. Roman remains and mosaics are on show in a tranquil Romanesque cloister; the same complex holds the ancient church of Sant'Elena.

Museo Archeologico
Regaste Redentore 2 (045 800 0360/www.comune. verona.it/castelvecchio/cvsito/mcivici2.htm). Open 1.45-7.30pm Mon; 8.30am-7.30pm Tue-Sun. Admission €3; €2 reductions (includes Teatro Romano). No credit cards.
This small museum, across the Adige from the Old Town, contains a fine collection of Roman remains. It also offers incomparable views over Verona and the river: take the lift from the theatre through the cliffs and up to the museum.

Sant'Anastasia
Piazza Sant'Anastasia (045 592 813/www.chiese verona.it). Open Mar-Oct 9am-6pm Mon-Sat; 1.30-6pm Sun. Nov-Feb 10am-4pm Tue-Sat; 1.30-4pm Sun. Admission €2.50. No credit cards.
This imposing brick Gothic church is best visited in the early morning, when sunlight streams in and illuminates Antonio Pisanello's glorious fresco (1433-38) in the sacristy to the right of the apse of St George preparing to set off in pursuit of the dragon. Back inside, two delightful *gobbi* (hunchbacks) crouch down to support the holy water font.

San Zeno Maggiore
Piazza San Zeno 2 (045 592 813/www.chieseverona.it). Open Mar-Oct 10am-6pm Mon-Sat; 1-6pm Sun. Nov-Feb 10am-5pm Tue-Sat; 1-5pm Sun. Admission €2.50. No credit cards.
One of the most spectacularly ornate Romanesque churches in northern Italy, San Zeno Maggiore was built between 1123 and 1138 to house the tomb and shrine of San Zeno, an African who became Verona's first bishop in 362 and is now the city's much-loved patron saint. The great bronze doors feature 48 panels depicting scenes from the Bible and from the life of San Zeno plus a few that experts can't explain, including a woman suckling two crocodiles.

Factfile

When to go
Verona's unique position gives the city a bizarre mix of weather conditions. Spring can be rainy but quite short, and summer tends to be muggy and mosquito-ridden. If you're coming in summer, make sure your hotel has air-conditioning, and book well in advance: the summer opera season draws huge numbers of visitors to the city. September is a very pleasant month, but rain may intrude in late October and November.

Getting there
Valerio Catullo Airport (045 809 5666, www.aeroportoverona.it).
A bus (0458 057911) runs between Verona airport and the train station every 20 minutes from 6.35am to 11.35pm. The 20-minute journey costs €4.50 (pay on board).
There are regular train services from Venice (045 892021, www.trenitalia.it). The journey takes around 45 minutes.

Getting around
AMT (045 887 1111, www.amt.it) runs the city's orange buses, most of which start and terminate at Porta Nuova. Tickets can be purchased at any tobacconist. A €1 ticket is valid for one hour and should be punched on each bus boarded.
The APT Verona bus company (045 805 7911, www.aptv.it) runs blue coaches to towns in the area around Verona, including Lake Garda and the Monti Lessini. Buses depart from the bus station in front of Porta Nuov.
The tourist office at the station offers bikes for free. Leave a passport or another document and return the bike before the office closes.

Tourist information
IAT Via degli Alpini 9 (045 806 8680/ www.tourism.verona.it). Open July, Aug 8.30am-7pm Mon-Sat; 9am-5pm Sun. Sept-June 8.30am-7pm Mon-Sat; 9am-3pm Sun.
IAT Railway station, piazza XXV Aprile (045 800 0861). Open 8am-7pm Mon-Sat; 9am-3pm Sun.
IAT Verona airport (045 861 9163). Open 9am-7pm Mon-Sat.

Internet
There are many internet points throughout the city, among them Internet Train (via Roma 17 (045 801 3394) and Internet Etc (via Quattro Spade, 3/B (045 800 0222).

Vicenza

If you're looking for a reason to visit Vicenza, its evocative nickname
is a good place to start. This small but stately town is known as the
Città di Palladio, a nod to the immeasurably influential 16th-century
architect, Andrea Palladio, who was born in nearby Padua but grew
to become an adopted son of the city. Palladio was responsible
for numerous beautiful buildings in and around Vicenza, which make
it an incredibly handsome place.

Clockwise from top left:
Basilica Palladiana; Teatro
Olimpico; detail from
Santa Corona; Vicenza
railway station; *baccalà*.

The Romans put this area on the map in 157 BC, naming the city Vicetia and planning its framework; a layout that is still virtually intact today. The city became an important Lombard and Frankish centre, but it was destroyed by Magyar marauders in 899. During the Middle Ages the city flourished as the astute locals took advantage of their position as a crossroads and link between two rivers. In 1404, Vicenza came under the rule of mighty Venice, and a no-expense-spared building boom began in earnest. The conquered noblemen assuaged their wounded pride by commissioning sumptuous townhouses and country villas, many of which are still in evidence today.

Palladio left his mark in the town in the 16th century. Many of his renowned townhouses still stand, joining row upon row of imposing *palazzi* to help make Vicenza a paradise for lovers of architecture. For a primer, you could do worse than start in piazza Matteotti, where two of Palladio's masterpieces await: the Palazzo Chiericati (1550), which is now the city's art gallery, and the Teatro Olimpico, the architect's imposing final work. The great man is even buried here in the amazing Gothic church of Santa Corona.

For those unmoved by its grand buildings and idyllic setting amid rolling, cypress-topped hills, Vicenza has other charms. There's an abundance of shady street cafés and traditional bars, and an array of excellent shops. Another of the city's nicknames, Città dell'oro (City of gold), came about thanks to its reputation for goldsmithery, something mirrored in the wealth of fine jewellery boutiques that dot the town; the city continues to host the world-famous VicenzaOro trade fair three times a year.

The suburbs surrounding Vicenza have succumbed to light industry (primarily textiles-based), and have little to offer the visitor. It's the magnificent, UNESCO-protected *centro storico*, easily navigated on foot, that really makes this one of Italy's must-see cities.

Vicenza

Vicenza

ITALY

Historic sites
● ● ● ● ○

Art & architecture
● ● ● ● ●

Hotels
● ● ● ○ ○

Eating & drinking
● ● ● ● ○

Nightlife
● ○ ○ ○ ○

Shopping
● ● ● ○ ○

Stay

Albergo Due Mori
Contrà do Rode 24 (0444 321 886/
www.albergoduemori.com). €.
Housed in an imposing 19th-century *palazzo* that was completely restored in 2002, and located just minutes from the piazza dei Signori, this art nouveau-style hotel is Vicenza's oldest and most central. The antique-filled bedrooms are characterful and pleasantly spacious; most have their own private bathrooms, and two are equipped with disabled facilities.

Albergo San Raffaele
Viale X Giugno 10 (0444 545 767/
www.albergosanraffaele.it). €.
Situated on the hill just below the Santuario di Monte Berico, the San Raffaele is a good 20 minutes from the station, but it's worth the trek for the fantastic views over the city (ask for a north-facing room). The atmosphere is unpretentious; furnishings verge on the spartan, with unfussy wooden furniture and hard flooring, although the beds are comfortable enough. Breakfast and parking are included, making this a good budget option.

Hotel Campo Marzio
Viale Roma 21 (0444 545 700/
www.hotelcampomarzio.com). €€.
A half-and-half mix of business travellers and people on holiday frequent this spacious hotel, which is conveniently located between the historic centre and train station. If you ignore the dated reception and other communal areas (smoked glass windows and lots of wood-effect panelling) and manage to bag one of the individually styled 'superior' rooms, you're in for a treat. With its pretty hand-painted wall stencils, baroque furniture and double-size spa bath, the best is room 311, but 'Canova' and 'Orientale' are also pleasant.

Hotel Castello
Contrà piazza Castello 24 (0444 323 585/
hotelcastelloitaly.com). €€.
The Castello, which became part of the Dimore d'Epoca chain three years ago, boasts a gorgeous roof terrace with great views over the old town and the surrounding hills. The rooms are attractively furnished with antiques, and retain some original features; leaving aside the dodgy carpets and labyrinthine stairs (there's no lift), the owners have done everything to make this 17th-century building into a quaint yet modern hotel. Massimo, the enthusiastic Sicilian manager, is an attraction in his own right.

Hotel Cristina
Corso San Felice 32 (0444 323 751/
www.hcristina.it). €€.
Located a few steps outside the Porta Castello, the friendly, family-run Hotel Cristina was founded in 1981, and it shows. However, a recent restructuring has added a new '*music e scrittori*' ('music and writers') wing containing tranquil, tastefully furnished rooms. Top marks, too, for the Cristina's

commitment to the environment: the hotel has received the Ecolabel designation for its energy-saving measures, serves all-organic breakfasts, and even lends bicycles to its guests. Several rooms are disabled-adapted.

"The Villa Saraceno, built originally for a gentleman-farmer, is a magnificent example of Palladio's pared-down classicism."

Villa Saraceno
Via Finale 8, Agugliaro (UK 01628 825 925/
www.landmarktrust.org.uk). €€€€.
The magnificent Villa Saraceno offers a unique opportunity to stay in an original Palladian property. Like many of Palladio's villas, the Saraceno was built for a gentleman farmer, with an attic-granary lit by large, grilled windows that kept the wheat ventilated. Designed towards the end of the 1540s, it's a magnificent example of the architect's pared-down classicism. Located about 20 miles south of Vicenza (take the bus for Noventa Vicentina and change at Ponte Botti for the local service), it can be rented out by the week and sleeps up to 16. Guided tours are available on Wednesdays between April and September (0444 891 371).

Eat

The *vicentini* have been eating *baccalà alla vicentina*, a dish of dried cod stewed in milk and oil, since at least 1269. There are two ways of preserving cod: it can be salted and partially dried (salt cod, or *baccalà*) or just dried (stockfish, or *stoccafisso*). When stockfish was introduced to the *vicentini* in the 15th century, they decided they preferred it to the already-established *baccalà*. But *stoccafisso* is not an easy word to pronounce in the local dialect, so they called it *baccalà* regardless.

Amici Miei Restaurant & Drinks
Piazza Biade 6 (0444 321 061/www.amicimiei.vi.it).
Open 6.30pm-midnight Mon; 11.30am-3pm, 6.30pm-
midnight Tue-Sat. Closed 2wks Aug. €€€€.
Traditional Italian/bar.
Overlooking piazza dei Signori, this stylish little bar boasts an impressive array of cocktails (all the classics, plus such conconctions as Chocolat Mint Tini and Rhapsody in Red) and extensive selections of wine and champagne. Lunches (pasta, omelettes, salads, and a fish of the day) are light but by no means lean, though chef

Davide Celio wheels out the big guns at dinner, with the likes of spelt fettuccine with purple artichoke hearts and king prawns, and three types of tartare. The desserts are wonderful, especially the ice-creams.

Antica Casa della Malvasia
Contrà delle Morette 5 (0444 543 704). Open 12.30-3.30pm, 7pm-1am Tue-Sat. €€. Traditional Italian.
This centrally located but also pleasantly secluded osteria offers an excellent-value lunch menu, and a good variety of wines by the glass. Although it lacks atmosphere in the evening, the attractive outdoor tables are a nice spot for an *aperitivo*.

Hisyou
Piazza delle Erbe 9 (0444 321 044). Open 7.30pm-midnight Mon; noon-3pm, 7.30-midnight Tue-Sun. Closed 2wks Aug. €€€. Japanese.
Considering the dazzling array of fresh fish on offer in the regional marketplaces, it's surprising that sushi isn't more popular. Hisyou is trying to put that situation to rights: choose from individual sushi or sashimi pieces and rolls to order, along with bentos and teppanyakis ranging from €9 to €16. Dark wooden benches and subtle paper lampshades create a calm, cosy atmosphere.

Osteria I Monelli
Contrà Ponte San Paolo 13 (0444 540 400). Open 10.30am-3.30pm, 6.30pm-2am Tue-Sun. Meals served 12.30-3pm, 7.30-11pm Tue-Sun. Closed 2wks July. €€. Traditional Italian.
This lively traditional osteria serves excellent and often meaty local cuisine, including a delectable *filetto di cavallo* (horse meat steak). But the varied menu also includes such delights as duck breast wrapped in speck (dried ham) with balsamic vinegar, and a hearty radicchio gnocchi with rosemary and bacon. Packed with locals, it's great for late-night drinking at weekends.

Osteria II Cursore
Stradella Pozzetto 10 (0444 323 504). Open noon-3pm, 7.30-10.30pm Mon, Wed-Sat; 6.30-10.30pm Sun. Closed 3wks July-Aug. €€. Traditional Italian.
This old-fashioned Vicentino drinking den across the ponte San Michele can be tricky to find, but it's worth the extra effort. Along with bar nibbles to accompany the early-evening aperitifs, the kitchen turns out excellent versions of local specialities such as *bigoli con sugo di anatra* (pasta with duck sauce) or the classic *baccalà alla vicentina*.

Papajoe's
Corso Palladio 7c-d (0444 325 327/www.papajoes.it). Open 6.30pm-1am Tue-Sun. €€. International.
Around 3,000 US troops are stationed just outside Vicenza at the Camp Ederle army base, which probably explains this all-American joint. Heaped plates of buffalo wings, steak 'n' chilli, chicken fajitas and all-you-can-eat salads are all on the menu, and the brightly painted walls are dotted with Mexican knick-knacks and vintage posters. Still, it's been a hit with the locals, perhaps because the food is of a very high standard.

Pasticceria Sorarù
Piazzetta Palladio 17 (0444 320 915). Open 8.30am-1pm, 3.30-8pm Mon, Tue, Thur-Sun. Closed 2wks Aug. No credit cards. €. Pasticceria.
This charming *pasticceria* is worth a look even if you don't have a sweet tooth: the columns, marble counters and ornate, mirror-backed shelves are all 19th-century originals. The cakes, firmly in the Austro-Hungarian tradition, range from basic pastries to sculptural, hand-crafted creations as elaborate as the interior. The outside tables make an ideal spot for breakfast in summer.

> ## "Pasticceria Sorarù is worth a look for original 19th-century columns, marble counters and ornate mirror-backed shelves alone."

Ristorante Pizzeria al Paradiso
Contrà Pescherie Vecchie (0444 322 320/www.alparadiso.net). Open 11am-3pm, 6pm-midnight daily. €. Traditional Italian/pizzeria.
Locals and tourists pack out this traditional *ristorante* with good reason: it's a lovely spot for alfresco dining, with an extensive, well-executed menu. Classics such as *melone con crudo* (piled high with melt-in-the-mouth cured ham) start at just €4.50, and bargain-priced plates of pasta and risotto are enthusiastically wolfed down at every table. Service is slow and moody – but with prices this good, who cares?

Explore

SIGHTS

Vicenza's main area of interest, the *centro storico*, is linked to the train station by park-flanked viale Roma. At the top, on the site of the city's original Roman gate, stands the imposing Porta Castello (1343). Piazza Castello is home to the odd-looking Palazzo Porto Breganze, a tall, awkward fragment in the southern corner that was designed by Palladio but never completed.

Palladio had a hand in designing five of the grandiose *palazzi* lining the city's main drag, corso Palladio (all closed to the public). The first of note, on the left if you're coming from piazza del Castello, is the magnificent Palazzo Thiene Bonin Longare, begun in 1562. At no.45 is Palazzo Capra, almost certainly designed by the young Palladio between 1540 and 1545 and now

Clockwise from top left:
Santa Corona; Villa
Valmarana ai Nani; Teatro
Olimpico (2).

home to a department store. Palazzo Pojana (1564-66), consisting of two separate buildings cunningly joined together, is at no.92.

South of the corso, in the elegant piazza dei Signori, looms the spectacular 82-metre Torre di Piazza clock tower, which dates from the 12th century; next to it is the imposing Basilica Palladiana. And further south in the labyrinth of streets is the Casa Pigafetta (contrà Pigafetta 9). Dating from 1444, this exotic townhouse was the birthplace of Antonio Pigafetta, one of only 21 survivors of Magellan's epoch-making circumnavigation of the globe in the early 16th century.

The church perched on the hilltops to the south, affording fantastic views over Vicenza, is the charming Santuario di Monte Berico. The Virgin is said to have appeared here twice, in 1426 and 1428, making it popular with pilgrims. An attractive 18th-century loggia built by Francesco Muttoni leads up viale X Giugno to the church, itself largely rebuilt in the 18th century. (Take bus 6 from outside the station, Monday to Saturdays, though it's infrequent. On Sundays, bus 18 runs every 25 minutes from Viale Roma.) Further east stand Villa Valmarana ai Nani and Palladio's revolutionary Villa Rotonda.

Admission to the Teatro Olimpico and Museo Civico is by *biglietto unico* only. Valid for three days, the pass also allows access to the Museo Naturalistico Archeologico and Museo del Risorgimento e della Resistenza. It can only be purchased at the Teatro Olimpico (€8, €5 reductions, €12 family, no credit cards).

"Palladio's alternative to scaffolding, composed of Serlian windows, neatly encases the original Gothic Palazzo della Ragione."

Basilica Palladiana (Palazzo della Ragione)

Piazza dei Signori (0444 323 681). Admission during exhibitions only; prices & times vary.
'It is not possible to describe the impression made by Palladio's Basilica,' commented Goethe on Palladio's most famous piece of urban restyling. The original Palazzo della Regione, seat of city government, was built in the 1450s, but the loggia that surrounded and supported it collapsed in 1496. An elegant way of shoring up the building was needed, so in 1525 the city fathers began canvassing the leading architects of the day. Luckily for Palladio, who was

only 17 at the time, they dithered for 20 years, before finally accepting the audacious solution he proposed: an impressive double-tiered loggia. This neat alternative to scaffolding, composed of Serlian windows, encases the original Gothic palazzo in a unifying Renaissance shell. Ordinarily open only for exhibitions, the basilica has recently undergone major restoration work, but should reopen in 2008.

Criptoportico Romano

Piazza Duomo 6 (0444 321 716). Open (guided tours only) 10-11.30am Wed, Sat. Admission free.
This well-preserved subterranean passageway is all that remains of a large, first-century *domus* (Roman townhouse). Well ventilated in summer and possibly heated in winter, the space may have been used to store food and wine. Admission is by tour (in Italian) only; wait by the gate.

Duomo

Piazza Duomo 8 (0444 320 996). Open 10.30am-noon, 3.30-5.30pm Mon-Fri; 10.30am-noon Sat. Admission free.
The site on which the cathedral stands is believed to have been occupied by a Christian basilica since the fifth century, but its present form is the result of reconstruction carried out between 1267 and 1290. Although the Duomo suffered extensive damage during World War II, its pink marble façade and Palladian dome were painstakingly restored. The banal brick interior houses a stunning 1366 altarpiece by Lorenzo Veneziano.

Museo Civico

Palazzo Chiericati, piazza Matteotti 37/39 (0444 321 348). Open July, Aug 10am-6pm Tue-Sun. Sept-June 9am-5pm Tue-Sun. Admission by biglietto unico only (see above).
Palladio's magnificent, statue-crowned Palazzo Chiericati contains a fine collection of works by local painters, in particular Bartolomeo Montagna (1450-1523), plus works by the likes of Van Dyck, Tintoretto, Veronese and Tiepolo, and a Crucifixion by the Flemish master Hans Memling (it's the central part of a triptych; the side panels are in New York). The highlight is a 1489 Cima da Conegliano altarpiece.

Santa Corona

Contrà Santa Corona (0444 321 924). Open 4-6pm Mon; 8.30am-noon, 3-6pm Tue-Sun. Admission free.
This Gothic brick church was built between 1260 and 1270 to house a stray thorn from Christ's corona (crown). Its three unequally sized naves contain an Adoration of the Magi (1573) by Paolo Veronese in the third chapel on the right, plus a handful of well-preserved frescoes. In the crypt, the Valmarana Chapel is one of the few examples of Palladio's religious architecture. Other treasures include the enormous late 17th-century high altar by Francesco Antonio Corberelli, and the beautiful (and recently restored) Baptism of Christ by Giovanni Bellini.

Teatro Olimpico

Piazza Matteotti 11 (0444 222 800). Open 9am-5pm Tue-Sun (may close occasionally in spring and autumn for rehearsals). Admission by biglietto unico only.

Palladio's final masterpiece was the first permanent indoor theatre to be built in Europe since the fall of the Roman Empire. After his death, son Silla and star pupil Vincenzo Scamozzi took considerable liberties with the original blueprint: note the contrast between the flamboyant wood-and-stucco interior and the modest entrance. It's based on the Roman model; Scamozzi's seven trompe l'œil street scenes of the stage set represent the city of Thebes in Sophocles' *Oedipus Rex*, the first play performed here.

Productions were halted by Counter-Reformation censorship, and it wasn't until after World War II that the theatre once again realised its potential. A season of classical drama in September and October usually includes a staging of *Oedipus Rex* (in Italian), with concerts in May and June. Take bus 4 from viale Roma.

Villa Rotonda

Via della Rotonda 45 (0444 321 793). Open Gardens Mar-Nov 10am-noon, 3-6pm Tue-Sun. Interior mid Apr-early Nov 10am-noon, 3-6pm Wed. Admission Gardens €5. Interior €10. No credit cards.

One of the most famous buildings in Western architecture, La Rotonda – designed between 1567 and 1570, but not completed until 1606 – is not, strictly speaking, a villa: it was planned as a pleasure pavilion for retired cleric Paolo Almerico. Daringly, the design was topped off with a dome, a form previously associated with ancient temples or Renaissance churches. The grandiose exterior alone is worth a visit; the garden, according to Palladio, is 'one of the most agreeable and delightful sites that one could hope to find'. To get here, take a number 8 or 13 bus from viale Roma, or walk from town, via Villa Valmarana ai Nani.

"Teatro Olimpico was the first permanent indoor theatre to be built in Europe after the fall of the Roman Empire."

Villa Valmarana ai Nani

Via dei Nani 2-8 (0444 321 803/ www.villavalmarana.com). Open Mid Mar-mid Nov 10am-noon, 3-6pm Tue-Sun. Mid Nov-mid Mar 10am-noon, 2.30-4.30pm Sat, Sun. Admission €6. No credit cards.

This delightful villa was designed by Antonio Muttoni in 1688, and still belongs to the Valmarana family. It's the interior that is the highlight, thanks to the series of frescoes painted in 1757 by Giambattista Tiepolo and his son Giandomenico. The statues of dwarves (nani) lining the exterior walls were added in 1785 by Elena Garzadori, who redesigned the garden; the story goes that the Valmarana family built the statues in order to give their own dwarf daughter some company. To walk from the centre, which takes about 30 minutes, climb the 192 steps from Palladio's Arco delle Scalette, then veer left and keep going along via dei Nani. A free map is available from local tourist offices (see below). To get here take bus 8 from viale Roma.

Factfile

When to go

Vicenza can be stiflingly hot and humid in the summer, and winters are bone-chillingly cold and damp. May, June and September are pleasant months in which to visit, though hotels are likely to be more expensive (if not fully booked) for the week-long duration of the three annual VicenzaOro trade fairs in January, May and September (see www.vicenzaoro.org). The city also tends to shut down in the fortnight after Christmas and for three weeks at the end of August.

Getting there

Vicenza is easily reached from the airports at Milan (*see p143*), Venice (*see p219*) or Verona (*see p335*). Regular trains run to and from Venice (1hr), Verona (30mins) and Milan (2hrs); the station is ten minutes' walk from the historic centre of Vicenza. In addition, FTV (0444 223 111, www.ftv.vi.it) runs a bus service between Padua and Vicenza, stopping near the railway station.

Getting around

Vicenza's buses are operated by AIM (0444 394 909, www.aimvicenza.it) and stop at viale Roma or the train station. A ticket valid for any number of trips in the space of 90 minutes costs €1.05 from a *tabaccaria*, or €2 from the driver.

Radiotaxi Vicenza (0444 920 600, www.taxi vicenza.com) operates metered cabs; bikes can be rented from Pronto Bici (11 Contrà Pedemuro San Biagio, 0444 526 336).

Tourist information

Piazza Matteotti 12 (0444 320 854/ www.vicenzae.org). Open 9am-1pm, 2-6pm daily.
Piazza dei Signori 8 (0444 544 122/ www.vicenzae.org). Open 10am-2pm, 2.30-6.30pm daily.

Internet

Piazza dei Signori 6 (0444 540 430/ www.vicenza.com). Open 10am-1.30pm, 4-7.30pm Mon-Sat.

Lakes & Mountains

Top: Abruzzo national park. Middle & bottom: L'Aquila.

Abruzzo

For centuries Abruzzo has been one of Italy's most isolated regions – and it shows. Despite being an hour or two's drive from Rome, the region couldn't be more different. The feverish pace of the capital slows to a countryside canter, and the enclosed streets gradually yield to illimitable open spaces. A third of Abruzzo is national nature reserve. The soul-soothing agglomeration of rugged mountains, sweeping plains and silent valleys is peppered with beautifully preserved medieval towns and Renaissance villages that help evoke the timeless quality the region is renowned for.

Top: Sextantio Albergo Diffuso (4). Bottom: B&B Santa Lucia (3).

Paradiso

Pescasséroli *Via Fonte Fracassi 4 (0863 910 422/ www.albergo-paradiso.it). €.*
There isn't an abundance of memorable accommodation options in Pescasséroli, but Paradiso is more welcoming than most. Run by Scottish-Italian couple Geraldine and Marco, it offers simple, clean rooms, wonderfully rural surroundings and great home cooking in the associated restaurant. There's also a great outdoor terrace for summer, a dedicated bar and a cosy 'taverna' with an open fireplace. You can reach a host of trails directly from the hotel, and there are family-friendly rooms for those with children.

Rifugio Della Rocca

Calascio, 30km E of L'Aquila *Località Rocca Calascio (338 805 9430 mobile/340 469 6928 mobile/www.rifugiodellarocca.it). €-€€.*
Created in the same conservationist spirit as Sextantio (though slightly less ambitious), Rocca's series of rooms, apartments and 16-bed dorm are hidden away in the abandoned village of Rocca Calascio. Restored with new and recovered materials, each house has its own entrance, bathroom facilities and heating. The interiors lean towards the traditional, with stone walls, fireplaces and wooden furniture, though the bathrooms are resolutely modern. Above the village are panoramic views, the famous Rocca fort (one of the highest in Europe) and the arresting Santa Maria della Pietà church. The surrounding area provides plenty of fantastic outdoor opportunities.

Sextantio Albergo Diffuso

Santo Stefano Di Sessanio, 25km E of L'Aquila *Via Boragno (0862 899 112/0854 972 324/ www.sextantio.it). €€€.*
Not so much a hotel as an admirably ambitious, sensitively-restored cultural village, Sextantio occupies a labyrinthine network of medieval rooms (32 in total) ensconced within the stunning ancient village of Santo Stefano Di Sessanio. The owners have been careful to maintain original medieval features where possible – cave-like interiors, heavy wooden doors, ancient fireplaces – enhancing them with designer bathrooms, heated floors and remote controlled lighting. There are also workshops, a restaurant serving local dishes made from ingredients grown in surrounding fields, exhibition spaces and a dedicated tearoom, all of them beautifully designed and realised.

Villa Dragonetti

Paganica, 8km E of L'Aquila *Via Oberdan 4 (0862 680 222/www.villadragonetti.it). €€€.*
Villa Dragonetti was built in the 16th century as a private summer residence. A couple of hundred years ago it was re-decorated by French artists, whose opulent, dramatic frescoes (which include a wide range of animals) still cover the villa from top to bottom, lending the place a luxurious time-warp feel. Surrounded by a 4,000sq m park and with only ten rooms, it's a quiet space, perfect for relaxation. The rooms are resolutely romantic with antique furnishings and quality fabrics (plus frescoes on the ceilings). Service is discreet, breakfast is bountiful and there's an outdoor pool plus a great restaurant with a fabulous domed ceiling.

Eat

One of the highlights of a trip to Abruzzo is the food. There is a wealth of both local farms producing tasty, organic produce and of restaurants serving it up. Local pastas such as *maccheroni alla chitarra* – made using a wooden frame with wires that resembles a guitar, called a *chitarra* – are served with delicious sauces, many of them featuring lamb and mutton. Vegetarians are well catered for, since the region is known for its wide variety of fresh vegetables and pulses: saffron, lentils, chickpeas and aubergine are local specialities, and feature heavily on most restaurant menus.

As for wines, the robust, the velvety Montepulciano d'Abruzzo comes in many great varieties. Cerasuolo, a light, complex rosé (also made from the Montepulciano grape) is also highly recommended, as is Trebbiano d'Abruzzo, the region's crisp white. The only nightlife to be found is in L'Aquila; try spots like Caffè Cavour, Caffè Eden, or the popular Evoè.

"The wealth of local farms producing fresh, tasty, organic produce – and the amount of restaurants serving it up – is simply staggering."

L'Antico Borgo

L'Aquila *Piazza San Vito 1 (0862 22005). Open noon-2.30pm, 5-11pm Mon, Tue, Thur-Sun. €€. Traditional.*
Cosy L'Antico Borgo offers classic Abruzzese fare with especially tasty salads, meat and soup dishes, backed up by a long international wine list (over 800 varieties at the last count). Considering its location right beside one of the city's main sights (Fontane delle 99 Cannelle; some of the tables look directly onto it), it's well priced. Since the restaurant isn't in the town centre as such, it requires a bit of a stroll to get to – but then again, you do get an opportunity to walk your meal off on the way back to your hotel.

Clemente

Sulmona *Vico Quercia 5 (0864 52284/www.ristorante clemente.com). Open 12.30-3pm, 8-11pm Mon-Wed, Fri, Sat; 12.30-3.30pm Sun. €€. Traditional/trattoria.*
Tucked away down a side street and ensconced in an old palazzo off the corso Ovidio, Ristorante Clemente has been quietly serving up quintessential Abruzzese food for 50 years – no small achievement in a business where ten years

is a good run. In keeping with the traditional style of the place, there's no written menu – just a daily list of specials based on the fresh ingredients available. Items include rabbit, seafood and meat dishes, as well as risottos, pastas and pizzas. Portions are generous, service good, and the food undeniably hearty.

Il Drappo

L'Aquila *Via Borgo Rivera 21/23 (0862 62817/ www.ristoranteildrappo.it). Open 12.30-3pm, 7pm-midnight Tue-Sun. €€€. Modern Italian.*
With its elegant dining salons, outdoor terrace, dapper soundtrack and funky colour scheme (mellow yellows, cool beiges), Il Drappo is one of the more contemporary places to eat in L'Aquila. Though recently annexed to boutique hotel 99 Cannelle, its operation stretches back eight years, and head chef Christian Granata continues to serve up classic dishes (*maccheroni alla chitarra, zuppa di lenticchie*) with trendy twists.

"The set menu at Osteria Della Posta poses an interesting conundrum: more food than you could possibly eat – but of such high calibre that you have to try."

Gino

Sulmona *Piazza Plebiscito 12 (0864 52289). Open 12.30-3pm Mon-Sat. €€. Modern Italian/traditional.*
Located on the pretty Piazza Plebiscito, off corso Ovidio, Gino's is something of an institution in Sulmona. Only open for lunch, it has arched rooms and neutral decor that lend it a fairly formal air, though the friendly staff and buzzy lunchtime ambience cut through the stiffness. The menu offers the usual run of regional specialities, all impeccably prepared. The *faro* dishes are definitely worth trying. Right across the square is the restaurant's own deli, Soldo Di Cacio, where you can stock up on local produce.

Gran Caffè della L'Aquila

L'Aquila *Piazza del Duomo 14 (0862 413 365). Open 7am-11pm daily. €. Café/gelateria/wine bar.*
The perennially bustling Gran Caffè on the central piazza Duomo is a great place at which to stop for breakfast or lunch. For much of the day, the place is overflowing with espresso-fuelled energy, serving up cappuccino, brioche and tasty croissants for the early birds, and baguettes and foccaccias throughout the rest of the day. A small outside terrace offers extra seating, and come the evening, the coolly contemporary upstairs space comes into its own as locals drop in for an aperitivo.

Locanda tra le Braccia di Morfeo

Santo Stefano Di Sessanio, 25km E of L'Aquila *Via Nazario Sauro (0862 899 110/www.tralebraccia dimorfeo.net). Open 8am-10.30pm Mon, Tue, Thur-Sun. Closed Nov. €€. Traditional/trattoria.*
It looks like just a tiny bar when you pass through the beaded curtains. But head towards the back and you'll discover a cosy little restaurant with around ten tables. The reassuringly rustic interior has wicker baskets, locally produced artwork and old-fashioned cooking equipment hanging from the walls. There's no menu – a member of staff runs through the daily offerings at your table, usually a selection of local specialities like lamb fettucini and lentil soup.

Osteria della Posta

Poggio Picenze, 14km E of L'Aquila *Via Palombaia 1 (0862 80474/0862 808 027/ www.albergolaposta.net). Open 8-11pm Mon, Wed-Fri; 1-3pm Sat, Sun. €€. Traditional/trattoria.*
The set menu at Osteria della Posta poses an interesting conundrum: it features more dishes than you could possibly eat, but all of such high calibre that it's certainly worth a try. Part restaurant, part 'showroom', this former mill has been converted into four large dining rooms, decorated in simple greens, yellows and reds. It serves exclusively traditional dishes, made from some of the tastiest ingredients in the area, including handmade pastas, locally produced truffles and game, and to-die-for desserts. (Non-foodies need not fret – there's an à la carte menu too).

Osteria di Costanza e Robert

Scanno *Via Roma 15 (0864 74345/368 511 473 mobile/www.costanzaeroberto.it). Open Summer 12.30-2.30pm, 7.30-11pm daily. Winter 12.30-2.30pm, 7.30-11pm Wed-Sun. Closed mid Nov-Dec. €€. Traditional/modern Italian.*
This centrally located restaurant is one of several cute eateries in Scanno. The interior is small but fairly plush, and wears its endearing duck theme well. Service is breezy and pleasant, and there's a wider than usual selection of antipasti and other dishes (the saltimbocca is very good) plus wines from all over Europe. English and French are spoken.

Da Paolino

Pescocostanza, 20km S of Sulmona *Strada Vulpes 34 (0864 640 080/www.ristorantedapaolino.com). Open 10am-3pm, 7.30-11pm Tue-Sun. €€. Traditional.*
Another great family run restaurant, Da Paolino has been serving up its tasty recipes for almost 30 years. The interior has a huddled, rustic feel with wooden beams and tables and traditional tiled floors, and service is notably warm and welcoming. All the food is great, but the handmade pastas are well worth investigating, in particular the chestnut-flour tagliolini.

Refugio della Rocca

Calascio, 30km E of L'Aquila *Località Rocca Calascio (338 805 9430/340 469 6928 mobile/ www.roccacalascio.it. Open Summer noon-3pm, 6pm-midnight daily. Winter noon-3pm, 6pm-midnight Mon, Tue, Thur-Sun. €€. Traditional/trattoria.*

Top: L'Antico Borgo.
Bottom: Clemente.

Clockwise from top left: Sulmona; Gran Sasso; L'Aquila; Santo Stefano di Sessanio; Scanno; Door in piazza Duomo, Scanno.

There isn't an embarrassment of decent dining options in this area, so thank goodness for the Refugio della Rocca. The restaurant is housed in a traditional setting in the main building, where the chefs knock up tasty cheese platters and salami, home-made pastas such as *chitarra* and pappardelle, and very good wild boar and duck sauces. In winter, there's a downstairs space with a cosy fire – a perfect romantic opportunity to share the restaurant's memorable chocolate flan. Reservations are required.

"The city got off to a shaky start with outbreaks of plague, ecumenical disputes and earthquakes making for turbulent beginnings."

Vinalia

L'Aquila *Via Andrea Bafile 15 (0862 414 545/ www.enotecavinialia.it). Open 11am-3pm, 6pm-midnight Mon, Tue, Thur-Sun. Closed Aug. €€€. Modern Italian.* Vinalia, as the name suggests, used to be a wine vault, and its history stretches all the way back to 1510. Over the centuries it has not only maintained its reputation as a world class *enoteca* but recently evolved its repertoire to become one of the city's most sophisticated restaurants as well. Backed by a wine list that stretches to quadruple figures (and a round-the-world water list that hits double), chef William Zonfa serves up perfectly prepared dishes such as foie gras with pear and saffron crêpes, all drawing playfully on established local classics.

Explore

L'AQUILA & THE GRAN SASSO

Nestled in a pleasant valley and overlooked by the jagged peaks of the Gran Sasso and Velino-Sirente mountain ranges, L'Aquila is Abruzzo's attractive administrative centre.

The city was built from scratch in the 13th century by the Holy Roman Emperor Frederick II, who brought together 99 local villages to help form the city (each of the villages contributed a *palazzo* and a church to the new development). It got off to a shaky start: plague epidemics, ecumenical disputes and earthquakes made for turbulent beginnings; but the locals were made of stern stuff and by the 15th century it was minting its own coins, founding a university and even setting up its own printing presses.

L'Aquila declined following invasion by the Spanish in the 16th century. A catastrophic earthquake in 1703 provided further calamity, as did some French sackings in 1799, but the city bounced back to play a part in the movement for Italian autonomy in the 1800s. It became capital of the region in 1860.

Today L'Aquila is a modern, relaxed and cosmopolitan place, combining medieval flair and contemporary sass in equal measure. A sizeable student population keeps the streets upbeat, and the maze of Renaissance palazzi, baroque churches and elegant piazzas lends the town an abundance of nostalgic charm.

The centre is easily navigable on foot. The main square, Piazza del Duomo, features a daily market (Mon-Sat 7am-1pm) and several places at which to refuel with a cappuccino or latte. Nearby corso Vittorio Emanuele, the main drag, combines fashion boutiques with lively nightlife, and nearby via San Bernadino hosts the eponymous basilica.

South of Piazza del Duomo, a series of picturesque streets lined with old houses and palaces leads to the gorgeous Palazzo Centi and Porta Bazzano, close to which is the wonderful church of Santa Maria di Collemaggio. North lie the Abruzzo National Museum and the San Giuliano Monastery, and further west you'll find the Piazza San Vito and the famous Fontana delle 99 Cannelle.

L'Aquila makes a convenient base for the spectacular Parco Nazionale del Gran Sasso, which offers a plethora of hiking and biking trails. Those wishing to ascend the Corno Grande, the highest peak in the Apenines, should be aware that routes range from moderate to very difficult. Advice on the ascent can be obtained from the small tourist office at the area's main base, Albergo Campo Imperatore (July & August, 9am-1pm daily, 0862 606 829), and the tourist and CAI offices in L'Aquila (via Sassa 34, 0862 24342, www.cailaquila.it, 6-8pm Mon-Fri).

Some routes start from the Albergo Campo Imperatore, which can be reached by bus then cable car from L'Aquila. You can get part-way up by car (although only from spring to autumn). Take the SS17 from Fonte Cerreto and follow the signposts. A well-marked series of winding roads ensures an unforgettably scenic drive through the area.

Basilica di San Bernardino

Via San Bernadino (0862 22255). Open May-Sept 9.30-11.45am, 4-6.30pm Mon-Sat; 4-6.30pm Sun. Oct-Apr 9.30-11.45am, 4-5.30pm Mon-Sat; 4-5.30pm Sun. Admission free.
San Bernadino, originally from Siena, lived for a while in L'Aquila and founded a congregation here (St Bernardine's Friars). This basilica was begun in 1454 at the request of St John of Capestrano, a disciple of his, a few years after the

The Dolomites

Tucked away in the north-east corner of Italy, the Dolomites might well be the most spectacular mountains in the whole of the Alps. There are no namby pamby gentle slopes here. Instead, the pale, sedimentary rock erupts from valley floors in breathtakingly sheer columns, turning into weird and wonderful natural sculptures as millennia of wind and rain do their work. As the light fails and the sun sets, these most beautiful of mountains have a final spectacular trick: they turn a brilliant, blazing pink.

Clockwise from top left:
Val Gardena (4);
Horse-drawn sleigh.

Sellavation

Staggeringly beautiful they may be, but European mountains can seem interchangeable to the untrained eye – the jagged peaks of Val d'Isére largely indistinguishable from those of Verbier or Villars. There are a few exceptions, of course: the glacial ice cream scoop of Mont Blanc; the heart-stopping plummet of the Eiger's north face; and the fairy-tale shards of the Dolomites, so otherworldly when the setting sun lends them their characteristic pink hue, that the only thing missing is an Elven castle.

Nowhere is the forbidding fantasy of these mountains more evident than at the Sella-Gruppe, a cluster of looming faces so sublime that pining skiers may find themselves dreamily shaping its likeness in mashed potato during the summer months. The surrounding area is a mass of cultural contradictions, thanks to its ties with the Austro-Hungarian Empire, which handed the land over to Italy in 1919 but lingers on in the predominant German tongue – although many locals remain defiantly Ladin at heart, with a dialect and associated culinary culture all their own.

These days, the Dolomiti Superski pass (from €34 per day, €167 for six days; www.dolomiti superski.com) opens up a staggering 1,220 kilometres of pistes accessed by 450 lifts – not the best organised ski circus on earth, but one that dwarfs better known systems like the Trois Vallées in France. Yet many visitors while away their weeks orbiting a single circuit at the base of the Sella-Gruppe – a circular traverse of wide, shallow snowfields that locals were using to visit neighbouring villages long before ski culture descended on the Dolomites.

The Sella Ronda, as this circuit is known, is hardly a white knuckle ride in terms of terrain – its gently undulating slopes are periodically flat enough to make the route pointless for snowboarders averse to hiking – but it continues to enchant skiers of all ages, thanks to its potential for long, easy cruises in the staggering shadow of the Sella-Gruppe. The 40-kilometre round trip takes between three and four hours (two spent on lifts, one to two on the slopes, depending on ability), but that takes no account of queuing at the lifts – less busy since the installation of high-speed chairs, but still prone to bottlenecks in peak season.

As a result, it's advisable to start the circuit – which goes clockwise and anticlockwise (follow orange signs for the former, green for the latter) – no later than 10am, and much earlier if you intend to draw out pit stops at the personable mountain refuges along the way. These include the Pralongia at Alta Badia (0471 836 072, www.pralogia.it), the Plan Boè in Arabba (0436 79339) and the Panorama atop the gondola at Dantercepies (0471 795 372) – the latter turning out heavy Ladin lunches to slow down even the swiftest of skiers. Just be sure you don't miss the last lifts (around 4pm), or you'll incur a hefty taxi fare back to your resort.

Rifugio Valparola

Livinallongo di Col di Lana, 25km W of Cortina d'Ampezzo *Passo Valparola (04 3686 6556). €€.*

At a road pass 2,168m above sea level and close to Passo Falzarego, this marvellously panoramic hotel features cosy rooms, some with en suite bathrooms and all with thick duvets. Mezza pensione (half board) is a good deal, and hearty fare is served. A summer bus stops outside the door.

Rosa Alpina

San Cassiano in Badia, 15km W of Cortina d'Ampezzo *Strada Micura de Rü 20 (0471 849 500/ www.rosalpina.it). €€€.*

Generations of the Pizzinini family (since 1780) have brought this local hotel to its impressive contemporary standard, recently appreciated by the likes of George Clooney. There are excellent spa facilities with massages galore, an indoor swimming pool, roaring wood fires and traditional pine furniture, and the beds have snug down duvets. St Hubertus (two Michelin stars) is one of three restaurants serving trout, fondue and regional fare.

Youth Hostel Bolzano

Bolzano *Via Renon 23 (04 7130 0865/ www.ostello.bz). €.*

The only budget accommodation in Bolzano is provided by this modern youth hostel minutes from the railway station. It offers small but spick and span rooms, all with en suites, and no age limit; families are welcome. Cheap meals too.

Zirmerhof

Redagno, 13km S of Bolzano *Redagno di Sopra 59 (04 7188 7215/www.zirmerhof.com). €€€.*

On the edge of the village of Redagno south of Bolzano, this is an inspiring place to stay – a favourite with writers – as well as handy for the Bletterbach canyon. Wonderful views across the Adige valley take in the glaciated Ortler massif. Comfort features include hay baths, sauna and a heated swimming pool.

Eat

Bar Suisse/Cantina del Suisse

Madonna di Campiglio, Brenta Dolomites *Piazza Righ (Bar 0465 441023/Cantina del Suisse 0465 442 632/www.cantinadelsuisse.com). Open Bar Suisse Dec-Easter, July-mid Sept 8am-1am daily. Cantina del Suisse Dec-Easter, July-mid Sept 4pm-2am daily. Bar Suisse €; Cantina del Suisse €€. Traditional Alpine (Bar Suisse)/Club (Cantina del Suisse).*

The 19th-century style hunting lodge that once belonged to the Austrian Emperor Franz Joseph has been tastefully converted into an atmospheric café serving mouthwatering chocolate pastries with lashings of cream. Close by is sister establishment, Cantina del Suisse, which has drinks, live music and tasty snacks. Set in the town's main square, it remains lively until the early hours of the morning.

Castel Roncolo Osteria

Bolzano *Via San Antonio 1 (04 7132 4073). Open 10am-7pm Tue-Sun. €. Traditional Italian.*

Enjoy a glass of local wine and delicious tavern lunch in a wonderful setting, the shady courtyard of Castel Roncolo. Schlutzkrapfen, luscious fresh pasta stuffed with spinach and ricotta, is a recommended first course, followed by roast meat – pork or lamb. For dessert, visitors in autumn are treated to traditional Krapfen, filled with chestnut purée and poppy seeds. It's best to reserve.

"There are massages galore, an indoor swimming pool and roaring wood fires, and the beds have snug down duvets."

Finsterwirt

Bressanone, 15km north of Val Gardena *Domgasse 3 (04 7283 5343/www.finsterwirt.com). Open Künstlerstübele noon-2.15pm, 7-9.15pm Tue-Sat; noon-2.15pm Sun. Garden 10am-11pm Tue-Sun. €€€. Traditional Tyrolean.*

A tavern back in the 1700s, Finsterwirt prides itself on its traditional Tyrolean cuisine that comes with an emphasis on local ingredients and a touch of the Mediterranean. Reservations are essential for the elegant timber-panelled Künstlerstübele, but simple al fresco meals are served all day in the shady garden.

Ristorante Tivoli

Cortina d'Ampezzo, Cortina Valley *Via Lacedel 34 (0436 866400/www.ristorantetivoli.it). Open Dec-Easter, June-Sept 12.30-2pm, 7.30-10pm Tue-Sun. €€€€. Modern Italian.*

With a fine terrace overlooking the spectacular Cortina basin, the elegant Michelin-starred Tivoli prides itself on seasonal fare served with an innovative touch. You may be offered *lasagnette con finferli* (ribbon pasta with local mushrooms) and variations on foie gras with cherry compote. Book ahead.

La Stube di Franz Joseph

Madonna di Campiglio, Brenta Dolomites *Viale Dolomiti di Brenta 1 (0465 440875). Open mid Nov-mid April, mid June-mid Sept 10am-2am daily. €. Pub.*

Great music (live on special occasions such as New Year's Eve) and a good choice of beer make for a good place to unwind in after a hard day's skiing. It also calls itself a *paninoteca*, meaning that the keen young staff will concoct a sandwich for you on the spot or make up a *tagliere*, the Italian equivalent of a ploughman's lunch.

El Toulà

Cortina d'Ampezzo, Cortina Valley *Località Ronco 123 (0436 3339/www.toula.it/cortina). Open late July-early Sept, 8 Dec-Easter 12.15-2.30pm, 8-10.30pm Tue-Sun. €€€€. Traditional Italian.*
A short way out of town, this beautifully converted barn (*toulà* means 'barn' in the local dialect) has superb views of the surrounding Dolomites. The luscious fresh pasta dishes include saccottini con speck e erbette, little parcels stuffed with smoked ham and greens. Best to book ahead.

Wirtshaus Vögele

Bolzano *Goethestrasse 3 (04 7197 3938/ www.voegele.it). Open 11.30am-2.30pm, 6-11pm Mon-Sat. €€€. Traditional Tyrolean.*
Guests at this sophisticated, centrally located restaurant have a vast choice of both food and decorated 'Stube' dining rooms. The cuisine is traditional Tyrolean, and the enthusiastic young owners change the menu daily to include seasonal products. Chances are you'll be able to feast on *canederli*, a sort of dumpling made with bread and egg and flavoured with speck (smoked pork), liver or cheeses. Meat main courses such as venison or beef come with cranberry sauce.

Explore

Note: the walking routes described are samples of what you can find in the vicinity; but before setting out, get hold of an up-to-date map, as well as the equipment necessary for a mountain hike: boots, drinking water, sun protection, wet weather gear and common sense. The *rifugio* huts found en route generally open from June to late September and provide dormitory-style accommodation as well as great meals with wonderful views.

BOLZANO

Walking around Bolzano, you could be forgiven for thinking you'd inadvertently crossed the border into Austria. The architecture, café signs and beer are overwhelmingly Germanic and even the cyclists here are law abiding. At the confluence of three strategic valleys linking northern Europe to Mediterranean lands, this laid-back regional capital, along with the whole of the South Tyrol region, has only been part of Italy since the end of World War One and the demise of Austria's Habsburg Empire. These days, street signs are bilingual. The same goes for many of the top grade wines grown on densely packed terraces over the steep, sun-blessed mountains: Pinot Nero, for instance, is also known as Blauburgunder.

Cafés and beer gardens abound, as do outdoor gear suppliers with high tech ski equipment. Bolzano is an excellent launching pad for exploring the Dolomites, but there are some sights at lower altitude.

Archaeological Museum

Via Museo (04 7132 0100/www.iceman.it). Open 10am-6pm Tue-Sun. Admission €8, plus €2 for recommended audioguide in English.
If you only have a few hours in Bolzano, spend them here. This custom-built museum is home to Ötzi, aka the Iceman, a mummified Copper Age hunter discovered in a glacier pocket in upper Val Senales in 1991. It was a remarkable find, as he came complete with his clothing consisting of a cape, bear fur cap and footwear, as well as arrows and a quiver of bark. Displays and explanations are excellent and you actually get to look Ötzi right in the eye. A prehistoric crime mystery has come to light, as recent investigations suggest he died from a spear wound.

Castel Roncolo

Lungotalvera *Via San Antonio 1 (04 7132 9808/ www.comune.bolzano.it/roncolo). Open 10am-6pm Tue-Sun. Admission €8.*
Take a riverside stroll or bus no.12 to this delightful manor house-cum-castle perched on a dramatic outcrop over the Talvera River on the city's northern edge. Well-preserved medieval frescoes in the main hall tell the story of Tristan and Isolde, as well as King Arthur, and an atmospheric tavern does lunch.

Piazza Walther

The main square comes alive in December, when it is transformed by the popular Christmas craft market. Here, you can admire the statue of 12th-century poet Walther von der Vogelweide, then wander over to the southern edge which is taken up by the solemn Gothic cathedral, the work of 15th-century Swabian craftsmen. Beyond is Piazza Domenicani, where one of South Tyrol's oldest churches boasts a richly frescoed chapel.

Via dei Portici

This especially attractive, narrow pedestrian shopping street lined with colourful arcaded Gothic buildings runs through the city's heart. The southern side was originally for German merchants, and the north for Italians. From the jutting upper floor windows known as Erker, both could monitor business in their street-level stores. Modern-day shopping possibilities cover outdoor gear and Tyrolean souvenirs such as traditional Dirndl frocks or dark green woolen Loden clothing.

SURROUNDS

RENON

Half the attraction of Renon is the fun of getting there. A vertiginous cable car from Bolzano's railway station skims over terraced vineyards and whisks you up 950 metres in 12 minutes to a medium altitude plateau hardly visible from the town. Far from the oppressive summer heat below, relaxation reigns. Gentle walks lead through pine woods and meadows, where the native Haflinger horses graze and traditional farms serve rustic al fresco meals for walkers.

Clockwise from top left:
Hotel Turm (3);
Meublé Montana (2).

Top to bottom:
Finsterwirt; view from the
restaurant at Hotel Turm.

In addition, a narrow gauge train trundles along between the villages. Whichever way you look are amazing views of the Dolomites, especially memorable at sunset when they turn pink, scarlet and purple.

Renon was long a haven to the region's wealthy classes and intellectuals in search of cool conditions to escape the steaming hot summers, with visitors like Freud and Mahler. The village of Maria Assunta is especially memorable, with aristocratic 17th-century houses and artistic sundials. Not to be missed are the sets of curious *Erdpyramiden* or earth pyramids, eroded columns of moraine deposits left by long-gone glaciers and topped with a protective rock slab. One easily accessible cluster is a 15-minute stroll out of Collalbo. Their bizarre shapes have given rise to scores of legends, for example that they are petrified witches, punished for their immoral Sabbath activities. (Bolzano itself was once under a kilometre-thick glacier when the Adige valley channelled ice southwards, spilling out onto the Po plain near Verona.)

Renon walk

3.5hrs. Recommended map: Tabacco no.034 scale 1:25,000.

Start out from Tre Vie and the Pemmern guesthouse (1,538m), a short bus trip from Collalbo. A chair lift will transport you to 2,071m but so does track no.1, which climbs north through conifer wood and pastureland. After Unterhornhaus (2,042m) it's an uphill slog to Rifugio Corno Renon (2,260m), lookout par excellence for its spectacular 360° views of the Alps, glaciated peaks and all. Once you've got your breath back and enjoyed some refreshment, turn south-west and descend on track no.2.

BLETTERBACH

Some 20km south of Bolzano a vast gash in the earth separates the villages of Aldino and Redagno. In this amazing canyon, 12 kilometres long and 400 metres deep, the largest in South Tyrol, over 15,000 years of erosion have laid bare the fossil-rich layers that underlie the Dolomite formations. The lowest rocks were formed 280 million years ago during the Permian and Triassic eras. Note that the canyon is closed during bad weather due to the danger of rockfalls.

Walking the Bletterbach

4hrs. Recommended map: Tabacco no.029 scale 1:25,000.

A short way north of the village of Aldino is the Bletterbach Visitors' Centre, well worth a visit. Before setting out on the following geological route, ask for the English translation of the informative numbered signboards that you'll come across along the way.

Take the signed path that leads down steps into the narrow Taubenleck section of the canyon, beneath tall, dark red porphyry walls. You proceed along the stream bed towards the deepest, most dramatic section of clearly layered coloured rocks, where fossilised reptiles and sea creatures such as squid have been discovered. Then, via dizzy but well-anchored ladders past a volcanic chimney, you climb to the top of a waterfall. Continue to the upper valley for views to the pale Corno Bianco peak that crowns the Bletterbach. Either return the way you came, or take the track back to the Visitors' Centre.

VAL GARDENA

Val Gardena is a superb Dolomite valley that branches east off the Adige valley, making it easy to access. Set amidst breathtaking mountains and a string of national parks, it is justifiably a prime destination, with a string of interesting villages along the valley, including Ortisei, Santa Cristina and Selva di Val Gardena, all of which retain a strong sense of tradition. Some 90 per cent of the locals use the ancient Ladin language, showy dress costumes come out for festivals, and each village even has its own brass band. Moreover, the age-old practice of artistic woodcarving is very much alive. Deep red timber from the Arolla pine features in attractive toys as well as crucifixes.

"To the west, the massive Seceda point rears its eroded head, alongside the weirdly wonderful Odle needles and spires."

SURROUNDS

PASSO GARDENA

Heading east uphill over the settlements, the main road divides into equally tortuous branches, each served by buses. The first climbs to Passo Gardena, flanking the high altitude Puez-Odle mountain group and nature park where rock spires alternate with gently undulating plateaux. Opposite is one of the most amazing Dolomite groups, the Sella, a solid rock fortress with desert-like landscapes. A renowned via ferrata (aided climbing route) clambers up this northern flank, and a cable car runs up to 2,950 metres on Sass Pordoi on its southern flanks, departing from Passo Pordoi (accessible via Passo Sella).

The Dolomites.

admired further on from Misurina and its pretty lake. This is the gateway to the well-known Tre Cime di Lavaredo and the Parco Naturale Dolomiti di Sesto, and is well served by buses.

Walking around the Tre Cime

4hrs. Recommended map: Tabacco no.010 scale1:25,000.

This spectacular loop circumnavigates one of the most beautiful landmarks in the Dolomites, the Tre Cime di Lavaredo (or Drei Zinnen in German). The threesome of sheer rock walls rise isolated from a vast scree basin, and were appropriately likened to 'Egyptian colossi' by 19th-century travellers.

BRENTA DOLOMITES

Separated from the main Dolomites block, the Brenta group is located on the western side of the main Bolzano-Verona valley, due north of Lake Garda. This superb range of soaring, magical rock spires is the summer playground of climbers and walkers. The area is a protected nature park, and even has some resident brown bears. These creatures are now breeding successfully, but are rarely seen, as they are extremely timid. However, visitors can expect to see plenty of other wildlife such as chamois and birds of prey.

Madonna di Campiglio is the main town and transport hub, which winter transforms into a very chic resort frequented by VIPs and film stars. You can ski right into town in style, and there are pistes for all levels. On the quieter south-eastern side of the range is lovely Molveno, set on the shore of a lake. When not ruffled by windsurfers, fishing rods and sailing boats, its waters reflect the surrounding peaks. Molveno is the gateway to the magnificent central Brenta group, with marked pathways. Opposite rises La Paganella, a massive elongated mountain with excellent skiing. On the Brenta's northern edge lies Lago di Tovel, a pretty lake ringed in conifers.

Factfile

When to go

For walking and climbing, summer is the time. If you plan to use the high altitude refuges, you'll need to come between late June and late September, their opening period. Wildflower lovers should plan for late June to July for the best blooms. If the weather holds, the Dolomites are divine well into October, when the larch and beech trees turn golden and Italy is still on daylight saving time. Ski enthusiasts usually have to wait until mid December for lifts to open and decent snow conditions, which usually last until March or April. However, artificial snow is guaranteed on the main pistes. Visitors during in-between periods will have the mountains to themselves, and may well enjoy slashed hotel rates, especially in the South Tyrol.

Snow buffs will appreciate details of the Dolomiti Superski network, with information on ski lifts and passes. Check the website at www.dolomitisuperski.com.

Getting there

Brescia, Verona, Treviso and Venice are the nearest airports. All have connecting buses to railway stations for ongoing trains and coaches. Bolzano itself also has a small airport (www.abd-airport.it) with domestic traffic and some international flights. Useful railway stations are Calalzo (for reaching Cortina), or Bolzano on the busy Verona-Innsbruck line (892 021/ www.trenitalia.com).

Getting around

The Dolomites boast an excellent local transport network, with very reasonably priced bus services provided by SAD (www.sad.it) and Dolomitibus (www.dolomitibus.it). During peak tourist periods (midsummer and the skiing season), the network is extended.

Madonna di Campiglio and Molveno are easily reached by coach from Trento (www.ttspa.it); shuttle buses also link Madonna di Campiglio with many north-eastern Italian airports.

Tourist information

All the towns have good tourist information facilities, starting with informative web sites that provide online accommodation booking.

Bolzano's helpful information office is in centrally located on piazza Walther 8 (04 7130 7000, www.bolzano-bozen.it).
Castel Presule (04 7160 1062, www.schloss-proesels.it).
Cortina d'Ampezzo (04 363 231, www.dolomiti.org).
Fiè allo Sciliar (04 7172 5047, www.fie-allo-sciliar.com).
Madonna di Campiglio (0465 447 501, www.campiglio.net).
Misurina (04 353 9016, www.infodolomiti.it).
Molveno (0461 586924, www.molveno.it).
Ortisei, Strada Rezia (04 7177 7600, www.valgardena.it).
Renon (04 7135 6100, www.renon.com).

Clockwise from top: Isola di San Giulio; Orta San Giulio; Lago di Como; Isola Bella (2).

The Lakes

A short drive north of Milan lies a region packed with pretty villages and breathtaking scenery. The highlights are undoubtedly the exceptionally lovely lakes – Maggiore, Como and Orta – which are Lombardy's most visited attractions. Shelley said that Lago di Como 'exceeds anything I ever beheld in beauty', and these world-famous beauty spots show Italy at its most romantic.

Lago Maggiore is picturesque from just about any angle. The area around it was inhabited in the Bronze and Iron Ages, and by the Middle Ages much of it was under the control of the powerful Visconti family and then the Borromeos. It is to them that the lake owes some of its most celebrated landmarks, including the island gardens and fortresses. During the 18th and 19th centuries the lake's mild climate and enchanting position attracted Italian nobility, the industrial bourgeoisie and wealthy foreigners, many of whom built themselves sumptuous lakefront villas and gardens.

A short distance to the west is Lago d'Orta. If you're determined to visit one of Lombardy's lakes but can't face the crowds, Orta is the one for you. Located in Piedmont, this smallish stretch of water is the only northern lake you can take in at a single glance. People come here for the romance of the medieval town of Orta San Giulio and to steep themselves in the area's natural beauties.

And then there's Lago di Como, which has been attracting the rich and famous for at least a couple of millennia. During the Middle Ages, it became famous for its stone masonry and later as a centre for silk weaving.

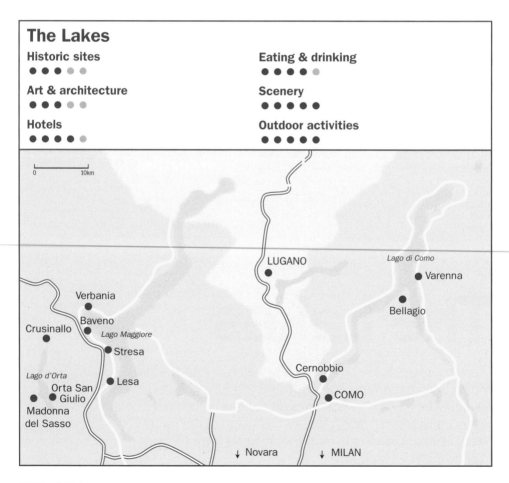

The Lakes

Historic sites
● ● ● ● ○

Art & architecture
● ● ● ● ○

Hotels
● ● ● ● ○

Eating & drinking
● ● ● ● ○

Scenery
● ● ● ● ●

Outdoor activities
● ● ● ● ●

0   10km

LUGANO

Lago di Como

Varenna

Verbania

Bellagio

Baveno

Crusinallo

Lago Maggiore

Stresa

Lago d'Orta

Cernobbio

Orta San Giulio

Lesa

COMO

Madonna del Sasso

↓ Novara   ↓ MILAN

Stay

Barchetta Excelsior

Como *Piazza Cavour 1 (031 3221/www.hotel barchetta.it). €€€.*
Although scruffy in patches, this hotel can't be faulted for its proximity to water, being located right on the edge of Lago di Como. The 84 rooms, including four suites, are decorated in a rather dated, chintzy style, and not all have views of the lake; still, there's TV and internet connection in every room and thoughtful touches like hypoallergenic pillows. The same management runs the smart Palace Hotel (031 23391, www.palacehotel.it) a stone's throw away; staff are friendly and efficient.

Grand Hotel des Iles Borromées

Stresa *Corso Umberto I 67 (0323 938 938/ www.borromees.it). Closed mid Dec-mid Jan. €€€€.*
Among Stresa's most sumptuous five-star belle époque hotels is the palatial Grand Hotel des Iles Borromées, built in 1861 and sensitively renovated 130 years later. Stay here and you'll be sleeping under the roof that once sheltered Gabriele D'Annunzio, Ernest Hemingway, John Steinbeck, George Bernard Shaw and Clark Gable. There are two outdoor heated pools, tennis courts and spa.

Grand Hotel Villa Serbelloni

Bellagio *Via Roma 1 (031 950 216/www.villa serbelloni.com). Closed Nov-Mar. €€€€.*
For a real treat, follow in the footsteps of Winston Churchill and John F Kennedy, and splash out on a room at the Grand Hotel Villa Serbelloni. Facilities at this five-star deluxe grande dame include indoor and outdoor pools, sauna, Turkish bath and day spa. The enormous grounds are a lovely place to explore, and the views of Lago di Como are, needless to say, stunning. Even if you're not a guest here, you can book a table at the Terrazza Serbelloni restaurant and sample the Michelin-starred molecular cuisine of chef Ettore Bocchia.

Hotel Panoramico Ristorante

Madonna del Sasso *Via Frua 31 (0322 981 312/ www.hotelpanoramico.it). Closed mid Jan-Mar. €-€€.*
The three-star Panoramico is a little short on character, and the rooms are nothing to sing about; still, they're comfortable enough, and there's a restaurant (average €28) with two outdoor terraces that have fine views of Lago d'Orta.

Hotel San Rocco

Orta San Giulio *Via Gippini 11 (0322 911 977/ www.hotelsanrocco.it). €€€.*
The historic four-star Hotel San Rocco is a former monastery with a wonderful location right on the shore of Lago d'Orta. It's a tastefully decorated, airy place: common areas have antiques, and its 74 rooms have clean and welcoming modern furnishings and colour schemes. The lovely colonnaded central courtyard is a strong reminder of the building's monastic past, and a full suit of armour welcomes guests at the entrance; there are ten deluxe rooms and a presidential suite in the self-contained baroque Villa Gippini next door.

Leon d'Oro

Orta San Giulio *Piazza Motta 43 (0322 911 991/ www.albergoleondoro.it). Closed Jan. €€.*
The stone-roofed Leon d'Oro has a distinctly Alpine look from the outside; the interior is rather more twee (there's a lot of pink), though it's looking spruce after a recent renovation. Rooms in the higher categories have wooden beams and wrought iron features; all have internet access and TVs. There's dining on an outdoor terrace, and the hotel's location on the waterfront, but still in the heart of Orta San Giulio, couldn't be more convenient.

Lido Palace Hotel Baveno

Baveno *SS Sempione 30 (0323 924 444/ www.lidopalace.com). Closed Oct-Mar. €€€.*
This luxurious hotel is housed in a 19th-century villa and its extensions, with a view over the Isole Borromeo. Rooms are done out with tasteful and sumptuous fabrics, brass lamps and gilt-framed mirrors (with internet access as standard), and suites are equipped with jacuzzis. There's an open-air swimming pool, gym, billiards room and tennis court, a bar (complete with a fine old 'eagle top' espresso machine), and a restaurant with water views. The hotel is distinctly anglophile, too: a telegram from Churchill is proudly on display, and a statue of Queen Victoria stands outside.

> ## "Stay here and you'll be sleeping under the roof that once sheltered Ernest Hemingway and John Steinbeck."

Villa Crespi

Orta San Giulio *Via G Fava 18 (0322 911 902/ www.villacrespi.it). Closed early Jan-Feb. €€€.*
This really is something out of the ordinary. The Villa Crespi is an over-the-top Moorish villa that was built in the 19th century by a wealthy Italian cotton trader. There are just six double rooms and eight suites, with such fairy-tale features as four-poster beds, parquet floors, painted ceilings, chandeliers and jacuzzis. The villa's restaurant – under young Neapolitan chef Antonino Cannavacciuolo – has two Michelin stars and is ranked as one of Italy's best.

Villa d'Este

Cernobbio *Via Regina 40 (031 3481/www.villadeste.it). Closed mid Nov-Feb. €€€€.*
For unbeatable luxury, and if you're happy to dress up for dinner, Villa d'Este is the place. It's an enormous complex: the main building, put up in the 16th century, has over 120 rooms, and that's not counting the nearby 27-room Villa Regina and the two gorgeous 19th-century private villas, Cima and Malakoff. The hotel has its own marina, there are seven restaurants and bars, squash court, swimming pool, indoor golf range and sauna.

Top: Hotel San Rocco (3).
Bottom: Villa Crespi (2).

Eat

With so much water at hand, it's no surprise that restaurants around the Italian lakes are so strong on freshwater fish. That said, meats are popular, especially poultry (duck in particular). Risotto and polenta are eaten more often than pasta, and the preference for butter and cream in cooking has only recently made way for olive oil. Wine is less of a strong point, and much of what you'll find on wine lists here comes from neighbouring Veneto, Emilia-Romagna and Piedmont, although the *metodo classico* sparkling wines of Franciacorta are well worth looking out for. Finally, no visitor should leave without sampling some of the local cheeses: gorgonzola comes from here, and other worthy cheeses include taleggio, mild quartirolo lombardo and tangy provolone valpadano.

Antico Maniero

Lesa *Via Alla Campagna 1 (0322 7411/www.antico maniero.com). Open 8-11pm daily (only with reservation). Closed Jan. €€€.*
The elegant Antico Maniero is housed in a crenellated villa – it looks rather like a storybook castle – just outside Lesa. The lace tablecloths, silverware, antique furniture, old paintings galore and stone fireplaces give the place a romantic, old-worldly feel; the seasonal menu includes the likes of delicate crab ravoli and duck carpaccio served with a drizzle of oil and fragrant flakes of parmesan.

Breeze Inn Ristorante

Como *Via Natta 29 (031 242 320/www.breeze-inn.com). Open noon-2.30pm, 7.30-11pm Tue-Sat; 7.30-11pm Mon. Closed 3wks Aug, 1wk Dec. €€.*
Although it's well back from the water's edge, in the centre of Como, this tiny restaurant is still worth a visit. Don't be fooled by the English name, this is no by-rote tourist joint. The menu consists primarily of local dishes, and changes every week, but might run to squid ink ravioli and the house speciality, *chicche al granchio fresco* (tiny crab gnocchi). Thick walls, beamed ceilings and homely wooden chairs and tables set the mood; cosiest of all is the small mezzanine.

Milano

Pallanza, nr Verbania *Corso Zanitello 2 (0323 556 816). Open noon-2.20pm, 7.15-9.15pm Mon, Wed-Sun. Closed mid Nov-mid Feb. €€€.*
Small restaurants have been popping up all along Lago Maggiore in the last few years, but this neo-Gothic building in the centre of Pallanza has passed the test of time. It serves classic dishes and excellent fish – indoors or, in the warmer months, on its waterfront terrace. Try fish fresh from the lake such as *pesce persico* (perch) and *salmerino* (char), all served with locally grown organic vegetables.

Osteria al Boeuc

Novara, Orta San Giulio *Via Bersani 28 (0322 915 854). Open 11am-3pm, 6.30pm-1am Mon, Wed-Sun. €.*
This 500-year-old wine bar serves bruschetta, cheese, cold cuts, *salsiccia ubriaca* ('drunken' sausage) and over 350 wines. If what's on the menu particularly titillates your taste buds, drop into the Boeuc's food store next door, La Dispensa, and stock up.

Silvio

Bellagio *Via Carcano 12 (031 950 322/www.bellagio silvio.com). Open 12.15-2.30pm, 7.15-10pm daily. Closed mid Nov-mid Dec, 6wks Jan-Feb. €€.*
This friendly hotel-restaurant has been in the Ponzini family for four generations. Today's owners, Silvio and Giuliana, specialise in dishes made with impeccably fresh fish caught in the lake: delicately flavoured fish stew, fillet of perch and own-made pastas; don't miss the various preparations of *missultini* (salted freshwater sardines flavoured with laurel leaves). If you want to try more dishes than you can eat in a single sitting, you can stay overnight in one of the 21 rooms (doubles €70-€100), or rent an apartment (www.bellagioapartments.it).

Taverna Antico Agnello

Orta San Giulio *Via Olina 18 (0322 90259). Open 12.30-2.30pm, 7.30-10pm Mon, Wed-Sun. Closed Dec-mid Feb. €€.*
The rustic, family-run Taverna Antico Agnello serves hearty regional food in a snug dining room: dishes like *cavallo* (horse) scented with rosemary and garlic, or various pasta dishes. You might even find *tapulon* on the menu – a regional speciality made from chopped donkey meat with garlic and oil. There's a good wine list, and the majority of the diners are locals, which says a great deal.

Vecchia Varenna

Varenna *Contrada Scoscesa 14 (0341 830 793/www.vecchiavarenna.it). Open 12.30-2pm, 8-10pm Tue-Sun. Closed Jan. €€€.*
The excitement at this destination restaurant, on the eastern shore of Lago di Como, is twofold: excellent food and excellent views of the lake (which is so close you can almost touch the water). The speciality is freshwater fish, including roast pink trout with garlic. It's refreshingly informal and has more than enough scenery to sustain contemplation for a very long lunch.

Explore

LAGO DI COMO

Lake Como – or Lario, as it has been known since Roman times – extends in an inverted Y shape from the Alps in the north to the plain just 70 kilometres from Milan in the south. Colico is at the northerly extreme, and the cities of Como and Lecco, some 50 kilometres away, are at the other two ends. The three 'arms' come together to form the promontory of Bellagio.

Despite the fact that the lake has a 178-kilometre perimeter, and is Italy's third largest (and Europe's deepest), it is never more than four and a half kilometres wide, which creates a sense of intimacy. Moreover, each of the lake's 'arms' is different. The Como section is relatively narrow; the mountains behind are somewhat uniform, with plenty of little towns and grand villas along the shoreline. The Lecco branch is more rugged, the jagged edges of the Grigne range providing a strong contrast. And the northern part features deep valleys and tall mountains, and is the most dramatic. The scenery is at its most spectacular in the central section of the lake, around the triangle of Bellagio, Menaggio and Varenna.

Golf is a local speciality, with no fewer than seven 18-hole courses within 20 kilometres of Como town. The best known is Golf Club Villa d'Este (031 200 200, www.golfvilladeste.com), popular with Europe's royal families.

And then, of course, there's silk. Although the raw thread is now imported, Como's reputation as a centre of excellence for silk textile manufacturing and printing lives on. Factories with retail outlets include Martinetti (via Torriani 41, 031 269 053, www.martinetti.it, closed Sun & 3wks Aug), which can be reached on foot from piazza Cavour. It's also worth checking out the collection called La Tessitura by Mantero, one of the top names in luxury silk design and production. Accessories for women, men and the home have been created by Mantero's in-house team of international designers using remnants of luxury silk that have been redyed, retextured, rewoven, reprinted or taken from one-off colour samples. La Tessitura's outlet at viale Roosevelt 2a (031 321 666, www.latessitura.com) also has a chic café.

Finally, no trip to Como is complete without a visit to Brunate, the village 720 metres above Como town. The funicular railway (adjacent to Como Nord Lago railway station, www.geocities.com/funicolarecomobrunate), will take you up there in just under seven minutes, at gradients of up to 55 per cent. However, if this seems like the easy way out, by all means walk it – it will take about an hour and a half to cover the five kilometres. It's worth going to Brunate for the views over the lake, but also for a stroll around. Outside the perimeter walls you can admire some of the villas built in the 19th and early 20th centuries, when Brunate became a resort for the well-heeled. The Grand Hotel Brunate and the Grand Hotel Milano, both of which have now been diverted to other functions, attest to that past glory.

Basilica di Sant'Abbondio
Como *Via Sant'Abbondio (031 338 8111). Open Oct-Mar 8am-4pm daily. Apr-Sept 8am-5pm daily. Admission free.*

This Benedictine abbey church is one of the greatest jewels of the Lombard Romanesque. Visiting monks from northern Europe are perhaps responsible for its innovative design – including the twin bell towers, a Norman touch – built in the 11th century to replace an earlier church. You can see the floorplan of the previous structure marked out on the pavement. There are 14th-century frescoes in the apse, and the relics of Saint Abundius, to whom the church is dedicated, are buried under the altar.

Duomo
Como *Piazza del Duomo (031 265 244). Open 9am-6.30pm daily. Admission free.*
Como's Duomo, begun in 1396, is unique and beautiful. Its late Gothic façade (1455-86) is even more striking because pride of place is given to two renowned pagans – the Plinies, Older and Younger. Note also Tommaso Rodari's Frog Door (Porta della Rana) leading into the left side of the nave. In the Latin-cross interior, the three-aisled nave is Gothic and the transept Renaissance, and the great dome was designed by Filippo Juvarra in baroque style in 1744. The rose window is a particularly fine example; artworks inside the Duomo include 16th- and 17th-century tapestries and 16th-century paintings by Bernardino Luini and Gaudenzio Ferrari.

Museo Didattico della Seta
Como *Via Castelnuovo 9 (031 303 180/www.museosetacomo.com). Open 9am-noon, 3-6pm Tue-Fri. Admission €8; €5.50 reductions.*
A little off the beaten track, but worth the effort, is this lovingly curated museum that brings the city's main industry – silk – to life. It's housed inside Como's silk-making school, and displays include examples of silk looms through the ages, printing equipment, dyeing processes and numerous examples of the end product.

San Fedele
Como *Piazza Medaglie d'Oro (031 267 295). Open 8am-noon, 3-7pm daily. Admission free.*
The church of San Fedele was built some time between the tenth and 12th centuries, and was named after the saint who brought Christianity to Como in the fourth century. It was Como's cathedral until the Duomo was built at the end of the 14th century. The rose window over the reconstructed main entrance is from the 16th century; the majority of the decorations inside are baroque.

Villa Melzi
Bellagio *Lungolario Marconi (031 950 204/www.bellagiolakecomo.com). Open mid Mar-Oct 9am-6pm daily. Admission €6; €5 reductions. No credit cards.*
Although the house is not open to the public, the gardens are a fantastic attraction in their own right. Villa Melzi boasts a pretty Japanese garden, some splendid water lilies and a Moorish-looking, lapis lazuli-blue coffee house.

Villa Serbelloni
Bellagio *Piazza della Chiesa (031 951 555/031 950 204/www.bellagiolakecomo.com). Open Apr-Nov 11am-4pm Tue-Sun. Admission €7; €5.50 reductions. No credit cards.*

Clockwise from top left:
Varenna; Lago di Como
(2); Bellagio; Varenna.

Clockwise from top:
Villa Taranto; Lago di
Como; Stresa; Villa
Pallavicino; Cannobio.

Open for guided tours twice a day, the 17th-century Villa Serbelloni – which is owned by the Rockefeller Foundation – stands high on the point above Bellagio's town centre. It may be on the site of Pliny the Younger's villa Tragedia (he had another villa called Commedia at Lenno). The trees in the gardens of Villa Serbelloni, added in the 19th century, are worth noting. Although they seem to blend effortlessly into the landscape, these were, in fact, among the first examples of magnolias, oleanders, palms and cedars ever planted in Italy.

LAGO MAGGIORE

Although the lake is handsome on the eastern side, it's the western shore that attracts most visitors. From Arona to Cannobio, small towns alternate with majestic villas and gardens, many of which are only visible from the water. At the lake's southern tip is Arona, a lively commercial town with a pretty, historic centre. San Carlo Borromeo was born here and a 17th-century, 35-metre tall copper statue of the saintly local hero, built using the same technique later employed to construct the Statue of Liberty, stands high on a hill above the town (piazzale San Carlo, closed Mon-Fri Nov-Mar). Those with steely nerves can climb a narrow internal spiral staircase and ten-metre vertical ladder to the statue's head to peer at the lake through the saint's eyes.

Stresa stands on the Golfo Borromeo, which, with its islands, forms the heart of the lake. The town became famous after Dickens and Byron gave it rave reviews; Hemingway also set part of *A Farewell to Arms* here. During the belle époque, Stresa's grandiose hotels, refined attractions and casino rivalled those of Monte Carlo and the Venice Lido. The 1,491-metre-high summit of Montagna Mottarone can be reached by cable car or a five-hour hike from Stresa. It becomes a ski resort in winter and, on a clear day, you can enjoy a sensational view of the Alps, several lakes, and – on really exceptional days – as far as Milan and Turin. The cable car also stops at the Giardino Alpinia (0323 20163, closed Mon & mid Oct-mid Apr), which boasts hundreds of alpine plant species.

From Stresa, ferries and water taxis take tourists to the three islands collectively known as the Isole Borromee: Isola Bella, Isola Madre and Isola dei Pescatori. So popular are these excursions that the islands can become unpleasantly crowded in high season. The Borromeo feudal lords took possession of these islands in the 16th century. Isola Bella (0323 30556, closed Nov-mid Mar) was named in honour of Isabella d'Adda, whose husband Carlo Borromeo III began transforming the island in 1632. The island's baroque Palazzo Borromeo (where Napoleon and Josephine slept

after his conquest of northern Italy) has a stately Italian-style garden with albino peacocks. Isola dei Pescatori is a strip of narrow lanes and whitewashed houses, ending in a park with benches and shady trees. The 16th-century Palazzo Borromeo on Isola Madre (the largest of the three Isole Borromee) has an 18th-century puppet theatre and is surrounded by a magnificent English-style garden (summer 0323 31261, winter 0323 30556, closed Nov-Feb).

Beyond Stresa, Baveno is home to the tenth-century church of the saints Gervasio e Protasio. The octagonal baptistery dates from the fifth century. The local pink marble is exported worldwide. Verbania, the provincial capital, is made up of several towns that were unified in 1939. Pallanza is renowned for its gardens and has an attractive lakeside promenade abundant with flowers. The gardens of the Villa Giulia (corso Sanitello 10, 0323 503 249) at the end of the promenade have views over the privately owned islet of San Giovanni Battista, where composer Arturo Toscanini spent his holidays (Villa Giulia itself is closed to the public).

One of Europe's largest wilderness areas, the Parco Nazionale della Val Grande, stretches behind Verbania and is reached from the town of Cicogna in the hills above. Dozens of hiking and bike trails lead to meadows, gorges and peaks where chamois goats far outnumber hikers (information office: via Sanremigio 19, Verbania, 0323 557 960, www.parcovalgrande.it or www.parks.it, closed Sat, Sun).

Villa Pallavicino
Stresa *Strada Statale 33 (0323 31533/0323 32407/www.parcozoopallavicino.it). Open 9am-6pm daily. Closed Nov-Feb. Admission €9; €6 reductions.*
The waterfront Villa Pallavicino is not open to the public, but it's surrounded by a vast and attractive English-style park, with rose garden, botanical enclosure and zoo. The residents of the last include flamingos, llamas, kangaroos and zebras, as well as sheep and goats.

Villa Taranto
Pallanza, nr Verbania *Via Vittorio Veneto 111 (0323 556 667/404 555/www.villataranto.it). Open Apr-Sept 8.30am-6.30pm daily. Oct 8.30am-5pm daily. Closed Nov-Mar. Admission €8.50; €5.50 reductions.*
The beautiful garden at Villa Taranto, complete with stately statues and water features, was laid out by the scion of a wealthy Scottish family, Captain Neil McEacharn, who bought the property in 1931. It contains over 20,000 species of plants, including many rarities, brought from all over the world. McEacharn is buried in a mausoleum on the site; the villa itself houses offices of the local municipality, and is not open to the public.

Clockwise from top:
Lago d'Orta; Isola di
San Giulio; Alessi (3).

LAGO D'ORTA

Visitors to the medieval lakeside town of Orta San Giulio could be forgiven for thinking they have somehow stumbled on to the set of a romantic film. A dramatic pathway sweeps from the main waterside square (piazza Motta) to the church of Santa Maria Assunta (1485), and crumbling villas flank the shorelines stretching out from the town. Back in the café-lined square, models are often found posing for photoshoots beneath the loggia of the 16th-century Palazzo della Comunità. It's no wonder Orta is popular for weddings (if you get the urge to tie the knot, there's even a resident British wedding organiser, Philippa Lane, mobile 338 461 0665).

Perched above the town, in the wooded Sacro Monte nature reserve, are 20 small chapels (1591-1770) containing remarkably lifelike terracotta tableaux depicting scenes from the life of St Francis. A pleasant pilgrims' path (30 minutes) winds uphill from piazza Motta, leading to the 17th-century Chiesa di San Nicolao and the Sacro Monte. Alternatively, you can drive up.

Lovers of local crafts shouldn't miss the tiny shop, Penelope (Piazza Motta 26, Orta San Giulio, 0322 905 600, www.orta.net/penelope, open 9am-8pm daily. Closed Oct-Feb) where luxurious, hand-woven kitchen linens and tablecloths, all hand-printed with antique wooden stamps and natural dyes, can be found. Designs include traditional Umbrian patterns, and motifs taken from Giotto's frescoes in the basilica of Assisi.

Alessi

Crusinallo *Via Privata Alessi (0323 868 611/ www.alessi.it). Open 2-6pm Mon; 9.30am-6pm Tue-Sat.* Tucked away at the end of the lake, at Crusinallo, are the museum, factory, offices, and outlet store of Alessi, the company whose gleaming kettles and Philippe Starck-designed juice squeezers crop up in stylish kitchens around the world. Visitors can't miss the aqua-and-orange factory with a giant sculpture of Alessi's archetypal, squat 1940s teapot outside; but although the on-site museum is jam-packed with more than 22,000 design objects, only industry specialists (designers and the like, strictly by appointment) are allowed inside. Fortunately, the factory outlet is open to all, and stocks Alessi pieces at knock-down prices.

Factfile

When to go

It's a common belief in Italy that lakes in general – not only the three covered here – are *tristi* (sad) from October to March. Make up your own mind, but it's worth noting that some hotels and restaurants may be closed during the winter.

Getting there

The nearest airport for Lago di Como is Aeroporto di Orio al Serio (035 326 323, www.orioaero porto.it), just outside Bergamo; for Maggiore and Orta, it's Milan's Aeroporto di Malpensa (02 7485 2200, www.sea-aeroportimilano.it).

To get to Lago d'Orta by train, take a mainline train service from Stazione Centrale or Porta Garibaldi to Novara, then the local service. For Maggiore, you'll need to take the Domodossola service from Porta Garibaldi, or an express from Stazione Centrale. Alternatively, take the twice-daily commuter bus from Porta Garibaldi: Autoservizi Nerini (0323 552 172, www. safduemila.com) or Baldioli (0332 530 271, www.baldioli.com). To get to Lago di Como, take the hourly state railway service (www.trenitalia.it) from Stazione Centrale.

Getting around

Once at your lake of choice, you'll find boat services around the shores will stop in at most decent-sized towns. At Lago d'Orta, operators are Navigazione Lago d'Orta (0322 844 862)

and Servizio Pubblico Motoscafi (333 605 0288 mobile, www.motoscafisti.com). At Lago di Como, the name to look out for is Navigazione Lago di Como (031 579 211, www.navigazionelaghi.it), which operates frequent ferry and hydrofoil services all year round. Special tourist cruises are also on offer.

Tourist information

IAT Tourist Office Piazza Cavour 17, Como (031 330 0111/www.provincia.como.it/turismo, www.lakecomo.org). Open June-Sept 9am-1pm, 2.30-6pm Mon-Sat; 9am-1pm Sun. Oct-May 9am-1pm, 2.30-6pm Mon-Sat.
Orta San Giulio tourist office, via Panoramica (0322 905 614/www.distrettolaghi.it). Open 9am-1pm, 2-6pm Wed-Sun.
Stresa tourist office, piazza Marconi 16 (0323 30 150/www.distrettolaghi.it). Open Apr-Oct 10am-12.30pm, 3-6.30pm daily. Nov-Mar 10am-12.30pm, 3-6.30pm Mon-Fri; 10am-12.30pm Sat.

Internet

Most of the main towns around the Italian lakes have at least one internet café. Centro Informagiovani, via Natta 16, Como (031 242 044). Open 2.30-6.30pm Tue-Fri; 9am-12.30pm Sat.
Internet Cafè, via Poli, Orta San Giulio (0322 905 532). Open 10am-7pm daily.

Need to know

Accommodation

CAMPING

Canvas Holidays 0870 192 1159/
www.canvasholidays.co.uk

Eurocamp 0870 366 7552/
www.eurocamp.co.uk

Vacansoleil 08700 778 779/
www.vacansoleil.co.uk

VILLAS & APARTMENTS

A&K Villas 0845 070 0618/
www.abercrombiekent.co.uk

Cottages to Castles 01622 775 236/
www.cottagestocastles.com

CV Travel 020 7384 5897/www.cvtravel.co.uk

Landmark Trust 01628 825 925/
www.landmarktrust.org.uk

Owners' Syndicate 020 7381 7492/
www.ownersyndicate.com

Simpson Travel 0845 811 6504/
www.simpsontravel.com

Solemar 020 8891 1294/www.solemar.it

Electricity

Italy uses 220V – compatible with British-bought
appliances (with a plug adaptor); US 110V
equipment requires a transformer.

Embassies

Australia Via Antonio Bosio 5, Rome
(06 852 721/www.italy.embassy.gov.au).

Canada Via Zara 30, Rome (06 854 441/
www.canada.it).

Ireland Piazza Campitelli, Rome (06 697 9121/
www.ambasciata-irlanda.it).

New Zealand Via Zara 28, Rome (06 441 7171/
www.nzembassy.com).

South Africa Via Tanaro 14, Rome (06 852 541/
www.sudafrica.it).

UK Via XX Settembre 80A, Rome
(06 4220 0001/www.britain.it).

US Via Vittorio Veneto 119, Rome (06 46 741/
www.usembassy.it).

Emergencies

Ambulance 118; **Fire brigade** 115;
Police 112

Lost credit cards

American Express 06 7290 0347/06 7228
0371/US cardholders 800 874 333; **Diner's
Club** 800 864 064; **MasterCard** 800 870 866;
Visa 800 877 232

Public holidays

New Year's Day (Capodanno) 1 January;
Epiphany (La Befana) 6 January; **Easter
Sunday** (Domenica di Pasqua); **Easter Monday**
(Lunedì di Pasqua); **Liberation Day** (LIberazione)
25 April; **Labour Day** (Primo Maggio) 1 May;
Republic Day (Festa della Repubblica) 2 June;
Feast of the Assumption (Ferragosto) 15 August;
All Saint's Day (Tutti Santi) 1 November;
Feast of the Immaculate Conception (Festa
dell'Immaculata) 8 December; **Christmas Day**
(Natale) 25 December; **Boxing Day** (Santo
Stefano) 26 December

Time

Italy is on Central European Time, which is one
hour ahead of GMT.

Tours & courses

ACTIVITY HOLIDAYS

Bettina Schroeder 020 7609 0843/
www.art-holidays.com

Naturetrek 01962 733 051/www.naturetrek.co.uk

Painting in Umbria 0800 458 9112/
www.paintinginitaly.com

CULINARY TOURS

Arblaster & Clarke 01730 263 111/
www.winetours.co.uk

Flavours 0131 625 7002/
www.flavoursholidays.co.uk

Saperi Gastronomic Adventures 07768 474 610

Tasting Places 020 8964 5333/
www.tastingplaces.com

CULTURAL TOURS

Cox & Kings 020 7873 5000/
www.coxandkings.co.uk

Martin Randall Travel 020 8742
335/www.martinrandall.com
Travel for the Arts 020 8799 8350

Voyages Jules Verne 0845 166 7003/
www.vjv.com

HIKING/BIKING/DRIVING

ATG-Oxford 01865 315678/
www.atg-oxford.co.uk

Collett's Mountain Holidays 01763 289660/
www.colletts.co.uk

Freewheel Holidays 0845 372 0315/
www.freewheelholidays.co.uk

Headwater 01606 720199/
www.headwater.com

HF Holidays 0845 470 7558/
www.hfholidays.co.uk

Inntravel 01653 617906/
www.inntravel.co.uk

Real Holidays 020 7359 3938/
www.realholidays.co.uk

Self Guided Adventures in Umbria/Tuscany
www.selfguidedadventures.com

Sherpa 020 8577 2717/
www.sherpa-walking-holidays.co.uk

LANGUAGE COURSES

LCA www.languagesabroad.co.uk

Scuola Leonardo da Vinci (Florence)
www.scuolaleonardo.com

Istituto Il David (Florence) www.davidschool.com

Tourism

Italian State Tourist Board www.enit.it

Travel

AIRLINES

Alltalia 0870 544 8259/www.alltalia.co.uk

British Airways 0870 850 9850/www.ba.com
Bmi 0870 6070 555/www.flybmi.com

Easyjet 0905 821 0905/www.easyjet.com

Ryanair 0871 246 0000/www.ryanair.com

Thomsonfly 0870 1900 737/
www.thomsonfly.com

CAR HIRE

Avis 08445 818181/www.avis.co.uk

Auto Europe www.autoeurope.co.uk

Europcar 0870 607 5000

Hertz 0870 844 8844

Suncars 0871 664 9672/www.suncars.com

TRAINS

Italiarail.co.uk 08700 841414

Italian State Railways www.trenitalia.com

Railchoice 020 8659 7300/
www.railchoice.com

Rail Europe 0844 848 4070/
www.raileurope.co.uk

Festivals & events

JANUARY

Abruzzo
Living Nativity Scene
Hundreds of costumed figures re-enact the arrival of the Three Kings at the manger in Rivisondoli.
www.comune.rivisondoli.aq.it

The Aeolian Islands
Live Representation of the Nativity
On the island of Vulcano.
www.regione.sicilia.it/turismo

Calabria
Red Onion Festival
Celebration of traditional red onion-based dishes (Tropea).

The Italian Riviera
San Remo in Fiore
A flower festival in San Remo.
www.sanremoinfiore.it

Milan
Corteo dei Rei Magi
Traditional procession of the Three Magi.
www.milanoinfotourist.com

Siena
Girogustando
Experimenting with new kinds of cuisine.
www.comune.siena.it

Vicenza
Mercato Dell'Antiquariato e del Collezionismo
Market of antiques and collectables in Vicenza.
www.turismo.provincia.vicenza.it

FEBRUARY

The Amalfi Coast
Grand Carnival
A fancy dress procession with small carnival floats.
www.amalfitouristoffice.it

The Aeolian Islands
Feast of San Bartolomeo
Celebration in Lipari in honour of San Bartolomeo, protector of fishermen.
www.regione.sicilia.it/turismo

Florence
Carnevale
Ten days ending on Shrove Tuesday. Held in many Tuscan towns, with floats and fancy dress.
www.firenzeturismo.it

Italian Riviera
Festival della Canzone Italiana
A popular Italian song contest held since 1951 at the Ariston Theatre in San Remo, the inspiration for the Eurovision Song Contest.
www.sanremo.rai.it

Milan
Carnevale Ambrosiano
Carnival Parade with dance and themed carriages.
www.milanoinfotourist.com

Sardinia
Sartiglia
Historical re-enactment with horse race and medieval parade in Oristano.
www.sardegnaturismo.it

Siena
Le Stagioni dell'Olio
Gastronomic week celebrating olive oil.
www.comune.siena.it

Venice
Il Carnevale di Venezia
The Carnival is the most magnificent of Venetian celebrations, re-instigated by the Municipality in 1980 after a break of almost two centuries.
www.carnivalofvenice.com

Verona
St Valentine's Day
Loved-up music and cultural events in the city of Romeo and Juliet.
www.tourism.verona.it

MARCH

Abruzzo
Madonna Che Scappa
A medieval pageant is held in Piazza Garibaldi in Sulmona every Easter morning.
www.comune.sulmona.aq.it

Calabria
Easter Procession
Religious procession on Good Friday in Catanzaro.
www.turismo.regione.calabria.it

Florence
World Sacred Music Week
Sixteen international music concerts at the Church of Santo Stefano al Ponte.
www.florenceyouthfestival.com

Genoa
World Championship of Genovese Pesto
Celebration of 'pesto alla genovese'.
www.turismoinliguria.it

The Italian Riviera
Criterium Velico di Pasqua
Easter Regatta held in the San Remo Gulf.
www.comunedisanremo.it

Lecce & around
St Orontius
Festival in honour of the saint in Lecce on Good Friday.
www.turismo.provincia.le.it

Lucca
Lucca Jazz Donna
Jazz women play in the old centre of Lucca.
www.luccajazzdonna.it

Lucca
Mostra dei Fiori e dei Dolci di Santa Zita
Santa Zita, the little saint of the flowers, is honoured with bouquets of jounquils, traditional vegetable cakes, and a flower market.
www.comune.lucca.it

Milan
MODIT: Milanovendemoda
The major fashion show for leading Italian and international designers.
www.milanoinfotourist.com

Sardinia
Sagra del Torrone
On Easter Day Tonara hosts a Festival of Nougat.
www.sardegnaturismo.it

Siena
Settimana della Musica Senese
Annual event with musicians performing traditional music.
www.comune.siena.it

Umbria
Dance International Week
Classical and modern dance in Spoleto (Perugia).
www.comune.spoleto.it

Urbino & around
Laborati in Piazza
Every Thursday afternoon from March to November, local artists and craftsmen explain their techniques in Urbino's Piazza San Francesco.
www.turismo.marche.it

APRIL

The Italian Riviera
Rally Automobilistico di San Remo
Only cars built up to 1981 are admitted and put through their paces in the hinterland of San Remo.
www.sanremorally.it

Florence
Maggio Musicale Fiorentino
An important festival of music, dance and theatre that has been running for more than 70 years.
www.maggiofiorentino.it

Lucca
Via Vinaria
An event celebrating regional wine production.
www.comune.montecarlo.lucca.it

Milan
Fiera dei Fiori
Flower fair in Via Moscova.
www.milanoinfotourist.com

Palermo
Dance of the Devils/ Holy Week (Prizzi)
Traditional battle between good and evil featuring huge iron masks, culminating in a villager representing Jesus entering on a horse.
www.comune.palermo.it

MAY

Abruzzo
Procession of the Ox
A costumed procession culminating in a sumptuously outfitted ox kneeling before the statue of St Zopito in Loreto Aprutino (Pescara).
www.comune.loretoaprutino.pe.it

Bologna
Festa di San Luca (Ascension Day)
Procession of the icon of San Luca from the hills through the town to the Cathedral of San Pietro, where it lies for a week.
www.comune.bologna.it

Florence
Settimana dei Beni Culturali

State museums (including the Uffizi, Accademia and Palatina galleries) let the public in free for a week. Dates are announced late to keep the queues down.
www.firenzeturismo.it

Florence
Gardens and Courtyards Open to All
About 30 city palaces and many outlying villas are opened up to the public for the day.
www.firenzeturismo.it

The Italian Riviera
Lemon Feast
On the Saturday preceding Ascension Sunday, a prize is awarded for the biggest local lemon and best window display of lemons, with live music throughout the day in Monterosso al Mare (La Spezia).
www.cinqueterre.it

Milan
Cortili Aperti
The most beautiful Milanese courtyards are opened to visitors.
www.milanoinfotourist.com

Naples
Maggio dei Monumenti
Many private exhibitions, churches and palaces open their doors to the public.
www.portanapoli.com

Sardinia
Cavalcata Sarda
Traditional horse parade in Sassari.
www.comune.sassari.it

Siena
Cantine Aperte
Open cellars, with tastings of local wines and food.
www.comune.siena.it

South Tuscan hill towns
Fiera di Sant'Agnese
Historical parade around the city streets with the statue of Sant'Agnese in Montepulciano.
www.montepulciano.com

Umbria & around
Calendimaggio
A medieval and Reinassance procession, with theatre, singing and music, dancing, displays given by archers, crossbowmen and flag wavers, in a contest between factions from 'Upper' and 'Lower' Assisi.
www.calendimaggiodiassisi.it

Urbino & around
Il Cortile del Gusto
Traditional food and wine from Pesaro and Urbino in the Raffaello courtyard in Urbino.
www.turismo.marche.it

JUNE

The Aeolian Islands
Folkmare
An international folk festival, with artists from all over the world coming to Lipari.
www.regione.sicilia.it/turismo

The Amalfi Coast
Historical Regatta
Founded in 1954 to commemorate the Four Maritime Republics of Italy.
www.amalfitouristoffice.it

Florence
Il Mese Medìceo
A celebration of the world and court of the Medici family.
www.mesemediceo.it

Genoa
Feste e Palio di San Pietro
Traditional boat race and fireworks.
www.turismoinliguria.it

The Italian Riviera
Corpus Christi
Celebrated yearly on the second Sunday after Pentecost, the old town centre of Monterosso al Mare (La Spezia) is decorated with flower petals for an evening procession.
www.cinqueterre.it

Milan
La Notte Bianca
For one night a year everything (restaurants, shops, bars, cinemas) stays open in the centre of Milan until 6am.
www.comune.milano.it

Parma
Palio of San Secondo
A jousting tournament dating back to 1523.
www.paliodellecontrade.com

Ravenna
Ravenna Festival
Various venues, including San Vitale Basilica and the Rossini Theatre, host opera, concerts, dance, jazz, ethnic music, drama and cinema during June and July.
www.ravennafestival.org

Rimini
La Notte Rosa
For one night only, hundreds of free events are put on along the Adriatic Riviera – concerts, fireworks displays and lots of pink lightbulbs.
www.riminiturismo.it

Rome
Opera at the Roman Baths of Caracalla
A great summer venue for the Teatro dell'Opera.
www.romaturismo.it

Turin
Torino Punti Verdi
Events in the Royal Gardens, Stura Park, Lingotto and many other places in and around Turin.
www.turismotorino.it

Umbria & around
Festival dei Due Mondi
The Spoleto Festival always attracts big names from the arts world.
www.spoletofestival.it

Urbino & around
Erbe Buone, Erbe delle Streghe
Near the Ducal Palace in Urbino, this culinary and music event promotes antique recipes based on homeopathic grasses (known as 'the grass of the witches').
www.turismo.marche.it

Verona
Verona Theatre Summer Festival
Shakespeare, ballet and jazz performed in the old Roman theatre.
www.turism.verona.it

JULY

The Aeolian Islands
Lipari Cinema Festival
www.regione.sicilia.it/turismo

Calabria
Swordfish Festival
This celebration of the year's swordfish catch attracts crowds to the small village of Bagnara.
www.turismo.regione.calabria.it

Florence
Mercantia
Certaldo's famous festival.
www.firenzeturismo.it

Lucca
Festa di St Jacopo di Altopascio
Celebration of the feast of the Protector Saint with a medieval dinner provided by the 'big pot' of Altopascio and a procession.
www.comune.altopascio.lucca.it

Palermo
Festino di Santa Rosalia
A mid-July riot of theatre and fireworks celebrate Palermo's patron saint.

Parma
Verdi Opera Festival
Very popular opera festival celebrating Verdi, a native of Parma.
www.turismo.parma.it

Ravenna
La Notte Rosa
A night when everything (shops, restaurants, museums, churches) stays open until the early hours of the morning.
www.turismo.ravenna.it

Rome
Festa de Noantri
An eight-day Roman street party in homage to the Madonna displayed at the church of San Crisongo in Trastevere.
www.romaturismo.it

Sardinia
Arresojas: Mostra Biennale del Coltello Sardo
Exhibition on traditional Sardinian knives called 'Arresojas' in Comune di Guspini (Cagliari).
www.sardegnaturismo.it

South Tuscan hill towns
Cantiere Internazionale d'Arte di Montepulciano
Opera, theatre, concerts, ballets and other entertainment all summer.
www.montepulciano.com

Umbria
Umbria Jazz
Huge array of jazz peformances, spilling out on to the streets in Perugia.
www.umbriajazz.com

Urbino & around
Festival Internazionale di Musica Antica – Sinfonia Divine
International festival of sacred and ancient music in Urbino's Basilica Cattedrale, Museo Diocesano Albani and Oratorio delle Grotte.
www.turismo.marche.it

Venice
Redentore
The Redentore is a feast day of thanksgiving for Venice's survival of the plague in the 16th century, with countless boats and a grand fireworks display on St Mark's Basin and the Giudecca Canal.
www.comune.venezia.it

AUGUST

Abruzzo
Pope Celestino's Pardon Ceremonies

Official celebrations in honour of Pope
Celestino V in L'Aquila.
www.turismoaq.com

The Aeolian Islands
**Festival dell'Allegria
(Feast of Happiness)**
Dances in San Calogero Square.
www.regione.sicilia.it/turismo

Bologna
Bologna Sogna/Viva Bologna
An arts festival that aims to invigorate the city when
much of the population is away.
www.comune.bologna.it

Calabria
Festival of Madonna della Grotta
Celebrations in honour of Madonna della Grotta with
music and cultural events, fireworks and loads of stalls
in Praia a Mare (Cosenza).
www.turismo.regione.calabria.it

Genoa
Procession dell'Assunta
Evening procession and firework display
at Nervi.

The Italian Riviera
Fireworks World Championship
Every summer San Remo is the venue for the World
Championship of Fireworks.
www.fioridifuoco.it

Naples
Neapolis Rock Festival
The two-day Neapolis Festival is one of the
most popular in Italy and takes place at an
outdoor arena.
www.napolimusica.it

Palermo
World Festival on the Beach
World Festival on the Beach combines windsurfing, jazz,
beach volleyball, sky diving, paragliding, kite surfing and
sailing on Mondello Beach.
www.wwfestival.com

Rimini
Otteocentro Festival
A street festival with a 19th-century theme in a walled
hilltop town about an hour from Rimini.
www.riminiturismo.it

Sardinia
**Al Confini Tra Sardegna
e Jazz 2007**
This jazz festival features top international jazz players in
Sant'Anna Arresi (Cagliari).
www.sardegnaturismo.it

Siena
Il Palio di Siena
Piazza del Campo is still used today for the well-known
Palio horse race.
www.ilpalio.org

South Tuscan hill towns
**Settimana degli Eventi del
Bravio delle Botti**
Historical re-enactment, with medieval costumes,
archers and a street race in Montepulciano.
www.montepulciano.com

Urbino & around
Festa del Duca
Historical re-enactment with archers and flagwavers
parading around Urbino city centre for four days.
www.turismo.marche.it

SEPTEMBER

Calabria
Calabrian Folklore Festival
Traditional dances, costumes, and local food
and wine animate this festival in Villaggio
Mancuso (Catanzaro).
www.turismo.regione.calabria.it

Florence
Annual Wine Championship
The annual Wine Championship is a wine-tasting
tournament open to the public and organised by
Slow Food Florence.
www.slowfoodfirenze.it

The Italian Riviera
Salted Anchovy and Olive Oil Feast
Celebrated each year over the second weekend of
September in Monterosso al Mare (La Spezia).
www.cinqueterre.it

Lucca
**Fiere di Santa Coce, San Michele,
San Matteo**
Traditional September fairs on Piazza San Michele and
Borgo Giannotti.
www.comune.lucca.it

Matera & around
Metaponto Beach Festival
Music festival on the beach in Bernalda-
Metaponto (Matera).
www.aptbasilicata.it

Milan
Monza Formula 1 Grand Prix
Monza has played host to more Formula 1 races than
any other circuit since 1950.
www.monzanet.it

Naples
Piedgrotta Festival
Several world-famous Neapolitan folk songs such as 'O Sole Mio' were originally composed for this festival.
www.portanapoli.com

Palermo
Feast of St Rosalia
Celebration of the city's patron saint, including fireworks, processions and music.
www.comune.palermo.it

Rimini
Fiera di San Michele
Celebration in honour of San Michele with procession, music and loads of stalls along the streets.

Rome
Opere Sotto le Stelle (Opera Under the Stars)
Rome ends its summer festivities with a season of contemporary opera.
www.romaturismo.it

South Tuscan hill towns
Palio dei Somari
Traditional games and local gastronomy in the historic town centre of Montepulciano.
www.montepulciano.com

Umbria
International Festival of Theatre in the Street
In Orvieto (Terni).
www.comune.orvieto.tr.it; www.orvietoturismo.it

Urbino & around
Festa dell'Aquilone
Kite festival in which different teams compete for the best kite performance on top of Monte delle Cesane.
www.turismo.marche.it

Venice
Regata Storica
Regatta dating back to the second half of the 13th century.
www.comune.venezia.it; www.turismovenezia.it

Venice
Venice Biennale
Founded in 1895 and now one of the most prestigious cultural events in the world.
www.labiennale.org

Vicenza
Le Piazze dei Sapori
Culinary event dedicated to the traditional tastes and aromas of Vicenza.
www.turismo.provincia.vicenza.it

OCTOBER

The Aeolian Islands
Settimana Enogastronomia Eoliana
Local gastronomy week on Salina.
www.regione.sicilia.it/turismo

Bologna
Festa di San Petronio Patrono di Bologna
Celebration in honour of Bologna's Patron, San Petronio. Holy Mass and procession around Bologna's main streets.
www.bologna.chiesacattolica.it

Calabria
Wild Mushroom Festival
Featuring tastings of local mushrooms cooked according to different Calabrian recipes in Camigliatello Silano (Cosenza).
www.turismo.regione.calabria.it

Genoa
Niccolo Paganini Prize
Festival and competition in honour of Paganini, with the winner getting to play the great man's violin.

Ravenna
Festival Europeo del Pane
Exhibition dedicated to bread.
www.turismo.ravenna.it

Sardinia
Sagra delle Castagne
Chestnut festival in Aritzo (Nuoro).
www.sardegnaturismo.it

South Tuscan hill towns
Sagra del Tordo (Feast of the Thrush)
The four neighbourhoods of Montalcino compete in an archery tournament on the last weekend of October.
www.prolocomontalcino.it

Umbria
Celebrations in Honour of San Francesco
Two days of cultural and religious events to celebrate the life of San Franc of Assisi.
www.umbria2000.it

Vicenza
Esta Popolare Marronata
A very popular folk event, the main attraction being the open-air tasting of the 'marroni' (a type of chestnut) cooked according to local recipes.
www.turismo.provincia.vicenza.it

NOVEMBER

Lecce & around
Historical Regatta
San Cesarea Terme (Lecce).
www.pugliaturismo.com

Lucca
Palio della Balestra per San Paolino
Celebration of the Protector of Lucca with a crossbow
tournament, processions, musicians and flag waving.
www.comune.lucca.it

Rome
Romaeuropa Festival
Rome's annual festival of international art, music,
dance and theatre.
www.romaturismo.it

Palermo
Morgana Festival
The stars of this festival are the historic Palermo *pupari*
or puppeteer families.
www.palermotourism.it

Sardinia
Sagra dello Zafferano
This very popular annual saffron festival
attracts around 50,000 visitors to San Gavino
Monreale (Cagliari).
www.sardegnaturismo.it

Turin
Torino Film Festival
www.torinofilmfest.org; www.turismotorino.it

Vicenza
Mostra del Libro, Stampa e Disegno Antichi
Book, press and antique drawing exhibition.
www.turismo.provincia.vicenza.it

Naples
Mostra Presepi
Via San Gregorio Armeno is completely dedicated to
the crib, with the craftsmen showing their creations.
Also in Via dei Tribunali.
www.portanapoli.com

South Tuscan hill towns
Piazza Grande
Art and antiques fair in Montepulciano.
www.montepulciano.com

South Tuscan hill towns
Natale Insieme
Religious and cultural events during Christmas
in Montalcino.
www.prolocomontalcino.it

Umbria
Umbria Jazz Winter
Winter jazz festival in Orvieto (Terni).
www.comune.orvieto.tr.it; www.orvietoturismo.it

Urbino & around
Le Vie dei Presepi
Historical representation of the Nativity in Urbino.
www.turismo.marche.it

DECEMBER

Bologna
Bologna Motor Show
One of Europe's most prestigious car and
motorcycle exhibitions.
www.motorshow.it

Florence
Ponte Vecchio Challenge
Golfing greats reveal their secrets.
www.pontevecchiochallenge.it

Genoa
Mostra Presepi
Crib exhibition. Traditional representation of the Nativity.
www.turismoinliguria.it

Advertisers' Index

Please refer to relevant sections for contact details

Editor's picks

Five-star destinations

Each destination in the book is rated by a series of categories. Here are the top performers in each:

ART & ARCHITECTURE

Florence p102-p119

Naples p144-p159

Rome p172-p185

Siena p314-p327

South Tuscan hill towns p62-p75

Umbria p76-p87

Urbino & around p88-p99

Vicenza p336-p343

EATING & DRINKING

The Amalfi Coast & Capri p236-p247

Bologna p280-p289

Calabria p20-p31

The Langhe & Asti p32-p41

Lecce & around p42-p51

Milan p128-p143

Naples p144-p159

Parma p298-p307

Northern Sardinia p266-p277

South Tuscan hill towns p62-p75

Urbino & around p88-p99

HISTORIC SITES

Matera & around p52-p61

Naples p144-p159

Rome p172-p185

Venice p200-p219

Verona p328-p335

HOTELS

Northern Sardinia p266-p277

South Tuscan hill towns p62-p75

NIGHTLIFE

Milan p128-p143

OUTDOOR ACTIVITIES

The Aeolian Islands p222-p235

The Dolomites p358-p371

The Lakes p372-p383

SCENERY

Abruzzo p346-p357

The Amalfi Coast & Capri p236-p247

The Dolomites p358-p371

The Lakes p372-p383

Northern Sardinia p266-p277

South Tuscan hill towns p62-p75

Umbria p76-p87

SHOPPING

Bologna p280-p289

Milan p128-p143

Accommodation

LAP OF LUXURY

Bentley Hotel, Genoa p123

Castello Banfi, South Tuscan hill towns p65

La Coluccia, Northern Sardinia p269

Excelsior, Venice p205

Four Seasons Hotel Milano, Milan p131

Furore Inn Resort, The Amalfi Coast & Capri p239

Golden Palace, Turin p189

Grand Hotel et de Milan, Milan p131

Grand Hotel Villa Serbelloni, The Lakes p375

Hassler Villa Medici, Rome p175

Helvetia & Bristol, Florence p107

Hotel Cala di Volpe, Northern Sardinia p269

Hotel Caruso, The Amalfi Coast & Capri p239

Hotel Philosophy, Rimini p261

Hotel Splendido, The Italian Riviera p251

Palazzo Personè, Lecce & around p45

Panta Rei, Calabria p23

Residenza del Moro, Florence p108

Royal Hotel, The Italian Riviera p251

St Regis Grand, Rome p175

Santa Caterina, The Amalfi Coast & Capri p239

Town House Galleria, Milan p133

Villa d'Este, The Lakes p375

MID-RANGE

Acquarossa, Lecce & around p45

Allakala, Palermo p163

Antica Dimora Johlea, Florence p107

Antica Locanda Leonardo, Milan p131

Carasco, The Aeolian Islands p225

Casa Howard, Rome p175

Daphne Trevi, Rome p175

Grand Hotel et Des Palmes, Palermo p163

Hotel Cimarosa, Naples p147

Hotel Verdi, Parma p301

Locanda di San Martino, Matera & around p55

Orso Poeta, Turin p189

Palazzo Abadessa, Venice p207

Palazzo Galletti, Florence p107

Al Ponte Mocenigo, Venice p205

Porto San Mamolo, Bologna p284

Villa Cicolina, South Tuscan hill towns p67

Villa Krupp, The Amalfi Coast & Capri p239

BUDGET BEDS

Albergo Due Mori, Vicenza p339

B&B Prestige, Lecce & around p45

Beehive, Rome p175

Le Calandre, Venice p203

Cestelli, Florence p107

La Chiocarella, South Tuscan hill towns p65

Hotel Europa, The Italian Riviera p251

Locanda Ca'Vernaccia, Urbino & around p91

Navettaetica, Genoa p123

Panormus, Palermo p163

Paradiso, Abruzzo p351

Poggio Sul Belbo, The Langhe & Asti p35

FAMILIES

Allakala, Palermo p163

La Chiocarella, South Tuscan hill towns p65

Lecce & around p42-p51

Palermo p160-p171

Ravenna p308-p313

Northern Sardinia p266-p277

Urbino & around p88-p99

ICE-CREAM

Da Alfredo, The Aeolian Islands p227

Fiorio, Turin p190

Il Gelato di San Crispino, Rome p177

Grom, Turin p190

Pianegiani, Umbria p82

Rome p172-p185

Vivoli, Florence p111

LEMONS

The Amalfi Coast & Capri p236-p247

Limone, Verona p333

Naples p144-p159

MICHELIN STARS

La Caravella, The Amalfi Coast & Capri p240

La Ciau de Tornavento, The Langhe & Asti p37

Cracco-Peck, Milan p133

Enoteca Pinchiorri, Florence p108

Da Fiore, Venice p208

Joia, Milan p135

Madonnina del Pescatore, Urbino
& around p93

L'Olivo, The Amalfi Coast & Capri p243

La Palma, The Italian Riviera p253

I Parizzi, Parma p302

Relais San Maurizio, The Langhe & Asti p35

Ristorante Tivoli, The Dolomites p363

Rossellinis, The Amalfi Coast & Capri p243

Al Tramezzo, Parma p302

Villa Crespi, The Lakes p375

Villa Las Tronas, Northern Sardinia p270

OLIVE OIL

Lecce & around p42-p51

Museo dell'Olio d'Oliva, Verona p333

South Tuscan hill towns p62-p75

Umbria p76-p87

SLOW FOOD

Bologna p280-p289

Eataly, Turin p197

Guido per Eataly – Casa Vicina,
Turin p191

Naples p144-p159

Osteria dell'Arco, The Langhe & Asti p37

Slow food movement, Parma p303

TRUFFLES

Acqualagna, Urbino & around p93

Alba, The Langhe & Asti p38

Osteria dell'Acquacheta, South Tuscan
hill towns p69

Procacci, Florence p111

Urbino & around p88-p99

WINE

Azienda Vitivinicola e Agrituristica Trerè,
Ravenna p311

Jesi, Urbino & around p93

The Langhe & Asti p32-p41

Manarola, The Italian Riviera p257

Matera & around p52-p61

Naples p144-p159

Ombre Rosse, Parma p302

I Parizzi, Parma p302

Sella & Mosca, Northern Sardinia p274

South Tuscan hill towns p62-p75

Verona p328-p335

Mind & body

PILATES
Agriturismo Cascina Papaveri, The Langhe & Asti p35

SPA HOTELS
Bulgari, Milan p131

Castello Banfi, South Tuscan hill towns p65

The Dolomites p358-p371

Furore Inn Resort, The Amalfi Coast & Capri p239

Il Gatto Blanco, Abruzzo p347-p357

Golden Palace, Turin p189

Grand Hotel Parker's, Naples p147

Grand Hotel Villa Serbelloni, The Lakes p375

Hotel Victoria, Turin p189

Masseria Torre Maizza, Lecce & around p45

Relais San Maurizio, The Langhe & Asti p35

Nature

AGRITURISMI
Abruzzo p349-p351

Agriturismo Cascina Papaveri, The Langhe & Asti p35

Cardillo, Matera & around p55

Fattoria di Vibio, Umbria p79

Northern Sardinia p266-p277

GARDENS
Giardini Hanbury, **La Mortola Inferiore**, The Italian Riviera p253

Orto Botanico, Palermo p168

Ravello, The Amalfi Coast & Capri p246-p247

Villa Taranto, The Lakes p381

Scenery

CLASSIC HILL TOWNS
South Tuscan hill towns p62-p75

LAKES
Abruzzo p346-p357

Lake Garda, Verona p333

The Lakes p372-p383

MOUNTAINS
Abruzzo p347-p357

The Aeolian Islands p222-p235

The Dolomites p358-p371

Monte Baldo, Verona p333

NATIONAL PARKS
Parco Nazionale Della Sila, Calabria p28

Parco Nazionale della Val Grande, The Lakes p381

NATURAL WONDERS
Blue Grotto, The Amalfi Coast & Capri p246

The Dolomites p358-p371

Le Grotte di Frasassi, Urbino p98

Stromboli, The Aeolian Islands p232

SEASIDE
The Aeolian Islands p222-p235

The Amalfi Coast & Capri p236-p247